# TROUBADOUR

Early & Late
Songs of
Bob Dylan

Andrew Muir

Woodstock Publications

First published in 2003 by Woodstock Publications
8 Laxton Grange, Bluntisham, Cambridgeshire PE28 3XU

First edition
Text copyright Andrew Muir © 2003
The moral right of the author has been asserted

Typesetting by Keith Wootton
Cover Design by Jez Brook
Printed by Bath Press

A CIP record for this book is available from the British Library

ISBN 0-9544945-0-4

# TROUBADOUR

Early & Late
Songs of
Bob Dylan

Andrew Muir

Woodstock Publications

*To my Mum and Dad*
*Thanks for staying forever young*

# Contents

# Preface: About this book

*Troubadour* is a mixture of brand new essays and updated versions of articles that have appeared in a variety of fanzines. These latter have all been reworked for the book. Changes range from correction and revision to complete re-writing, as in the restructured chapter on *"Love And Theft"*; unrecognisable and some five times longer than the reviews it was based on.

The book is in two distinct parts, with a bridging chapter. Part one covers Dylan's early output (1962-1966) plus 'If You See Her, Say Hello' (written in 1974) which offers a mature exploration of some of the themes encountered in the opening chapters. Two of the chapters are on mid-1960s imagery and themes, while the rest discuss individual songs or pairs of songs.

A chapter examining Dylan's use of nonsense verse bridges the two parts. This looks both at earlier songs (especially from *The Basement Tapes*) and 1990's *under the red sky*. In contrast to part one, the book then takes the reader through every album from *under the red sky* to *"Love And Theft"* in depth, concentrating on the development of a new style of song-writing and the role the Never Ending Tour and the two early 1990's 'cover albums' played in this.

Although roughly in chronological order as regards Dylan's performing and recording career, the book is not designed to be read in one continuous sitting. I have tried therefore to keep the chapters self-contained, while still endeavouring to keep repetition to a minimum. Due to the length of the chapter on *"Love And Theft"*, I have tried to achieve a similar effect by sectioning it into themes.

# Introduction

For those unfamiliar with any previous writing I have done, I would like to explain my critical stance. I defined it in my first magazine on Dylan, **Homer,** *the slut,* as 'analytical but understandable' but the best explanation of it comes from elsewhere. There is a series of books entitled *Literature In Perspective* whose general introduction states:

> *...the critics and analysts, mostly academics, use a language that only their fellows in the same discipline can understand. Consequently criticism, which should be 'as inevitable as breathing' - an activity for which we are all qualified - has become the private field of a few warring factions...*

I concur heartily with this view and believe the damage caused in the field of artistic appreciation in general has been enormous. The same problem has affected Dylan criticism too. For example, I cannot imagine many readers enjoying Aidan Day's book *Jokerman*, in fact I know of few people who managed to read it all the way through. The saddest thing about this is that it contained more insights and illuminating hypotheses than most books on Dylan. The use of 'a language that only their fellows in the same discipline can understand' meant it failed to engage most of those who were keen to read it.

That is a problem related not only to Dylan but to all academic writing on any subject. More specific to Dylan is the question of whether a literary criticism-type approach, however expressed, can be beneficial in discussing his songs. The case against it is often put, and it reared its head again in a volume of, ironically enough, mainly academic pieces on Dylan that came out as I was approaching the end of this book. In his contribution, 'Rock Of Ages', Simon Armitage wrote:

> *'Tangled Up In Blue' is a great song. But peering in to it like this tells us that it's something of a mess, or that literary criticism is the wrong tool when it comes to the analysis of song lyrics. There are moments in the textual life of 'Tangled Up In Blue' that are pure poetry and that any poet would have been glad to have written. ...But for every highlight there is a contrived rhyme, a cornball cliché, an embarrassing tautology, a redundant syllable, a tired simile, a lame comment and a cheesy pun. Towards the end the song slews unnecessarily between pronouns. Dylan's sabotaging of the linear progression of the story is intriguing, even exciting in performance, but on paper it doesn't look so clever...*
>
> *But lest we forget, writing about music is like dancing about architecture, and Bob Dylan doesn't need the literary establishment to accredit his writing. He doesn't need to be seen in that light or spoken of in those terms. His virtue is in his Style, his attitude, his disposition to the world and his delivery of his words. Even the way he pronounces 'illusion' on that track is enough to make something happen...*[1]

Given its schizophrenic approach towards the subject at hand, where the overall effect is of an approach to Dylan that is neither fully academic nor sure of exactly what it should be, Mr Armitage is not proven wrong about the efficacy or otherwise of talking about Dylan's songs in a literary critical style by the collection in which his words appear. Others have proven his claims unfounded, however. Professor Ricks, for one. Ricks began a 2002 speech at Boston university with the following comments:

> *If he ever gets the critic that he deserves, it would be somebody who could talk about the music and the words and the voice - and voicing - and independently respect them and be imaginative about their independence. I am not that person. I talk only about the words. I am not trained in the study of music and voices have always - legendarily - defeated the word. It is extraordinarily difficult to put voices into words, as it is to put the difference of taste between white wine and red wine or an apple or a pear into words.*

Superficially it would appear that Professor Ricks is agreeing with Armitage, that he is using the 'wrong tool' because it is inadequate to the multifarious elements that make up Dylan's art. Ricks, though, is being modest, we should not miss this by being too used to the immodest in the world of Dylan criticism. What he is saying is that he is 'only' expertly trained to talk about the words, it is not that he is unable to talk about the other elements at all. Indeed it is impossible to think that a man so trained in one discipline of art appreciation would be unable to transfer some of his discernment and insight into other spheres. Leaving that aside though, and just highlighting an example that any listener can come up with, Professor Ricks went on to talk about George Harrison's version of Dylan's 'If Not For You'. He spoke of it being 'slow' and 'languorous', which he pointed out makes it sound 'odd' as though it were being sung in the 'midst of a painful divorce'. He was not talking here as a literary critic, he was responding to Harrison's musical and vocal treatment of the song in comparison to Dylan's. His response on this level alerted the literary critic in him to the realisation that the 'rhymes are different', the very words changed in meaning by the music and voice. (Harrison's version he said, with understandable bewilderment at the idea, 'sounds sad and blue'.)

So to return to Armitage's first criticism, it is not so much that 'literary criticism is the wrong tool when it comes to the analysis of song lyrics' but that it is wrong to use it as the only tool. Common sense surely makes that clear in any case. As listeners we know that 'Tangled Up In Blue' is never 'contrived, cornball, embarrassing, redundant, tired, lame' or 'cheesy'. Simon Armitage knows it too and he only arrives at these words by deliberately judging Dylan's lyrics in a way he knows is inappropriate, to 'prove' a point.

Yet he does not prove that the tool of literary criticism is of no use at all, all he does is show that to ignore the fact that the tool is being used on song lyrics rather than poetry produces ridiculous results. That is surely clear in any case, and yet the point has been belaboured in recent years with an avalanche of writing pointing out that Dylan's words are not poetry and it is the performance that matters not the lyrics.

I can understand why this has happened, I should do since I've been moved to similar sentiment myself. Dylan fans have always known that the general view that Dylan can't sing is only true in the sense that what he vocally achieves seems so far beyond mere singing. 'Dylan can't sing in the same way that Picasso can't paint' just about sums up the weary retorts from embattled believers. The relatively recent stress on openly admitting this and placing it at the heart of his art has, however, had the knock-on effect in some circles of downplaying his compositional powers. I'd like to explore why that has happened and then return to what I see as a more balanced approach to discussing his songs. An approach that allows for what is evidently the case, that his art is a fusion of elements - music, voice and words - and to elevate one element should not necessarily lead to downplaying the others. This is I think a stance we all instinctively realise is true and take naturally, it is only in championing a particular element that we move away from it.

Although I often write using the tools of literary criticism, I don't forget the voice or that I am discussing song lyrics rather than poems and that they have to be heard not read. It should also be clear that they need to be heard as sung by Dylan. Cover versions are sometimes pleasant, occasionally even something more; Hendrix's 'All Along The Watchtower' always springs to mind - but of the thousands of others very few are contenders for being considered similarly worthy. This is another argument for the importance of Dylan's vocal and musical abilities. Even Hendrix's 'All Along The Watchtower' is brilliant musically, not vocally and by the very success of its treatment portrays the song in a one-dimensional way, exhilarating as it is. You miss the depths of meaning that Dylan's vocals bring to any song he is engaged with.

There was until relatively recently an understandable defensiveness in Dylan fans and favourable critics towards this subject. Its glory is so commonly misunderstood that someone like Jann Wenner, writing in *Rolling Stone* felt the need to point out: 'more than his ability with words, and more than his insight, his voice is God's greatest gift to him'.

A number of critics have taken this further though and downplayed his words altogether. The rallying point for this school of interpretation is 'I'm Not There (1956)' from *The Basement Tapes*. This is one of Dylan's most haunting musical and vocal achievements. As the song, in the only take known to exist, has unfinished lyrics, it is often used as an example to show the primacy of those elements in Dylan's overall art. Unfortunately, in extolling the virtues of Dylan's performance on this song, a number of illogical conclusions have been jumped to.

Before discussing those conclusions, there are some things that should be cleared up regarding what has been written about the song. The literature on it continually suggests there are virtually no lyrics at all, or at least none that make sense. This is simply not true. Over and above the already-pregnant-with meaning title - (especially if you are biographically interested, think what the date could allude to in the composer's fifteenth year) - and refrain, the song boasts a number of coherent and moving lines and phrases. Lyrics such as: '*In my neighbourhood she cried both day and night*' leap out at you in the opening seconds. The central verses trace a discernible argument '*but I don't belong there/no I don't belong to her*', '*when I'm there she's alright/ but she's not when I'm gone*' and a complex situation is sketched out with '*I was born to love her but she knows that the Kingdom weighs so high above her*'. These are just a few of the many demonstrable lines. Now I know that some of the writings on the song were based on a poor quality tape, but the conclusions they draw from Dylan singing 'non-words' were simply based on a mistaken assumption that because they couldn't hear many words clearly that few were there. This led them to critically undervalue the importance of meaningful words in the song's effect.

Before looking at that, let me agree that it *is* undoubtedly a song with unfinished lyrics but what we have is more than a mere skeleton. There's a lot of meat on the bones. In any case, conclusions that are arrived at by using this incomplete work to 'prove' that 'words are irrelevant' fly in the face of common sense. Try replacing, 'The ghost of electricity howls in the bones of her face' in 'Visions Of Johanna' with 'A phust of eccentricity spoils in the haste of she trace' and tell me the song would mean the same so long as Dylan sang it in an identical way. Change every line in the song to gibberish and about a quarter of the words to meaningless sounds, or try the same with 'Mr. Tambourine Man' or any other song - it doesn't matter how well he were then to sing or play them, they would not be as worthy songs.

We all know this, and I am not pointing out the obvious to take away from the beauty of the voice and music of 'I'm Not There (1956)' but we know the emotional intent of the song not just through the music and vocals. Their luminous beauty is inspired and augmented by what text there is too; there is more than enough audible lyrical content to set the mind off making its own connections.

There's also enough to show that Dylan may not have finished the song but he knew what it was about and where it would go when finished. This shapes his vocalisation and music; they don't come out of a sectioned off area with 'Lyrics not allowed' written on the door. Simply put, Dylan knows what 'I'm Not There (1956)' *says* and he transmits that to us, partly through the lyrics that we hear. They are part of the whole song. In this haunting case the lyrics are not completely finished, in other cases you can think of it's the music or vocals that aren't quite 'finished'. One of the reasons collecting Dylan bootlegs is so rewarding - and frustrating - is the amount of times you come across versions where they are perfect - just not all three of them on the same takes!

The swing against lyrics in critical writing on Dylan went too far. The immediacy and primacy of his voice is so beguiling and had hitherto been undiscussed at length so attention was drawn to this oversight. In the process elements of Dylan's art were treated as separate entities rather than the inextricably linked components that they are. I'd like to bring this introduction round to myself now, and how I see the balance of voice, music and lyrics. You will notice from this that I am in agreement with the 'performance school of thought' in their main points, it is just that I think the lyrics need to be properly positioned and accredited for their indispensable role in the whole experience.

When I first heard early and mid sixties' Dylan songs it was on an album called *A Rare Batch Of Little White Wonder*. One of those quasi-legal releases that are bootlegs in most countries but legal in some - in this case, Italy. It completely captivated me - all of it; the acoustic side as well as the sensational band sessions. In my naivety, I knew of no big acoustic/electric split, I just heard the voice I had been waiting all my life to hear on every track of this precious vinyl thing.

The sheer power of the music and the appealing, if mysterious, lyrics of the electric tracks were something totally outwith my previous experience; I'd never heard anything like it. A tired old phrase normally but literally true on this occasion. Life has never been the same since.

I knew right away from his voice - it's always those uniquely communicative vocals that catch you first - and the sumptuous, joyful music, that he was delving into deep 'truths' in the songs he had written himself and this led me to instinctively believe that the lyrics portrayed profound insight. It's important, though, to know that before I even knew what they were saying to me lyrically, Bob Dylan had pierced my heart and soul. There and then I knew this was it for good, there'd be no going back, from now on the mid-60s classic sound was imprinted forever. My contention is, however, that this magic imprinting was only possible because the words *were* 'special'; because they inspired the voice and the music which needed them as *words* as much as the words needed them. I knew what was being communicated was important, illuminating, fun and life-enhancing. I just could not yet comprehend intellectually why it was so. Yet I knew I would in time, that promise was an integral part of the instinctive reaction to the music and vocals - and what they were saying.

It is one of the most rewarding mysteries of art's effect on us. Here is Ted Hughes talking of the same thing in relation to hearing the poems of T.S. Eliot:

> *I prefer poems to make an effect on being heard, and I don't think that's really a case of them being simple because for instance Eliot's poems make a tremendous effect when you hear them, and when I first heard them they did, and when I was too young to understand very much about them they had an enormous effect on me, and this was an effect quite apart from anything that I'd call, you know, understanding, or being able to explain them, or knowing what was going on. It's just some sort of charge and charm and series of operations that it works on you, and I think quite complicated poetry, such as Eliot's, can do this on you immediately.*[2]

Bob Dylan's songs certainly 'did this on me', and the first half of this book in particular is my attempt to share part of what those mysterious and powerful lyrics say to me now when I hear them; what I 'understand by them' now, in Hughes' terms. This understanding has multiplied the 'tremendous effect when I hear them' exponentially.

Yet it was not the first time I had heard Dylan. Although *A Rare Batch Of Little White Wonder* was my introduction to the true Dylan experience, this was preceded for me by (in the order I heard them): *Self Portrait, Nashville Skyline* and *Dylan.*[3] I was interested in these, I liked certain songs a great deal but I wasn't transported. There was no epiphany as there was when hearing 'Lay Down Your Weary Tune' and 'Can You Please Crawl Out Your Window'.

This proves to me that the effect is an inextricable mixture; he wrote the songs because those were the songs he needed to sing, to express his vision(s). Then these combinations of words and music inspired him to create the perfect vocal vehicle to express them. All elements are needed to some degree or another.

The first 'Like A Rolling Stone' I heard was from the Isle of Wight performance. It had no effect whatsoever that I can remember. Words which now mean so much to me simply didn't register because of the way they were sung. (Perhaps, 'not sung' would be more appropriate.) As Ricks said of Harrison's version of 'If Not For You', the 'words had changed'. Again this shows the primacy of Dylan's vocal delivery; without it nothing works. Conversely, when he is fully engaged, the most mundane words can take on the power of the best poetry. I agree in all of this with critics who have been stressing performance over lyrics, *but at the same time* if you add his delivery powers to lines that carry such power on their own already, that's when you have classic Dylan. I contend too that the richness of the lyrics and the thoughts and emotions they contain inspire the best in his vocals and music; notwithstanding the fact that he can and often has turned his full delivery powers on songs of (seemingly) minor lyrical worth.

So, without denying the primacy of performance, for me the lyrics of the songs Dylan has written are part of the performance of how he sings them, most usually an integral part at that. I find it illogical to talk of the lyrics in isolation from the performance. After doing so with 'Tangled Up In Blue', Armitage himself notes: 'Even the way he pronounces 'illusion' on that track is enough to make something happen...' Exactly so, which is what a critic should talk about, integrating such thoughts into what a literary-critical approach can bring to the table.

To claim that literary criticism is of no help in 'Tangled Up In Blue' because it doesn't work on paper as well as it does in song only makes sense if, for some bizarre reason, the critic is discussing the text of the lyrics while never having heard the song. (And doing that for an audience who haven't either, for that matter.) The 'critic he deserves' that Ricks mentions would be an expert in discussing the lyrics, the vocals and all the other musical elements. This is not to say that an expert in one field, as Ricks is, with an appreciation of the others cannot be illuminating. It is only 'dancing about architecture' if one only talks about any one and totally ignores the other two. You can talk about how the music affects you emotionally even if you do not have the expertise to talk about it technically. (Which may be as well, as the only music critics I have read on Dylan have even more trouble in discussing it in a way non-trained people would understand than literary critics have in discussing text. One lives in hope, though, that others who can communicate such insights clearly will appear in the future.)

Similarly, you *can* talk about 'voice, and voicing' - we all know what is meant by a 'rasp, a growl, a croon, a caress, a whisper, a roar' etc. You can go a lot further and refer to a whole range of subtle effects when you know your readers are intimately familiar with the recordings you are writing about.

To this endeavour I bring a literary background and an interest in discussing it, a history of listening to all kinds of popular and traditional music, and over a decade's experience of writing on Dylan's (and occasionally others') music. A line from Dylan can recall a verse from Donne or a song by Neil Young to me - or both at the same time. So, the following chapters range from those using more or less pure literary criticism to those utilising different 'tools' altogether. It changes if, for example, I am discussing a complex, well known vision from the 1960s or the cover of an obscure country blues song some thirty years later. I come with my own predispositions; my influences are worn on my sleeve so you know where I am coming from.

I am telling you how the songs make me think and feel and why and how I think they come to do so. I hope by doing this that I in some way deepen your understanding of and/or appreciation of Dylan's songs. That's a big challenge and responsibility. I can only hope to achieve the 'deepen your understanding' part, it would be immodest to claim that as a certainty. On the other hand, I trust that by telling you what I hear when listening to Dylan and why I think I am hearing it that way it will at least supplement your own appreciation.

John Ruskin wrote sagely of criticism: 'The greatest thing a human soul can do in this world is to see something, and tell what it saw in a plain way... 'I've seen this,' says the helpful critic. 'Here's how you can see it too.''

Then again, it is possible you won't like the way I see it. Love of songs is a very personal and emotional area after all. If that is the case there should be no harm done. It is not as though someone else's view of a song can spoil it for you. If I tell you the way I hear it, and why, but you find my view insupportable, or not applicable to yourself or simply something you don't want to think about in relation to a song that has a private meaning for yourself, then fine, so be it, move on to the next song.

I don't go along with the idea that if something is precious to my emotional life I should be frightened to point my intellect at it. If the emotional response is an authentic one, intellect cannot cause it any harm; either it has no effect upon it or it enhances it. Analysis and criticism are, we have seen, as 'natural as breathing'. We all engage in them the minute we start talking about Dylan, the minute we say 'I love one track more than another', or 'I don't like this song as much as the others'. Criticism is simply a way of putting this on paper, hopefully in a structured manner that allows us to share with others the reasons someone's art moves us so much.

I happen to enjoy analysis: I believe that criticism has enhanced my appreciation of great artists from Donne to Dylan. The appeal of someone like Dostoyevsky, who for personal reasons is extremely precious to me in a private sense and whom I read and re-read to deepen my own appreciation, has been increased by others' criticism.

So I hope to do with you, dear reader, and the songs of Bob Dylan. As I have been extolling the virtues of good criticism, I would like to end this introduction by quoting an insightful paragraph from the music critic Benny Green, who wrote the following in *The Observer*:

> *What few people apart from musicians, have never seemed to grasp is that he is not simply the best popular singer of his generation... but the culminating point in an evolutionary process which has refined the art of interpreting words set to music. Nor is there even the remotest possibility that he will have a successor. He was the result of a fusing of a set of historical circumstances which can never be repeated.*

These would have been amongst the truest words ever written about Dylan. Except they weren't. Mr. Green was writing about Frank Sinatra. It must have seemed at the time that Frank Sinatra was that culmination. However, along came Bob Dylan writing new 'words set to music' that needed to be 'interpreted'. Words that carried a power and complexity comparable to that of the best poetry, even though they were song lyrics rather than Armitage's 'pure poetry'. Later Dylan placed these in the tradition of song he sees as his 'lexicon'. Bob Dylan's extension of the 'evolutionary process' is still on-going, and lately has had a particular interaction with the Sinatra legacy on his album *"Love And Theft"*.

From the current vantage point on the evolution of popular (Western) music it appears that Mr. Green was only about one generation out. For this writer Bob Dylan is the 'culminating point' of the 'evolutionary process'. Dylan certainly sees himself as having caught the end of a tradition that nurtured singers and writers for generations but has now come to a conclusion:

> *To me, music either expresses ideas of liberty, or it's made under the oppression of dictatorship. The only stuff I've heard that has that freedom is traditional Anglo-American music. That's all I know. That's all I've ever known. I was fortunate to come up at a time when the last of it existed. It doesn't exist anymore...*[4]

Let us now turn to look at some of this troubadour's songs, his 'traditional Anglo-American music' that 'expresses ideas of liberty'.

1. *'Do You Mr. Jones?' Bob Dylan with the Poets and Professors,* Ed. Neil Corcoran, Chatto & Windus 2002

2. This is from a recording published as 'The Poet Speaks, No. 5', and is transcribed and reprinted in Terry Gifford and Neil Roberts, *Ted Hughes. A Critical Study* (London: Faber and Faber, 1981), p.33.

3. You can read the full story of my introduction to Dylan on Troubadour's website at *www.amuir.co.uk/troubadour*

4. Edna Gundersen, *USA Today*, August, 2001

# One

# Anthems

## Blowin' In The Wind

*'Blowin' In The Wind', first published in* Broadside Magazine *in 1962...was an indisputably strong song, simple and timeless from the first listening. It would become the fastest selling single in Warner Brothers history in the hands of Peter, Paul and Mary, and the first to bring a new social awareness to the pop charts. To this day it's Dylan's most covered composition, from Bobby Darin to Marlene Dietrich. When folk music found its largest audience, it was because of this song.*

Cameron Crowe, Liner Notes to *Biograph*, 1985

'Blowin' In The Wind' was a major breakthrough for Dylan. It became an anthem for a whole generation; it seeped into general consciousness and built up a head of steam that resulted in a #2 hit for Peter, Paul and Mary. It was Dylan's first big leap forward and remains one of his most famous songs, and one of the most covered in pop history. As Robert Shelton writes in *No Direction Home*:

*'Blowin' in the Wind' had a dual life as a pop standard and civil rights anthem. Within a year of the 'Peter, Paul, and Mary' hit, nearly sixty other versions were recorded by the likes of Duke Ellington, Lena Horne, Marlene Dietrich, Spike Jones, Percy Faith, Trini Lopez, and Glen Campbell. Many more sang the song than those who recorded it.*

Dylan himself soon tired of it - or at least he did at the height of his rock 'n' roll incarnation in 1966 (interview with Martin Bronstein 20/2/66):

> MB: *What particular thing - song - would you say you remember being a breakthrough for you? Was it 'Blowin' In The Wind'?*
>
> BD: *No, no, it was...the most...d'you mean the most honest and straight thing which I'd ever put across? That reached popularity you mean? There's been a few. There's been a few. 'Blowin' In The Wind' was - to a degree, but I was just a kid, you know, I mean I didn't know anything about anything at that point. I just wrote that and that wasn't it really. ...*[1]

'Just a kid' he may have been, but it was a devastatingly effective song and Dylan's own return to it in all the later years of touring perhaps belies the above. It has to be taken into account that Dylan in his electric '60's phase was often derisive of his earlier songs. By the time of the 1974 'comeback' concerts he was encoring with 'Like A Rolling Stone' and 'Blowin' In The Wind', thereby sending his fans off with, respectively, his most famous rock and most famous folk song. Since then 'Blowin' In The Wind' has been performed many hundreds of times, becoming one of the most regularly featured songs in Mr. Dylan's performances (it was second most played in 2001, with 103 appearances in that year alone).

The following interview sees Dylan speaking from a longer perspective than the one above.

> Ron Rosenbaum: *How did it feel doing 'Blowin' In The Wind' after all those years during your last couple of tours?*
>
> Bob Dylan: *I think I'll always be able to do that. There are certain songs that I will always be able to do. They will always have just as much meaning, if not more, as time goes by.*[2]

Writing an anthem is no easy matter. It relies on many things: it must hit home straight away and it must have musical and verbal staying power.

It had no difficulty in the first - it was just so damn catchy! The sceptical Dave Van Ronk found this out quickly:

> *'Jesus, Bobby,' he later recalled telling him, what an incredibly dumb song! I mean what the hell is blowing in the wind?' He was soon to learn that he'd misread the situation. 'I was walking through Washington Square Park and heard a kid singing,*
>
> *'How much wood could a woodchuck chuck*
> *if a woodchuck could chuck wood*
> *The answer my friend is blowin' in the wind.'*
>
> *At that point I knew Bobby had a smash on his hands.'*[3]

The melody comes from the old Negro anti-slavery song 'No More Auction Block' (you can hear Dylan's brilliant rendition of this on *The Bootleg Series*). Then there was Dylan's voice and the harmonica: sounding simultaneously old and young, sounding like he'd learned a lot from Woody Guthrie, sounding like nothing you'd ever really heard before. Although it would be sanitised cover versions that first took the song to a mass audience, they were pale shadows of the Dylan version. No one else could sing the word 'blowin'' quite like Bob did; you would be forgiven for thinking that possibly the only other thing that could sound the same would be a blowing wind. He makes it sound like the phrases of the chorus are being swept up and along like scraps of paper in a wind.

Nonetheless, as the quote at the head of this chapter states, it was Peter, Paul and Mary who first capitalised on the song's hit potential. They noticed its immediacy right away, that it would 'hit home straight away'. The 'Peter' of the threesome, Peter Yarrow:

> *A big controversy started when Albert [Grossman] brought in the acetate of Bobby's new solos. Albert thought the big song was 'Don't Think Twice'. That, he said, was the hit. We went crazy over 'Blowin' In The Wind'... We went into the studio and released [it] as a single. We didn't wait for an album, we just put it out. Instinctively, we knew the song carried the moment of its own time.[4]*

Their instincts were right, and handsomely rewarded. Dylan recalled the excitement of its runaway success when speaking to Cameron Crowe for the liner notes to the songs on 1985's compilation, *Biograph*:

> *I remember running into Peter of Peter Paul and Mary on the street, after they had recorded it. 'Man,' he said, 'you're going to make 5,000 dollars.' And I said 'What? Five thousand dollars?' Five thousand dollars, it seemed like a million at the time. He said, 'It's amazing man. You've really hit it big.' Of course I'd been playing the song for a while anyway and people had always responded to it in a positive way to say the least. [5] Money was never my motivation to write anything. I never write anything with 'this is gonna be a hit or this isn't' type of attitude. I'm not that smart anyway...'*

As for 'staying power', it had - and still has - that. Not only is it still appearing on albums, and still featuring very often in Dylan's own set, but others play it too. During the 1991 Gulf War, Neil Young sang an ominous version of it on his *Weld* tour (it is on the live album of that name) and explained that he did so because the song was the 'anthem' of his people, his generation. The ideal of the 'Woodstock generation' as a family clearly still holds validity for some, and they have no doubts as to what their anthem is.[6]

This is no surprise given Dylan's role (however reluctant) as the leader of that lost tribe, but it is curious that it is this song which is always held up as the (pronounced theee) song about civil rights and peace. 'Curious' not because this is incorrect but because of how the song manages to convey this. This is no finger pointing protest song, nor a self-consciously righteous 'marching anthem' like 'The Times They Are A-Changin''. This is a simple little hypnotic piece that just asks questions; it is the listener who supplies the answers. This enigmatic structure gives the song cohesion and lasting power and its 'poetry', if that's the word, stems from its structure more than anything else. Then there's that hummable tune bringing to mind, time and again, the pointed questions; *'Yes, 'n how many times...', 'Yes, 'n how many roads'.* It was as though an entire generation fell under the hypnotic spell of this song, that through allusive questions and an inscrutable chorus was asking them: 'How much longer are you gonna let this go on?'

If you have any doubt of the importance of this song in the civil rights movement, bear in mind that the year after its composition saw the famous Washington March to hear Martin Luther King's epoch-making 'I have a dream' speech. Dylan was there on stage, singing 'Blowin' in the Wind' and his insightful look at all the victims and perpetrators of racism, 'Only A Pawn In Their Game'.

Mary Travers (of Peter, Paul and Mary) counts 'Blowin' In The Wind' as her favourite song because of that historic occasion:

> *If I had to pick one song, my softest spot, it would be 'Blowin' In The Wind.' If you could imagine the March on Washington with Martin Luther King and singing that song in front of a quarter of a million people, black and white, who believed they could make America more generous and compassionate in a non-violent way, you begin to know how incredible that belief was.*

She also has no doubts about the song's continuing relevance and enduring appeal, continuing:

> *And still is. To sing the line, 'How many years can some people exist before they're allowed to be free?' in front of some crummy little building that refuses to admit Jews in 1983, the song elicits the same response now as it did then. It addresses the same questions. 'How many deaths will it take till they know that too many people have died?' Sing that line in a prison yard where political prisoners from El Salvador are being kept. Or sing it with Bishop Tutu. Same response. Same questions.[7]*

The song's meaning and impact is known by those who oppose its message as well as those who support it. During his world tour of 1978 Dylan played at Nuremberg, site of the infamous Hitler rallies. A group of Neo-Nazis 'welcomed' this - as they saw it - left-wing, Jewish, 'Peacenik spokesperson' by demonstrating with predictable hatred, especially during songs they deemed most offensive. Dylan sang a spiritual version[8] of the song that year and one wonders what he thought singing it at that venue facing, as the stage does, the concrete edifice from which Adolf Hitler delivered his bile. One wonders, too, how aware he was of Hitler's 1978 followers by the stage. Whatever the answer to those questions, he added an extra word to the line at the end of the song, emphasising its continuing importance and relevance: 'the answer my friend is *still* blowin' in the wind'.

Immediate impact and lasting influence; how did Dylan create this?

The song is tightly organised. Each verse opens with two lines that pose questions. There then follows four lines of questions that are 'despairing' questions, inasmuch as the answers are so obvious that it is shocking that the questions are still being asked. The song as a whole promotes the idea that aeons are passing/have passed and still the simple answers have not been found. Paradoxically, though, the very fact that the questions can be asked gives hope that one day the answers will be found, and by the end of the song the hope is that they will be - must be - found now. As we shall see later, the intermingled pull of despair and hope is perfectly realised in the refrain that ends each verse.

I will now look at the song as it is structured; each verse has opening questions, followed by those of the quatrains, and then there is the refrain. The questions that open each stanza bring out key concerns of the time and the young songwriter. Verse one begins:

> How many roads must a man walk down
> Before you call him a man?

This seems to bring up the problem of youth not being taken seriously - something that seemed to bother Dylan then. As he was to sing elsewhere on the same album:

> How much do I know
> To talk out of turn
> You might say that I'm young
> You might say I'm unlearned
> But there's one thing I know
> Though I'm younger than you
>                 'Masters of War'

As we shall see, it is a theme that would be taken up in the next huge anthem, 'The Times They Are A-Changin''.

The second⁹ verse opens with:

*Yes'n, how many years can a mountain exist*
*Before it is washed to the sea?*

Time and questions about and surrounding it were to become a major theme in Dylan's oeuvre. In this early image he alerts the listener to the scale of the song (and thus the depth of importance attached to its questions) by the sheer length of time it conjures up.

Stanza three continues the time-based questions by asking how many times a man must look up before he can see the sky, by which time the point is well and truly made, the song is hollering at every listener - just how long can it take to observe something so obvious?

Before we look into this in more depth, though, let's explore the central questions in each stanza, allusive yet pertinent to the emerging Peace and Civil Rights Movements' questions.

The opening verse poses the question of how many seas a white dove has to travel before it finds restful peace, and then asks:

*Yes'n, how many times must the cannon balls fly*
*Before they're forever banned?*

This works off the basic contrast of war (cannon balls) and peace (white dove), and by using the question format it does so without 'browbeating' the listener. The use of 'cannon balls' is clever: There can be no doubt that its intended - and first - audience would immediately think of the nuclear bomb, but Dylan makes it a wider point than just nuclear disarmament; he makes it all war in all times.

Still, to reiterate, no-one who heard the song in the time of its creation, near the height of the Cold War tensions, could ignore the particular 'cannon balls' it brought to mind. This implicit reference resonates stronger with the partial rhyme of 'banned', as in 'ban the bomb'. This verse immediately became - and has remained ever since - an anti-war, and by extension an anti-nuclear war, cry.

Stanza two as sung, if you remember, is the one that makes it clear that the time involved in answering the very obvious questions the song asks is to be measured, frustratingly, in aeons. (*'How many years can a mountain exist, before it is washed to the sea?'*)

It is worth pointing out, though, that the sea does eventually wash the mountain away, so there is hope that evil will eventually be overcome.

Combine this with the very act of the singer singing the song and the audience answering the questions and you get a 'why not do it now?' effect. Again, the effect of an anthem perfectly realised; in two verses we have already been given the impetus to say: 'No to war' and 'No to racism'.

I say 'No to racism' because the question here, again by allusion only, is clearly as anti-racist as the previous lines have been anti- war:

> Yes'n, how many years can some people exist
> Before they're allowed to be free?

By using such oblique references and questions a much more powerful and long-lasting song (an anthem for all time) is created. Had Dylan specifically denounced past and on-going slavery and racial oppression it would have seemed more like haranguing his audience (however worthily), and may have become limited by explicit references' subsequent lack of topicality.

This is something Dylan has obviously grasped early in his writing life: on the same album the trenchantly anti-racist song 'Oxford Town' does not make a single specific reference to James Meredith. In a similar way to everyone hearing this verse from 'Blowin' In The Wind' in 1962 and thinking of the civil rights movement, it was surely the Meredith case which everyone hearing 'Oxford Town' in 1962 was immediately meant to think of.[10]

In the concluding stanza the mysteriously unseen sky (poetically evoking Man's inability to see not only the obvious but the elevated) is followed by the corollary of questioning that wonders how it is that we who have ears cannot 'hear people cry'.

All the song's questions climax in the next two lines:

> Yes'n, how many deaths will it take till he knows
> That too many people have died?

These unnecessary deaths that are mentioned link irresistibly to the war imagery in stanza one and the curse of racial prejudice (and, therefore, slavery, lynchings and mass murder) of verse two.

Just how long can we allow all this to continue? That's the question the song has been asking again and again. As to why this is happening, that has already been answered by the very questions the song poses:

> Yes'n, how many times can a man turn his head
> And pretend that he just doesn't see?

These lines detail exactly why racism and, by implication, militarism and war-mongering succeed. As Dylan said in interview to Gil Turner, not long after writing the song:

> *I still say that some of the biggest criminals are those that turn their heads away when they see wrong and know it's wrong. I'm only 21 years old and I know that there's been too many wars... You people over 21 should know better... 'cos after all, you're older and smarter.'[11]*

Both here and in his songs Dylan displays a very mature and sophisticated understanding, for one so young, of the way in which evil and repression rely on silence and cowardly evasion and facelessness to prosper.

Another thing that this verse does is to put the responsibility back on to the listener. The question that asks *'how many ears'* a man must have *'before he can hear people cry?'* begs the answer that we have two, where one should easily be enough. The implication of the opening questions of the verses tells us that despite this obvious answer the opposite is happening. Get a grip folks, the song is saying, the answer is palpably present everywhere you look. So where is this answer? As the song keeps telling us, it is 'Blowin' In The Wind'. All these questions are answered by the refrain that turns the song into such a powerful anthem, repeatedly telling us that the answer is 'blowin' in the wind'.

The answers are everywhere - all you have to do is pluck them from the air as the wind blows them by. Yet the nagging questions and the images of aeons passing both point to the fact that, although the answers may float by, they can also be snatched away by the wind just before you pick them up. This paradoxical reading is at the heart of the song; the answers are always within reach, it would seem, but they are always just out of reach too.

It is like a newspaper blowing in front of you, you half see the headline but you are not concentrating, and before you can read it properly the wind blows again and up and away goes the news.

Dylan is saying, indirectly, that by not paying attention to obvious answers all around us we are condemning humanity to ask itself in bewilderment, time after time, just how such ludicrous things as war and racism can exist. There are none so blind as those who will not see; there are none more guilty than those who pretend not to see.

Most Dylan commentators feel that, at least subconsciously, Dylan was recalling the following passage from *Bound For Glory*, the book, much-loved by Dylan, written by his 'last idol', Woody Guthrie:

> *I begun to pace back and forth, keeping my gaze out the window, way down, watching the diapers and the underwear blow from fire escapes and clothes lines on the back sides of the buildings... Limp papers whipped and beat upwards, rose into the air and fell head over heels, curving over backwards and sideways, over and over, loose sheets of newspaper with pictures*

*of people and stories of people printed somewhere on them, turning loops in the air. And it was blow little paper blow! Twist and turn and stay up as long as you can, and when you come down, come down on a penthouse porch, come down easy so's not to hurt yourself. Come down and lay there in the rain and the wind and the soot and smoke and the grit that gets in your eyes in the big city - and lay there in the sun and get faded and rotten. But keep on trying to tell your message, and keep on trying to be a picture of a man, because without that story and without that message printed on you there, you wouldn't be much. Remember, it's just maybe someday, some time, somebody will pick you up and look at your picture and read your message...[12]*

In the previously quoted Gil Turner interview, Dylan gives us a direct statement of how the song came about and what he was trying to say. Here's the full, relevant passage:

*There ain't too much I can say about this song except that the answer is blowing in the wind. It ain't in no book or movie or TV show or discussion group. Man, it's in the wind - and it's blowing in the wind. Too many of these hip people are telling me where the answer is but, oh, I won't believe that. I still say it's in the wind and just like a restless piece of paper - it's got to come down some time.*

*But the only trouble is that no-one picks up the answer when it comes down so not too many people get to see and know it... and then it flies away again... I still say that some of the biggest criminals are those that turn their heads away when they see wrong and know it's wrong. I'm only 21 years old and I know: there's been too many wars... You people over 21 should know better... 'cos after all, you're older and smarter.[13]*

This seems a clear reference to where the inspiration for the song's central imagery came from. Either independently or inspired, consciously or subconsciously, by the above passage from *Bound For Glory*. This does not discount the possibility that Dylan had also read Emerson's lines:

*Some stars, lilies, leopards, a crescent, a lion, an eagle, or other figure, which came into credit God knows how, on an old rag of bunting, blowing in the wind, on a fort, at the ends of the earth, shall make the blood tingle under the rudest, or the most conventional exterior. The people fancy they hate poetry, and they are all poets and mystics![14]*

While that description of flags - the Stars and Stripes in particular and what military people will do in its name - is strikingly apt, it could well just be coincidence. The Guthrie quoted above seems a far surer touchstone.[15]

As to why Dylan chose to write the song in question format, perhaps he tells us that answer directly in the liner notes to his fourth album, *Another Side Of Bob Dylan - (Some Other Kinds of Songs):*

> *you ask me questions*
> *an' i say that every question*
> *if it's a truthful question*
> *can be answered by askin' it*

In one sense 'Blowin' In The Wind's' questions are answered by the way Dylan asks them. The answers are so obvious; it is as easy as that. Yet still, the song reminds us, it isn't that easy and never has been. Sadly, the questions are just as 'truthful' and relevant when sung today. Dylan's first, great anthem is as alive and vital as ever, though one cannot help but wish that it did not still need to be heard.

It changed everything, for pop music and for Dylan. Cameron Crowe writes, in the liner notes to *Biograph:*

> *It is now almost a casual observation in the works of pop and rock histo-rians that 'Bob Dylan changed the face of popular music'. That difficult task hinged on the authorship and success of 'Blowin' In The Wind'. A simple melody with a subtle and questioning lyric, the song resonated with all the deeply felt civil rights issues of the early sixties. These issues, until then, had never been heard in pop music.*

Here we can also read Dylan recollecting that:

> *It was just another song I wrote, and got thrown into all the songs I was doing at the time. I wrote it in a cafe across the street from the Gaslight. Although I thought it was special, I didn't know to what degree, I wrote it for the moment, ya know.*

He wrote it for the moment, and became because of it the leader of a movement:

> *In my opinion, the history of America in the '60s does not make sense, unless we recognise that Dylan communicated more effectively with his generation than any official leader did, and that his songs, especially 'Blowin' in the Wind', influenced the attitudes and conduct of millions of people who might otherwise never have become involved with politics and dissent.*

*During 1962 and 1963, as 'Blowin' In The Wind' circulated by word of mouth and in print, it sowed the one idea that was essential to the peace movement, because the peace movement linked the civil rights movement and the antiwar movement, and transcended both of them - which is that racism, militarism, and authoritarianism are interrelated, and are evil. It does not state this idea or explain it, but it does contain it...*[16]

The problem with all of this is that leaders have roles to fulfil, song-writing leaders are expected to write anthems - whether that is what they want to be doing or not. Dylan soon did produce another 'big' anthem, 'The Times They Are A-Changin'', which we are going to look at now. However, it was not a role he felt comfortable in, nor was he prepared to undertake it for much longer.

## The Times They Are A-Changin'

'The Times' has many similarities with 'Blowin''. It too appears in a US compilation in the first years of the new millennium[17]. It too is still often played. If it is the lesser-known of the two, it is only slightly so. There are, however, major differences too. 'The Times' is clearly not as rich a song, lacking the enigmatic mystique and allusive poetry of the former. 'Blowin' In The Wind' was a spontaneous creation capturing the mood of the moment. 'Times' is an anthem written to order for what people wanted to hear at that moment. 'Blowin'' invited the listener in, and each listener's contribution is crucial to the song working for them; 'Times' preaches at one audience while flattering the egos of another.

'The Times They Are A-Changin'' was written to fulfil his role as 'Spokesman for a Generation', to give people what they wanted to hear rather than what he felt inspired to write. Notwithstanding that, it became nearly as well known as the former anthem and has lasted just as well. Almost despite himself - given the position he found himself in - Dylan imbued the song with a central imagery and genuine apocalyptic tone that has allowed him to return to the song time and again and find a surprising elasticity in it, permitting him to sing it in a variety of moods and settings. These strengths in the song help overcome its obvious limitations.

Those 'limitations' (and I am speaking here as though the song were being judged as a work of art, which was not Dylan's primary intention) make some people very uptight about this song. They see it as naive and unworthy of a writer who was to progress to songs such as 'Visions Of Johanna'. However, so long as you accept that it is a purpose-built sloganeering anthem then it has a lot going for it. If you are of the opinion that there is a place in the world for such things then it has much to recommend it and, unsurprisingly, it is not altogether devoid of greater depth and poetic power.

Initially at least, it was almost too succesful for Dylan. The messianic tone he adopted here was so very effective that it lived with him, much to his annoyance, for many years.

Indeed, the self-righteous folk singer armed only with a guitar and harmonica, denouncing the iniquities of the old, ruling order is an image of Dylan that became so pervasive that it is still, after all these years, and all his many accomplishments in other areas, the one that many people have of him.

Dylan would look back from his next album and scold himself for singing 'Lies that life is black and white'. Be that as it may, as an anthem for the emerging youth culture, the success of the signature tune of the Sixties cannot be underestimated.

And, although simplistic, the song is very well structured.

Like 'Blowin' In The Wind', it is an anthem, and it shares with that earlier song a pre-occupation with time and an under-pinning of biblical allusion and language;[18] more overtly so in this instance.

It is a ringing declamation, a marching song; the prophetic tone gains authority by its Biblical references and phrasing. The whole performance is threateningly ominous; the recurring beat propels the towering self-right-eousness of the performance in a way that allows us to be carried away, to believe the singer.

The title phrase itself is a master-stroke; it sounds like it has been around forever. It serves as a famous example of a felicitous streak in Dylan's writing - the saying or aphorism that perfectly encapsulates a known truth or deeply held desire. It has entered our everyday consciousness just as a saying. You can see it on adverts for bus station timetable alterations; the company I worked for at the end of the 1990s produced an internal brochure aimed at height-ening awareness of the millennium date problem for computers - guess what it was called? You will hear it in TV adverts, you will read it in newspapers and magazines, you can hear people quote it as though it were as a wise old saying.

The opening verse is purposefully vague in who it is addressing or, rather, until we hear the rest of the song at least, it purports to address everyone. 'Come gather round, people'.

Two concepts introduced are firstly, the central one of time, with the assertion that 'current' time is about to be replaced with something new. The other is that of an all-changing flood, which inescapably brings with it Biblical connotations of The Flood.

Those from the soon-to-be old time are warned that unless they start moving they will be doomed. It is a warning bell that will toll repeatedly for them, and not only, though most insistently, in the refrain.

Verse two opens with a more particular group of people: *'writers and critics'* - specifically those that should know, and warn, of this impending change. *'The chance won't come again'* hints of an apocalyptic change, as does the 'Flood' of stanza one. Of course, this runs counter to the whole idea of time being circular (*wheel still in spin*). There cannot be one 'end' of time if time is envisioned as spinning in a never-ending circle. Today's present is, irrefutably, tomorrow's past - a point the song repeatedly stresses (and also seemingly contradicts on more than one occasion).

This seeming contradiction has allowed the song to live long (and prosper) in Dylan's live performances, but to restrict ourselves to the original version presented here, it is not a contradiction that invalidates the song's core messages. Indeed, as we will see, it is an inevitable outcome of them.

For the 'writers and critics' Dylan refers to in these lines are those alive and writing at the time he composed this song. There will be writers and critics in future generations too - after the cataclysmic change Dylan sings of here - and the same may well need to be sung about them. Eventually, in a traditional Western religious sense, there will be an end to this cycle: a 'finishing end' or a 'final end' as Dylan might refer to it. You know, the really, finally, ultimately, finishing end - but this song does not address that issue, or at least that is not how I hear it. Rather it addresses one generation's view (or, more accurately, verbalises the latent thoughts of the generation); a generation that has always thought of itself as unique.

> *Come senators, congressmen*
> *Please heed the call*
> *Don't stand in the doorway*
> *Don't block up the hall*

Dylan progresses now to addressing the elected representatives of the old order; as many times before, even in so young a career, politicians find themselves in Dylan's firing line. From the opening verse's generality of 'people' we have moved to the more specific 'writers and critics' (those who should be alerting us to the imminent change) and now to that particular group who should be leading the change. Instead, though, they are either ignoring or vainly trying to block this march of history.

This third verse urges, as did the first, that movement is crucial because *'he who has stalled'* *'gets hurt'*. The battle is out on the streets, but sheltering behind the windows and walls of one's property will not afford protection against the rising tide of change. A change that is painted again in 'ragin'', cosmic terms.

Stanza four opens with exactly what youth always loves to hear - an attack on the parents that never 'understand' them.

> *Come mothers and fathers*
> *Throughout the land*
> *And don't criticize*
> *What you can't understand*

while the immediately following words say what all youngsters throughout history have yearned to hear, *'your sons and your daughters are beyond your command'*.

Dylan then neatly summarises the song so far; again stressing the changing of the ageing present time into something new, and warning that those who do not move with the change should get out of the way before it is too late:

> *Your old road is*
> *Rapidly agin'.*
> *Please get out of the new one*
> *If you can't lend your hand*

After this poetic synopsis of the song so far, Dylan crystallises the biblical, portentous tone into what can only be heard as a direct reference to *Matthew 19:30 (Many that are first shall be last, and the last shall be first.)*:

> *The order is*
> *Rapidly fadin'.*
> *And the first one now*
> *Will later be last*

The old road is about to be replaced. Dylan leaves us in no doubt by what: the losers of current time are about to be winners, who now is first will soon be last. The spin of time is causing chaos, destabilising the present society, but Dylan sees through the current chaos to a new order in which, to quote from Matthew again, *'the meek shall inherit the Earth'*:

> *...For the loser now/Will be later to win...*
> *...The slow one now/Will later be fast...*
> *...And the first one now/Will later be last...*

Youth will overthrow the old order. However, this youth will inevitably age and then, in turn, need to be replaced. That idea is made explicit by the central image of time being a spinning circle; notwithstanding the countering effect of the finality of other images such as *'the chance won't come again'*.

In the original version, the song is a clarion call for the coming of the New Dawn of cultural, youthful change. By placing the song at the opening of his third album and, even more so, by opening every show with it from shortly after its release until he stopped touring solo, Dylan was emphasising this message, and his position as the leader of this incipient change.

> *...the civil rights movement and the folk music movement were pretty close and allied together for a while at that time. Everybody knew almost everybody else. I had to play this song the same night that President Kennedy died. It sort of took over as the opening song and stayed that way for a long time.*[19]

Being Dylan, it was a position he quite clearly stood for, and yet simultaneously felt trapped by and rebelled against. In the chapter on 'Restless Farewell', we will see that Dylan quickly cast off this mantle and then, as he turned into an amplified rock star, how his repudiation of his immediate past grew. 'The Times They Are A -Changin'' was one of the songs to suffer most from the immediate backlash.

Some of his comments, while illuminating on one level, are, to put it kindly, disingenuous:

> *It happened that maybe those were the only words I could find to separate aliveness from deadness. It had nothing to do with age.*[20]

The concept of 'aliveness v deadness' is well worth pointing up (though one would be within one's rights to see it strongly connected with youth v. age under any circumstances) but whatever Dylan's intentions or wishes (and one has to bear in mind his own tendency to rewrite his own past, indeed his need as a creative artist compels him at times to do so) the song itself quite specifically and repeatedly had a great deal to do with age. Children and parents are set up as opposite if not warring factions, and a new road is heralded as coming to replace the 'rapidly aging' old one.

The message was unmistakable. It is inconceivable that Dylan did not appreciate fully this part of the song's meaning and impact both when he wrote the song and when he was still opening his shows with it in 1964. Speaking for the interview that accompanied 1985's *Biograph*, he recalled:

> *This was definitely a song with a purpose. I knew exactly what I wanted to say and for whom I wanted to say it to. I wanted to write a big song,*

> *some kind of theme song, ya know, with short concise verses that piled up on each other in a hypnotic way...*

The audience certainly was in no doubt. Paul Williams:

> *'The Times They Are A-Changin' expresses a feeling that was in the air but had not yet been put into words (not in a popular, accessible medium), that all these political and cultural (and personal) changes going on were part of one large Movement, a sea change, something of historical proportions, the sort of thing spoken of in biblical prophecy. This song may have been the decade's first public identification of what later came to be called the 'generation gap' - the new road of the children against the old road of their parents. Dylan took his own advice, seized the chance and wrote a hymn that would continue to be relevant throughout the changes of the next six years (at least). Naming the album after the song was a natural move, and served to heighten the dramatic impact of both album and song.*[21]

Which is not to say that the song does not suffer from the idea of being written to order. Compared to 'Blowin' In The Wind' it does lack depth. Nor should one downplay Dylan's honesty in disavowing a role he felt uncomfortable with. Indeed it seems he was ill-at-ease with the song almost from the first. Clinton Heylin, in *Behind the Shades*, quotes Dave Glover:

> *...Glover recalls seeing some typed pages of song lyrics and poems lying on Dylan's table. Picking one up, he read a line from a new song: 'Come senators, congressmen, please heed the call'. Turning to Dylan he said, 'What is this shit, man?' Dylan simply shrugged his shoulders and said, 'Well, you know, it seems to be what the people like to hear.'*

Naturally one has to beware taking one comment from one person's memory and without knowing Dylan's tone (diffident, put-on, scornful, resigned, playing along, defensive?) and placing too much emphasis on it, but all the weaknesses in the song when compared to 'Blowin' In The Wind' for example would seem to flow from Dylan writing it in this frame of mind.

Or at least partly thinking this, as other quotes show him in a very different mindset. Talking of this time Dylan later was to say:

> *I felt passionate about all those songs because I had to sing them. They were written for me to sing. To stand in front of people and sing, I have to care about the songs. As I remember, I cared about all the stuff I wrote about.*[22]

The mantle of leader of the young, harbinger of the upcoming, palpably felt 'one big Movement' was bound to make Dylan uncomfortable, and yet the writing, release and prominent position he gave (and continued to give when his dissatisfaction was full blown) to this song played a large part in cementing him in that role. One which he was to struggle to escape for a long time to come. Contradictions surround him; they have throughout his career. It is something I will remark upon in more than one of the following chapters, because Dylan uses them as a creative force. As Jack Nicholson memorably and perspicaciously said in introducing him at the 1991 Grammy Awards:

> I started leafing through the dictionary. All the words seemed to apply to him! Under 'P', two words under 'paradigm' which means 'model', 'paradox' the fairest word for him, I think. It means 'a statement seemingly self-contradictory but in reality possibly expressing a truth'.

In this, as in so many other things, Dylan brings Ralph Waldo Emerson to mind, he who once talked of 'foolish consistency' being the 'hobgoblin of little minds'.

Time allowed him to return to the song, and a counter-balance to the rejections of his own work can be poignantly heard on the official album *Live At Budokan*[23] (1978):

> 'I wrote this... about 15 years ago - it still means a lot to me...I know it still means a lot to you, too'

As the years passed, Dylan, along with many in the audience, was no longer the young and the new but rather the ageing and the old, and he sang the song with longing, regret, irony, defiance and a host of other emotions depending on which facet of his reflection on time's passing and his (and our) and his anthem's place in it he most wanted to convey.

Remarking, in 2001, on the often overlooked depths to his song, Dylan commented:

> People focus on the senators and congressmen in 'The Times They Are A-Changin' but never the Nietzschean aspects. The spirit of 'God is dead' was in the air, but Nietzsche was the son of a bourgeois pastor. That turns the rationale on its head.[24]

At the time of the song's release, for the generation Dylan was speaking for - if not, in fact, shaping - this was the moment of great change; for the 'writers and critics' referred to here this was their last chance. Dylan was playing it very much as an end-of-time warning of apocalyptic change. Time though, as the song tells us, will pass and the great circle will turn again - an image that allowed Dylan to perform it very differently in later years, investing the song with different moods and emotions. As a parent many times over himself, (perhaps he himself stands as a symbol for many youths of an old order that they want to overthrow), but most of all as someone who has experienced that life again and again can dash naive hope, Dylan subtly alters the lines:

> For the loser now
> Will be later to win

to

> For the loser now
> Might be later to win

1. Martin Bronstein, Feb. 1966 Montreal, reprinted in *The Fiddler Now Upspoke* series; Desolation Row Publications, UK.

2. Ron Rosenbaum (*Playboy*) interview Nov. 1977.

3. Quoted by Jasper Rees in Tim De Lisle (ed.), *Lives of the Great Songs*, Penguin, 1995, p. 143-144.

4. Joe Smith, *Off The Record*, London, 1989, p. 162.

5. This had been true from the very beginning. Both Dylan and David Blue have recounted how the song was first played live, straight after being completed by Gil Turner. Blue remembered it like this:

> Bob was nervous and he was doing his Chaplin shuffle as he caught Gil's attention. 'I got a song you should hear, man,' Bob said, grinning from ear to ear. 'Sure thing, Bob,' Gil said. He moved closer to hear better. A crowd sort of circled the two of them. Bob sang it out with great passion. When he finished there was silence all around. Gil Turner was stunned. 'I've got to do that song myself,' he said. 'Now!' 'Sure, Gil, that's great. You want to do it tonight?' 'Yes,' said Turner, picking up his guitar, 'teach it to me now.'
> Bob showed him the chords and Gil roughly learned the words. He took the copy Bob made for him and went upstairs. We followed, excited by the magic that was beginning to spread. Gil mounted the stage and taped the words on to the mike stand. 'Ladies and gentlemen,' he said, 'I'd like to sing a new song by one of our great songwriters. It's hot off the pencil and here it goes.'
>
> He sang the song, sometimes straining to read the words off the paper. When he was through, the entire audience stood on its feet and cheered. Bob was leaning against the bar near the back smiling and laughing. (See *Hoot! A 25-Year History of the Greenwich Village Music Scene*, New York, NY, 1986, p. 83-84).

6. Its enduring appeal continues. Following the atrocities inflicted on America on September 11th 2001, Columbia Records released a (partial fund raising) album of 'patriotic and emotional songs', *God Bless America*. Among the chosen tracks were: 'God Bless America' - Celine Dion, 'Land of Hope and Dreams' (live) - Bruce Springsteen & the E Street Band, 'Amazing Grace' - Tramaine Hawkins, 'Bridge Over Troubled Water' - Simon & Garfunkel, 'America the Beautiful' - Frank Sinatra, 'This Land Is Your Land' - Pete Seeger, 'We Shall Overcome' - Mahalia Jackson and 'Blowin' In The Wind' - Bob Dylan.

7. Joe Smith, *Off The Record*, London 1989, p. 161

8. *'Blowin' In The Wind' has always been a spiritual. I took it off a song, I don't know if you ever heard, called 'No More Auction Block.' That's a spiritual. 'Blowin' In The Wind' follows the same feeling... I've always seen it and heard it that way, it's just taken me... I just did it on my acoustical guitar when I recorded it, which didn't really make it sound spiritual. But the feeling, the idea, was always, you know, that's where it was coming from, so now I'm doing it in full like a spiritual...*

Bob Dylan talking to Marc Rowland, 23 Sept 1978, Rochester, New York

9. Verses two and three are transposed in the official Lyrics book. As mentioned elsewhere, these lyrics are so riddled with errors and inconsistencies that it is impossible to know when to place significance upon such changes. I am discussing the song in the order Dylan sings it.

10. In late 1962 Meredith became the first black student at the University of Mississippi. He was risking his life to prove that non-segregation was not only illegal in fact but could be overcome in practice. This landmark episode in the civil rights movement left two people dead amidst wide-spread rioting. As far as we know Dylan has played the song live but once, at the University of Mississippi on the 25th of October 1990.

11. Gil Turner interview Oct.-Nov. 1962 issue of *Sing Out*, reprinted in liner notes for *Broadside* (*Broadside* 301; 1963)

12. Woody Guthrie, *Bound For Glory*. The probable connection with 'Blowin' In The Wind' was first made, I believe, by Wayne Hampton in *Guerrilla Minstrels*.

13. Quoted in *The Telegraph* 44; winter 1992

14. Ralph Waldo Emerson: *The Poet*

15. Also apt is that Emerson's next line begins *'Beyond this universality of the symbolic language'*, apt inasmuch as that is a good description of 'Blowin' In The Wind's' strength. As far as I am aware the first person to mention Emerson's use of 'blowing in the wind' and link it to Dylan's song was Gordon Friesen in *Broadside* 108, 1970.

16. Jenny Ledeen, *Prophecy in the New Era* (chapter one), 1995 Peaceberry Press, St Louis

17. Columbia/Legacy released the box set *Freedom: Songs From the Heart of America* on Nov. 19th 2002. Featured artists included Bruce Springsteen ('Chimes of Freedom'), Bob Dylan ('The Times They Are A-Changin' '), and Johnny Cash ('Song of the Patriot').

18. Not only does 'Blowin' In The Wind' have a white dove (bringing to mind the tale of Noah) but also for Bert Cartwright in (*The Telegraph* 44) the title phrase is 'reminiscent of "wind bloweth where it listeth, and thou can'st not tell whence it cometh or whither it goeth"' (John 3:8 King James Version). See also Jenny Ledeen *Prophecy in the New Era* (throughout) 1995 Peaceberry Press, St Louis. All of which ties in nicely with the Dylan quote in note 8, above.

19. *Biograph* interview-sleeve notes, 1985

20. Quoted by Clinton Heylin, *Behind The Shades, Take Two*. Quoting an interview by Mary Merryfield, Chicago Tribune 1964

21. Paul Williams, *Performing Artist*, Underwood -Miller 1990

22. Joe Smith, *Off The Record*, London, 1989, p. 164

23. He does the same, and provides yet another counter-balance to his early rejections, by including an out-take version from the original album sessions on the bonus disc released with 2001's *"Love And Theft"*. Incidentally, the second disc of *Live At Budokan* opens with 'Blowin' in the Wind' and ends with 'The Times They Are a-Changin''.

24. *Dylan is positively on top of his game*, Edna Gundersen, *USA Today* October 9[th] 2001`

# Two

# Don't Think Twice, It's All Right

## Foreword

*In the first Dylan magazine I edited,* **Homer,** *the slut, I had a section called 'Focus On'. This consisted of a collection of all the commentary I could find on a particular song. Originally it was also the intention that readers would contribute their thoughts on each song in question, and to encourage contributions I would append my own thoughts on the particular song under the spotlight. This article is an amended and updated version of the one that appeared in that position in* **Homer,** *the slut issue 4. The* **Afterword,** *new to this volume, looks at the development of the song's core theme in a later song, 'It Ain't Me, Babe'.*

When Dylan came to write this song, articulating feelings generally ascribed to his personal relationship with Suze Rotolo at that time, he used the tune from a song Paul Clayton discovered called 'Who's Gonna Buy You Chickens, When I'm Gone?' That old controversy is not the concern of this article, that kind of 'love and theft' was going on long before Dylan began his career and will continue long after it. The route of the melody from the mists of obscurity to Appalachia then spread worldwide via Bob Dylan and innumerable covers of his song is nonetheless a diverting, if far from unique, tale.

Johnny Cash used the same melody for 'Understand Your Man' which he released as a single backed with the known-to-Dylan fans 'Dark As A Dungeon'. 'Understand Your Man' provides a fascinating comparison with Dylan's song. Cash performs it with that trademark voice of his, conjuring up a John Wayne, square-jaw approach to life. (I think one of the main things to come out of his later duets with Dylan is how affecting and sensitive Dylan's vocals are in comparison.) However, his tough man stance is apt here as the singer of Cash's song has some harsh things to say, such as:

> *Lay there in your bed and keep your mouth shut*
> *Till I'm gone*

'Understand Your Man' paints a very unsympathetic portrait of the woman: 'cryin', cuss & moan' / 'bad mouthin''. We presume that when she does understand her man - and it is clear that this enlightened state will only be reached when he's gone, she's too dumb to have appreciated the treasure she had when he was there - she'll be very sorry.

It is condescending and one-sided in the extreme.

However this is a scene, a vignette from the country song life cycle: it is an episode in the life of a man who has had a harsh but warm upbringing in rural America. A man who will go on to marry his childhood sweetheart but whose initially ideal marriage will be rocked by affairs and heavy drinking. The downward side will be accentuated when first their dog and then their favourite daughter are killed in freak, easily avoidable accidents. Many traumas later the bottle will let them down & the old rugged cross will give them something everlasting to hold on to.

Does it sound like I'm just being sarcastic? Well maybe, maybe not. It is just that the tradition, the conventions of white folk-country at this time are so very different from the way we apprehend Dylan singing 'Don't Think Twice, It's All Right'. These situations I've jestingly described above are clichés, scenes from a stereotypical life. What is a cliché, though, but a universal truth frozen in time? What is country music doing with these banal clichés? Sometimes - mostly - making banal songs, but at others touching on the universal truth behind the cliche. As Allen Jones said on the *Arena Special* on the making of Elvis Costello's country album, *Almost Blue:*

> '...*although the popular conception of country music condemns it as being sentimental, bland and lachrymose, the best of it contains a real soul and depth of feeling that people don't often recognise. George Jones or Hank Williams, say, could take what appears to be a trite lyric and turn it into something really quite monumentally moving.*'

This transformation from banal cliché to 'something really quite monumen- tally moving...' will almost certainly have happened due to the performance of the song - or of a new song using conventional country musical and verbal structures and images - rather than anything transcendentally different in the music or lyrics. I could take a number of Dylan performances of recent years as proof of this, without even listing a few country greats. You can find examples of it from the most unlikely sources, such as Nick Cave singing 'By The Time I Get To Phoenix' on his *Kicking Against The Pricks* album. Again a one-sided situation - (the dumb broad is gonna realise that he's really left now and again she'll be sorry) - and a song that has been played as cheaply and banally as almost any that spring to mind. Here it is transformed by Cave's devastating delivery into 'something really quite monumentally moving...'

His performance eloquently conveys the impression that he is not only sorry not to be there, it is driving him mad that he is not.

The songs mentioned above are the property of any singer, they are stylised scenes, impersonal to the performer except as a test of his ability to perform them. Unless, that is, he *lives* the song as he performs it and thereby imbues with personal meaning. Cash threatens to do this but once - listen to how he breathes the word 'breathed' in:

> While I'm breathin' air that ain't been breathed before.

The rest of the time, though, Cash is playing the wise, tough man-of-the world. He even stresses that he is playing the part in a stock scene from this stereotypical life-film. The pronunciation of 'I'll' as 'Ah'll' in line four is a bit over exaggerated, the jaunty playing in the 'hoe down' interlude that splits the song in two, but most of all the laughter while singing the title line after his first aside:

> Understand your man
> (I'm tired of your bad mouthin')
> Understand your man.

All of these emphasise that he is just a singer singing a stock song. This is the convention. But not only was it the convention of country music then, it was the given situation. This is pre-Dylan style, the heyday of Tin Pan Alley; writers didn't write from the heart, performers weren't communicating with their audience on a personal basis.

No-one listening to 'Understand Your Man' can feel that the song means anything specifically personal to Cash. Although he happened to write it, it may as well be what we'd now call a cover, and one picked with no particular relevance to the singer; no-one listening to Dylan singing 'Don't Think Twice, It's All Right' can feel that the song is anything other than the result of an intensely heartfelt and personal experience for Bob Dylan. It is a startling reminder of the changes he was making to the course of popular music even at this early stage.

I'm quite well aware that there were more covers of 'Don't Think Twice, It's All Right' than any Johnny Cash song, but with Dylan's arrival on the scene, there was this new difference between a 'cover' and the 'real thing'. With 'Understand Your Man' most listeners probably didn't know or *care* who had written it.

There is a feeling of wistful regret in Dylan's song that isn't evident in Cash's song. 'Understand Your Man' would never have the following lines:

> *But I wish there was something you would do or say*
> *To try to make me change my mind and stay,*

But the next line:

> *But we never did too much talkin' anyway*

hints at similar problems of non-communication, though here the blame seems mutual, or the situation almost inevitable rather than the fault of the caricatured cussin', moanin' and bad mouthin' woman of the previous song.

Which is not to say that this line cannot be sung in a totally different, non-regretful, way. As he has shown in many live performances, Dylan can use it to point the finger of blame in almost crude, but invigoratingly gleeful - and still intensely personal - rejections. The title line itself can have a double reading: 'Don't think twice, you heartless bitch, I'll survive without you' or 'Don't think twice, we're doing the right thing, we're just one too many mornings...' The enduring magic of this and most other Dylan performances of the song is that both are present simultaneously, just as they are in the real life experience.

Certainly, though, rejection is always there. She is after all 'the reason he's travelin' on', she has 'wasted his precious time': this is what the song is about. However, this is surely just a statement of a feeling and situation that everyone experiences, not (on the original, at least) a simplistically vindictive put down or a crowing celebration of leaving her behind.

He has to go on and put it down to experience to continue to grow as a person. There is no doubt that if things could be worked out he'd be back with her like a shot, as the earlier quote demonstrates. There is a double edged truth to the 'precious time' line, Dylan leaves an ever so delicate and deliberate pause before emphasising the word 'precious'. The result is slightly self mocking, and the harmonica confirms that the time with the girl is what comes across as precious, regardless of the literal meaning of the words.

Perhaps the strongest *verbal* evidence that Dylan provides to show that, underneath the brash 'movin' on down the road', he is hurt and regretful, comes when he throws away a superb line of rejection and replaces it with a very forced term of endearment. The opening line of the last verse in *Lyrics* reads:

> *I'm walkin' down that long, lonesome road, babe*

And in the (earlier) Gaslight Tapes version was sung as:

> *So, I'm ramblin' all by myself, babe*

It is here rendered - and it is no mean vocal feat as it takes up the same musical interval - as:

> *So long, honey babe* [1]

This use of '*honey* babe' has the effect of softening all the other uses of 'babe' in the song, but it does so at the expense of a line that encapsulated perfectly the feeling he'd been searching for a few weeks earlier while singing the Gaslight version.

The woman addressed here may not have the devastating effect on recall that the woman of 'Most Of The Time' has, but she'll cause more than a few wistful moments in the singer's life, further down the road. The recurring 'its all right' takes on a number of tones throughout the song (as it later would in 'It's Alright, Ma') not least the very common usage which indicates the exact opposite. It is a phrase much used when all parties present know that everything is very far from 'all right'.

There are complicated shifts of mood in situations like these, shifting from blame ('like you never done before'), self-justification, regret, wishing it didn't have to be this way and back again. This version of 'Don't Think Twice, It's All Right' encompasses all of these in the lyrics and the music both.

The key line in the song, though, occurs in the third verse, couched in characteristic, man of the people tones ('give' for 'gave'):

> *I give her my heart but she wanted my soul*

This line is a touchstone for many Dylan's lyrics to come, especially in the ensuing four years. The pull is between romantic love, (and the heart's near over-powering hold has been well established in this very song), and something even stronger, something calling him away - his 'soul'. It is a classic theme for 'Love' ('heart') to be forsaken for a higher calling, religion or duty (Dido and Aeneas spring to mind ). For Dylan it is a higher calling and a duty too; the duty to himself as an individual - even more crucially as an artistic individual. The pull described in the songs to come is between the she that loves him romantically (as he does her) and the devotion demanded by his artistic calling, his muse - a 'she' he is enthralled and ravished by. The dichotomy was flagged early in Dylan's lyrics here by 'heart' and 'soul'; they are very useful terms to keep in mind while listening to his songs, populated as they are by mysterious 'she's and 'you's, in the mid-sixties.

As a musical performance it is a tour-de-force, with Dylan's young-yet-old voice phrasing perfectly - check out the enunciation of 'heart' in the famous penultimate line, third verse - and his harmonica playing evoking *everything* the song has attempted to capture in words.

There is no need to speculate on what Dylan was hoping to achieve with the song because he tells us that in the liner notes to the album:

> '*A lot of people,' he says, 'make it sort of a love song-slow and easy-going. But it isn't a love song. It's a statement that maybe you can say to make yourself feel better. It's as if you were talking to yourself. It's a hard song to sing. I can sing it sometimes, but I ain't that good yet. I don't carry myself yet the way that Big Joe Williams, Woody Guthrie, Leadbelly and Lightnin' Hopkins have carried themselves. I hope to be able to someday, but they're older people. I sometimes am able to do it, but it happens, when it happens, unconsciously. You see, in time, with those old singers, music was a tool - a way to live more, a way to make themselves feel better at certain points. As for me, I can make myself feel better some times, but at other times, it's still hard to go to sleep at night.*'

As this book unfolds we'll see how Dylan grew to 'carry himself that way', but this song is already quite a feat. It is not easy to create in song '*a statement that maybe you can say to make yourself feel better*' and give it, like others from *Freewheelin'*, enduring value and appeal.

I would like to add one last point in relation to the earlier performance we have from The Gaslight Tapes as a reminder of the craftsmanship and inspiration he needed to call upon to achieve this. Most of the main lines and images are in place, though the refrain line itself is changed, but there is one major change that illuminates both the care with which the young Dylan crafted his songs and his unerring artistry.

The passage in The Gaslight Tapes version that runs:

> *Well, it ain't no use in turnin' on your lights, babe*
> *Lights I never knowed*
> *And it ain't no use in burnin' your lamp, babe*
> *I'm on the dark side of the road.*

becomes the following on *Freewheelin'*:

> *And it ain't no use in a-turnin' on your light, babe*
> *The light I never knowed*
> *And it ain't no use in turnin' on your light, babe*
> *I'm on the dark side of the road*

There is nothing 'wrong' or clumsy with the earlier version, indeed the 'burning the lamp' image is excellent. It does, however, disrupt the structure of the song because the third line, in all the verses except the last, is a re-iteration of the first.[2] So Dylan has to choose between *turnin' on your lights* and *burnin' your lamp*. They are quite different, if both compelling, images. 'Burning" leads to ashes, there is also the forlorn connotation of 'burning out', while *'turnin' on your light'* is more like the 'strike another match' image from 'It's All Over Now, Baby Blue'; that is, active and dynamic, suggesting starting afresh as well as enlightenment. The 'light' image, therefore, is preferable to the 'lamp' one.

I have, however, slipped in a crucial alteration in my comment there, that of changing 'lights' to 'light'. It's interesting to speculate that it might only have been at the late stage of deciding between the 'lights' and 'lamp' images that Dylan realised the rich double meaning in turning on the light in the singular, the physical light and the spiritual light, the woman's inner essence. The same double meaning that leads Shakespeare's *Othello* to exclaim:

> *Put out the light, and then put out the light;*
>
> Act V Scene i

## Afterword - 'It Ain't Me, Babe'

'Don't Think Twice, It's All Right''s central declaration of the freedom of the individual from constraints was one that Dylan was to return to again and again. Not only, but perhaps most obviously, in his love songs. Two albums later, it found probably its most direct expression in 'It Ain't Me, Babe'. This song is a specific statement of the self freeing itself from the entrapments of a love relationship.

I am fully aware that, even more than 'Don't Think Twice, It's All Right' there are performances that support different interpretations of this song, but let me begin by stating categorically that when Dylan wrote this song and played the version on *Another Side Of Bob Dylan*, it was quite clearly about a love relationship.[3]

I am not denying that, especially in context, a farewell to other constraints can be read into the song, nor even that they subconsciously influenced its overpowering tone of rejection, but I remain unmoved in my belief that it is first and foremost a song about the ending of a personal relationship.

Not that I am interested in the specific relationship *per se*. We are dealing, after all, with art not journalism. We should not treat his songs as a diary of Dylan's life; they may well be the result of something happening in a relationship he is going through but they have been written and re-written; carefully crafted to project the universalised expression of a personal insight garnered through experience.

The fore-shadowing of 'It Ain't Me, Babe' can be traced back even further than 'Don't Think Twice, It's All Right'. In the early 'Hero Blues' he satirises women who want their lovers to become war heroes:

> *She wants me to go out*
> *And find somebody to fight*
>
> *She wants me to walk out running*
> *She wants me to crawl back dead*

Although the song is, intentionally, a very simplistic satire, it does have early forewarnings of some of the lines and thoughts in 'It Ain't Me, Babe':

> *You need a different kinda man, babe*
> *One that can grab and hold your heart*

Like 'Don't Think Twice, It's All Right', 'It Ain't Me, Babe' is a song about the need to move on to preserve the integrity of self while also highlighting the regret of doing so and the opposing attractions of staying. 'It Ain't Me, Babe' shows this regret in the way Dylan sings the repetitive 'no' in the refrain. Although parts of the song are quite harsh toward the woman he is leaving, the harshness is mollified by this and we are left with a mature, balanced look at a situation from which the man must move on to develop his true potential. As there is no sense of authorial distancing I believe we can safely assume Dylan to be singing from his own standpoint and, since he is a growing artist, the need to break free is even stronger.

Taken on its own, the song may seem one-sided, but Dylan was already thinking in complex terms about relationships - terms he would fully explore in some of his greatest songs on the following three albums. 'It Ain't Me, Babe' recognises a danger in the stultification that can affect both the protagonists in a love affair. The liner notes to the album make it quite clear that Dylan realises that he too must beware of entrapping a lover of his:

> *i have seen what i've loved*
> *slip away an' vanish. i still*
> *love what i've lost but t' run*
> *an' try t' catch it'd*

27

> *be very greedy*
> *for the rest of my life*
> *i will never chase a livin' soul*
> *into the prison grasp*
> *of my own self-love*

What he is saying in this song is that he will not allow her to ensnare him in the same 'prison grasp'.

This was a big deal at the time; you may think it quite ordinary now but back then popular artists simply did not sing in these terms far less write in them. The theme of the dangers posed to individual (especially artists') freedom from possessive love entanglements is, naturally, a recurring one in poetry. You will find it in the work of many, but perhaps none ever captured it more tellingly than William Blake in his masterly *Sick Rose*.[4] The same poet's oft quoted 'Proverb' is also pertinent:

> *He who binds to himself a joy*
> *Does the winged life destroy,*

Which is exactly the warning Dylan was giving in the sleeve notes quoted above. It is now a theme you can find explored in the work of people from the same field as Bob Dylan; back then, though, 'pop music' utterly ignored such depths. As Michael Gray wrote:

> *When I first heard 'It Ain't Me Babe' I specially liked that line*
> *'A lover for your life and nothing more' because in pop songs*
> *there never was anything more: to be 'a lover for your life' was*
> *the ultimate ideal.*[5]

Not only should Dylan be applauded for this kind of breakthrough but also for the fine way this, the final verse line, sums up the ideas and emotions behind the entire song.

'A lover for your life and nothing more' succinctly puts his case for the integrity of the self. The phrase, 'nothing more' not only satirises the excessive demands of the lover (reminding us again of 'Hero Blues') but also points to the potential doom-laden future of the narrator. If he does not leave her, he will be her lover and 'nothing more' - he will have given up his own personality and have no other identity than 'her lover'.

'It Ain't Me, Babe' was to be played in many Dylan concerts and was an ideal song to develop new meanings with ever evolving performances. The song became seen as a declaration of freedom not only from love's entanglement but from all restraints. As Dylan's name became bigger and bigger in the entertainment world more people wanted him to be their figure-head; from the outraged folkies when he went electric to everyone who wanted him to be a spokesperson for something or another, Dylan would sing: 'no, no, no, it ain't me babe'.

It came to seem at concerts that Dylan was directly addressing his audience and, as that audience developed, those that remained with Dylan through his changes began to sing the song back at their idol-who-was-telling-them-he-was-no-idol. It was as though they were saying, 'Yes, we understand now; you were right when you told us: 'don't look back', 'don't follow leaders', 'trust yourself'. But wait a minute, it you told us all this, we know this *by* following your lead'.

Remarkably the song that so exulted in a rock cry of individual freedom (on 1974's *Before The Flood* album for instance) became a communal expression of shared views (on 1984's *Real Live*). The ability of the one song to hold so many emotions and opposed points of view is something celebrated on many nights of what became known as Dylan's 'Never Ending Tour'.[6] The song also appeared - in yet another guise - in the *Renaldo And Clara* film and was one of the four tracks selected for the promotional EP; a truly sublime performance[7] mixing a huge variety of emotions in a new musical setting and a singular vocal delivery.

---

1. Would you have believed that the line: 'I'm walkin' down that long, lonesome road, babe' wasn't on the original LP without checking? I was astonished.
2. This change has the added benefit of signalling the song is coming to an end, the kind of thing Christopher Ricks has spoken of Dylan doing in his songs in a number of illuminating talks.
3. I do remember reading an interpretation in *Isis* magazine asserting that the 'Babe' of the song was the American Flag. Ingenious thought this was I am sticking to my own belief
4. We return to these same themes in the later chapter on 'If You See Her, Say Hello'
5. Michael Gray, *Song And Dance Man*, Hart-Davis MacGibbon, 1972
6. A catch all term for the style of touring that Dylan first introduced in the summer of 1988 and which is still ongoing over 15 years later as this book approaches publication.
7. *Renaldo & Clara* promo EP TAS 422 'It Ain't Me, Babe' is from Cambridge, 20/11/75. As this book was reaching its conclusion, *The Bootleg Series Volume 5* double CD plus bonus DVD celebrating the 1975 tour was released and it included this performance.

# Three

---

# Restless Farewell

### Foreword

*Nearing the end of November 1995, I put a message on my information line to say that Dylan had performed the perfectly appropriate, if startlingly unpredictable, song 'Restless Farewell' at Frank Sinatra's 80th birthday tribute. No-one who phoned, except for Michael Gray, seemed to agree with my comment on its aptness.*

*As I was due to write a column for* On The Tracks *I thought it seemed only natural to write about the song that was the talk-of-the-moment. I went back and played the original album version and waited for the video to arrive of the Sinatra tribute.*

*It is always my hope that, whenever possible, a reader listens to the song in question before reading one of these articles. If you are about to go and play the track from* The Times They Are A-Changin' *I suggest you play it on vinyl rather than CD; the early Dylan albums were not transferred to the CD medium successfully. Warmth and depth were replaced with a pinched coldness - ironically pushing Dylan's voice closer to the public at large's misconception of it. Or, at least, this is the position as I write, the long rumoured and much-needed re-mastering of Dylan's back catalogue on CD not yet having taken place. I hope it has by the time you read this; an album like* Bringing It All Back Home - *to pick the most extreme example - is being so badly misrepresented that it almost beggars belief.*

*However, let's get back to 'Restless Farewell'; this is the article I wrote, now updated and expanded to take into account material that has come to light subsequently, as well as what others have written about the song in the interim.*

I have often thought that I'd like to write an article on the last songs on Dylan's albums. They are usually very special, pointing either backwards to reflect on the album they conclude or forward to the artist's next progression. This song could well stand as the archetype of these 'ending songs'; a 'Restless Farewell' indeed, almost a repudiation of all that has gone before, and a pointer to the artist's future steps on the road ahead.

The song echoes sentiments and phrases from other Dylan songs; the title itself sets off various associations. 'Restless' is an uncomfortable feeling even when it is the springboard to positive action. Which it is here, as it was in 'One Too Many Mornings', an earlier song on this album (*The Times They Are A-Changin'*):

> *It's a restless hungry feeling that don't mean no-one no good*

except that the listener discovers that it did 'mean' the people involved in that song's relationship 'good'. Implicit in 'One Too Many Mornings' is the realisation that the relationship must end for the future growth of the two people involved. The acceptance of a complex world where 'you are right from your side and I am right from mine' also shows a maturity beyond some of the sloganeering evident elsewhere on this protest album to end all protest albums. These insights are repeated in the song under discussion also, although not in such a convincing way. This is because the earlier song is a more complete creation, fully worked out, whereas 'Restless Farewell' is something altogether different.

'Restless Farewell' is a song about transition that is being created almost in front of our eyes. It was tacked on to the end of the LP (as they were then referred to) a week after the rest was recorded; the album needed another track and Dylan had something to get off his chest. It was a rushed job, too,[1] and the kind of thing Dylan would normally have gone back to finish properly, or save a verse or two from, or abandon altogether as he moved on to something else. The sort of thing we often get on bootlegs. Instead we find it as the closer to the album and, as already stated, these are commonly key songs on Dylan's albums.

This transitional piece allows us a fascinating glimpse into Dylan's art because not only is it a far from worthless song in its own right but, similarly to the juvenile writings of a great artist, it affords its own pleasures and, by comparison, highlights why the mature masterpieces are so perfect. (Not that this is a piece of juvenilia.)

By happy coincidence - unless it is deliberate and I am doing Mr. Dylan a disservice - the half-formed song here is perfectly apt, epitomising, as it does,

**31**

the restless state the creator is describing. Just as the song itself seems in a state of flux until Dylan gets to the final verse, so the feelings it describes move from a restless state to a resolution of firm farewell.

I will be writing of a certain sloppiness in this song but it is not my intention to criticise negatively for the sake of it, rather to stress the hurried nature of this song's creation and the way it propels untidily toward a ringing conclusion. Dylan himself has said:

> Of course some songs like 'Restless Farewell' I've written just to fill up an album.

Dangerous as it is to rely too much on the veracity of a quote from a Dylan interview, all the evidence points to this being true (see the Afterword to this article). The song is not without overall structure and control, however. The rhyme scheme, although irregular, is based on the opening verse's *ababccdeed*, along with some very effective internal rhymes as the verses move from description to rejection. Each verse opens with 'oh every...' (or variant therof) as he bids farewell, in turn, to Friends, Lovers, Foes, Current Songs - and then looks forward to an independent future in the last stanza. Each verse has the same pattern, where an opening four lines of description are followed by short, sharp lines stating the need for the singer to move on; and each verse ends with '...I'll bid farewell...'

At this point I can almost hear the complaints of 'what's he on about, this is all old fuddy-duddy stuff like we got at school, all this *ababc* business.' Well that stuff was taught for a very good reason; to illuminate the craftsmanship behind inspirational poems. The lyrics to a song, too, are a mixture of inspiration and craftsmanship (a pretty unstable mixture at times - I'll admit - but always so, nonetheless).

It is pretty clear, in the case of 'Restless Farewell', that when you compare it to previous songs from the same album - 'The Lonesome Death Of Hattie Carroll' or 'One Too Many Mornings', for instance - that this is an *unpolished* little gem of a song.

You may well ask 'what about the musical arrangement?' Pure early-sixties Dylan, the lone singer with his guitar and harmonica - and a borrowed melody!

Dylan has used the melody from 'The Parting Glass', an Irish drinking song. Naturally, the melody of that farewell song fits Dylan's purposes exactly, as farewells are a time of extreme and mixed emotions, the pull of the present-about-to-be-past versus the lure of the future.

So it is here, and the ebb and flow of the melody match the to-ing and fro-ing of Dylan's thoughts in the lyrics. (It is perhaps worth admitting up front that Dylan has copped more than just the melody; you can add the lyrical structure, the sentiments and some of the images themselves.)

And so we find ourselves in Verse One in prime 'parting glass' territory, as it is time for Dylan to bid farewell to his friends after the bottles have all been emptied. The song opens rather clumsily with a convoluted first line (all he is saying is 'All the money I have spent') - a mish-mash, in fact, of the opening of 'The Parting Glass' ('Of all the money ere I had, I spent it in good company') followed by a few vague sentiments also echoed from that song. It picks up most effectively with a moving and well realised scene that always makes me think back to 'Bob Dylan's Dream':

> *But the bottles are done*
> *We've killed each one*
> *And the table's full and overflowed.*
> *And the corner sign*
> *Says it's closing time*
> *So I'll bid farewell and be down the road.*

Verse Two declares farewell to past loves, a theme Dylan has already covered more impressively elsewhere ('Don't Think Twice, It's All Right' and 'One Too Many Mornings' spring to mind) and this seems a rather brusque good-bye in comparison - a brusqueness tempered only by the oddly old-fashioned 'touched':

> *Oh ev'ry girl that ever I've touched*
> *I did not do it harmfully*

The song becomes more interesting - to this listener anyway - when the next group are bid farewell. Dylan follows friends and lovers with foes - an interesting order for one thing - but what foes are they exactly? They could be personal foes or they could be the political foes that he has been decrying in the protest songs that make up the bulk of the album (where the cause most certainly *was* 'there before they came').

I see it as a mixture of the two but leaning more toward the latter - for two reasons. Firstly, every farewell in this song is part of a 'Restless Farewell' to the previous tracks on the album. Secondly, Dylan will address his personal foes in verse five.

It is intriguing to hear Dylan singing proudly that he has no regret or shame over any cause he fought for, which if it does not exactly contradict, certainly stands in sharp contrast to his 1964 comment:

> *'I used to write songs, like I'd say, 'Yeah, what's bad, pick out something*

> *bad, like segregation, OK, here we go...I wrote a song about Emmett Till,*
> *which in all honesty was a bullshit song...I realise now that my reasons*
> *and motives behind it were phony.'*

Intriguing, also, is his need to slip out in the night; one can understand why the sight of his lover in 'Don't Think Twice, It's All Right' would make him stay behind if he waits until dawn, but why does he have to sneak out in the dark here? Is it because the arguments his foes would put up would prove so irresistibly engaging that he'd have to stay behind and counter them? This does not seem likely by the end of the song - by then a defiant proclamation of 'I'll make my stand' has replaced any thought of slipping out under cover of darkness. I suggest, rather, that it is another sign of its hasty composition, harking back to the drinker who never leaves the bar because he has to stay for yet another 'last drink for the road'. Or simply that Dylan has half-integrated the repeated refrain from 'The Parting Glass' where the singer at the conclusion of each of the three verses bids the revellers 'goodnight and joy be with you all'.

The next verse opens with a splendid couplet that snaps things back into focus:

> *Oh every thought that's strung a knot in my mind*
> *I might go insane if it couldn't be sprung*

Dylan here portrays the *need* for the artist to communicate and the effort required to do so - the unwieldy metaphor and language brilliantly reflect the somewhat untidy springing of the knot that is 'Restless Farewell'.

In addition, for the Dylan listener, these lines provoke an immediate recall of the lines in 'It's Alright Ma, I'm Only Bleeding' when he acknowledges it is safer to keep his thoughts hidden:

> *And if my thought-dreams could be seen*
> *They'd probably put my head in a guillotine*

The next line is one I find hard to believe:

> *But it's not to stand naked under unknowin' eyes*

I have to wonder if Dylan can really believe this. I cannot see how it can be true, as that is exactly what putting his songs out in a mass-market format leads him to do. However, this particular song, as we shall see later, finds Dylan questioning why he is doing this at all, and whether he should continue. This line could be taken for a lament for how it should have been, or, given the violent imagery and urgency of this composition, a declaration that he will not allow things to continue as they are. As he would write ten years later:

*I'm crestfallen, the world of illusion is at my door*
*I ain't a-haulin' any of my lambs to the marketplace anymore*

The same thoughts were troubling him here. He is all but thinking aloud in front of us and raising questions that are central to the work he produces around this time. Soon he'll be writing:

*A song is anything that can walk by itself*
*A poem is a naked person*

Now that is true, and also points to the full complexity of the situation. Dylan's struggle with his own fame has often been commented on; this song presents us with his thoughts on the matter, but they are only the fleeting thoughts of the moment. I do not doubt for a second that Dylan is sincere when he sings the following line:

*It's for myself and my friends my stories are sung*

but this does not begin to deal with the crux of the dilemma facing any artist presenting his inner visions to a public consisting mainly of strangers. (Although Dylan is right to stress that as far as he is concerned his songs are for those 'friends' who get where he is coming from, not the niggardly nay-sayers and negative reporters and those not on his wavelength, that is not how it works in the mass media.) This matter becomes most pressing for the *popular* artist. On the other hand, Clinton Heylin has written that perhaps Dylan was on the brink of ceasing to be a popular singing artist:

> Originally called 'Bob Dylan's Restless Epitaph,'... it suggested that, at the age of twenty-two, Dylan already felt time was not on his side. 'Restless Farewell' gave fair warning that he was no longer content to remain the Woody Guthrie of his generation. Dylan may even have envisaged a restless farewell to song. In the next three months, he would write a profusion of other 'epitaphs' (eleven of which would appear on the back cover, and as a special insert, to his third album) but none of them carried melodies, original or appropriated.[2]

This touches upon a central paradox between Dylan's avowed love of privacy and his existence as a public performer - one who *to this day* will go out of his way to draw attention to himself and to get reported in the very parts of the media he so claims to despise. (Let me add that, like the true artist he is, Dylan most commonly uses paradox as fodder for his art - I'd be tempted to say that at times Dylan's very mode of communicating his vision to us is via a series of refracted paradoxes.)

Returning to the song: the dismissal in this verse seems almost petulant to me, and certainly hard to justify. On the other hand it accurately reflects the problem he is having with 'his position and his place'. It is quickly followed up by what I hear as a rather trite rephrasing of 'time is short' (*But the time ain't tall*).

My friend and fellow Dylan commentator, Robert Forryan, on the other hand, hears it differently:

> *A typically Dylanish twist of language to say 'tall' instead of the more usual 'long'. Or is it a deliberate diminishing of Time, since it may seem that height, as in tall-ness, is more limited by gravity, than length which, since it is horizontal, may seem to be potentially longer (or should that be taller?)? 'Yet on time you depend' emphasises the all-pervading importance of Time to each of us, and that it isn't really as 'tall' as we wish it was.*[3]

Then we have some lines that in the Sinatra tribute he makes sound like the loveliest and most profound poetic thought:

> *Yet on time you depend and no word is possessed*
> *By no special friend*
> *And though the line is cut*
> *It ain't quite the end*

What is he actually saying when you put this verse all together? He is certainly claiming that these songs that he has felt compelled to write are for him and his friends only. (Is it the same friends he has just bid farewell to in stanza one, one wonders? And is he then suggesting that none of his words can be owned by any of his friends/fans?) He has 'cut the line' - there will be no more of these protest songs. Or so conventional readings of the song go, but is it not tantalising of Dylan to sing: 'but it ain't quite the end'? It hardly ever (never?) is with Dylan. There are 'ends' but he also expresses 'finishing ends' and 'final ends' as though a 'single end' never is '*quite* the end' unless one has a multiple expression of finality, and even then one often feels the 'real end' is still to come .

This verse is not really the great kiss-off it is reputed to be - where friends and lovers are told he's off down the road/line away from them; and foes are slipped away from under cover of darkness - his current songs are bid adieu only 'till we meet again.' We are very far from 'Positively 4th Street' style Dylan dismissal here; mind you, the next verse gets closer!

The last verse is undoubtedly where Dylan was wanting to get to. We are now clearly on the verge of a completed artistic statement and we are unquestionably right in the middle of what Dylan wants to say.

The opening line resonates in the context of the album it closes - from the ringing social call-to-arms of the opening, title-track, 'The Times They Are A-Changin'' to this more personal comment. The second line is a bald statement of his annoyance and impatience, followed by a couplet that gets right to the nub of his irritation:

> *And the dirt of gossip blows into my face*
> *And the dust of rumours covers me*

Those familiar with Dylan's life at the time will rightly see this as a reaction to the infamous *Newsweek* article that had just come out, a hatchet job that included - amongst other slanders - the repeating of the shameful rumour that 'Blowin' In The Wind' was written by someone else, granting that rumour credence by implication. Indeed, every scrap of evidence one can find points to this song being conceived, written and recorded in the few days after that article's publication. But you don't *need* to know the specifics: it fascinates me that where commentators understandably pick out the personal nature of this song,[4] the listener unfamiliar with Dylan's life-story hears a much more universalised cry of outrage. Listening to the song is a meaningful and moving experience whether you know the circumstances of its origin or not.

At the time, though, Dylan further underlined the personal nature of the comments by some of the lines in the 8th and 9th of *Eleven Outlined Epitaphs*. This was a series of poems, written at the same time as the album:

> *Yes, I am a thief of thoughts*
> *not, I pray, a stealer of souls*
> *I have built an' rebuilt*
> *upon what is waitin'...*

etc.

> *...your questions're ridiculous*
> *an' most of your magazines're also ridiculous*
> *caterin' t' people*
> *who want t' see*
> *the boy nex' door*
> *no I shall not cooperate with reporters' whims...*

Perhaps Dylan assumed his future listeners would also read these 'epitaphs' and make the connection, perhaps they were originally scheduled to be part of the LP packaging or perhaps they were just another way of 'springing the knot in his mind'.

Whichever, it is one of Dylan's greatest gifts to universalise his personal feelings in song, and how well the lines here do that. The following:

> But if the arrow is straight
> And the point is slick
> It can pierce through dust
> no matter how thick

make you fast forward to that other spine-tingling, state-of-the-artist acoustic-album closer 'When He Returns'.[5]

> Truth is an arrow
> and the gate is narrow
> that it passes through

While the next line, (*So I'll make my stand*) rewinds your thoughts to the conclusion of 'A Hard Rain's A-Gonna Fall'.

What a quintessentially 'Dylan' ending we have to this song, this album, this phase of his career:

> So I'll make my stand
> And remain as I am
> And bid farewell and not give a damn.

If you take the first and third of these lines it sounds like he is doing what he has said he is going to do all through the song, get up from the drinking table and leave. The middle line, however, contradicts all this talk of leaving; Dylan is determined to 'remain' as he is, as he has always been. It's others who are trying to force him into a backward path, and he's not having it. Instead, remaining true to himself he moves forward by leaving the backstabbers and nay-sayers and gossipers behind, along with anyone who thinks they can tell him how and what to sing and say. He says he's 'gonna do it his way' - and, of course, he did exactly that. Time and again he sings to us 'trust yourself' and 'take me as I am or let me go'; usually we reply 'no, no we want to take you as you were'. And so we leave him bidding farewell, not giving a damn...

## Afterword

Where did all this start? Oh yes, the Sinatra tribute: a great performance wasn't it? Very different from the original, the mix of contrived archaisms ('never did spend') and colloquial speech ('ain't') coming together exceedingly well as one old timer tips his hat to an even older one who had also done things his way. That's what Michael and I meant by its appropriateness; a greater 'My Way' from a near-forgotten, half-formed back page.

In his in-depth look at Dylan's life at the time, Clinton Heylin[6] points out that the song was originally introduced by the lines:

*The time can't be found t fit / all the things that I want t do*

Which certainly fits with the urgent feeling of having to push on and let no 'false clock' dictate how his precious moments will be spent. These lines come from what are known as the 'Margolis and Moss Manuscripts', a collection of Dylan writings from 1963 that show him trying new ways of writing: poems, free form autobiography, even a stab at a play.

In an important section, detailing how these papers include Dylan's response to the assassination of John F. Kennedy, Mr. Heylin pin-points the genesis of the next song I look at, 'Chimes Of Freedom'. The foreword to that article will take up the story from here...

1. Clinton Heylin's *The Recording Sessions* St. Martin's Press, 1995 and *Behind The Shades: Take Two* Viking 2000 for full details.
2. Clinton Heylin, *Behind The Shades: Take Two* Viking, 2000
3. Robert Forryan: 'Time' *Freewheelin' Quarterly* Volume 22, January 2002.
4. Paul Williams, *Performing Artist, vol. one* Underwood-Miller, 1990 and Clinton Heylin, *The Recording Sessions* St. Martin's Press, 1995
5. It is a curious fact that yet another acoustic album-closer, 'Dark Eyes', also has a reference to the art of archery: '*Oh, time is short and the days are sweet and passion rules the arrow that flies*'.
6. Clinton Heylin, *Behind The Shades: Take Two* Viking, 2000

# Four

# Chimes Of Freedom

## Foreword

*This began life as another article for the* **Homer,** *the slut section called 'Focus On', though much later than the 'Don't Think Twice, It's All Right' one discussed earlier. The section had proved to be very popular, but very few actually contributed to it and as the magazine grew I was unable to find the time to do so either. Then Paula Radice kindly volunteered to take over the running of 'Focus On', which allowed me the opportunity to comment on the song chosen for the final issue, 'Chimes Of Freedom'.*

*The January of that year had found Dylan appearing at the Bill Clinton Inauguration Concert at the Lincoln Memorial in Washington, DC. The controversy sparked among Dylan fans by this appearance made the song an obvious choice for the 'Focus On' section. And leaving that controversy to one side, I have to admit that there was something moving about seeing Dylan in such a setting; so many resonances abounded that one hardly had time to reflect on Dylan playing for a President younger than himself. The times sure had a-changed since Dylan had sung 'Only A Pawn In Their Game' at the same venue during the Washington Rights March. Some thirty years' worth of astonishing changes.*

*The performance was splendid enough in a completely Dylanesque way; that is, it did not kow-tow to the setting nor the unused-to-live-Dylan audience at all. The President seemed to be pleased that Dylan was there, Hilary seemed to think the whole thing was a joke (a view shared by many, I'd venture) and Chelsea looked as though Bob had descended from another planet (potentially another popular view).*

*It was an inspired choice of song, though, one that Bruce Springsteen and Amnesty International had used for presumably some of the same reasons as Dylan did here. It was also one that - when first written - was a significant artistic breakthrough for the young Dylan, leading to his great poetic statements of the mid-Sixties. We will return to the reasons for this significance after looking at the song itself. In the meantime, it is worth noting how the song follows on from the subject of the previous chapter, 'Restless Farewell'.*

*I closed there by remarking that Clinton Heylin had 'pinpointed the genesis' of 'Chimes Of Freedom' in the Margolis and Moss manuscripts from 1963. Mr. Heylin quotes from a passage concerning the effect of watching - as the whole world was doing - the assassination of President John F Kennedy:*

> ...on one of the sheets in the Margolis & Moss papers, matched to a poem about his own response to the Kennedy assassination, was a six-line coda with a familiar ring to it:

> the colors of friday were dull / as cathedral bells were gently burnin / strikin for the gentle / strikin for the kind / strikin for the crippled ones / an strikin for the blind.

> This reads like a refrain. It is also the onset of 'Chimes of Freedom,' and ...there can be no real doubt which Friday's colours were dull - Friday, November 22.

*Now he was playing it, albeit in a hard-to-decipher manner, for another President, all those years later.*

*The genesis of the song, as portrayed above, is a revealing insight into the way some songs come to Dylan. It seemed to have almost insisted on coming to him as he wrote free form and prose poems at a time when he was unhappy with being labelled a 'protest singing spokesman' and recoiling at his first bitter taste of the poisoned fruit of celebrity status. In trying to escape being pigeon-holed he was attempting to write in new formats - prose, poetry and even a play. As he expressed his feelings on the momentous slaying of the president his imagination found rhythm and beat and tapped into his well-spring of lyricism - the song began to be released almost in spite of the artist.*

*We are going to look at why and how 'Chimes Of Freedom' was such an important song to Dylan, but an even more celebrated 'breakthrough' song was to come in 1965 when he composed 'Like A Rolling Stone'. I mention it here because of the similarities in the way these two crucial songs came about.*

*In 1965 Dylan again found himself in an artistic cul-de-sac, born in part out of frustration during the UK tour. Due to a time lag in singles' release, 'The Times They Are A-Changin'' was in the UK charts as late as 1965. So Dylan toured as a solo acoustic performer, but inside his head he had already moved onto another sound. The depression and bitterness this caused him was so intense that he claimed he 'quit' song-writing. (Although these resignations from his calling could be counted in months, they were still sincere and deeply felt. He changed from having songs pour out of him on almost a daily basis to months of nothing being produced.)*

*How did he get out of the impasse? He tells us repeatedly in interviews that it was by typing page after page of 'vomit' (The number of pages varies from interview to interview - sometimes, 14 another time, 20 then again 8 pages - but it is always 'pages of vomit'). Eventually the 'paper began to sing' to him, and the song was born. After that he realised he could say all he wanted to in song. There seems little point in me telling you the story when Dylan tells it so well. Here are some of the interviews[1].*

Martin Bronstein Feb. 1966 Montreal
...I wrote that after I quit..., ...you know, I mean nobody had ever done that before...I've never met anybody or heard anything...I think 'Like A Rolling Stone' is definitely the thing I do...

Ralph Gleason, December 1965:
I wrote 'Rolling Stone' after England. I boiled it down, but it's all there. I had to quit after England. I had to stop and I knew I had to sing it with a band. I always sing when I write, even prose, and I heard it like that.

Nat Hentoff, Playboy 1966
I was playing a lot of songs I didn't want to play. I was singing words I didn't really want to sing. I don't mean words like 'God' and 'mother' and 'president' and 'suicide' and 'meat cleaver'. I mean simple little words like 'if' and 'hope' and 'you'. But 'Like A Rolling Stone' changed it all; I didn't care any more after that about writing books or poems or whatever. I mean it was something that I myself could dig.

*The leaps forward represented by 'Chimes Of Freedom' and 'Like A Rolling Stone' appear similar. He was being pigeon-holed, he was unhappy with what he was singing, he tried something new, something other than popular song to express himself. Yet his muse was always to be song and would bring him back to his vocation whenever the right phrases set off the rhythm in his mind.*

*I should point out that in the case of 'Chimes Of Freedom' it was more of an awakening to an ongoing development in his composing that he had been temporarily diverted from than a total change of direction. But we can consider that later in the **Afterword**, once I have shared my thoughts on the song itself.*

*This article is based on the piece I wrote for* **Homer**, *the slut issue 11 but has been much updated to take account of the new information discussed, especially in the fore- and afterwords. Also, in the magazine it came after a number of other commentaries on the song, and I avoided repeating there such things as the story the song tells.*

**M**any commentators on this song remark on the way the poetic images strike through the song just as the lightning strikes through the storm, an accurate observation. In addition, just as the lightning pierces the misty rain so it illuminates - in these poetic flashes - the songwriter's thoughts and sensibilities (and, it is to be hoped, the listener's). I would also be hardly the first to point out that the imagery of the song cascades toward the listener in much the same way as the rain pours down in the storm - breathtaking and overwhelming. What no-one seems to have mentioned is how Dylan manages this without the poor listener drowning in the torrent of synaesthetic imagery. Instead we are able to leave the song 'starry-eyed and laughing', just as the participants in the storm leave their shelter; uplifted and full of wonder rather than overpowered or merely impressed with verbal trickery.

What Dylan does is to provide the listener with a shelter too. It may be unobtrusive, but we are held and protected throughout the avalanche of rich images by the tight structure of the song. I think that before we look at the verses of the song it is essential to spend a little time on the overall structure.

We have six verses of eight lines each, the last two preceded by harmonica breaks of varying lengths depicting the gradual lifting of the storm. The rhyming scheme, *abcb ddd e*,[2] is maintained more or less consistently throughout; added to which the repeated last lines, with 'flashing' as the final word, unify the overall structure.

In each verse the first quatrain of abcb describes the physical situation of the songwriter as a participant in a city storm scene. The second quatrain consists of three lines - *ddd* - followed by the never-changing last line:

*And we gazed upon the chimes of freedom flashing*

It is a tightly crafted song. It has to be, otherwise all the poetic tricks, techniques and effects that the young Dylan employed in this enthusiastic burst of poetry that so characterises this album would seem just that - clever verbal trickery.

The song also has a narrative - a point often overlooked due to the sumptuous imagery. Dylan and friend(s) are caught by a storm when out in the city one evening. They shelter in an urban doorway as the storm's natural grandeur illuminates the society huddled in the buildings below it, and the artist's imagination is fired as he watches the dramatic tempest. As the song progresses the storm starts to lift, releasing the sheltering watchers (and the listeners) back into the relative mundanity of 'real' life. Yet we are changed because we take with us what the tempest-inspired visions have told us, and a memory of its awe-inspiring splendour. Since it is on a record we do not need to rely on memory alone - we can re-live it any time we want to.

It seems strange to think of Dylan being decried, at the time of this album's release, for deserting 'Protest songs' when one listens to this protest song par excellence - a song later to be used as an anthem for Amnesty International. All the fuss is caused by the lack of specificity and the overtly poetic language. Dylan here is a young lyricist striving for effect and some have claimed this shows to his detriment - as it does in the contemporaneous 'My Back Pages'. However, both these songs are the result of highly wrought craftsmanship; this is no untutored genius springing from the city streets, whatever he might have wanted us to believe at the time. The album also betrays evidence of wide reading; on this album Dylan wears his influences on his sleeve.

Just as the seminal Scottish poet Robert Burns cultivated the image of a poet sprung almost divinely from the soil (when all his work displays great craftsmanship and knowledge of the classics), so Dylan's image as a poet sprung from the city streets is somewhat at odds with the care with which the songs on this album are constructed, and the obvious poetic influences of various Romantic, Symbolist, Modernist and traditional American poets.

We do not know that Dylan was overly familiar with all of these at this time. As in folk and blues music, what seems a straightforward influence is not necessarily a direct one. We do know that Dylan was influenced by the Beat writers and they in turn are imbued with the poetry of 19th Century Romanticism and the works of US poetic forerunners like Emerson and Whitman.

As well as the Beats, a writer who held some sway over Dylan at the time was Arthur Rimbaud. Dylan biographer Robert Shelton interviewed Dave Van Ronk about what poetry Dylan was reading in the early sixties:

> 'Did Dylan ever say he admired Dylan Thomas?' 'He assiduously avoided it,' replied Dave. 'I think the reasons are obvious. I did come on to Bob about François Villon. I also told him about Rimbaud and Apollinaire. I once asked Bobby: "Have you ever heard about Rimbaud?" He said: "Who?" I repeated: "Rimbaud-R-I-M-B-A-U-D. He's a French poet. You really ought to read him," I said. Bobby kind of twitched a little; he seemed to be thinking about it. He just said: "Yeah, yeah." I raised Rimbaud with him a couple of times after that. Much later, I was up at his place. I always

*look at people's books. On his shelf I discovered a book of translations of*
*French symbolist poets that had obviously been thumbed through over a*
*period of years! I think he probably knew Rimbaud backward and forward*
*before I even mentioned him. I didn't mention Rimbaud to him again until*
*I heard his "A Hard Rain's A-Gonna Fall", his first symbolist verse. I said*
*to Bob: "You know, that song of yours is heavy in symbolism, don't you?"*
*He said: "Huh?"*[3]

'Chimes Of Freedom' carries an even greater debt to Rimbaud and his
declaration: *'The poet makes himself voyant by a long, immense, and calculated*
*derailment of all the senses'*[4]. However, in this song, Dylan uses this to a very
specific end, one more in line with the poetry of the Whitman tradition. Out
of many influences Dylan is creating his own voice and vision in this key song,
on what is forever described as a 'transitional' album.

As ever with Dylan, musical influences are intertwined with and underpin
all others. Although he was, on the surface at least, moving away from earlier
musical influences, the ghost of Guthrie is still present. A Guthrie line like : *'In*
*the misty crystal glitter of that wild and windward spray'* would fit into 'Chimes
Of Freedom' on every level of metre and poetic effects. With Guthrie, though,
it is merely descriptive (though highly effective), whereas with Dylan his
similar lines are actually causing the listener to undergo an experience analogous to that they are depicting.

It is an experience the listener can relive each time s/he plays the track,
with or without any knowledge of other poets or musicians. What follows is a
description of how and why the song works its magic on me.

The opening verse of the song has me revising, slightly, my earlier declaration of the consistency of structure, as I will immediately point out that
Verse One is a little exceptional in this regard! (It is in content too, but more
of that later.) This is precisely because it is the opening verse. The first four
lines set the scene in each verse, but naturally the writer has to be more
specific in the introductory verse, and he drives his point home by making the
fourth and eighth lines almost identical. The first verse tells us what has
happened and sets up the way the whole song will work.

The opening line:

*Far between sundown's finish an' midnight's broken toll*

gives us the time of day - or at least it would if we knew when the sun went
down! In fact it is quite vague - where exactly is 'far between' the sun finally
setting and midnight (unless he just means the mid-point between these
times)? The effect that Dylan is after is something far greater than telling us

that it is '21:32 and 15 seconds'. The line serves the dual purpose of preparing us for the suspension of normal time, and with the slightly ominous use of 'finish' and 'broken' introduce us to the beginning of a battering of some intensity. The opening line ends with the word toll and it proves to be a crucial one as the song develops.

The listener is also introduced to the song's characteristic imagery - alliterative and synaesthetic as in: *bells of bolts struck shadows in the sounds.* Synaesthesia is the linking together of multiple senses, such as hearing colours or seeing sounds[5]. It is nowadays seen as an abnormal psychological state, although some see it as a throwback to an earlier stage in humankind's development - or, as here, as a poetic technique. If indeed there was such an earlier stage in our development, Dylan's mid sixties use of this technique makes me inclined to think we took a(nother) wrong turning somewhere!

What the poet, artist, songwriter or whatever term you prefer tries to do with this technique is to heighten his audience's perceptions, in our particular case to try to make the listener feel what he felt.[6] This technique was a particular favourite of the Romantic school of poetry, whose practitioners were often prone to achieve and report on states of heightened perception. It was also prevalent in the writings of the Beats. In both cases the heightened perception was not always inspired solely by the poet's vision or nature's majesty - drugs were another way of raising perceptions to another level. Synaesthetic techniques were to be used to great effect by Dylan in other songs of this time, sometimes leading, as here, to a feeling that time has stopped; a concept that was to dominate Dylan's artistic aims in future years.

To return to 'Chimes Of Freedom', as with 'Mr. Tambourine Man' this song has not necessarily got anything to do with drugs or a drug-induced experience[7], but it is not difficult to see why many people have used this song as a 'tripping' song - in this case the state is achieved courtesy of Mother Nature's storm and Dylan's poetic account of it.

The first verse is unique in the way in which the *ddd* lines are all connected by 'soldier' type imagery; perhaps Dylan didn't want to throw too much at us in the first verse in fear of disorientating us, or perhaps he planned at this stage to have each verse tied to a specific 'theme'. It is worth noting in passing the phrase *'the warriors whose strength is not to fight'* which, in addition to being very thought-provoking in its own right, perhaps had particular connotations for Dylan in relation to the 'Folk Protest Movement' of the time, whose supporters wanted him to 'lead the marches', 'man the barricades' etc.[8]

In the second stanza, the physical scene is well-painted in the opening four lines, as the singer and his companion(s) press closer to the wall for protection:

*Through the city's melted furnace, unexpectedly we watched*
*With faces hidden as the walls were tightening*
*As the echo of the wedding bells before the blowing rain*
*Dissolved into the bells of the lightning*

The reference to 'wedding bells' here seems to point out the fragility of human hopes and institutions in the face of nature's power - it may appear at first as just another piece of stage-setting but it will also have a contrasting echo later in the song. Dissolved is a key word in this quatrain, the song is full of shifting, misty, formless images.

The triple *d* rhymes passage here contains an interesting collection of characters for whom the bells are tolling. Some of the characters are complementary, some are typical of Dylan throughout his career, some seem to have stepped directly out of the songs in his preceding work. It is interesting too that the tautology of *'the abandoned and forsaked'* works so effectively here - it is not always so in this song.

Despite my claim that some of this song is naive, young man's poetic strutting, the opening to the third verse is magical:

*Through the mad mystic hammering of the wild ripping hail*
*The sky cracked its poems in naked wonder*

This is pretty impressive on the page and is absolutely magnificent when sung with Dylan's unequalled gifts of expression. Any fool can string words together that alliterate, but to come up with an alliterative phrase like mad mystic hammering that also harmonises with the meaning of the passage, while all the time having the exact onomatopoeic effect desired, is the stamp of genius.

The second line constitutes an exact summation of the whole experience from the participant's viewpoint. In years to come I hope there is an exam question asking 'What is "Chimes Of Freedom" about?', just so someone can answer 'It is about how the sky cracked its poems in naked wonder'.

The second quatrain, even ignoring the bizarre alteration to what he sings that appears in the official Lyrics, is somewhat confusing. It is a very odd collection of characters: *'the gentle'* and *'the kind'* certainly fit as do *'the poet and the painter'* who are out of time. It is more common, of course, for artists to be misunderstood because they are ahead of their time, and it is intriguing that the word 'beyond' is used in *Lyrics.*[9]

However, the middle of these three lines has always struck me as rather odd for Dylan at this time. He seems to be placing *'the guardians and protectors of the mind'* in some good company while in other songs of the time he was coming down pretty hard on teachers, professors etc. I realise that the phrase does not necessarily equate to such instructors but the connotations of *'guardians and protectors'* are of restriction, not enlightenment. Also the tautology here seems unnecessary and wasteful.

The fourth verse begins with another stunningly poetic couple of lines:

> *In the wild cathedral evening the rain unravelled tales*
> *For the disrobed faceless forms of no position*

- *'wild cathedral evening'* always seems to get all the praise but *'rain unravelled tales'* is just as good. The third line, *'Tolling for the tongues with no place to bring their thoughts'* seems out of place both in terms of meaning and structure, yet it is important as a reference point for a line in the following verse.

The first couplet of our familiar *ddd* triplet is marvellous; line one lists three sensorily deprived groups of people while line two is about one section of the 'downtrodden'. It is a line that should have been well heeded but is still ignored as hypocritical governments and their lapdog press unite to turn these particular *'abandoned and forsaked'* into societal scapegoats:

> *For the mistreated mateless mother, the mistitled prostitute*

Of all the clever uses of alliteration in this song, I find this the most dazzling. The mixture of the soft, comforting 'm' sounds with the harsh, sibilant 's's perfectly encapsulates the line's meaning. This is one heck of a line for a so called misogynist to write. It is also a line any poet would be proud of as it scans perfectly, uses internal rhythm and alliteration to maximum benefit and even includes an outrageously successful pun in *'mistitled prostitute'* ('miss, titled prostitute') that sums up the entire import of the line.

The penultimate line of the stanza is a nonsense - but he somehow gets away with it:

> *For the misdemeanour outlaw, chained and cheated by pursuit*

It reminds me of what Paul Williams wrote about Dylan's ability to put things in such a way that, unless we study it carefully, we hear something different - possibly contradictory - to what the words actually say:

> *I don't suggest that this is intentional on his part. On the contrary, I use it as an example of Dylan being in control of his communication (what we actually hear, what we think he said) but not his words.*[10]

I happen to think that Dylan does sometimes intentionally utilise this technique, though he often uses it as Mr. Williams describes. I never doubted what this line meant from the first time I heard it until I came to write about it for the first time. Still, doesn't it sound great? Aren't you on the side of this poor, hunted outlaw who probably has a heart of gold anyway? What's a 'misdemeanour' anyway - nothing to be hounded about, that's for sure.

Dylan plays a harmonica break of five seconds to supplement the guitar break between verses – the storm is beginning to slowly lift as the fifth verse beckons. Again the physical theatre is marvellously evoked; again alliterative onomatopoeia is employed to spell-binding effect. Just read aloud the following phrase:

*Electric light still struck like*

You can almost feel the arrows striking.

This is followed by a typical Dylan double-bind of a line:

*Condemned to drift or else be kept from drifting.*

A drifter is often a heroic figure in Dylan's Guthriesque landscapes. He is the honest man unshackled by society's constraints, we want him to drift and, if caught, to break free when the lightning strikes. Here, although the lightning is striking, the figure is *'kept from drifting'* - a tragedy. It is also a tragedy to be *'condemned to drift'* - to be made homeless, *'abandoned and forsaked'*, not out of choice but out of injustice and persecution. It is another message, unfortunately, that does not lack relevance for our own time from this timeless, all-embracing, protest song.

The *ddd* triplet opens with:

*Tolling for the searching ones, on their speechless seeking trail*

I used to think that this was merely a nice image but it relates back to verse 4, line 3:

*Tolling for the tongues with no place to bring their thoughts*

which makes it altogether more powerful. Even those with something to say are denied a platform. The triplet in this verse contains the following characters:

- Searchers
- Those denied a voice
- Trail seekers
- Lonely lovers
- Gentle souls unfairly jailed

It is almost as though these three lines are designed to contain a list of archetypal Dylan characters.

Listening to this you cannot help but be reminded of Walt Whitman's all-encompassing identification in 'A Song Of Myself' (which contains many similar characters such as wrongly blamed prostitutes, outcasts and criminals):

> I am posses'd!
> Embody all presences outlaw'd or suffering,
> See myself in prison shaped like another man,
> And feel the dull unintermitted pain.
>
> ...For me the keepers of convicts shoulder their carbines and keep watch,
> It is I let out in the morning and barr'd at night.
>
> ...Not a mutineer walks handcuff'd to jail but I am handcuff'd to him and walk by his side,
>
> ...Not a cholera patient lies at the last gasp but I also lie at the last gasp,

The closing verse opens with beautiful imagery describing the ending of the storm as experienced by the friends whose comradeship has been strengthened by the experience. The opening words *'Starry-eyed and laughing'* catch the wonder and hesitancy one feels after such an experience. This feeling of largesse leads to the awesome, all-embracing sympathy for everyone who needs the chimes of freedom to flash for them:

> Tolling for the aching whose wounds cannot be nursed
> For the countless confused accused misused strung-out ones and worse
> And for every hung-up person in the whole wide universe

This is a bravura peak of emotion even amongst Dylan's mountain ranges of such, and it is all the more effective for the inexorable way the song's design has built to it. Unlike many lines I have previously quoted these do not necessarily come across on the page; in performance they are equal to anything else in the song and, given the delivery, a perfect culmination. Dylan listeners will probably 'read' the *nursed/worse/universe* lines in that familiar voice anyway!

The song is brought to a very definite conclusion by a six-second burst of harmonica. The listener, like the protagonists of the song, is released from an awe-inspiring experience, unsure of how much time has passed as he 'hung suspended'.

It's a magnificent achievement and again Whitman comes to mind with the long list of characters in 'A Song of Myself' which his self identifies with, envelopes and becomes. Men and women, regardless of colour, young, old, criminals or not are gathered into his cosmic, poetic embrace - *'every hung up person in the whole wide universe'* would cover it, if only Mr Whitman had thought of the phrase.

The somewhat similar 'The Sleepers' is, if anything, at times even closer to the Dylan of 'Chimes Of Freedom' as the following quotation shows:

> *Onward we move, a gay gang of blackguards! with mirth shouting music*
> *and wild-flapping pennants of joy!*
> *I am the actor and the actress, the voter, the politician,*
> *The emigrant and the exile, the criminal that stood in the box,*
> *He who has been famous, and he who shall be famous after today,*
> *The stammerer, the well-formed person, the wasted or feeble person.*

The 'mad mystic hammering' of Dylan's song takes us – like the storm takes him and his companions – out of day-to-day reality, out of time itself. Normal human perception is transformed into a state where we listeners can imaginatively embrace, just as Whitman did in the poems above, and the singer did while huddling from the storm, *'every hung up person in the whole wide universe'.*

## Afterword - place in the progression of visionary songs

I was writing in the **Foreword** about how 'Chimes Of Freedom' proved a catalyst that propelled Dylan from a creative impasse into the full flowering of his artistic visions in songs such as 'Mr. Tambourine Man', 'Desolation and 'Visions Of Johanna'. Although this is true on one level, it does not – as I intimated earlier - tell the whole story. Just as love songs such as 'Don't Think Twice, It's All Right' and 'One Too Many Mornings' flourished in the 'protest' years, paving the way for 'All I Really Want To Do' and 'It Ain't Me, Babe' on the same album as 'Chimes Of Freedom' (which in turn pointed toward 'She Belongs To Me' and 'Love Minus Zero/No Limit'), so there was also a strain of visionary songs already being written amidst the 'finger pointing' songs. On Dylan's second album, the magnificent 'A Hard Rain's A-Gonna Fall' was the first of his songs to betray the influences of Beat poetry (think of the long-line, bardic style of Ginsberg's 'Howl') and the first clear imprint of Rimbaud's work.[11]

This strain of writing *seemed* to have been in abeyance until 'Chimes Of Freedom', but it was only a *seeming*. The sessions for the third album included 'Lay Down Your Weary Tune', one of Dylan's most glorious creations, both ravishing and profound at the same time. It's the kind of song that once you have heard it you cannot imagine a time when you did not know it, or at least it is unimaginable that it once hadn't existed. It stands as a touchstone of what Dylan's art represents, yet in some ways is unlike any other song he has written.

One can only imagine that it was left off *The Times They Are A-Changin'* because it was not seen to correspond with that album's main pre-occupations. This could be seen as a mistake, as at least on one crucial level it was; musically, however, one cannot reconcile its sumptuous beauty with the monochrome visual and aural ambience of that stark third album.

Notwithstanding that rationale, the song's exclusion was a loss to the officially-released catalogue for too long a time, but a boon to the underground record industry which feasted on such unused gems from Dylan's pen. 'Lay Down Your Weary Tune' via Dylan's lyrics and vocals transforms the Scottish tune[12] on which it is based into something so new as to sound a totally new creation.

The song contrasts the human voice (of Dylan/Everyman) bound by laws, driven by sexual possessiveness and need for applause with the transcendent and regenerating powers of creation itself as depicted in the harmonious 'symphony' of nature. The song is visionary not just in the obvious pantheistic sense but also in the way that Dylan depicts the effect this vision has on him, on anyone who listens to the tune 'no voice can hope to hum'. To rest 'neath these strings is to allow your identity to be subsumed into the overall harmony of creation and arise, refreshed, enriched and strengthened. Paradoxically, human individuality has to be overwhelmed by the vision encapsulated in the song to fully realise itself.

The correlation with 'Chimes Of Freedom' is obvious, albeit that 'Chimes' has an urban setting. In both cases Nature allows human perception to make a leap into a transforming vision.

The relationship between these songs and 'Mr. Tambourine Man' is an intriguing one. For many years it was thought that 'Mr. Tambourine Man' came after 'Chimes Of Freedom'. Following Dylan's career and artistic development there seemed a natural (no pun intended!) progression from 'Blowin' In The Wind', 'A Hard Rain's A-Gonna Fall', 'Lay Down Your Weary Tune', 'Chimes Of Freedom' to 'Mr. Tambourine Man'. This released chronology turns out to be misleading in the case of the last two. Both 'Chimes of Freedom' and 'Mr. Tambourine Man' (according to Dylan himself) were written on the same 1964 trip across country and to New Orleans' Mardi Gras. Not only that but 'Mr. Tambourine Man' was one of the first songs attempted on the *Another Side Of Bob Dylan* sessions, and although it did not appear (in a different version) until the fifth album, a complete take of it was made with Ramblin' Jack Elliot accompanying Dylan for *Another Side Of Bob Dylan*.[13]

The released chronology does, however, represent correctly the development of Dylan as an artist because, for all the many delights of 'Chimes Of Freedom', 'Mr. Tambourine Man' represents another leap forward in Dylan's art; it took him (and us, the grateful audience) further.

The link between the songs can be heard in musical and lyrical ways, but also in the sense of the artist sharing a rare and exceptional vision with his audience. On one level this link becomes strongest through the last word of the title of 'Chimes' - 'Freedom'. Paul Williams wrote of 'Mr. Tambourine Man':

> *The song is for anyone who can feel it, and it's about something so simple we can even put a word to it without too much fear of being misunderstood. The word is freedom.*[14]

Yet even that doesn't quite cover it because it is about a special kind of freedom. It is an ecstatic liberating dance revolving around attraction and repulsion, to say nothing of complete surrender. And it is an invocation to the muse in the nineteenth century romantic poetic tradition; a tradition that acknowledges not just the exhilarating liberation of the creative muse (this is the 'freedom' part) but also the pain and self-abnegation that the human person must go through to allow the muse to transform him into an Artist.

To quote from the back of Dylan's *Lyrics 1962 - 1985*:

> *'As a lyric poet of intensity, and as a human being of political and humanistic feeling, Dylan stands proud with the revolutionary romantics of the early 19ᵗʰ-century.'* (Richard Gott, *The Guardian*)

Never has this connection between Dylan and 'the revolutionary romantics' been truer than in this song, an invocation that follows in the footsteps most particularly of Shelley and Keats. I am not for a moment claiming that Dylan either read any of their many poems on the same subject - though he may have done - or that he is consciously following them. I am merely pointing out that the lyrics of this song – and the superbly complementary melody - invoke analogous thoughts and sentiments. (As does another song on the *Bringing It All Back Home* album, the ironically titled 'She Belongs To Me' - which also deals with submission of the self to the artistic muse.) Other critics - Stephen Scobie and Aidan Day being amongst the most prominent - also see the song as Dylan's plea to his muse to come and inspire him. This is hardly surprising given their literary backgrounds. It seems to me, too, that this is the obvious interpretation of the song when one looks at what the singer requests of the tambourine man:

*...play a song for me*

*...Take me on a trip upon your magic swirlin' ship*

*...cast your dancing spell my way*

*...take me disappearin' through the smoke rings of my mind*

That last line indicates that the singer is aware that for the tambourine man (the muse) to fulfil his request he must allow this creative daemon to possess him. Other lines indicate this self-abnegation too:

*...My senses have been stripped,*

*...I'm ready for to fade*

*...I'll come followin' you.*

*...With all memory and fate driven deep beneath the waves*

*...cast your dancing spell my way/I promise to go under it*

There is a preparatory pain for such self-abnegation (another thing the poets mentioned earlier agree upon); indeed what the singer goes through approaches torture:

He is stripped, branded, blinded and numbed.

Yet he wants to go through this - *I'll come followin' you / I promise to go under it.* What could be worth enduring such pain? Pleasure of course, the ecstatic pleasure of liberation from self and time in the creative act of writing the very song we are listening to. The paradox at the centre of this song is that the intoxicating dance is only prefigured - none of this has yet been achieved, the song is a plea to the muse to provide it. Simultaneously, though, the song itself is the answer to the plea. Rapture has been achieved, time here does not merely 'hang suspended', it has been obliterated:

*Then take me disappearin' through the smoke rings of my mind*
*Down the foggy ruins of time, far past the frozen leaves*
*The haunted, frightened trees, out to the windy beach*

He can *'forget about today until tomorrow'*; and, caught up in the glorious swirling melody, we listeners are granted (as when we listen to 'Chimes Of Freedom', 'trapped by no hours') the gift of stepping out of time also. Everyday cares cannot touch us when we are in the thrall of the song: we too are, to some extent, *Far from the twisted reach of crazy sorrow* and temporarily free from 'memory and fate'.

1 All interview quotes taken from John Baldwin's excellent series *The Fiddler Now Upspoke*; Desolation Row Publications, UK.

2. The last line is the same in every verse and can often appear as another b rhyme or half rhyme – particularly as it ends with an 'ing' sound which is prevalent throughout the song. Nonetheless it stands as a separate line in the structure of the poem, although it can be used to special effect with the b rhyme as in Verse One.

3. Robert Shelton, *No Direction Home*, William Morrow & Co Inc, 1986.

4. 'The Visionary Letter' to Paul Demeny , 15 May 1871.

5 In the same Margolis and Moss manuscripts mentioned earlier there is a passage in what are referred to as 'The Kennedy Poems' that utilises this technique at the same time as delivering a deft pun as Dylan describes his feelings while looking at images of the assassination:

> *'why am I deliberately lied wild lies*
> *about what I see with sound eyes'*

6. Unfortunately - like so many literary techniques that Dylan employed - the following years saw imitators employ them simply for their own sake and immature excess and gibberish resulted.

7. In *The Illustrated Record* (Harmony Books 1978) Alan Rinzler writes:

> '... the classic Mr. Tambourine Man, one of the most explicit drug songs Dylan has produced and probably the best song ever written on the subject.
>
> > *Though I know that evenin's empire has returned into sand*
> > *Vanished from my hand*
> > *Left me blindly here to stand but still not sleeping*
> > *My weariness amazes me, I'm branded on my feet*
> > *I have no one to meet*
> > *And the ancient empty street's too dead for dreaming*
>
> What a brilliant evocation of the drug experience. What wonderfully accurate images:
> *In the jingle jangle morning...senses have been stripped...take me disappearin' through the smoke rings of my mind...*
>
> Strung out, desperate to get off, Dylan's melody has all the yearning and plaintiveness of the pleasure seeking lotus-eater. The words have become gospel, through this and many other famous recordings, most notably the electric, rock and roll version by The Byrds.'

I feel obliged to remind Mr Rinzler of what Dylan said live on stage in the UK in 1966: referring to another of his masterpieces that had been given the limiting label of drug song, 'Visions Of Johanna', Dylan told the audience: *it's all wrong...this is a typical example...*(of songs labelled 'drug songs') *I don't write drug songs; I never have, I wouldn't know how to go about it...it's just vulgar to think so* (Being Dylan he delivers this in the most druggy, strung out voice imaginable).

It is indeed not only 'vulgar' but absurdly reductionist to think of either of these great songs as 'a drug song'. I grant you that 'Mr. Tambourine Man' was - and still is - played as background music to many a tripping listener and that Dylan was surely aware of the above interpretation. To be fair to Rinzler, the descriptions are uncannily - and surely not coincidentally, accurate - but the song is about something much deeper than that, as I hope the afterword to this chapter demonstrates.

8. It is a theme that Dylan explores in *Some Other Kinds Of Songs*; prose poems written at the time, some of which featured on the rear sleeve of the album:

> *run go get out of here*
> *quick*
> *leave joshua*
> *split*
> *go fit your battle*
> *do your thing*
> *i lost my glasses*
> *can't see jericho*

*the wind is tyin' knots in my hair*
*nothin' seems*
*t' be straight*
*out there*
*no i shan't go with you*
*i can't go with you*

9. Just to be completely mystifying, the word 'behind' is not removed but the poet is and the painter becomes 'unpawned', thus transforming *'And the poet and the painter far behind his rightful time'* into *'And the unpawned painter behind beyond his rightful time'*!

10. Paul Williams, writing about 'Talkin' New York' in *Performing Artist Volume One.*

11. As well as the Van Ronk quotation used earlier, Robert Shelton also comments that: 'In her paper, *Bob Dylan and French Symbolist Poetry*, Belle D. Levinson found in 'Hard Rain' and 'Chimes Of Freedom' a Dylan whose style as well as theme is close to Rimbaud's. I find 'Chimes Of Freedom' a landmark lyric in which Dylan has progressed from 'Hard Rain' towards his full poetic powers.'

12. In the *Biograph* interview with Cameron Crowe, Dylan comments: *'I had heard a Scottish ballad on an old 78 record that I was trying to really capture the feeling of, that was haunting me. I couldn't get it out of my head. There were no lyrics or anything, it was just a melody, had bagpipes and a lot of stuff in it. I wanted lyrics that would feel the same way, I don't remember what the original record was, but this was pretty similar to that, the melody anyway.'*

13. Surprising as it may sound, it was a good decision to hold the song back for the fifth album, as musically it was not yet nailed. Much sought after as this out-take became in the minds of fans, it is of historical and academic interest more than anything else.

14. Paul Williams, *Performing Artist Volume One*, Underwood-Miller 1990. I am only quoting one sentence here; to get Paul's full views (which differ from mine) you would have to read this excellent book.

# Five

# Subterranean Homesick Blues

## Foreword

In compiling these articles I found that I had often concentrated on what I saw as 'key' songs that had been relatively overlooked in critical works on Dylan. Hence, rather than write an article on 'Mr. Tambourine Man' I offered my thoughts on that song only after looking at the place of 'Chimes Of Freedom' in the development of Dylan's visionary songs of the early 1960s.

Given the prolific nature of Dylan's output in his early career, it is not surprising that some songs get less attention than others. 'Mr. Tambourine Man', 'Like A Rolling Stone' and 'Visions Of Johanna' would have great claim to be the most 'important' songs; a horrible word in this context, but meaning to give the sense of import, influence, culmination of artistic development(s) and breakthrough, for both Dylan as artist and ourselves as audience. Not to say that 'It's Alright Ma', 'Desolation Row' and 'Absolutely Sweet Marie' could not also put forward claims to 'greatness', 'import' or whatever.

It is also not surprising that I have leant towards those songs not quite so often written about previously. I also tend to be drawn to songs that open or close albums; not surprisingly in the days when album sequencing was so significant to Dylan, these tend to carry special consequence.

Hopefully this also ensures that a coherent thread runs through the 1960s section of this collection of articles. With this in mind, I have included the following commentary on 'Subterranean Homesick Blues', which kicked off the 'non-folk' (to drag oneself down to the pigeon-holing categorisation of that time) side of Bringing It All Back Home.

'Subterranean Homesick Blues' was a minor hit but a great controversy stirrer at the time of its release. The controversy was due to Bob Dylan, hitherto the darling of lovers of acoustic music, moving to the world of amplified, popular - and therefore, to the eyes of many of his former admirers, materialistic and irrelevant - music. Writing personal, subjective rather than finger-pointing songs on *Another Side Of Bob Dylan* was bad enough, but moving to the world of 'pop' was heresy.

Nevertheless, 'Subterranean' has proved to be one of Dylan's best-known songs among modern audiences. The reasons for this are threefold:

Firstly, in this TV dominated age, the opening sequence for the documentary film *Dont Look Back*, which features this song, is often broadcast. Secondly, the song has frequently been referred to as a forerunner of Rap; and finally, though it is far from unique in this, it has occasioned many tribute and cover versions.

The opening sequence of *Dont Look Back* is, in essence, a promo film, and it has been shown world-wide in this age of MTV and its clones. Filmed against the background of a back alley full of rubbish sacks in London, the film works as a perfect adjunct to the song, showing similar wit, verve, humour and pointed messages to the 'kids'. There is something terribly ironic in it being Dylan's idea to utilise the magnificently successful lyric-bearing cards as the forum for putting his message across visually.

I say 'terribly ironic' because, since this early trailblazing in the form of promo video, Dylan - despite an obvious interest in the cinematic form - has produced, or allowed his songs to be promoted by, a succession of mainly banal and derivative videos. This 'pre-video-promo-video' has, however, spawned imitators and tribute versions aplenty, like the song itself. Again, as with the song itself, it holds up remarkably well after all these years, still fresh and invigorating.

Many people - including various rappers - have commented on how the song seems a forerunner of rap and that Dylan is, indeed, as Paul Williams notes: a *'natural rapper'*. I don't believe that this song caused or affected rap in any meaningful way, but it is more than a happy coincidence that they share the same approach and style.

Dylan's song is born out of numerous traditions, one of which is that of the rapping comedians of the Village scene. Another possible forerunner was the Guthrie/Seeger song 'Takin' It Easy' (covered by Cisco Houston among others). This, like other folk songs, built on nursery rhyme structure, and certainly prefigures 'Subterranean Homesick Blues' with lines like: *'Pa was in the cellar mixing up the hops/Brother's at the window, he's watching for the cops'*.

Another clear musical influence is the Chuck Berry of 'Maybelline', 'School Days' and, most obviously of all, 'Too Much Monkey Business'.

For influences outwith music itself, one would have to include that of the cinema and even cross-fertilisation with the kind of hip, beat writing style that Dylan had already used in writings that adorned album sleeves, concert programmes etc. For example, a similarity of style can be seen in the liner notes to the preceding album, where Dylan writes:

> *baby black*
> *hits back*
> *robs. pawns*
> *lives by trade*
> *sits an' waits on fire plug*
> *digs the heat*
> *eyes meet*
> *picket line*
> *across the street*
> *head rings*
> *of bed springs*

Some of the traditions that helped to shape 'Subterranean Homesick Blues' are shared by exponents of modern rap, whose stylistic approach probably helped Dylan's song sound fresh and new when Rap was dominating the music scene. Though the main credit for that lies in the song itself, the strength of which has attracted other performing artists to cover it.

Besides cover versions there have been modern rewrites and, in addition, new songs that build on the Dylan song in a similar manner to his does on 'Too Much Monkey Business'. I am thinking of songs like REM's 'It's The End Of The World As We Know It (And I Feel Fine)' and, in particular, Elvis Costello's 'Pump It Up', which not only stands as a kind of musical tribute to 'Subterranean Homesick Blues', but also cleverly puns its title on the closing couplet of Dylan's song.

All these things have kept the song in the public's eye. Turning now to look at the song itself, you put the needle down on the album's first track (ok, I am romantically remembering the vinyl - and still best sounding, especially the first release in mono - version; press the CD or tape play button if you will) and you are instantly catapulted into the world of the song.

It explodes into life in a dazzling display of infectiously joyous verbal dexterity; cawed by that perfectly expressive voice over a raucous yet controlled backing that careers forward as the singer pistol-whips us with his barbed lines. It seems for all the world like some demented nightmare nursery rhyme, that we had tried to bury away but which was now hitting us with the dizzying realization of speed-fuelled paranoia. As the chorus warns, LOOK OUT KID - danger is everywhere, they are out to get you.

> *Johnny's in the basement*
> *Mixing up the medicine*

Starts us off firmly in the world of drugs but also of the subterranean or, as it was to become widely known, 'the Underground'. An Underground that was just about to blossom into a range of political activity that broadened the canvas of activism way beyond that of the folk movement which Dylan was seen as betraying by recording this rockabilly/half-rock/rapping/bluesy piece.

So the singer, knowing that the drugs are being prepared in the underground, finds himself, instead of being in that subterranean home:

> *...on the pavement*
> *Thinking about the government*

Why is this person *'thinking about the government'*? Is he some kind of political activist? There seems little evidence of it elsewhere, perhaps he is just musing about those in power - authority is regarded with a great deal of paranoia in this song.

So, although it is perhaps a reference to his 'protest' days (after all Bob Dylan, of all people, would have been expected to be 'thinking about the government') it could also be seen as an indication that this is what protesters have become - drug makers and takers hiding underground.[2] Alternatively, perhaps he is merely introducing the drug culture's paranoia that he is about to memorably depict.

'Look out *kid*' – the song's repeated warning is specifically a warning to *youth*. Dylan clearly has this particular age group in mind as his rightful audience, just as he had in the opening anthem and title song to his protest album, *The Times They Are A-Changin'*. Some of the audience could not follow him from acoustic strumming to rockabilly rebellion, but some did, and many more would join as Dylan became, much to his ultimate annoyance, truly the 'voice of a generation'.

Dylan here embraces that spokesman role with the first warning:

> *Look out kid*
> *It's somethin' you did*
> *God knows when*
> *But you're doin' it again*

This is very much the voice of a hip older - but still young - brother who knows what 'they' (parents, schoolteachers, cops, the government) are like with their endless, unfounded criticisms and restraints.

The preceding description of the 'man in the trench coat' is highly visual. Or, rather, perhaps I should say it is cinematic. I *see* this man as though I am watching an American cop film from the fifties, hell - I even see it in black and white. Why is this? Shared cultural references, I suppose, but the technique is clearly intentional on Dylan's part. So successful was he that in his own film for the song he had to hold up the words he was singing to reinforce the vocal message - the lines themselves being so filmic that they required no acting out.

There is a darker cynicism in the cop wanting to be *'paid off'*; though when this realization occurs to the listener is a moot point as s/he can only get so many of the depth-charge couplets at a time. Which lines strike home on first, second or subsequent listens presumably varies from listener to listener.

However, in every verse the closing couplet stands out and, during the musical breaks between the verses, leaves the listener still struck by the ideas it engenders.

The opening stanza memorably concludes with the coon-skin cap wearing man demanding *'eleven dollar bills, you only got ten'*. These closing lines paint a drugs scene - perhaps again evoking films (at least for those who have not personally tried to score from a seller who ups the price in the face of the junkie's need). Maybe this is also a metaphor for life (as seen by this song) - a vain struggle to achieve something that always demands more than one has to give.

The second verse rattles in with full-blown, drug/underworld, paranoia about the cops coming to get you - and it sounds like it is going to happen any minute now:

> *Talkin' that the heat put*
> *Plants in the bed but*
> *The phone's tapped anyway*
> *Maggie says that many say*
> *They must bust in early May*

These are marvellous lines, with their internal rhyming and echoing phonetic effects. It is almost a nursery rhyme diction rat-a-tatted out with Dylan's machine-gun delivery. And all the while they still depict the typical paranoia of the drug taker and/or underground person with breathtaking economy. On the other hand , perhaps we should remember the old saying: 'just because you are paranoid doesn't mean they aren't out to get you'. In this song, as in life, menacing authority figures are never far away.

The wise older brother provides another warning:

*Look out kid*
*Don't matter what you did*
*Walk on your tip toes*
*Don't try 'No Doz'*

This is mocking typical parental advice: the kids are to blame for whatever they did and are told to walk on their tip toes for fear of treading too heavily on something. (A neat image of the petty, restricting nature of authority). Drugs, as you would expect, are a complete 'No-No'; the order is to avoid even the least kind of upper, 'No Doz' being a form of caffeine pills which, ironically enough, were commonly consumed by kids cutting down on sleep to cram for exams to get results that would please the very parents warning against their usage. (Just for the record (sic) their consumption has since been designated as a health danger.)[3]

The lines fly by, but each verse ends with a sledgehammer effect of unforgettable couplets that have impinged themselves on the general consciousness of our times. The epigrammatic close to this stanza:

*You don't need a weather man*
*To know which way the wind blows*

is a prime example of this, and the famous saying became ironically enhanced by the splinter group of the SDS[4] movement taking their name from it. In doing so they reversed the meaning, claiming that you did indeed need The Weathermen - with capitals - to tell you what was happening.

In stanza three, life's trials and tribulations tumble out in a rhyming, rhythmic tour de force. If you are not listening to the record just now, read the lines aloud from *Lyrics* or the song book and you'll see what I mean.

As in the Chuck Berry song 'Too Much Monkey Business', school imagery (*ink well / ring bell*) plays a central role, appropriately enough for a song structured around warnings to 'the kids'. Again there is a darker cynicism - all the more so for being blatantly pointed out - in the inescapable conclusion that the army is a refuge for those who *fail* in their schooling or careers. The pun of getting 'barred' then getting back only to end up behind bars ('get jailed') is typical of the song's inventive and muscular wit.

As ever in this song, however insightful the previous lines, the most thought provoking are the stanza's closing couplet. Here we are treated to:

*Don't follow leaders*
*Watch the parkin' meters*

It is another strikingly resonant phrase, *parkin' meters* being another perfect symbol of petty, restricting authority.

For Dylan himself there is an unsettling paradox here: in telling people not to follow leaders he is contradicting himself in the very act of singing what he sings. In his previous album Dylan had shown acute self-analysis in the masterful song 'My Back Pages', which included the lines:

> *...fearing not that*
> *I'd become my enemy in the instant that I preached...*

Unfortunately for him it was a lesson he was about to re-learn, as songs like 'Subterranean Homesick Blues' bound him to a role he has never quite managed to shake off, no matter how he has tried. It is hardly surprising that this unique voice of the emerging youth culture, warning its constituents of life's pitfalls in this hip language via their music, should be taken to heart as the voice of the generation. He truly was a spokesman, who, in David Bowie's tribute 'Song for Bob Dylan':

> *Stood behind a million pairs of eyes*
> *And told them how they saw...*

The last verse has a stunning opening: the life the kids are being pushed into by everyone (but advised against by Dylan) is summarised as economically as could be imagined. It sounds like a whole sitcom series about growing up is flashing before your eyes (or rather, ears). About five years worth of 'Roseanne' (a programme with numerous Dylan references and quotes[5]) is summed up at lightening pace:

> *Ah get born, keep warm*
> *Short pants, romance, learn to dance*
> *Get dressed, get blessed*
> *Try to be a success*
> *Please her, please him, buy gifts*
> *Don't steal, don't lift*
> *Twenty years of schoolin'*
> *And they put you on the day shift*

This describes the very antithesis of Dylan's ideal existence where one should 'trust yourself'. The life satirised here is a Dylan nightmare, however funnily or wittily put. In the promo film, 'Success' is spelt out as 'Suck-cess' punning on the 'sucking up' one has to perform, along with obeying all the rules here enumerated, to gain the middle-class, middle-America notion of 'success'.

It is worth noting also that 'buying gifts' is an action viewed with great suspicion by Dylan - it is portrayed as a dishonest way of currying favour/sexual gratification. For example, in 'Love Minus Zero/No Limit' from the same album we have the contrast between the idealised 'my love' and the materialistic no-hopers who don't realise that she cannot be bought by valentines or fooled by people carrying roses:

> *People carry roses*
> *And make promises by the hours*
> *My love she laughs like the flowers*
> *Valentines can't buy her.*

If buying gifts is to be viewed with suspicion, the forces of advertising are to be met with outright resistance. Also on *Bringing It All Back Home*, on 'It's Alright Ma (I'm Only Bleeding)', we are warned of their pernicious wiles:

> *Advertising signs that con you*
> *Into thinking you're the one*
> *That can do what's never been done*
> *That can win what's never been won*
> *Meantime life outside goes on*
> *All around you.*

I think of that verse when I hear the following lines in 'Subterranean Homesick Blues' :

> *Don't wear sandals*
> *Try to avoid the scandals*
> *Don't wanna be a bum*
> *You better chew gum*

These parody both the ridiculous nagging advice from parents and modern life's ever present rubbishy advertising speech. It is a deep and depressing irony that this song and its accompanying film have been utilised for adverts in the years since. I suppose that, given Dylan's mastery of advertising-speak and rapid-fire delivery of advice, this development was inevitable. One thing that cannot ever be diluted, however, is the cynical, ultra-hip-but-with deeper import-too ending of:

> *The pump don't work*
> *'Cause the vandals took the handles*

Again, this is a much quoted epigram, which is a testament to its various levels of significance. It symbolises not only the breakdown of the society that the middle-class version of the American dream (which Dylan has been busily debunking) actually results in, but also knowingly deflates any overblown concept of youthful rebellion by exemplifying the kind of minor vandalism that bored, unfulfilled teenagers indulge in. Heck, they'll be vandalising telephone kiosks next, the naughty scamps.

It is all a very far cry from 'The Times They Are A-Changin'' or 'When The Ship Comes In' with their apocalyptic, Biblical visions of the young overthrowing the moribund oldies' society. Then again this is Dylan in a more worldly-wise yet playful role - a hip big brother rather than a fire-brand preacher - and, ultimately, one which would allow him greater scope to effect a more far-reaching critique of modern society.

## Afterword

'Subterranean Homesick Blues' was the song Dylan chose to launch his new style of touring in June 1988; the beginning of a period of touring that has continued through every year since, gaining in the process the name 'the Never Ending Tour'. A name coined by Dylan, but one which he feels is no longer relevant. However one refers to this yearly gigging since just after his 47th birthday to into his 60s, it was apt that the ground-breaking 'Subterranean Homesick Blues' was performed for the first time live as the opening song of the opening show.

An intriguing hint as to the inspiration for the song's imagery was posted on a Dylan newsgroup on the internet[6]:

> 'I attended Bard College in the late '60's and early '70's and rumor has it that this song was (at least partially) about that venerable institution. 'Must bust early May, orders from the D.A.' which refers to the annual drug busts of Bard students by then Dutchess County Sheriff Quinlan.

> 'The pump don't work 'cause the vandals took the handle' refers to a pump which sit in a triangle in the middle of Annandale Road which, to this day, cannot keep its handle.'

We do not have enough information on Dylan's life at that time to say much more about this, but he undoubtedly was in the right area at the time for there to be something in it.

Further references to the same story have surfaced from time to time, including a piece by Lynn Samuels in Long Island Voice (August 28th 1997), entitled 'Get High on Education, Kids!'. The relevant passage reads:

> *'My biggest college claim to fame has nothing to do with me at all. You know at the end of Dylan's (Bob not Jakob) Subterranean Homesick Blues,' where he says, 'The pump don't work cause the vandals took the handle'? Well, I went to the actual place, Bard College, where the handle-less pump was located. Apparently Bob, who was not a student, hung out at Bard during the very years I was there. We are talking pre-hippie here.- it was still beatnik time and somewhere among the scraggly boys with guitars and bad voices that matched their bad skin was the future poet laureate of a generation. For all I know, I drank beer with him, or even - oh, never mind, my mother reads this.'*

You can look at Bard College at http://www.bard.edu/ if this has piqued your curiosity.

1. It is interesting to note, in passing, that the sinister nursery rhyme is something Dylan would return to in *under the red sky* and *"Love And Theft"*.

2. Which forms an ironic contrast to the moral righteousness of the singer in 'Let Me Die In My Footsteps' ('I will not go down under the ground...').

3. Though you can read a more positive spin on No Doz by those trying to sell it at http://www.keypharmaceuticals.com.au/no_doze.htm

4. Students For A Democratic Society (SDS) was an organisation best known for its activism against the Vietnam War. It came to national prominence after organising a march to the capital in April 1965.

5. John Goodman, who played the part of Roseanne's husband (and who will appear in a 2003 film, *Masked And Anonymous*, playing promoter to Dylan's Jack Fate character) on more than one occasion could be heard singing snatches of Dylan songs, a fairly lengthy excerpt from 'All I Really Want To Do' brightening up a shower for him in one episode. That was soon followed by daughter Darlene (mis) quoting some lines about tax men to her mother. When asked where she got that from, Darlene replied *'from the back of one of your old Dylan LPs'*.

There was also a mooted scene when the series was coming to a close where God would appear in a vision to Roseanne, and God would be played by Dylan. I am a bit disappointed we never got that...

6. Posted on the newsgroup rec.music.dylan, 5/07/1995

# Six

# Maggie's Farm

### Foreword

*In 1994 I was about to start writing a column for a then-new Dylan fanzine, On The Tracks. Although I knew the general tone I sought for the column, I also wanted to start with a flourish. So, I mused over various "biggies" - like 'Visions Of Johanna', 'Tangled Up In Blue' and 'Every Grain Of Sand'.*

*Then it occurred to me that I was going about things the wrong way. The column ought to be of interest to the readers - all Dylan aficionados, after all - no matter what the song in question might be.*

*In a complete change around, I thought I would start with a 'toughie' - the, at that time, generally derided 'Maggie's Farm'. Derided, that is, by some of those who attend or listen to concert after concert; it was usually greeted rapturously by others. This audience split between aversion to /enthusiasm for certain famous songs was later to crystallise spectacularly around 'All Along The Watchtower'. Stuck, it seemed for all eternity, in the third slot of the set list, this later, classic song became an albatross around the neck of multiple concert-goers. Nonetheless, it usually received the biggest cheer of each night. As the years passed this division between those going to show after show and the rest of the audience naturally grew more pronounced, and is particularly acute when Dylan plays an area he has not visited before (or for many years). Two different audiences to please; those who go infrequently to see him when he is in town, those who go to a number of shows every year. As someone famous once said 'You can't please all the people all of the time'.*

*At Cardiff International Arena in 1995 I saw it more clearly than ever; the audience that night was mainly made up of people there to see a big name, a 'legend', and they went bananas when 'All Along The Watchtower' began. There was a hard core of followers who groaned at the same moment. The same thing happened later that night with 'Maggie's Farm', which brought the main set to a close.*

*For those who do not go to many shows this must seem a churlish reaction. Imagine, though, the position of those who do, and who are highly likely to listen to most - if not all - of the shows on tape (remember there are 100+ per year) and getting that same damn song in the third position each and every time. At Hyde Park, London 1996, a major concert-going friend of mine, Peter Vincent, was more excited by the fact that 'All Along The Watchtower' was played as the second song, rather than in the third slot, than by anything else that day. (I was not sure that festival set lists really counted.) Finally, in the fall of 1997, Dylan relented and stopped having the song as a permanent feature. This was after the song had been played 1029 times since 1974, over half of these performances coming in the 1990s at number 3 in the set.*

*Anyway, that is another story, though it gives you an idea of the similar low esteem in which the previous bête noir, 'Maggie's Farm', was held. 'Maggie's Farm' was for a long period the most played song since 1974, when accurate records began to be kept. For many concertgoers their only request was 'anything but 'Maggie's Farm', Bob.' So I thought it would be a good idea to start my new column with a look at this song, in an effort to reclaim it from derision and perhaps discover why it seemed so important a song to Dylan.*

*The following is a reworking of that article, with an **afterword**.*

So why, in the first instance, do I believe this song means something special to Dylan? First of all, he has played it almost 600 times between January 1974 and when I first wrote this some twenty years later. On that Newport night when Dylan first performed with electric guitar and backing band, it was the opening song. It appears on the following seven official albums, including three successive live albums:

> *Bringing It All Back Home*
> *Greatest Hits Volume II*
> *Masterpieces*
> *The Essential Bob Dylan*
> *(live):*
> *Hard Rain*
> *Live At Budokan*
> *Real Live*

I listen to Dylan singing it in 1994 and he has revitalised it again. It is still fresh and powerful after all these years, all these performances - clearly, it is an important song to Bob Dylan.

I was not alone in focusing on this particular song. Ed Ricardo and Sorabh Saxena were concurrently delving into its historical genesis via Dylan Internet groups. They were interested in the story of Dylan singing 'Only A Pawn In Their Game' at Silas Magee's Farm on 6th July 1963, a clip of which appears in the documentary film *Don't Look Back*. Many people believe this visit is what 'Maggie's Farm' is all about.

That it is not what I want to write about here. My purpose is to tell you how it felt to me in my sixteenth summer (I was late into Dylan). A summer that saw my first exposure to Dostoyevsky (Notes From The Underground), Sartre (all the fiction, some of the plays and philosophy) and Dylan (all the mid-sixties classics). Everywhere I read, saw and heard a cry for the freedom of the individual.

It may raise some scholarly eyebrows to list Dylan with Dostoyevsky and Sartre; others may think it pretentious to do so. I don't find it either surprising or pretentious, as I am simply telling you what happened, and in that summer those three artists filled my days. They were all opening up my mind to the inviolability and importance of the self. Not least the gorgeously expressive voice tied to the Rockabilly-style beat drilling into my head:

*I ain't gonna work on Maggie's Farm no more...*

It is quite a simple song. Simple in the sense of its structure, its melody and its message - which is not to say it does not carry deep import. Yes, there are specific references to farm labourers, slaves and servants; but what I heard first of all was the cry of the 'I'. Through that summer I also noticed how interlinked and self-supporting Dylan's imagery was in the great 1964-68 years. More of that later, because before I heard the imagery, I heard the sound. The voice, the instruments, the rock 'n' roll beat. It sounded like a great single to me. It's the right length, has a great hook and short, sharp, punchy lines screaming against drudgery and confinement.

That scream has universal application, from downtrodden slaves to anyone who listens and feels the same. Mid-sixties pop music, that's what Dylan was creating; music played on the radio to adolescents, listened to by teenagers who hated being locked up in an institution day after day, their lives controlled by someone else's timetable. Teenagers who hated always being told what to do and when to do it. School children are too smart to believe the 'these are the best days of your life' crap - hell, they know their lives haven't started yet. If you look back on those days and think that they were, well your life never really did start. Me? I hated it then and went AWOL as often as possible, muttering under my breath

> *I try my best*
> *To be just like I am*
> *But everybody wants you*
> *To be just like them.*

That is how I remember the last years of school; you've just become a person, an individual in your own right, but everyone, everywhere, wants you to be just like them. The only good thing about those days was the soundtrack - the magic inherent in the classic pop single. Bruce Springsteen got it right when he sang:

> *We learned more from a three minute record, babe*
> *Than we ever did in school*

A three minute record like 'Maggie's Farm'. Maybe it's time to take a closer look at it. Or, even better, you should play a really loud, fast, rocking version and idiot-dance to it for a while, or play the version on *Hard Rain* and imagine Dylan's face as he pulls off some outrageously effective line endings.

Back with me? Good. I do not wish to try your patience by detailing the metrical and rhythmic structures but it is worth noting that these give us four short and punchy middle lines in each stanza, followed by a longer line for Dylan to deliver however the mood takes him in concert. Around these the opening line comes three times, twice at the beginning and once at the end, with the addition of 'No' on first repetition. For my purposes in this article, it is highly relevant that Verses 1 and 5 deal with 'I', (in relation to 'Maggie' and 'They' respectively) while enclosing three verses that deal with 'you' (in relation to the 'Brother, Pa, and Ma').

Verse One:

This verse certainly has specific references to servitude: *It's a shame the way she makes me scrub the floor.* Also, does the comment pray for rain denote a plea for cooling rain while slaving in the burning Mississippi sun, as someone suggested to me recently?

However, it also contains lines that surely come straight from the heart of Bob Dylan. Oh, I know I should talk about 'the singer-as-narrator' and all that, but I always hear it as the author's voice.

> *I got a head full of ideas*
> *That are drivin' me insane.*

70

Suddenly we seem to be on a whole other level; this is the man who sings on the same album (and, again, I perceive no screening of the author; for me this is Bob Dylan speaking, whatever he claims):

> And if my thought-dreams could be seen
> They'd probably put my head in a guillotine.

There we have two quotes from two songs - one rock, one folk - by one artist. These were viewed at the time as being 'fun' and 'serious' respectively. We forget how deep the pop/folk divide then was. For me, that debate had all been long before my time and what I listened to was 'popular music'. Of course 'Maggie's Farm' is a very funny song, at least at times. I don't know which version you played at my earlier prompting, but if you didn't play the original go and stick the track on now. Isn't it great? Listen to the invention in the playing and the phrasing. It is catchy, appealing, witty - and, yes, pretty funny in parts. It confused most critics at the time; I don't mind the reviewer in the *New York Herald Tribune* writing 'There is the genuinely funny 'Maggie's Farm'...' (12/12/65) but I certainly would take issue with P.M. Clepper describing it as 'one of his most farcical songs...' in the *Washington Star* (27/3/66). Still, for a 'funny' song it is about to make a few disturbing observations. This is no surprise to listeners to mid-sixties Dylan, but it was an unknown experience for many reporters at the time. To say nothing of those who did/still do think that only the folk side of the album could possibly be 'serious' in any way.[1]

Verse 2 -'The Brother'

Not a nice chap, Maggie's brother. He seems heavily into money as power, using it to demean via charity (something Bob has always been strong on), to pay a pittance for hard labour or for fining people for expressing the temper he has ignited in them. If this man gave money to a charity it would surely be a tax-deductible one.

Picking up from where verse 1 left off we have another demeaning reference; this time to the payment in petty cash - *a nickel, a dime* - that he 'hands you'. Most listeners seem to equate the 'you' the money is being handed over to as the 'me' who 'scrubbed the floor' - a kind of tip for doing the menial work. It certainly seems to be a meagre wage for such work, but I'm not sure it *needs* to be payment for the specific 'scrubbing of the floor' referred to in verse 1.

There is something very unsettling in his 'grin'; in fact, people who grin in Dylan songs are usually a bad lot. The same disquiet you feel from:

> he asks you with a grin
> If you're havin' a good time

is also present in the second verse of 'Lily, Rosemary And The Jack Of Hearts':

> *Then he walked up to a stranger and he asked him with a grin*
> *'Could you kindly tell me, friend, what time the show begins'*

You may also remember the crowds in Roman times with their 'bloodshot grins' ('Long Ago, Far Away'), and what was his 'friend' doing when he was 'down' in 'Positively 4th Street'? Yes, that's right, standing there *grinning*. My favourite lines - well, they're all great lines, really - in 'Clothes Line Saga' are:

> *'Have you heard the news?' he said, with a grin*
> *'The vice-president's gone mad.'*

Depending on how Dylan sings it, the word 'grin' and the phrase 'good time' can suggest a very nasty side to the brother, but it is all a bit petty compared to when he grows up and becomes 'the Pa'. You see, Magee's farm in Mississippi has already been left behind; surely we are hearing now of all our relatives, of all society's restraints and victimization?

Verse 3 - 'The Pa'

Now this is a real nasty piece of work, and a fellow whose unfortunate traits and characteristics resound throughout Dylan's mid-sixties work. I don't find much funny here, and definitely nothing 'farcical'. The whole song darkens as the latent viciousness of the power-holder comes to the fore:

> *Well, he puts his cigar*
> *Out in your face just for kicks.*

(It would be a cigar, of course, a cigarette would be too common. A 'cigar' spells as much trouble as a 'grin'. See 'Who Killed Davey Moore?' for an early example.)

This is the work of a sadist. The lines always remind me of the frightening, if pitiful, persona in 'Can You Please Crawl Out Your Window?' who is *preoccupied with his vengeance*. In both songs, too, the implication of cruel, perverse sexuality is also there. I'm not surprised 'Maggie's Pa' has his bedroom window bricked up, otherwise we might see him testing out some of those 'inventions'. What we need here is Lenny Bruce to come along and *shine a light in their beds.*

Lenny Bruce isn't there, though, so we are left to wonder in what deviant ways this stunted, twisted personality gets his kicks. The brother grown up, still hung up on power, all the negative aspects of man; hell, if he needed a third eye he'd just grow one.

The National Guard standing around his door seems to be opening the song out into even wider contexts. (In Britain, as the full injustice and iniquities of the

Thatcher years became apparent even to the dimmest observers, this song became very popular. There were numerous cover versions, including one which railed against a 'Maggie's Pa' who had his door guarded by the 'SPG'[2].)

Verse 1 - 'The Ma'

What a difference we find in this character. Dylan takes us from those unsettling images of the sadistic 'Pa' to 'Ma' - a vain old fusspot. OK, some people may tell you that she is *the brains behind pa*, but, I doubt it, I think it's just an image. Like the image she has of herself as being a bit of a philosopher, while the glibness of the following line tells us she is babbling nonsense:

*About man and God and law*

The verse has its serious side, too. It re-introduces the servitude motif, and Ma's self-delusion about her age could be taken as being important, but Dylan usually plays it for laughs. (This could be viewed as a fairly sexist slander, but I must say that the 'ma' character is considerably less offensive than the 'brother' or the 'pa'.) The ma is anti-life, but not in the overtly malicious way of pa or the sneering brother. She epitomises Aunt Sally in *Adventures of Huckleberry Finn*, when Huck says:

> *...because Aunt Sally she's going to adopt me and sivilize me, and I can't stand it.*

Or at least that is how I hear the song now. Previous to writing this article, I'd thought of the song's verses as *rising* in menace. The sneering brother led to the sadistic pa who was controlled by the mastermind of evil known as ma. Listening to it more closely, the above interpretation struck me more forcibly. After some 20 years of listening to this song I find myself looking at a whole verse in a different light; interesting, and a good argument for going back to original versions, re-listening and sharing your views with others. Why the change in my case? One of the main reasons is that when I now listen to the song I hear Dylan's playful, over-the-top 1976 versions with his favoured live line:

*She's sixty-eight but she says she's twenty-four*

rather than the original 'fifty-four'[3], which exaggerates her vanity beyond credibility. On the other hand, the song was greeted as 'humorous' at the time of its release. That view was surely based only on this verse. Perhaps the song is flexible enough to be taken either way; after all, the whole point of Aunt Sally's attempts to 'sivilize' Huck is to destroy his very nature, however well-intentioned she is. Certainly this elasticity of interpretation is exploited by

Dylan in live versions: the 'Ma' here can be seen as a bumbling old lady' or as a force that destroys man's core being. We are back to whether you take it as a 'funny' or a 'serious' song - I refuse to limit my options, but allow myself instead to be guided by the particular Dylan performance I am listening to. The way Dylan deftly exposes her vanity and self-importance even in the original version inclines me towards the comic interpretation - though that has its own serious repercussions, in the setting of the rest of the family running the farm.

Verse 5

Part of the reason I wrote this article was to try to explain why Dylan plays this particular song so often, what pull it has got on him to appear almost constantly in his set lists. To anticipate that somewhat, I think it has a lot to do with the last verse. I was listening to the 3rd May 1976 version where he has so much fun with the line:

*They sing while you slave I get bored*
*ohh -soo-bo-o-o-red*

but yet doesn't rob it of its meaning. What a great line this is, it is literally true for slaves and both literally (in a different way) and metaphorically true for Dylan, the innovative performer often criticised for singing songs differently from how they appear on record. The perfect line to sum up the two strands of the song, the perfect line to sing night after night on stage. Before that we have a four-line summary of a theme dear to Dylan's heart:

*Well, I try my best*
*To be just like I am*
*But everybody wants you*
*To be just like them*

This is the voice that spoke to me way back when I first heard the song, and speaks to me still. I hear it as a straightforward statement from Bob Dylan, the man who wrote:

*stay in line. stay in step. people*
*are afraid of someone who is not*
*in step with them.*
            'Advice for Geraldine on Her Miscellaneous Birthday'.

And, many years later,

*Well you're on your own, you always were,*
*In a land of wolves and thieves,*

*Don't put your hope in ungodly man*
*Or be a slave to what somebody else believes.*
                                        'Trust Yourself'.

Trust yourself, be yourself, and play it again, Bob.

There are many other interesting things about this song. For one, there is the setting of the track in *Bringing It All Back Home*. Succeeding, as it does, a song which includes images of serfdom, which itself is preceded by a song including a character called Maggie. If it is simply an oblique reference to Silas Magee's farm in Mississippi, why do I feel Maggie is such a feminine character? Her farm may be taken as a metaphor for all manner of things: the Establishment, white-dominated society, the US of A. Ultimately, though, I see it as representing any restricting, corrupt society or system. In my gloomier moods I see it as being inevitable that any society will, by its very nature, turn into a 'Maggie's Farm' that forever tries to entrap and torment the individual spirit of humankind.

Why, though, is this particular song so important to Dylan? Well, I really think it has got a lot to do with the first and last verses. I realise, though, that many will be horrified by me taking these lines as pertaining to Dylan at all. I am fully aware that the whole song can be seen as the view of a black slave (literal or economic) from a farm such as Silas Magee's. Indeed, once this has been pointed out, it becomes, on one level, clearly a story told by someone steeling himself to break free from his servitude. The details are deftly drawn, the physicality of brutish labour unmistakable, the repeated lines parody the chain gang songs that were sung 'while they slaved'. However, that is not the only level the song works on, and I'm telling you *how I first heard it, how it felt to me*. It still does come to that, most times I hear it. In any case, I do not see how a 'solely voice of a slave' interpretation would account for the song's enduring appeal to Dylan the performer. I suspect that comes from its crucial place in Dylan's oeuvre, in addition to all I've said above.

The song has a pivotal place in his folk-folk/rock-rock move (I remind you again that he opened with this song at Newport '65). The version on *Bringing It All Back Home* couldn't be classified as 'Rock'; it sounds more like some sort of folk-rock, being neither one thing nor the other. Then again, it is more rockabilly than either - the music Dylan must associate with his growing up, with the impact of much of the early Elvis.

So, the song is a kind of musical bridge between folk and rock. I also see it as being a lyrical bridge between the concerns for the farms from the period of *The Times They Are A-Changin'* to the later intensely psychological investigations of the personal prisons that we all create by denying the freedom of the individual. To take you back to my ' summer of discovery' all those years ago, Dylan was about to write songs which were 'notes from the underground', and discover that, very often, 'hell is other people'.

Dylan may always play it as an out-and-out rocker nowadays, but the original 'Maggie's Farm', in every sense, stands midway between the early 'protest' songs with literal farms:

> *There's seven people dead*
> *On a South Dakota Farm*
> *There's seven people dead*
> *On a South Dakota Farm*
> *Somewhere in the distance*
> *There's seven new people born*
>> 'Ballad of Hollis Brown', from *The Times They Are*
>> *A-Changin'*, 1963

and the mid-sixties, electric (in every sense) Dylan for whom the word 'farm' symbolised a corrupt society, repressive to the individual:

> *And then you told me later, as I apologized*
> *That you were just kidding me, you weren't really from the farm*
> *An' I told you, as you clawed out my eyes*
> *That I never really meant to do you any harm*
>> 'One Of Us Must Know (Sooner Or Later)'
>> from *Blonde On Blonde*, 1966

## Afterword

Despite the song's omnipresence in the set lists, there was an occasion when I was more excited by 'Maggie's Farm' than by anything that had preceded it in the show. It was a couple of years after I wrote this article, in Konstanz, Germany on July 3, 1996 at the Zeltfestival (Tent Festival).

This is one of the strangest shows I've been to: a boring set list, a very indifferent performance from Dylan for most of the show, but immensely entertaining and fun by the end.

I should point out that other people loved every song on this show without exception. I think they were carried away by the setting and atmosphere. The setting was a tiny tent perched on a beautiful lakeside, the atmosphere was one of intense and unrestrained appreciation of Dylan, no-one in the crowd could be described as far away from the stage, and they certainly all responded to the intimate atmosphere.

At the end of the acoustic set, Dylan finally stretched his voice - hesitantly at first, then with more confidence on 'One Too Many Mornings'. Things were looking up, though my interest was dimmed by the opening chords of 'Maggie's Farm'. I should not have despaired; help was at hand from an unlikely source.

Now anyone who knows me will vouch for me being of all people the most anti-guests on stage with Bob Dylan. Notwithstanding that, it was a guest who saved this show, someone I didn't even know the name of. All I knew was he was the electric violin player from the supporting Dave Matthews Band.[4] A cool dude he was too, a tall, muscular black man with a huge grin and an extrovert stage presence; he bounded onto the stage and suddenly Bob had to wake up. Here was someone on stage who not only was attracting the audience's eyes from Dylan, but who could also play like fury and had no inhibitions about showing it. 'Maggie's Farm' really took off and ended in a duet/duel between Dylan's guitar and the tall Dude's manic violin. It was exhilarating to be there and see the sheer joy in Dylan's face as it happened. The song ended with Dylan high-fiving the violinist.

The whole show was suddenly freed from being just another show on the rather uninspiring (in the main) 1996 treadmill. Now it was transformed into something with joy, invention and endless possibilities. It seemed fitting to me that this transformation took place with 'Maggie's Farm'.

1. The cassette release of this album changed the running order to 'even up' the sides. An act of vandalism as far as this writer is concerned.

2. Special Patrol Group.

3. Interestingly, the official lyrics now say 'twenty-four', though there's no doubt about what Dylan sang on Bringing It All Back Home.

4. Here's a piece of information from the Dave Matthews Band Web Site:

> Boyd Tinsley: (violin, vocals) finds it strange sometimes that he abandoned the reserved precision of classical violin for the spontaneity of contemporary musical performance. 'This was an area I hadn't explored before,' says Tinsley, who has been playing popular music since 1985. 'When I'm really into the music, my whole body, my whole soul is into it.' In fact, one of his trademarks are his 'jams' with Dave Matthews. The best thing, though, he says, is how much it matters to the audience, and to the players. 'People are drawn to it,' he says. 'There's a passion here.'

# Seven

# Inside The Gates Of Eden

## Foreword

*This first appeared in* On The Tracks *issue 9. It has been expanded and updated slightly for publication here.*

*I had intended this article to be about the lyrics of 'Gates Of Eden' and, indeed, it begins in that manner. However, as I was writing it I realised that there was a wider element I wanted to discuss, involving key lines from other songs of around the same time. So, my article begins by looking at 'Gates Of Eden' and then concentrates on a theme that is no more than implied in this song.*

*As you can tell from my frequent caveats, I was rather cautious of making any less-than-fully-admiring comments on a song that so many rate a 'classic', 'an all time favourite'. From my experiences after writing on* Time Out Of Mind *and certain aspects of the Never Ending Tour, this caution was well merited. However, I was told by a friend whose opinion I not only rate highly, but who follows the traditional British fashion in being loath to praise a friend about anything, that he thought this was my best piece of writing on Dylan. Given the high regard in which he holds the song I treasured this as praise indeed.*

*I won't name him as I trust he is blushing already...*

Listening to 'Gates Of Eden' recently, I was struck by how dated and contrived some of the lines sounded to me now, while simultaneously marvelling at other images that still sound as moving and insightful as ever.

Now I realise that for many of you this will be one of your favourite songs; one you treasure, one you regard as a masterpiece, a classic. I know this because it has been - and in many ways still is - the same for me. I remember during my first year at university that they had one Dylan single on the café jukebox: it was 'Like A Rolling Stone' b/w 'Gates Of Eden'. I used to programme them to play time after time - my own little electric/acoustic set! The magic of the songs never lessened for me no matter how many times I programmed that machine to play 'A7' followed by 'A8' (though the same could not be said for the sadly numerous people who groaned or, as time passed, actually got up and left whenever I arrived).

So do not imagine that I am deliberately going out of my way to antagonise or put Dylan down when I make a disapproving remark in the following lines . Far from it, I am merely doing my job as a critic (in the analytical rather than censorious sense), explaining why the magic remains completely intact for me for 'Like A Rolling Stone' and only nearly so for 'Gates Of Eden'. 'Only nearly an all time classic' is praise rather than condemnation. If you read on you'll find out exactly how high that praise is; these words of caution are only for those who would be put off from continuing at the merest sign of any disapprobation.

Anyway, the only reason that I feel 'Gates Of Eden' is 'not quite an absolute classic' is that it is, at times, obscure beyond understanding, usually when Dylan has over-reached for effect in his imagery and conceits. This obscurity never completely overwhelms the form of the song, however. Mainly because it is a song, rather than a poem, and Dylan's exquisite performance conveys his intent, his 'message', even on the occasions when his lyrics baffle us. Still, this is enough for me to place the song outside the category of absolute classic Dylan songs; it does not quite attain the fusion of perfect lyrics, perfect music and perfect performance that sets the likes of 'Visions Of Johanna', 'Tangled Up In Blue' etc. apart. In fact, one does not need to go any further than the song's original album setting to notice what I mean. Side two of *Bringing It All Back Home*, the acoustic side, contains four successive masterpieces: 'Mr. Tambourine Man', 'Gates Of Eden', 'It's Alright Ma (I'm Only Bleeding)' and 'It's All Over Now, Baby Blue'. It is only the second song that sounds a little dated.

In any case, it would be fairer to describe 'Gates Of Eden' as 'obscure but understandable' rather than labour on the obscurantism. 'Understandable' due to the underlying dynamics of the lyrics, which are dynamics built around contrasts. Structurally speaking, the contrasts occur within each sestet (opening six lines) and then all of those lines are contrasted with the reality within the gates of Eden.

In addition, obscurity is not always a sign of poor writing; lyrics can be obscure but effective - a phrase which could be used to sum up the entire song - or indeed transcendent, as in:

*Upon the beach where hound dogs bay*
*At ships with tattooed sails*
*Heading for the gates of Eden.*

This is consummate surrealism, you can feel it, you can see it and you could not use any other words to explain it or to inspire the same effect. It is magnificent lyric writing; but not all the song is, even famous lines like:

*The motorcycle black Madonna*
*Two-wheeled gypsy queen*
*And her silver-studded phantom cause*
*The gray flannel dwarf to scream*

seem to me merely very clever (though dazzlingly so) rather than truly imaginative as in the lines quoted previously. This is the kind of thing I meant by 'dated'; it is still good, of course, a straight contrast between the wild female embodiment of freedom and passion and the biting caricature of Mr. Normal Citizen (Mr. Jones/Nowhere Man) but it is just a touch contrived.

Other lines are contrived without being this good - for example:

*The lamppost stands with folded arms*
*Its iron claws attached*
*To curbs 'neath holes where babies wail*

is too stylised to be completely effective, and then Dylan overreaches for effect by following up with

*Though it shadows metal badge*

So, lyrically, we have a mix of the obscure, the sublime, the witty and the awkward. All of these are yoked together and moved along by the performance and by what I have termed 'the underlying dynamics of contrasts'; A term I would now like to explain.

There are various different types of contrasts within the song, three of the main ones being:

- contrasts within the sestet
- contrasts between the sestet and the closing line of each verse
- individual (and often delightful) contrasts between symbols and images.

An example of the first has already been quoted with the black Madonna/gray dwarf contrast; the same verse also illustrates the second type, as both 'Madonna' and 'dwarf' are contrasted with the inside of the 'Gates Of Eden', where there is no sin. Examples of the third category of contrasts would include the delicate 'sparrow/kings' and the arch 'friends and other strangers'.

The whole song is propelled by large-scale contrasts:

Money v. Spirituality

Conformity v. Freedom

Phoney Religious Organizations v. Authentic religious experience

Nature v. Art

Ownership v. Self-fulfilment

Tumult v. Silence

I grant you that this is quite a list, but it is not a surprising one for someone whose writing is imbued with the Romantics via the French symbolists and the Beats. It does, though, give an idea of the scale on which Dylan is working. It also presumably explains the endless list of Dylan commentators who refer to the lyric as 'Blakean'. There are obvious reasons why they do, but Blake would never produce a lyric as uneven and loose as this. 'Blake via the Beats' is a view I can see however, and I can also put into perspective my view on this song's worth for those of you still shocked by my ranking it as 'not a stonewall classic'. Judged as a piece of Beat art, this one song seems to me worth more than anything produced by anyone else.

However, going back to 'the contrasts' - a catalogue of these, comparing what's outside and inside the 'Gates Of Eden', is our only way of discovering what is inside the Gates. Or, rather, at least what is not.

From the opening stanza's description of the turmoil of life, followed by the struggle between peace and war which has no place within the Gates, through the meaningless din of urban life set against the silence within, via natural laughter from inside the Gates as opposed to the dour instructions of invented religions, we keep getting told what is not inside the gates. There are no phoney religions, no wars, no ownership struggles, (so, no Kings), no philosophical debate, no trials . We do know that there is silence, but also laughter (somehow this is not contradictory); we also know there are no truths outside the Gates, implying heavily that they are to be found inside them. (And you just know that the truths in question are Truths with a capital 'T'.)

There is certainly no need for debate or struggle inside, for perfection seems to be within those gates. And for me - and I am proposing for Dylan (at least the Dylan of the mid-sixties) - this means it is a non-human realm. A realm mankind must yearn for, must dream about attaining, must, most crucially, measure himself against but not really one he wants to attain, except perhaps through death. There is no room for the living human within those Gates: no debate, no struggle, none of the sound and fury of our - admittedly meaningless - existence, no sins for goodness sake! Doesn't that sound just a little, well, boring?

### Perfect must die

Which brings me finally to the greatest contrast of them all in the song: a contrast between the human and the non-human realm of perfection. Not an idea I get solely from 'Gates Of Eden', I hasten to add; it is here that I find it necessary to involve key lines from other, contemporaneous, songs.

There is a similar - and more direct - contrast evident in the magnificent 'Lay Down Your Weary Tune' where weary, inharmonious Man is exhorted to rest for a moment in the perfection of harmonious Nature. Again man is being judged - or rather is judging himself - against this ideal but not with any expectation (or even hope) of being a part of it.

> Lay down your weary tune, lay down
> Lay down the song you strum
> And rest yourself 'neath the strength of strings
> No voice can hope to hum.

There is no indication that man can ever become an element in the ideal harmony; the ideal tune contains many things but not our voice. Man instead toils and labours outside but sustains himself with the unreachable, non-human ideal. Just as in 'Gates Of Eden' the aspiration to attain what is inside inspires the players (us - Dylan and his listeners) outside to keep on striving.

Listen again to 'Lay Down Your Weary Tune' and 'Gates Of Eden' with a view that what is being described is too perfect for the human - and if you see my point you'll accept the next that, indeed, to attain that very perfection is to die. (This is explicitly stated in 'Farewell Angelina' and is discussed in the next chapter.)

> What cannot be imitated
> Perfect must die

And now we have finally moved from the world of contrasts to that familiar Dylan landscape of paradox. The artists (as in the case just quoted and Mankind as a whole in 'Gates Of Eden') strive for perfection to sustain their very existence. If achieved, however, perfection brings death to the creative artist or growing individual (whose growth comes from development). When the art has been perfected it may as well be hung in museums where infinity goes up on trial.

This is a bind that Dylan seems to comprehend with almost frightening clarity: Man cannot exist inside the gates of Eden, he cannot hum the great Tune (terrible thing for a singer to have to admit); an artist must strive to produce the unique (as an individual must strive to be just that) but, here's the rub, the minute you do, it dies.

'Farewell Angelina' is an outtake from the same album as 'Gates Of Eden', where the preceding track is 'Mr. Tambourine Man'. Writing of that song Aidan Day commented on the nature of its 'diamond sky':

> 'There is the "diamond sky": the crystalline perfection of an anaes-
> thetized nature. Like "Marbles of the dancing floor" in the city of Yeats's
> Byzantium, Dylan's "diamond sky" is intimidating in its cold,
> unyielding brilliance. But its worth lies precisely in its transmutation of
> natural laws.'

He could have been talking about what is inside those gates of Eden.

So what is behind those Gates? Why Heaven, of course - or maybe we should call it Hell?

## Afterword

I realised after writing the piece that my hesitancy in questioning its 'absolute classic' status was not only to do with upsetting potential readers. It is also that taken as a whole, the experience of hearing the song, its visionary sweep in the grand Romantic tradition and the overall effect make one not wish to draw any attention to (perceived) defects.

The warning is clear from the author of the piece that he does not approve of this 'shovelling of the glimpses' in search for meaning. A more than fair point, nonetheless I can appreciate and laud the way he presents the glimpse in the following lines, without putting my hand anywhere near a shovel:

> Upon the beach where hound dogs bay
> At ships with tattooed sails
> Heading for the Gates of Eden

It's just that this does not hold true throughout the whole - still, his perfor-mance can often make that seem an unimportant distinction.

# Eight

# Farewell Angelina

### Foreword

*I was running a Dylan information telephone service when the* Bootleg Series Volumes 1-3 *advance tape came out. No-one who phoned at that time could fail to note my enthusiasm for this song. I ended the message by playing the new verse. It was quite some time before I could bring myself to take it off. I know of at least one caller who phoned five times in rapid succession just to hear that snippet.*

*All of this will come as no surprise to Dylan aficionados for whom this track had been a Holy Grail for years. 'It doesn't exist.' 'It does exist, a cousin of a friend of mine heard Stephen Pickering's version.' 'Baez says he never recorded it.' How many of you reading this bought Baez's single? How many more bought the album of that title? How many really did play the single at 33rpm to make it sound more like you were hearing Dylan singing it? How many others - and I stand accused - bought yet another Joker album (semi-legal albums from Italy with endearingly mistake-ridden track listings) with 'Farewell' on it because the covers claimed it was 'Farewell Angelina', and this one might just mean it?*

*Suddenly, here it was, all these years later, 'really real'. How exciting! With great anticipation and expectation I played the tape... and played it again... and again.*

*Then I wrote the following for issue 4 of* **Homer**, the slut. *It has been updated for this collection.*

It certainly didn't disappoint, even in the face of these seemingly overpowering expectations; instead, within the opening few lines, it felt exactly as I'd always imagined it would. There was even a gorgeous little laugh while he sang 'erupting' at the end of the penultimate line, conjuring up images of the about-to-be-rock-star-with-a-band, totally compelling and in-control solo Dylan that we glimpse in *Don't Look Back*.

What I wasn't expecting, though, was a brand new verse; I also had to adjust to the many changes of lyric from the version I'd carried all this time in my head.

Given the special nature of this release I make no apologies for spending this review in a detailed comparison of the long-expected and the actual. Since he performs it exactly as you had always thought and hoped he would, it will be an examination concentrating on the lyrical differences. Through this comparative examination I'm hoping to shed light on some of the meaning in this performance.

Naturally, Dylan's performance of the song is essential too. Baez's was all very nice but it is a different matter altogether to hear Dylan deliver it. Listen, for example, to the onomatopoeia of his singing of *'flooding over'* and *'flutters from fear'*. Marvellous stuff, but I am presuming you all know the song well and hopeful that you go and play it just now to refresh your memory; because I am now going to contrast the lyrics as sung and the lyrics we believed to be the song's real ones for all those years.

This is not to claim that Dylan is scrupulously adjusting each difference I point out in some precise manner equating to a grand master plan. Rather, he is expressing the song at the moment of performance. The concentration on detail here is of my own making - it comes from the contrast between what I had been expecting to hear and what I did hear. At the same time, the consistency of the changes discussed betrays a deliberate approach, and that thought has gone into how they could be effective.

In stanza one we have only three alterations from the lyrics originally printed in *Writings and Drawings*. In that collection the last five lines appear as:

> The triangle tingles
> And the trumpets play slow
> Farewell Angelina
> The sky is on fire
> And I must go

What he actually sings is:

> The triangle tingles
> The music plays slow
> But farewell Angelina
> The night is on fire
> And I must go

The dropping of the 'And' preceding the fourth last line is a common alteration, indeed it only remains where the word is actually doing something. This attention to detail continues throughout the recorded version; a great deal of thought appears to have been given to the use of conjunctions such as 'and' and 'but'.

In that altered line we lose the sound of 'trumpets' which had followed on so sweetly from *'The triangle tingles'*. I must admit that I prefer the alliterative 'trumpets' version, although 'music' is perhaps more literally what Dylan had in mind.

The addition of 'But' before the conclusion to the verse is deliberate and effective. It occurs in all but one of the stanzas sung (the *Lyrics* version contains no instances of this) and would have been inappropriate in the other (new) one. The purpose of the 'but' is to separate the narrator's actions from the scenarios he is depicting. As I hope to demonstrate later, another crucial function it performs is to polarise the depiction and the sky.

Which brings me to the last difference - we have no 'sky' in the performed song's first verse. This is surely just a simple transposition in Dylan's mind of an apocalyptic image; I can't discern any change in meaning or emphasis here, perhaps he even meant to sing 'sky'. If that were true, it is an interesting 'slip' in the light of such later songs as 'Under The Red Sky' and 'When The Night Comes Falling From The Sky'.

The second verse contains some major changes: the written version goes like this:

> There's no need for anger
> There's no need for blame
> There's nothing to prove
> Ev'rything's still the same
> Just a table standing empty
> By the edge of the sea
> Farewell Angelina
> The sky is trembling
> And I must leave

What he sings is:

> There is no use in talking
> And there's no need for blame
> There is nothing to prove
> Ev'rything still is the same
> A table stands empty

*By the edge of the stream*
*But farewell Angelina*
*The sky's changing colours*
*And I must leave*

The meaning of the first four lines is not much altered, they contain standard nuggets of Dylan wisdom of the time - compare with 'All I Really Want To Do', 'One Too Many Mornings' etc. However, in the performed version they have been shaped to maximum effect. The use of the full 'is' links lines one and three very forcefully, while the change in line four – accentuated very strongly in Dylan's delivery - throws the emphasis on the word 'is'. This stress could not have come at a more critical time, as it directly precedes a major lyrical line change.

The fifth and sixth lines make up what was surely the most oft-quoted Dylan couplet that had never been heard from him. When we finally get a take of him singing the song, it is radically altered. This is initially a shock both in itself and inasmuch as the visual image is not as arresting. There is a very good reason for this; the written version stands perfectly as an isolated image, while the sung version is stylistically and meaningfully integrated into the song as a whole. Gone, then, is the 'just' that isolates the image. The most crucial change of all is from 'standing' to 'stands'; herein lies the key to the way the song works and the reason behind most of the sung alterations.

The move away from the 'ing' endings here and with the cross-eyed pirates (from 'sitting' to 'sit') makes for a much better contrast with the changing sky. (Flooding, erupting, etc.). In each stanza Dylan presents us with a snapshot scene, a tableau, behind or over which the sky is threateningly evolving and forcing the narrator to move on before it is too late, before he is frozen into the tableau forever. A classic Dylan nightmare; a situation to be avoided at almost any cost. As mentioned previously, the 'buts' that are added in the sung version underline the contrast. (Interestingly enough, the only 'ing' that remains in the sung version is in the opening stanza where the bells *'are being'* stolen; interesting because, although the grammatical form used here doesn't contradict my point, the sky here is 'night' and is *'on fire'* not 'burning' or some such word. The contrast is still there, only it is inverted in this instance.)

The change from *'the sea'* to *'the stream'* lessens the scope of the image, makes it less dramatic. The image in isolation loses out, but by this alteration Dylan improves the verse as a whole, while integrating it within the overall song. Perhaps because he intuitively felt that, for this verse, 'the sea' was too much the equal of the threatening sky and that the stream would seem more

**87**

vulnerable. More importantly in terms of the whole performance, imagine the fixed tableau with the *'sky changing colours'*; if there were *'the sea'* it too would change colours, reflecting the sky, and there would be no contrast. Indeed, the image would run counter to the whole song.

As will be clear from later remarks it is stylistically surprising that he chose the definite article here, 'a stream' seeming the more apt. On the other hand, he may simply have still had *'the sea'* in mind when he sang it. As we have only the one performance of this song to go on we cannot compare a range of performances and hear what he 'most often' sings.

The third verse has fewer discrepancies between the printed and sung lyrics. In the second line *'Have forsaked'* becomes *'They forsake'*, which is in keeping with the simple present tense state of the scenario that I've been at pains to stress. The guards become singular, a better image, while the change in the last line from *'in a while'* to *'after a while'* facilitates the performance without any change of meaning or emphasis. (It is almost as if Dylan has forced himself to use the two syllable 'after' by the omission - for the only time in the song - of 'and' as the first word in the stanza's last line.)

If you'll permit me to step out of my self-imposed brief of comparative study, I'd like to make a couple of points about this verse. Although Dylan is here in the midst of his most Romantic phase of writing, this verse contains a perfect Classical image of the modern degeneration of the Golden Age; all cards are now the same, there is no longer an ace. However, he presents the image in a Romantic light with that image of freedom in *'ran wild'*. (Dylan's use of language here is breathtaking in its economy, note the oppositional *'file past'*.) The idea of the cards all being the same ties in with the first verse's *'bells of the crown/Are being stolen by bandits'*; although the 'Royal' cards aren't directly mentioned these mutually supportive images bring them to our minds.

The only difference in the opening four lines of stanza 4 is the already noted *'pirates sitting'* to *'pirates sit'*. It is worth observing that Dylan opens this verse with 'See', thereby strengthening my idea of 'snapshots', or, given the surrealist images he presents, perhaps 'paintings' would be even closer to the mark. The other changes occur in the final five lines, from:

> *And the neighbours they clap*
> *And they cheer with each blast*
> *Farewell Angelina*
> *The sky's changing colour*
> *And I must leave fast*

To:

> And the corporals and neighbours
> Clap and cheer with each blast
> But farewell Angelina
> The sky it is trembling
> And I must leave fast

The sung description of the sky - the previous verse having already used *'changing colours'* - is ambiguous. Are we to take it that the 'blasts' are making the sky tremble with fear and apprehension or, as would match the rest of the song, that the sky is trembling with rage?

The introduction of corporals forces a restructuring of the first two lines above, beneficially as the 'And they' before 'cheer' was merely filling the line out. It also introduces a set of characters at home both in the song and in Dylan's sixties work. (*'Corporals and Neighbours'* would be a good title for a *Freewheelin'* to *The Basement Tapes* compilation.)

In the next stanza we have three changes. Firstly *'on the rooftops'* becomes *'in the rooftops'*, which better fits the way I've always visualised King Kong and the little elves. Secondly instead of:

> While the make-up man's hands
> Shut the eyes of the dead

we get

> While the hero's clean hands
> Shut the eyes of the dead

There's not much in it here, both have the necessary cinematic connotations for the stanza, though the use of 'clean' makes the latter a more complex image.

Lastly, the beautiful *'the sky is embarrassed'* is dropped in favour of *'the sky's flooding over'*; presumably because of the use of embarrass only two lines previously. This is a great pity, as the sky's reaction in being 'embarrassed' would have cast aspersions on the cleanliness of the hero's hands, giving us an obverse use of the same cliché in 'Lay Lady Lay':

> His clothes are dirty
> But his hands are clean

To add to the debit column for this alteration, the next verse repeats the use of *'flooding over'* to describe the sky. Still, you cannot expect every sung change to work flawlessly in one take. Overall the song has already gained by the changes made - to say nothing of the joy and depth brought by hearing Dylan perform it.

Which brings us to that verse, the 'new' verse, one that faces head-on the concerns of this particular song and the central concerns Dylan explored in his 'classic' years of the early to mid sixties.

> *The camouflaged parrot*
> *He flutters from fear*
> *When something he doesn't know about*
> *Suddenly appears*
> *What cannot be imitated*
> *Perfect must die*
> *Farewell Angelina*
> *The sky's flooding over*
> *And I must go where it is dry*

What an extraordinary verse this is. It opens with *'The camouflaged parrot'*. How are we to take this? A parrot is a bird known - in some varieties - for its spectacular plumage, plumage that in its natural habitat is partly for camouflage. Yet here there is something very dubious about the camouflage, I almost hear it as meaning the parrot is camouflaged as something else. A parrot is also - indeed primarily - renowned for its ability to imitate other sounds; coming hard on the heels of the Hollywood images we link the parrot with major questions of art imitating life - and popular art at that; just what has been the purpose of the tableaux Dylan has provided us with? What is he telling us now?

We know that the parrot is frightened, thanks to that lovely, alliterative, description *'flutters from fear'*; and we are told it is frightened of anything new or unknown. The parrot seems, therefore, to symbolise the merely imitative, frozen anti-life, an anti-creative force, anathema to the artist.

Yet the carpet is pulled from this comforting conclusion with:

> *What cannot be imitated*
> *Perfect must die*

Your senses do somersaults here; if something can't be imitated it is inviolate from the anti-life, anti-art parrot but because then it is in this way 'perfect' it will inevitably die. Why? Because perfection petrifies, it is no place for the human. It is *'the diamond sky'* of 'Mr. Tambourine Man', it is behind the *'Gates Of Eden'* from where no sound ever comes. (Two songs on the album from which this song is an outtake. Please see the chapter on 'Gates Of

Eden' for a more detailed discussion of these themes.) What escapes this parrot belongs in a place that Christopher Ricks has called *'hell for Bob Dylan'*, a place of perfection and therefore stasis, eternal and unchanging - nothing left for the artist to create, nowhere for the human to move onto; the times they have stopped a-changin'.

So is this parrot - timid and imitative though it is - extraordinarily and paradoxically a force for art and human values? Is it the parrot's sound that Dylan must follow in the first verse? Well, yes and no; and remember his *'Advice to Geraldine'*:

> do Not create anything, it will be
> misinterpreted. it will not change.

Now you see it, now you don't, a well-camouflaged parrot indeed. A paradox at the centre of art in general and Dylan's in particular. The imitative parrot is fearful of anything new and cannot mimic perfection. However, the moment the artist creates perfection - it dies. Dylan's challenge as a performing musician (*'a song and dance man'* as he put it) is to make songs that are as near 'perfect' (realised artistic creations) as they can be, but that still allow room for growth. In late 1997, in an interview with Jon Pareles for *The New York Times*, Dylan offered an interesting insight:

> *Many of my records are more or less blueprints for the songs.*

On the other hand 'Farewell Angelina' not only remained unplayed to its full potential live, but also, indeed, lay hidden away in Columbia's vaults for years, unheard even as a 'blueprint'. (I have no idea what colour of print Ms Baez's version can be considered to be!)

Back to the song itself, and all that I have been discussing in regard to the camouflaged parrot has happened in a verse where Dylan has been painting his picture underneath the threatening sky. Perhaps, therefore, the parrot who flutters is merely part of another tableau? If so, a particularly telling tableau and one that is not separated from the concluding lines with a 'But' before *'Farewell Angelina'*. (The new verse ironically using the written version's structure.)

We then have the wonderfully expressive ending of *'flooding over... where it is dry'* -except for the unhappy use of *'flooding over'* in the previous stanza. Since there is no divisive 'But', Dylan could have used a simple present, as in 'on fire' here, but the contrast he gives is, aptly, an irresistible conclusion to this pivotal passage.

The final verse has a number of variations. The preliminary two lines have the word 'the' dropped from its opening position. This is perfectly in fitting with the indeterminate surrealism of the whole piece and is why I mentioned the expectation of 'a stream' in the second verse. 'Machine guns' link with 'corporals' and the pirates who shoot and the pirates themselves link back to the bandits who steal the bells of the crown at the song's beginning. Puppets - because of the shared perspective of height - irresistibly associate in our minds with the little elves dancing in the rooftops.

The following lines:

> The fiends nail time bombs
> To the hands of the clocks

become:

> At misunderstood visions
> And at the faces of clocks

The misunderstood visions are the works of an artist misinterpreted by the public or the audience. And these lines also have a precise meaning for Dylan at this stage of artistic development. It's a powerful image, apparently damning the robot-like nature of the so-called 'radical left', which could be taken as America's folk equivalent of today's 'oh so liberal, trendy lefties'. That is, those who espouse certain apparently socialist ideas and ideals while acting in a different or contrary manner to that which they pay lip service to. Certainly the line 'Puppets heave rocks/At misunderstood visions' is about as economical and accurate a summation of what Dylan was suffering - and from what kind of people - for repudiating 'finger pointin'' songs as could ever be imagined.

The misunderstood visions, then, are the works Geraldine is advised not to create. If she does they will be misinterpreted, they will also never change no matter how many rocks are heaved at the faces of clocks. They will outlast even the museums where infinity goes up on trial, but they will be dead.

However, are not all artists constantly striving to create this very perfection, a vision that 'cannot be imitated' and therefore 'perfect must die'? Is not the song we are listening to such a work? And is not the singer and the song's creator, Bob Dylan falling into the trap, ignoring his own warnings? But, wait a minute, isn't Bob Dylan actually Robert Allen Zimmerman in camouflage? There is a wry little chuckle as he finishes singing:

> Call me any name you like
> I will never deny it
> But farewell Angelina
> The sky is erupting
> An' I must go where it is quiet

From *'I must follow the sound'* to *'I must go where it is quiet'*. Quite some journey Bob, thanks for the ride.

As you can see I felt the wait well worth it, but, despite all the above, I would not have had it replace any song from the second side of *Bringing It All Back Home.*

Well, think about it - just what would you have left off to make room for it?

## Afterword

Not long after this article first appeared I was at a pre-concert get together when someone approached me and told me he disagreed with my article because he thought that the new verse 'spoiled' the song. As these events are always so busy, I never got a chance to tell him that I agreed with him and that it was just my initial enthusiasm for the fine writing that had blinded me to this.

It does 'spoil' the song, it imbalances it and is too dense an argument for the song to carry. It's a very good piece of verse, and reflects on central concerns of Dylan's writings at the time - and yet the song is better without it.

If we fast forward many years - to 1996 in fact - a similar initial excitement was later quelled into an attitude of 'interesting, but...' The film soundtrack for *Jerry Maguire* contained an alternate version of 'Shelter From The Storm' that included a verse as yet unheard. This was a matter of tremendous note as most Dylan fans believe his writing was at its highest peak for the *Blood On The Tracks* album, where the song originally appeared. The 'new' verse was certainly worthy of attention but only in a kind of detached way, it was mostly of academic interest (both meanings).

In the 'Shelter From The Storm' example the new verse, well written though it was, is simply not up to the quality of the rest of the song, it's an idea not fully integrated into the song. In 'Farewell Angelina' the idea is integrated, the writing more than matches the verses we already knew about - yet it disturbs the whole and was therefore edited out.

We can forget - and literature on Dylan is riddled with examples of this - when discussing Dylan's lyrics away from the song, as though on the printed page, that he is a songwriter and the needs of the overall song are of paramount concern. Dylan is a careful and insightful editor of his own songs. He might not always pick the best songs for the albums (though until the effects of the CD market became all-pervasive, his attention to album sequencing was exemplary), but he's generally spot on in editing out extraneous material.

# Nine

# Too Much Confusion

## Foreword

*This was another article that I wrote for* On The Tracks. *It appeared there spread over three issues which, given the subject matter, must have made it difficult to follow unless the reader saved them until the last one appeared and read them all together. On the other hand, I could not have made it any shorter. Indeed, knowing the space restrictions, it was already pared back as far as it could be. The areas under discussion are so all-encompassing and Dylan's lyrics of the time offer so many illuminating insights into them that I could – and would, given the space - have made connection after connection and quoted example after example. If my article succeeds, though, Dylan listeners will think of those for themselves. So I came to believe that a concise version was ultimately for the best and have not greatly expanded on the original here, aside from the fore- and afterwords.*

*The afterword details one of the theoretical reasons why I would have expanded this ad infinitum. Another is a more instinctive one; because, in many ways, this is the article I had been progressing towards writing since first hearing the second side of* A Rare Batch of Little White Wonder, *as described in the introduction to this book.*

*A note of caution about this article; it is not to be read as though I am claiming that Dylan set out to write an orderly philosophic system to deal with all the issues I raise. Poets, dramatists, novelists and songwriters do not, generally speaking, work that way. Instead their visions are embedded in their creations. You cannot discuss, say, Browning's philosophy without discussing his poetry, nor Dylan's 'view of Life' without discussing his songs. Through them we hear him communicate his visions and insights on everything from his ex-girlfriend's sister to the Nature of Man and Reality.*

We are encouraged, not least by Dylan himself, not to categorise, not to glibly pigeon-hole artists or periods in artists' careers. It is, however, almost impossible to discuss, say, Picasso without mentioning his various 'periods', Wordsworth without contrasting the 'younger' and 'elder', or Bob Dylan without delineating his various 'phases'. In the case of the last it is particularly hard not to take an almost clichéd view of his development in the sixties: Guthrie clone, Prince of Protest, Personal Poet, ultra-cool James Dean Electric Hipster and then the post-crash journey from personal salvation to the cocooned world of conservative country music.

So it is all too easy to slip into this clichéd mode but, as I've written elsewhere, a cliché is only a universal truth frozen in time. The contempt comes from overuse; the kernel of truth usually remains. So it is with 1960's Bob Dylan – the reason I can glibly roll off the above definitions is that they are basically true. True about the projected persona 'Bob Dylan', at least. Just a glance at any selection of photographs of Dylan from the relevant years shows why these periods are so ingrained in our view of his development: he looks and breathes each part. Or take an auditory sampling of 'Ballad Of Hollis Brown' or 'Like A Rolling Stone' (65, 66, 69). Again you'll find that Dylan is projecting pigeon-holing generalisations of himself far more than any hack biographer could!

I am not, though, primarily interested here in the biography; I am more concerned with the songs which tell the above story in an infinitely more complex way. I want to look in this chapter at one area of Dylan's mid-'sixties work in particular. The area that I think that most fascinates the majority of us, and from where come the songs that to this day form the backbone to many of his sets. I am referring to the time just before 'the crash'; when the 'wheel was on fire, rolling down the road...'

It is the contention of this essay that Dylan had pushed things just too far, that the biographical accounts of the man 'not so much burning a candle at both ends but taking a blowtorch to the middle' are paralleled by the artist who pushed his vision(s) to a frightening point of no return.

'i accept chaos. i am not sure whether it accepts me.' Thus wrote Bob Dylan in the liner notes of *Bringing It All Back Home*. It is a good quote too, the type the confident young artist seemed to make so effortlessly as he neared the height of his powers, a world hanging on his every utterance. At the same time, however, as I hope to demonstrate to you, chaos accepts anyone and everyone and probably welcomes our visionaries most readily of all. Over the next three albums we hear of chaos embracing Bob Dylan and of how, in the end - at the very last - he refused to accept chaos, he retreated from its embrace. The wonder is how he took it so far and emerged in one piece; the glory we revel in is the sound and the words as he reports back from his odyssey.

Does it sound like I'm over-dramatising? Well, I hope you don't think so by the end of this essay, but in the meantime, cast your mind back to the clichéd history, conjure up some of the images of the wasted mannequin figure from *Eat The Document* and let me temporarily return to biography to let you re-read the following quotes presented by Anthony Scaduto:

> Joan Baez:
> *Bobby may be on a death trip........I always pictured Bobby with a skull and cross-bones on his head.[1]*

> An Australian Actress (1966):
> *I came to believe that Dylan was Christ revisited. I felt that everything fitted, without being Christian-religious or anything, I felt that what he had to say about living and communication with people was the truest, most honest and most Christ-like thing I've ever heard. I began to feel that Dylan was sacrificing himself in his whole philosophy, his thinking. That he would eventually die or that something horrible would happen to him. I felt it physically, I felt it strongly. I must have been going slightly unhinged. But I know that other people felt that Dylan was Christ revisited, sacrificing himself. Adrian Rawlings came to that conclusion the same time I did. Other people felt it.[2]*

These feelings were not caused solely by the actions of the pop person, they came from the music and lyrics[3] - from the 'Visions Of Johanna' that Dylan was conveying to his audience in shards. (Or, in the case of the 1966 tour, in great molten blasts.)

My contention is that Dylan careered into the mid-sixties, fully confident in his abilities, in tune with his muse, using his visions to enlighten us all to the true nature of society and relationships, probing the paradoxes and strug-gles of identity, communication and selfhood. And then the more he probed, the more he pushed, the nearer to an impasse he got. After you've seen through everything, what do you do next?

If we agree that 'My Back Pages' signalled a rejection of straightforward protest and that *'girls' faces formed the forward path'* seemed to be what Dylan was after, can we also agree that he felt forced to return to an exploration of what was wrong with society in many of the songs of the following albums?

Dylan's infamous 'truth attacks' were not reserved for people alone but also for people collectively. Modern society - often, by implication, specifically

American - is put under intense scrutiny throughout *Bringing It All Back Home, Highway 61 Revisited* and, to a lesser extent, *Blonde On Blonde*. Everywhere Dylan cast his eye he saw breakdown: of authority, of identity, of language, (or 'eye/I' and 'mouth(s)' as Dylan often put it) of rationality and, as a consequence, an alienation from reality itself.

In the following sections I will briefly examine how each of these 'breakdowns' are manifest in the songs of the time.

### Breakdown of authority

*i) In society*

Figures of corrupt officialdom were, naturally, prevalent in Dylan's 'protest songs' (both prior to and post the period under review); rock 'n' roll too has never exactly been regarded as a medium that respects the authorities! However the sheer overwhelming stink of corruption in 'the establishment' - the diseased head of a sick society - in songs of this period reflects, I believe, a more serious dislocation. In songs dealing with injustices as clear as in 'The Death of Emmett Till' Dylan can still appeal to an inherent sense of justice that should reside in the American people. Also, he often pointed out wrongs while by implication showing how these could be righted. In the period I'm writing about this possibility of appealing to something better becomes lost. (Or perhaps submerged would be a more accurate word.)

Everywhere you look there is disturbing news, from *'Jack the Ripper who sits/At the head of the chamber of commerce'* to *'the judge, he holds a grudge'*. As for politicians, I suggest you don't call up your local senator because:

> *Now the senator came down here*
> *Showing everyone his gun*
> *Handing out free tickets*
> *To the wedding of his son*

Nor should you expect judges to fulfil their role:

> *Old lady judges watch people in pairs*
> *Limited in sex they dare*
> *To push fake morals, insult and stare*

Yes it is bad news all round, as:

> *Now all the authorities*
> *They just stand around and boast*
> *How they blackmailed the sergeant-at-arms*
> *Into leaving his post*

Lawyers aren't likely to get you out of a jam either - they'd prefer discussing *'lepers and crooks'* from a sanctimonious distance. Meanwhile *'to live outside the law you must be honest'*.

Society's appointed healers will not be of any help, as Dylan's catalogue of disastrous doctors include one who 'won't tell him what it is he's got' and the unforgettable:

> *Dr Filth he keeps his world*
> *Inside of a leather cup*

While turning to religious, rather than physical, succour is equally difficult, as the following quote testifies:

> *Now the preacher looked so baffled*
> *When I asked him why he dressed*
> *With twenty pounds of headlines*
> *Stapled to his chest*
> *But he cursed me when I proved it to him*
> *Then I whispered 'Not even you can hide*
> *You see, you're just like me*
> *I hope you're satisfied.'*

Plus the as devastating as can be imagined :

> *The phantom of the opera*
> *A perfect image of a priest*

Indeed, like doctors, religious figures may be part of the problem. Although John the Baptist at least seems moved to revulsion by his Inquisition-style tactics:

> *Well John the Baptist after torturing a thief*
> *Looks up at his hero the commander-in-chief*
> *Saying 'Tell me great hero but please make it brief*
> *Is there a hole for me to get sick in?'*

The following verse:

> *The commander-in-chief answers him while chasing a fly*
> *Saying 'death to all those who would whimper and cry'*
> *And dropping a barbell he points to the sky*
> *Saying 'the sun's not yellow it's chicken'*

is a crushing enough caricature of an unfeeling military leader. However the scenario becomes even darker when one imagines the vastly overpowered fly as a small, industrially backward state being pursued by the gloriously brave might of America. The scene becomes pitch black when one remembers that this is *John the Baptist's commander-in-chief* who is speaking.

On and on this litany goes. I am sure everyone reading this will have many other examples that spring readily to mind. However, I do not expect this to convince you of my claim that Dylan was becoming alienated to a dangerous degree. I would, though, ask you to keep in mind how dislocated society was in Dylan's view, and hopefully the cumulative effect of the following sections will incline you to my proposal.

### ii) In culture

There was a concomitant, cynical view of the effect and relevance of major cultural figures too. Ones that are crucial to Dylan's writings through the years at that - from the Literary Tradition, from music through the years, from myth and fairy tales, from folk-protest.

From the 'Great Tradition' we find Shakespeare as a clown:

> *Well Shakespeare, he's in the alley*
> *with his pointed shoes and his bells*

And Pound and Eliot alienated from reality and squabbling over irrelevancies:

> *And Ezra Pound and T. S. Eliot*
> *Fighting in the captain's tower*
> *While calypso singers laugh at them*
> *And fishermen hold flowers*

Although there is no slight to the works of F. Scott Fitzgerald *per se*, his books appear here only to be 'gone through', not read, they are not there to engage the imagination. It is akin to all the homes around the world with complete works of Shakespeare on the shelf for no reason other than for show, because it is expected of them. Meanwhile, the tragic, suicidal Ophelia is reduced to a figure blamed for her lifelessness, whilst the romantic Romeo is so out of place in our deranged society that he is told *'You're in the wrong place my friend, you better leave'.*

Great musical genius doesn't fit either:

> *Where Ma Rainey and Beethoven once unwrapped their bedroll*
> *Tuba players now rehearse around the flagpole*

Fairy stories, the comforting conduits of much of our traditions, are inverted as the tale of Cinderella loses its happy ending:

*And the only sound that's left*
*After the ambulances go*
*Is Cinderella sweeping up on Desolation Row*

Dylan had raged against the inequities of society and its custodians during his 'protest phase', but the comforting homilies of that movement (remember Dylan later described the term 'liberal humanist' as 'a bullshit term') are dismissed with the scathing view of a Seeger-led crowd on the Titanic (and what wonderful wit these lines demonstrate):

*The Titanic sails at dawn*
*And everybody's shouting*
*'Which side are you on?'*

and with the blind ignorance of:

*...the good Samaritan he's dressing*
*He's getting ready for the show*
*He's going to the carnival tonight on Desolation Row*

This world of Dylan's mid-sixties work seems to have much in similar with Whitman's towering denunciation of America in *Democratic Vistas*:

*I say we had best look our times and lands searchingly in the face, like a physician diagnosing some deep disease. Never was there, perhaps, more hollowness at heart than at present, and here in the United States. Genuine belief seems to have left us. The underlying principles of the States are not honestly believ'd in, (for all this hectic glow, and these melodramatic screamings,) nor is humanity itself believ'd in. What penetrating eye does not everywhere see through the mask? The spectacle is appaling. We live in an atmosphere of hypocrisy throughout. The men believe not in the women, nor the women in the men. A scornful super-ciliousness rules in literature. The aim of all the littérateurs is to find something to make fun of. A lot of churches, sects, &c., the most dismal phantasms I know, usurp the name of religion. Conversation is a mass of badinage. From deceit in the spirit, the mother of all false deeds, the offspring is already incalculable.*

A very youthful disdain for the fallen world and all its creations is not unique to Dylan. It is almost mandatory for an artist of Romantic tendencies, and it most certainly is obligatory for a follower of Rimbaud, to have 'a season in hell'. What happens, however, after the season ends? Let us leave that till the end of the article - I've far from demonstrated my main thesis yet.

### Breakdown of Language

Possibly the most distinguishing facet of modern poetry is its heightened awareness of, if not at times obsessional interest in, the nature of that which it uses to communicate· language itself. Following on from ground-breaking philosophers, writers began to investigate their language. The more they looked, the less clear it became; old exactitudes were shown to be a sham, words were not what they seemed.

As Iris Murdoch cogently wrote:

> Language as exact communication seems possible only against the background of a common world, to whose reliable features the uses of words can be related by firm conventions. In the realms of morals and theology, and even political philosophy, a greater sophistication about the function of words seemed to lead to a weakening of that sense of a common world. `Good' was no longer thought to name an objective quality, nor `democracy' an identifiable form of government...[4]

It is a point not lost on Bob Dylan in 1965 (albeit in interview put-on mode) in the following exchange captured on the documentary-film *Don't Look Back:*

REPORTER:   *'Would you say that you cared about people particularly?'*

BOB DYLAN: *'Well, yeah, but.. but, you know, I mean, we all have our own definitions of all those words; you know, 'care' and `people' and...*

REPORTER:   *'Well, we surely...I mean we all know what people are.*

BOB DYLAN: *'Well...eh, do we ?'*

The perceived position of much of both modern poetry and Bob Dylan's mid–1960s work as being wilfully obscurantist was engendered in part by the legacy of the symbolists' attempts to portray the world as they saw it; a world that was full of rich impressions but had no order. How does one convey this through the medium of language? One has to use an ordered referential system to communicate the *non-*ordered, sensory impressions of a meaningless (without defined purpose) existence.

One way was to overburden the language of the poem until the referential nature of the language broke under the strain. The 'sense' was buried under an avalanche of images and impressions. Another was the approach of the Surrealists:

> Surrealism was born after the 1914 war, under the godmotherly influence of Tristan Tzara's Dadaism, a destructive hate movement, anti-social,

> *anti-literary, anarchical. It developed, under the leadership of André Breton, into a curious revolutionary enterprise. Literature had begun to encroach upon life. The Surrealists set to work to reverse the process. They professed themselves indifferent to art and morality; they were animated by a profound hatred of their society, and an abounding belief in the liberating value of an untrammelled exploration of the uncon- scious. Poetry was a voyage into dream, language itself simply a medium for automatic utterance, a net for trawling in the depths of the mind, and so extending the bounds of the real; an end which could equally well be reached by other means: collages, the fabrication of unnerving objects, or the impact of shocking or pointless acts...[5]*

The Surrealists had a very antagonistic view towards language. Rimbaud had been their trailblazer: they immersed themselves in the richness of language, abandoning reason to sensory overload. In addition, Rimbaud, at a shockingly young age, stopped writing completely. Life was for living, art a sham. Hence the split in the Surrealists: those who wrote and those who made performances of their lives (usually in association with revolutionary left wing politics). Those who did write approached the language they employed almost as an enemy; twisting the images to startling effect, attempting in words to achieve in language the startlingly incongruous images that some of the ground-breaking painters were creating.

Mid-Sixties' Dylan, having spurned direct political action, displays many of the signs of a writer grappling with just the same problems of the Symbolists and Surrealists - 'how do I portray what I see and feel in this ordered language ?' Hence the Rimbaudesque effects and surrealist images in so many songs of the period, for example this from 'Farewell Angelina':

> *Just a table standing empty*
> *By the edge of the sea*
> *Farewell Angelina*
> *The sky is trembling*
> *And I must leave*

From 'Gates of Eden':

> *Upon the beach where hound dogs bay*
> *At ships with tattooed sails*
> *Heading for the Gates of Eden*

From 'Visions of Johanna'

> *See the primitive wallflower freeze*

*When the jelly-faced women all sneeze*
*Hear the one with the mustache say, 'Jeeze*
*I can't find my knees'*
*Oh, jewels and binoculars hang from the head of the mule*
*But these visions of Johanna, they make it all seem so cruel*

And from 'Stuck Inside of Mobile With The Memphis Blues Again'

*But everybody still talks about*
*How badly they were shocked*
*But me, I expected it to happen*
*I knew he'd lost control*
*When he built a fire on Main Street*
*And shot it full of holes*

I am sure you can all think of further examples.

Before we move on to another 'breakdown', I would like to highlight two verses of 'Ballad Of A Thin Man' that demonstrate this crisis in language. In stanza two we find:

*You raise up your head*
*And you ask - 'Is this where it is'*
*Then somebody points to you and says 'it's his' And you say 'What's mine?'*
*And somebody else says 'Where what is?'*
*And you say 'Oh my God*
*Am I here all alone?'*

The questions posed here are reduced from meaning into a jumble of non sequiturs. This is because Mister Jones's question, *'Is this where it is?'* is not asked so that he can empathise with - or properly understand - what is happening, but because he wants to write it down. ('This is where it is at and I was there'). This looks forward to the masterful debunking of the three kings on the sleeve of *John Wesley Harding*:

*'Frank,' he began, 'Mr. Dylan has come out with a new record. This record of course features none but his own songs and we understand that you're the key.' 'That's right,' said Frank, 'I am.' "Well then,' said the king in a bit of excitement, 'could you please open it up for us?' Frank, who all this time had been reclining with his eyes closed, suddenly opened them both up as wide as a tiger. 'And just how far would you like to go in?' he asked and the three kings all looked at each other. 'Not too far but just far enough so's we can say that we've been there,' said the first chief. 'All right,' said Frank, 'I'll see what I can do,' and he*

*commenced to doing it. First of all, he sat down and crossed his legs, then he
sprung up, ripped off his shirt and began waving it in the air. A lightbulb fell
from one of his pockets and he stamped it out with his foot. Then he took a deep
breath, moaned and punched his fist through the plate-glass window. Settling
back in his chair, he pulled out a knife, 'Far enough?' he asked.*

In 'Ballad Of A Thin Man' Mister Jones asks questions that are profound,
but because of the way he approaches life they become ironically trivial or
meaningless. *'Oh my God, am I here all alone?'* could be just a trite phrase,
almost devoid of meaning; on the other hand it could suggest that he is on the
brink of an existential crisis, or that Mr. Jones's God - by the context and by
what unfolds in the song - is a false one.

If we jump ahead to stanza seven from the same song we are taken back to
this breakdown in language:

> *Now you see this one-eyed midget*
> *Shouting the word 'Now'*
> *And you say 'For what reason?'*
> *And he says 'How?'*
> *And you say 'What does this mean'*
> *And he screams back 'You're a cow*
> *Give me some milk*
> *Or else go home.'*

Again Mr Jones is searching for surface 'meanings' and 'reasons'. The one
-eyed midget tries vainly to communicate and then dismisses him - in an
absurd image - as the domesticated animal he has been shown to be. We will
come back to Mr. Jones's search for rational explanations in the next section;
meanwhile I'd like to point out that Dylan's increasingly impressionistic
lyrics and visions were leading him to the very limits of communicative
language. A surreal view can lead one to grotesquerie and absurdity. One of
the best commentators on the grotesque that I have come across is Wolfgang
Kayser. I'd like to quote two of his fundamental definitions of the style:[6]

> *The grotesque is the expression of the estranged or alienated world, i.e.
> the familiar world is seen from a perspective which suddenly renders it
> strange...*

and

> *The grotesque is a game with the absurd, in the sense that the grotesque
> artist plays, half laughingly, half horrified, with the deep absurdities of
> existence.*

Without even changing song we can find an example of this in the final verse of 'Ballad Of A Thin Man':

> Well you walk into the room
> Like a camel and then you frown
> You put your eyes in your pocket
> And your nose on the ground
> There ought to be a law
> Against you coming around
> You should be made to wear earphones.

With a flash of grotesque/surrealist wit, and the only complicated image in the song, Dylan shows Mr Jones from the vantage point of reality as an absurd bloodhound character. And this is a very successful use of the grotesque, being a mixture of the comic and the disturbing while presenting a perfect finale to the themes and images of the preceding verses.

Dylan at this point of his career is struggling in the quintessential modernist way with trying to communicate the incommunicable. Around the time I first wrote this article, I read a newspaper article that referred to Dylan in the mid-sixties as *'seeming eminently capable of naming the unnameable'*[7]. This feeling came, I suggest, from the impression that this artist was pushing his vision to the limit, that he was engaged in a struggle with language itself in an attempt to convey his personal visions to a mass audience.

Dylan was not alone in this, but he had the incalculable benefit over modernist poets of having music as part of his medium[8]. When Dylan is over-burdening the language in his verse he has his 'melody' that can *'ease you and cool you and cease the pain of your useless and pointless knowledge'*. Thus, when the language is overburdened:

> The kings of Tyrus with their convict list
> Are waiting in line for their geranium kiss,
> And you wouldn't know it would happen like this,
> But who among them really wants just to kiss you?
> With your childhood flames on your midnight rug,
> And your Spanish manners and your mother's drugs,
> And your cowboy mouth and your curfew plugs,
> Who among them do you think could resist you?

we can experience emotionally Dylan's 'message' of love, of lust, of wonder, of a tinge of jealousy and rapture by immersing ourselves in the sounds of the melody and his voice, letting the connotations the words evoke flow. Even with music the balance between word-sounds and sense can be an extraordinarily delicate thing; some songs rely on the music more than others, some more on the lyrics. In the best they are inseparable. Take the music away, though, and it becomes more difficult for Dylan, who as an artist is primarily a song-writer.

Although it is true that the liner notes to *Highway 61 Revisited*, to pick one example, are triumphantly successful, other attempts at non-song art are not so. A reading of *Tarantula* would suffice to make this clear, or at least the parts of that book that do not succeed. There are, unquestionably, passages which work marvellously well, where the wit and insight shine through. One doubts if there has ever been a more viciously amusing and successful attack on critics by an artist than the 'butter sculpture' scene, for example, but too often (and this is applicable, also, to 'Sad Eyed Lady') one recalls T.S. Eliot's critique of Swinburne's verse:

> '...the object has ceased to exist, because the meaning is merely the hallucination of meaning, because language, uprooted, has adapted itself to an independent life of atmospheric nourishment.'

In that book Dylan almost deconstructs the very language he is using, the mode of communication is wrenched so far as to convey only bewilderment. Many of the images can be worked out (but I'd contend we are 'shovelling the glimpses' rather than intuitively grasping them) and although there are underlying motifs to follow (or, more likely, trace), most of the pages leave the reader lost; perhaps admiring the clever juxtaposition of persons, images, words or clichés but none the wiser on any emotional or truly imaginative level. Most readers cannot follow many of the passages (perhaps only Dylan can) and, as Henry Miller correctly noted:

> And it is gibberish if, out of two billion people who make up the world, only a few thousand pretend to understand what the individual poet is saying. The cult of art reaches its end when it exists only for a precious handful of men and women. Then it is no longer art but the cipher language of a secret society for the propagation of meaningless individuality. Art is something which stirs men's passions, which gives vision, lucidity, courage and faith.[9]

Dylan had reached the point where the windows of communication, the very words themselves, obscure the artist's vision. In a typically paradoxical manner, Dylan himself conveyed this best - in the breath-taking poetry of:

*Now the wintertime is coming*
*The windows are filled with frost*
*I went to tell everybody*
*But I could not get across*

What a gorgeous image this is of the poet (in the wide sense of the word) facing up to his inability to convey his visions. Just as the windows designed to let us see out and others see in are blocked by frost, so the words the songwriter is using to communicate become themselves an obscuring barrier to communication.

### Breakdown of Rationality

Again I approach a subject that can - and probably has - filled a book on its own. Dylan, at this time in his career an archetypal Romantic artist, repeatedly illustrated the limitations of the rationalist world-view. Take the whole of 'Ballad Of A Thin Man', right from stanza one, where Mister Jones is in a bewildering situation. He is equipped with a pencil to attempt to collect facts (*'useless and pointless knowledge'*). A journalist-type, he is making no attempt to experience the situation, he just wants to know what to report back home.[10]

*You have many contacts*
*Among the lumberjacks*
*To get you facts*
*When someone attacks your imagination*

These lines assail his total lack of imagination and empathy. Again we find Mister Jones attempting to collect facts, making the use of the word, 'imagination' staggeringly ironic. How scornful, too, is that *'contacts among the lumberjacks'*. ('Some of my best friends are working class, you know.') His 'charity' is revealed as a tax-evasion ploy, he just does what is expected of him and, as we find out in the song, will forever be unable to do anything else.

All the way through to the final verse where, blind to experience, with his 'eyes in his pocket', Mr. Jones continues his search for facts, convinced that his view of the world is normal. The singer, speaking from a more enlightened perception of reality, wants him stopped - wants the flow of *'useless and pointless knowledge'* cut off.

However, there is also the beginnings here of Dylan's realisation that these insights bring him no resolution to the questions of mankind's condition . The clearer his visions reveal themselves, the more obscure the *'reality of man'* becomes. The final chorus tells us not only that Mr Jones doesn't understand what is going on, but that he never will. There is no resolution to this song;

Mr Jones sees the world outside of gathered facts as nonsense, and from the vantage point of this world Mr Jones and his search for facts is totally absurd.

This is not to say that Dylan's piercing view of where a reliance on rationalism can lead is in any way diluted – look at the perversions it causes in 'Can You Please Crawl Out Your Window?' for example. It is just that for him to comprehend and communicate all this does not necessarily lead to a solution to the mysteries of existence.

For example, take the justly famous lines:

> *The geometry of innocent flesh on the bone*
> *Causes Galileo's math book to get thrown*

This is a marvellous expression of how post-pubescent school attendees are more interested in discovering the joys of each other's bodies rather than the dry facts they have to learn by rote. Given its context in the song it could fairly be taken as an all-embracing life v. reductive rationalism statement also. However what seems nearly always to be forgotten is that the second half of the verse:

> *At Delilah who sits worthlessly alone*
> *But the tears on her cheeks are from laughter*

completely takes away any comfort that the first half brings.

Implicit in the most quoted verse of the song:

> *I wish I could write you a melody so plain*
> *That could hold you dear lady from going insane*
> *That could ease you and cool you and cease the pain*
> *Of your useless and pointless knowledge*

is the idea that the imaginative artist cannot produce a work that will *'cease the pain'*.

The clearest expression of the imaginative cul-de-sac that Dylan has found himself in at this point is the song 'Desolation Row', whose very length (especially for the time) and location as the final song on *Highway 61 Revisited* clearly indicate that we are to view it as a summation of the artist's world-view at that time. Many commentators have tied themselves in knots trying to reconcile the shifts of perspective in the song. The way I am describing Dylan's vision in this article means that there is no reconciliation possible and that *this is the whole point*.

The shifting perspective in 'Desolation Row' makes this clear: Desolation Row is both the place where the breakdowns I've traced above have brought about a meaningless, corrupt and worthless society and, most disturbingly of all, the *only* place from which this truth can be recognised. Frank Kermode was probably one of the first to write about this - and he certainly puts it clearer than most:

> ...*this is a deliberate cultural jumble - history seen flat, without depth, cultural heroes of all kind known only by their names, their attributes lost by intergenerational erosion - all of them so much unreality against the background of Desolation Row, the flat and dusty truth, the myth before the myth began.*[11]

While Aidan Day interprets the song in a manner fitting for my case:

> *But occupancy of Desolation Row as a position from which the chaos can be viewed does not emancipate the viewer from horror. The rearrangement of faces and names mentioned in the last stanza describes metafictionally the poetic procedures - the tampering with character and story - of the preceding nine stanzas themselves. Those tamperings constitute a rewriting of the received forms of stories in an attempt to demonstrate the essential incoherence of the culture that lives by such stories. The speaker in the last stanza insists on the inability to read the received narratives and asserts that only rewritten versions - versions scripted, like those of this lyric, from desolation's perspective - are acceptable. But the desolating double-bind explored by this lyric is that the rearrangement - the felt necessity to rewrite - can itself stand as a manifestation of the ill pervading the culture rather than a revolutionary act which transcends that ill.*[12]

This 'double-bind' of 'Desolation Row' certainly brings us closer to the edge I referred to earlier, but we are not quite there yet. There is still one other area of 'breakdown' to be looked at, that of identity.

### Breakdown of Identity

In his songs Dylan sought to define identity in relation to female acquaintances which, led inexorably to his relationship with his artistic muse and thus his Self.

On leaving his explicitly folk-protest days behind Dylan declared that *'girls' faces formed the forward path'*. They certainly seemed to do so at first. There are a number of ravishing love songs from Dylan at this time that delicately trod the thin line between proclaiming the inviolability of the individual and the mutual interdependencies of those in love.

This thin line separates two mutually repelling states and Dylan's love songs become battlegrounds as protagonists are forever being urged to break free from the restraints of stultifying relationships. The horrific results of not doing so are pointed out with increasing vigour via 'It's All Over Now, Baby Blue', 'Can You Please Crawl Out Your Window?', 'She's Your Lover Now' and in the unforgettable mutual destruction of 'One Of Us Must Know (Sooner Or Later)':

> *I couldn't see when it started snowing*
> *Your voice was all that I heard*
> *I couldn't see where we were going*
> *But you said you knew and I took your word*
> *And then you told me later as I apologised*
> *That you were just kidding me, you weren't really from the farm*
> *And I told you as you clawed out my eyes*
> *That I never really meant to do you any harm*

I would like to point out, in passing, that I do not for a minute mean to reduce all of Dylan's magnificent love songs from this period to a graph-like progression to fit my thesis. It is a product of me dealing in generalities and dominant themes rather than, as elsewhere in this book, specific songs. At all times, it is worth recalling D.H. Lawrence's wise observation:

> *It is no use thinking you can put a stamp on the relation between man and woman, to keep it in the status quo. You can't. You might as well try to put a stamp on the rainbow or rain.*[13]

And Dylan's songs more than testify to this! There is, however, an evident move toward more complex and dangerous relationships. By the time of *Highway 61 Revisited* and *Blonde On Blonde* we are surrounded by characters of unusual sexual persuasions. I take it the reader will be familiar with at least some of the images of transvestism, incest and homosexuality that abound, what with all those queens that are *'hungry like a man in drag'*. Anyone needing a refresher course is directed to what is going on in 'Temporary Like Achilles'.

However let us leave those thoughts for another chapter, because more pertinent to this one is the way that Dylan's relationship to the female characters in his songs blends inevitably into that with his muse. This is an even trickier relationship as it has its roots, its very being, in the artist's dependency on *the other*.

Here Dylan is yet again firmly in the Romantic tradition in his attraction/repulsion dance with his muse. Just compare his so-called 'drug songs' with some of the poetry of the early 19th Century in England and you'll see why he thought this reductive term so 'vulgar'.[14]

Where Dylan's 'love' songs begin to address the muse as opposed to a female, or 'the feminine principle', goodness only knows. I doubt if Dylan himself would. Sometimes it seems to be both simultaneously. Suffice to say that I believe many lines (including some Dylan has been criticised for) are not directed at real people but at his muse, and that there is always a 'power struggle' going on between the artist's freedom-loving Self and his thraldom to his muse (see, for example, 'She Belongs To Me'). The muse inevitably wins such a power struggle. The climax to this relationship comes in 'Visions of Johanna', the song ending with the ego vanquished, the muse totally triumphant:

> *...While my conscience explodes*
> *The harmonicas play the skeleton keys and the rain*
> *And these visions of Johanna are now all that remain*

Dylan's evasion of 'I' is one of his defining characteristics; Mr. Stephen Scobie has written an entire book on Dylan as Alias, the mask-changer. But there is no escape at the end of 'Visions of Johanna' - only the visions of the muse, the inner eye, remain - the 'I' has left the scene. *'I cannot say the word eye, anymore...when I speak this word eye it is as if I am speaking of somebody's eye that I faintly remember...there is no eye'* wrote Dylan in the liner notes to *Highway 61 Revisited*.

In *Tarantula* the 'eye' and 'I' are fragmented beyond repair, the distorting filter of Dylan's vision loses the reader, indeed in this work the 'I' even writes its own epitaph:

> *here lies bob dylan*
> *murdered*
> *from behind*
> *by trembling flesh...*
>
> *...bob dylan - killed by a discarded Oedipus*
> *who turned*
> *around*
> *to investigate a ghost*
> *& discovered that*
> *the ghost too*
> *was more than one person.*

### Everything's Been Returned Which was Owed

And so I approach the end of this article, leaving Dylan at the point where T.S. Eliot might remark: *'Humankind can only bear so much reality'* - or, as

**111**

Louise would say, delightfully punning the physical and metaphysical: '*Ya can't look at much, can ya man?*'

Dylan is not the first, nor will he be the last, to discover that you can chip and hammer away at the building blocks of rationality, you can undermine society, you can dismiss its cultural history as no longer relevant - only to be left all alone and defenceless in the face of the absurd. Self is all that is left, self facing Chaos, or even wilfully embracing chaos - but is it strong enough to survive? Not if the self *itself* has been broken down, if it cannot say the word 'eye' anymore, if the artist is alienated from his muse. In chaos, the heart of darkness, the alienated self cannot exist, the artist can no longer report back on his visions, he can only talk to himself or repeat the bare, unelucidated statement: *the horror, the horror.*

We tend to look on this as being a particularly 20$^{th}$ Century state, though the tormented geniuses of the 19$^{th}$ Century are the real starting points - they posed questions whose answers we are seeking still. I'll return to Henry Miller's book on Dylan's avowed influence Rimbaud for two pertinent quotes:

> *The poet today is obliged to surrender his calling because he has already evinced his despair, because he has already acknowledged his inability to communicate. To be a poet was once the highest calling; today it is the most futile one. It is so not because the world is immune to the poet's pleading, but because the poet himself no longer believes in his divine mission. He has been singing off-key now for a century...*
>
> *...When the poet stands at nadir the world must indeed be upside down. If the poet can no longer speak for society but only for himself, then we are at the last ditch. On the poetic corpse of Rimbaud we have begun erecting a tower of Babel.*

The last ditch indeed, the poet can speak '*only for himself*', the visions of Johanna are now all that remain.

So what did Rimbaud do next? He stopped writing altogether - a nigh on unbelievable suicide of his artistic self. As grandiose, brave and *proudly human* an act as has been recorded - but of what use that in the face of the dry, emotionless letters he wrote home afterwards? What triumph is there in the visionary poet's resolution of artistic paradoxes by retreating into silence at the age of eighteen - leaving us after that only with the balance sheets of a gun runner fixated with saving more money to stick up his anus in a bag?

Whatever you decide on that question, Dylan himself has said : '*I was not ready to follow Rimbaud yet.*'

So what did Dylan do next?

I could finish my article by neatly pointing out the contrast the 1969 Dylan persona gave us. Consider this: by 1969 the lyrics had changed from *'the ghost of 'lectricity howls in the bones of her face'* to *'Oh me oh my/Love that country pie'*. And the screaming wraith like dog-tooth suit clad figure had become the crooning, white-suited Isle of Wight incarnation. The man who had tried to accept chaos now stated:

> *I believe there should be an order to everything.*[15]

Yet that would just take me back to 'pigeon-holing': I could go on to say that Dylan used the 'crash' to reinvent himself because he realised that he'd reached an impasse of non-communication and that 'Sad-Eyed Lady Of The Lowlands' and *Tarantula* prove that if he'd followed this path we'd have been unable to comprehend his intensely private visions. Then, though, I'd be cheating by selecting the 'facts' to suit my case. It is not that these facts, quotes or observations would be untrue, but that they are only part of this artist's story.

Dylan goes to such extremes, and so completely inhabits the persona of any given time, that I *could* utilise such glib contrasts. Yet it must be remembered that Bob Dylan did not go straight from the '66 incarnation to the '69 incarnation. What he really did next was *The Basement Tapes* - a magnificent collection of nonsense/myth/bawdy songs shot through with messages of pain and loss. Then he put those multitudinous works on the shelf and released the extraordinarily assured *John Wesley Harding*.

Bob Dylan, like any great artist, is an enigma. The contrasts are there as a guide, a guide Bob Dylan himself gives us as he moves through his life and career. I am merely trying to highlight what I feel when I hear (some of) the performances from, for me, still his most fecund period and inarguably one of the most extreme.

'Extremes', yes, that's where you find Bob Dylan, a man of extremes, and some of these extremes can be frightening.[16] The 65-66 extreme was, in an artistic sense, a perilous journey that nearly took Dylan too far. I leave it to biographers to comment on how this was paralleled in the physical person and how much that may have influenced his art during these times. My point is that to survive he had to move on from *'these cruel nitemares where brick masons introduce me to hideous connections'*[17]. I must admit, though, that his songs depicting those 'nitemares' and *'hideous connections'* still enthral me to such an extent that they permeate my very existence.

## Afterword

The mid-sixties' years still strike me as Dylan's best. I do not mean to fall into the incorrect, if common, view that *all* his best work was created in the sixties, but, despite all the magnificent songs of later decades, the sole album disturber of the sixties hegemony is *Blood On The Tracks*. It happens also to be his very best. However, in my imaginary 'top ten' (a dreadful concept, I know, but we all do it) there would follow *Blonde On Blonde, Highway 61 Revisited, Bringing It All Back Home, John Wesley Harding, Freewheelin'* and *The Basement Tapes* (whose overall position is unclear due to the impoverished and misleading nature of the official release). All of these are without question; what would come next is so far from clear cut as to be not worth going into here, but *Another Side Of Bob Dylan* and *The Times They Are A-Changin'* would be among the first contenders in my mind.

Something changes in Dylan's writing after the sixties (approximately speaking). Something Dylan put his finger on in a 1978 interview:

> *Now, in the old days, they [the songs] used to do it automatically, but it's like I had amnesia, all of a sudden in 1966. I couldn't remember how to do it. I tried to force re-learn it, and I couldn't learn what I had been able to do naturally, like* Highway 61 Revisited, *I mean you can't sit down and write that consciously...*
>
> *To do it consciously is a trick, you know, and I did it on* Blood On The Tracks *for the first time...I knew how to do it because it was a technique I learned, I actually had a teacher for it...*Blood On The Tracks *did consciously what I used to do unconsciously.*[18]

As far as *Blood On The Tracks* itself was concerned this was the opposite of a problem. This testament from the author's own lips seemed the only explanation for how that album had superseded even his classic albums of the 1960s. That turned out to be the exception, however, to a rule that has bedevilled him since. As he moved away from the teacher and the lessons that had so successfully resurrected his writing skills to the level of genius, so the 'trick' of the 'technique' would become more visible. The 'unconscious' touch was often replaced by carefully constructed songs that betrayed or even drew attention to the craft necessary to write them. This is not to say there was no craftsmanship before - far from it - but that intuitive touch which led to a naturally formed, cohesive web of imagery and symbolism was what lit those songs from within their crafted stanzas. The lack of this affected some of even the finest of Dylan's later songs, such as 'Jokerman'. Others, though, such as 'Blind Willie McTell' and 'Every

Grain Of Sand', stand above and beyond this reproach, if reproach it be. In more recent years, however, he has created an altogether new way of writing songs, as we will see in this book's closing chapters.

1. Anthony Scaduto: *Bob Dylan*, W.H. Allen & Co. Ltd. 1972. Reprinted 1996, Helter Skelter Publishing, London.

2. Ibid

3. Dylan has always had an apocalyptic tone, of course, but it was the personal nature of the nightmare visions of this time that caused this singular response.

4. Iris Murdoch, *Sartre*, Fontana Books. First published by Bowes & Bowes Ltd. 1953.

5. Ibid.

6. Wolfgang Kayser, *The Grotesque in Art and Literature*, translated by Ulrich Weisstein, Bloomington, 1963.

7. I think it was in *The* (Glasgow) *Herald* - and was an unreasoned article on how far Dylan had fallen since his heyday, blah, blah etc. However, this phrase stuck with me as being particularly apt and true.

8. Even music, however, has its limitations in this regard. Not so much for Dylan specifically, but all music is based upon conventions and rules and depends on the audience knowing them. Ultimately music could no more solve Rimbaud's artistic impasse than language. Music whose 'rules' we have not learnt can confuse us, communication is not guaranteed. An example most Dylan fans will be aware of that illustrates this is the Concert for Bangladesh. Rock fans with no background in Indian music enthusiastically applaud after the first break to show their support for Ravi Shankar and co.'s music.
As Ravi says: 'Thank you. If you enjoy the tuning so much I hope you'll enjoy the playing more.'

9. *The Time Of The Assassins*

10. The song is replete with phallic images and here there are homosexual overtones in the pencil and the naked man; perhaps implying that it is 'abnormal' sexual practices that Mister Jones can't understand however 'hard he tries'.

11. Frank Kermode (and Stephen Spender) 'The metaphor at the end of the funnel', *Esquire*, May 1972

12. Aidan Day, *Jokerman*, Basil Blackwell, 1988

13. D.H. Lawrence, *Collected Letters*

14. Bob Dylan, on-stage, 27/05/1966 Royal Albert Hall, London, UK. Introducing Visions Of Johanna, Dylan said: "I'm not going to play any more concerts here in England and I'd just like to say that it's all wrong to... er, to... er... This is probably one song that your English music newspapers here call a drug song. Well I don't, I don't write drug songs. I never have. I wouldn't know how to go about it. But this is not a drug song. I'm not saying this for any kind of defense or reason or anything like that. It's just not a drug song, I don't, it's just vulgar."

15. *Rolling Stone* interview, November 1969

16. 1979 springs to mind, as well as 1966.

17. Bob Dylan, *Tarantula*, MacGibbon & Kee Ltd., 1971

18. Jonathon Cott, *Rolling Stone* interview, 1978.

# Ten

# Four And Twenty Windows

## Foreword

*In the previous article I talked about the rich and* 'cohesive web of imagery and symbolism' *woven around the songs of Dylan's mid-sixties period. In this article I'd like to take one strand of that web and explore some of its most effective appearances. The word I discuss is* 'window', *and this article is about some of the uses Dylan puts it to in his songs. It came about due to two circumstances: firstly how resonant I felt the line* 'the windows are filled with frost' *was when I wrote the preceding article; and secondly how different that effect was to the resonances of the same word in other famous lines and songs. So here you have an article about (some of) the uses Dylan puts the word* window(s) *to.*

*Perhaps unsurprisingly, though no less disappointingly for that, this article provoked letters of complaint when it first appeared in the pages of* Dignity. *Needless to say, the fuss was caused by the discussion of sexual metaphors; the other part of the article was ignored. I have expanded that part of the article to include an illustration of how pervasive such imagery is in pop and blues songwriting history, in the hope that this will forestall similar objections this time around. However, if you believe that any and all lyrics dealing with sex are demeaning to the listener and/or unworthy of the writer then the first part of this article is not for you.*

*I do not share that view and cannot see any problem with such lyrics. Not every song has to be about lofty topics. Dylan does indeed excel at various times in dealing with the deepest theological, moral and aesthetic questions. He can be illuminating on the nature of art and the reality of man and so forth, but that does not mean he always does this, nor should he have to. He can write songs about any and all subjects, he can write them just for the fun of it, for something to dance to, or just to rock out. He can write about fishing or travelling or about any and every thing he wishes, and why would sex not be one of these topics? Is sex to be divorced from the human equation? What is wrong with sex anyway, or singing about it?*

*Another complaint was that Dylan is too great an artist to write extended sexual metaphors or make ribald remarks. Yet Shakespeare's works are replete with nudge, nudge, wink, wink jokes. Shakespeare adroitly shows off his wit by making his 'smutty innuendoes' please all manner of audience members; from the literary types in the circles appreciating the ingenuity of the verbal wordplay, to those in the pit who revel in the innuendoes for their own sake. All those jokes in the Comedies about young ladies' rings were working on numerous levels, from the most basic to the most sophisticated. Shakespeare was not only capable of giving us the most sublime poetic exploration of the human condition and the smuttiest of innuendoes within the same play - he was sometimes even up to combining the two in one dazzling piece of wordplay. John Donne, a poet we often find has similarities to Dylan, and whom we know Dylan reads and regards highly, wrote (in his pre-ordination days, of course) a lovely passage of poetry that combined a surface meaning with a thinly disguised description of cunnilingus - much like Dylan does in a* Blonde On Blonde *song.*

*The kind of things I talk about in this article imbue the world of Dylan songs, in particular those of the mid-sixties. In a book on the black-face singer Emmet Miller that holds particular interest for listeners to Dylan's* "Love And Theft", *Nick Tosches touches on aspects relevant both here and to this book's final chapter's discussion of minstrelsy and other popular music traditions:*

New York City became the biggest hick town in the world, the racke-teer Vito Genovese (1897-1969) owned several celebrated nightclubs in Greenwich Village: the Club Savannah, at 68 West Third Street; the 82 Club, at 82 East Fourth Street; the Moroccan Village, the 181 Club, and others...Vito's joints presented entertainment in which the allure of real black female performers and that of transvestites effected a sexual blur whose draw proved mesmerizing. The Savannah featured a high-yellow chorus line of '14 Beautiful Savannah Peaches' and shows produced by Clarence Robinson, the black choreographer who had staged revues at the old Cotton Club in Harlem. The 82 featured transvestite acts. Vito, whose empire was built on dope, understood people and gave them what they wanted. His was a new minstrelsy, a transmuted minstrelsy, a sexual minstrelsy of flesh and fantasy, syncopation and Psyche, peaches and profits. As metaphor, the peach was a fruit of many meanings. In standard slang, a pretty girl was a peach. In the common vernacular of the blues, peaches alluded to the male genitalia: 'If you don't like my peaches, don't shake my tree.' In more obscure variations of that language, there were connotations of homosexuality, as in Guilford Payne's 'Peach Tree Man Blues' of 1923. In Vito's joints, the orchard of ambiguity bloomed in full splendor in the neon night. The shadowland – the language, characters, and occur- rences - of the Mobjoint milieu of which Vito's joints were a lingering part of Greenwich Village in the early sixties would imbue the lyrics and spirit of several of Bob Dylan's watershed songs: 'Subterranean Homesick Blues,' 'Like A Rolling Stone,' 'Highway 61 Revisited,' and 'Positively Fourth Street.' There are more underworlds through which a poet-singer may pass than that to which Orpheus descended and from which he emerged.[1]

*Finally, although I would have thought this did not need pointing out, experience suggests I should; just because I discuss in one part of this article the use of window as a metaphor for vagina it does not follow that I am saying that Dylan always uses the word window as some sort of Weberman[2] codeword for vagina. My article specifically mentions a variety of ways Dylan uses the word, but in any case that would be an absurd concept. Not only are there obvious contextual reasons for this in the instance of this one word, but also discussing a strand of imagery is not the same as 'decoding' text. I feel that the latter is the most destructive type of 'criticism' possible and one all artists and people of taste spurn, and I hope that the introduction to this collection, as well as the articles themselves, reinforces that contention.*

*With all those caveats in place, it is time to proceed with the article itself.*

The word 'window' can be an extraordinarily rich figure of speech. For example, as we will see below, it can be used as a metaphor for a vagina - an opening for a man to enter, an image enriched by the associated idea of the woman opening her window to let in a secret lover. This can lead to a deeper, even more intimate metaphor of the *window*, one allowing access to the private place of a person. Their room, their private space - standing for the very core of their individuality, their *soul*, if you will.

The particular power of *window* as a figure of speech is that it can always work in at least two basic ways. You can see in through a window and you can also look out. A window can be opened to let you in, but it can also be closed to deny you access. It does not take much imagination to expand both the functionality of windows, and, by extension, the range of possible metaphoric uses. A locked window can keep someone trapped inside. If the curtains are drawn or frost covers the windows you can see neither in nor out. If you've not got enough money for glass you have to cover up your windows with cardboard. If you've really got something to hide you'd better brick those windows up to make sure no-one sees what you get up to.

Windows are commonly referred to as 'the eyes of the soul', and 'eye' imagery is as prevalent and important in Dylan's writing as are 'windows', so the uses and associations multiply. So, *window* is a powerful and rich figure of speech and it is no surprise to find it is a main - and sometimes dominant - image in many of Dylan's most famous songs. This chapter discusses what I believe to be some of his most successful uses of this image.

As I mentioned above, *window* can be a very effective metaphor for vagina. This usage is particularly prevalent in the blues music that has so shaped and informed Dylan's art. So much so, actually, that the image became a stock one and therefore lost a lot of its power and appeal, but not before the richness of its potential was well and truly mined by the vigour and vitality of this great oral tradition. For example, one of the many variants of 'Rock Me Mama' - a song Dylan sings exquisitely in the out-takes from *Pat Garrett & Billy The Kid* - ends with the lines:

> *See me comin' raise your window high*
> *See me comin' raise your window high*
> *When you see me leavin', hang yo' head an' cry*

The repeated line works as a straightforward sexual metaphor, following on from previous verses with other examples of the same, such as:

> *Rock me mama. rock me all night long*
> *Rock me mama, rock me all night long*
> *Rock me like my back ain't got no back bone*
> *Rock me mama, like you roll your dough*
> *Rock me mama, like you roll your dough*
> *Oh I want you to roll me, roll me over slow*

The imagery in the song's last verse strikes deeper than the other two[3], because the play on words is both on 'coming' and 'window'. Not only does it describe the man's wish for when he reaches orgasm, but it also lets us know that this lover is a secret one. The first of the repeated lines could be telling us that the woman had to welcome him into the room by raising her window when she saw him approach. Why doesn't he enter by the door? (I ask this partly to get you thinking about the hundreds of blues songs you know that use door as a straightforward sexual metaphor.) Blues songwriters shared the same store of images, conceits, lines and even whole verses. These were picked up and used by one singer or another in whatever setting he wanted. This same verse that closes 'Rock Me Mama' appears in numerous other country blues songs; sometimes the setting makes it explicit that the lover is a secret one, giving a poignant edge to *'hang yo' head an' cry'*.

Doors and windows are standard blues metaphors for sexual apertures. If the lines quoted above do not come across so well on the written page, think of the melody of 'Rock Me Mama' and imagine a blues singer performing them with a leer in his voice. However, this vein of imagery was, as I've said, mined so deeply as to be less than startling by the mid-1960s. So what does Dylan do with it, how does he revitalise the stale tradition? The answer is that he digs deeper.

For sheer bravado and outrageous sexual metaphors 'Temporary Like Achilles' is hard to beat. It begins with seductive blues music and an opening line whose import does not become clear until the succeeding lines are heard:

> *Standing on your window*

At first this may not seem a sexual allusion but as the lines develop you are forced to re-appraise what you first heard. As the first verse progresses you get the impression that the song may be about a sexual encounter - how could you not with a reference to *'second door'* and the question *'Honey, why are you so hard?'*

However, it is only as the song unfolds that each piece falls into place and the full extent of the conceit becomes clear. Dylan extends the use of the window-as-vagina metaphor into a series of household components standing for female body parts. He tops this off by playing around with the perspective the verses are being sung from.

The second verse finds the man performing oral sex in a (seemingly vain) attempt to stimulate the unresponsive woman. Comically, he attempts to see the expression on her face but he cannot possibly do so from his current position:

> *Kneeling 'neath your ceiling,*
> *Yes, I guess I'll be here for a while.*
> *I'm tryin' to read your portrait, but,*
> *I'm helpless, like a rich man's child*

This tells us that on both a literal and a deeper level, he cannot 'read her'. His implied regret over the time he must spend here adds to our sense of his impatience and frustration.

This second stanza, especially when coupled with the later lines, '*I rush into your hallway/lean against your velvet door*', make the listener re-appraise the first verse the next time they listen to it. It is only after hearing the rest of the song that we realise that there was something odd about what we (or I, anyway) had presumed to be a description of oral sex. (Due not only to the second verse, but also to the line: '*looking at your second door*'.) Then it dawns on us that the opening stanza is not so much from the man's perspective as his manhood's. Verse three returns to this viewpoint and now we get as far as the '*velvet door*'. The last verse finds him musing - with marvellous comic irony - on the fatally flawed Achilles, with whom he shares the temporary condition of '*pointing to the sky*'.

Now, in case you think that the above interpretation in some way reduces the worth of the song, then think again, for it is part of its joy. The sheer over-the-top fun of the imagery, the appealing music and vocal delivery, all work together to make it a great piece of entertainment. Just like sex itself, not always necessarily profound, but always fun.

This song comes from the album *Blonde On Blonde,* a marvellous mixture of pop, rock and blues. In all of these there is a tradition of getting lyrics referring to sexual matters past the censor. At its lowest this is merely the pop field aiming 'coded smut' at schoolgirls to make money from their furtive longings (I say schoolgirls as they tend to be smarter than the boys when it comes to words. The boys in any case are bombarded by images and more or less encouraged in their longings). It has wittier and more entertaining outings too, however. Richard Goldstein wrote of the rock/pop convention in his collection *Poetry Of Rock*[4]:

> Such ambiguity has existed in rock since its earliest days, and for the most elemental reason. To sell, a pop song had to be meaningful, but to get on the radio, it had to sound harmless. Disc jockeys with a more rigid sense of propriety than the most bluenosed censor actually helped foster in young writers a profound awareness of slang and its implications. The ability of today's lyricist to say extraordinary things in ordinary words has its roots in the enforced ambiguity of top-40 radio, where composers tried to express the forbidden in the context of the permissible.

I am a back door man,
I am a back door man,
Well, the men don't know
But the little girls understand

**121**

Indeed they do, as the *NME* wrote, at the same time I first conceived of this piece, quoting this very line in explaining why the album they were reviewing by 'boy band' Bros, aimed at little girls, was called *Push*. Years pass but the custom survives.

As far as the blues tradition goes, the range of things that were treated as extensive sexual metaphors was huge. Horseracing, baking, household parts and items, trains and above all cars were among the favourites:

> *The use of horseback riding as a sexual metaphor is relatively archaic. Possessing an automobile is of special importance to Negroes; barred by social and economic barriers from satisfying jobs and from living in decent housing, the Negro male loves big heavy automobiles. Driving his old Buick or Cadillac he is swift, powerful, graceful, manly, irresistible; he finds a partial substitute for gratifications of comfort, importance, and power. By extension, a man about to have an orgasm is racing furiously along the highway, a rival lover is another driver at the wheel, a fickle woman is a cheap decrepit car, a desirable lover is a smooth chauffeur.[5]*

The classic 'Car Trouble Blues' and 'Terraplane Blues' probably could demonstrate all of the above automobile metaphors. Joe Turner, a singer name-checked more than once by Dylan, often demonstrated a sophisticated control over other extended sexual metaphors.

Although the main driving force behind describing sexual encounters in this manner was undoubtedly to get past the airplay censors it is also part of the art - or at the very least entertainment. The extended treatment given to the stock blues imagery by Dylan in this song is a marvellous little piece of wit worthy of the Metaphysical poets in one of their coarser, playful moods. OK, bits of the song sound a bit *sleazy,* and there is an uncomfortable, dark edge to some of the sexual imagery both here and throughout *Blonde On Blonde* as a whole. Yet surely to write a song about sex that is fun, a bit sleazy, a touch disturbing, backed with this captivating music, is to write a witty, pointed blues song.

Just as fun sex can develop into something more profound where not only the body, but the inner being is shared, so the metaphoric use of *window* can grow to reflect this. However to share your inner self with someone is a very big step to take and this is amply demonstrated by the difficulties characters have in using *windows* in this manner in Dylan's song's. Of course, some people have no soul to share anyway. Maggie's Pa's sex life has degenerated into something so sleazy and devoid of *real* human contact that '*his bedroom window is made out of bricks'.*

More often than not, though, we find ourselves listening to songs about people caught in between this extreme and the other of opening our windows in mutual trust and love; in other words people caught in the flux of life and love. Each of us living behind our windows, looking out and wondering what goes on behind all the other windows. Trying to decide whether we should or shouldn't let someone climb in ours.

So we found, in chapter two's 'It Ain't Me, Babe', the singer defending his individuality from a lover whose cloying embrace he views as narrow and stultifying by singing:

> Go 'way from my window[6]

Similarly, as seen in that same chapter, when the singer in 'Don't Think Twice, It's All Right' hits the road again to preserve the individual core of his self identity, he leaves behind his girlfriend, telling her:

> Look out your window and I'll be gone

In other words: you keep in your space, I'm moving on. No merging of souls here. The singer feels the urgent need to travel on, to keep moving, keep growing. But things can change, we can meet a soul mate and open our windows to them. Particularly when that person or being has been hurt - and is in need of help to regain their full selfhood:

> My love she's like some raven
> At my window with a broken wing

I, for one, have no doubt that he opened his window and let her in.

We grow older too. The young man who had a burning need to travel, to hit the road in an attempt to find his true self, grows to think that he's found that very thing. And now he beseeches:

> Throw my ticket out the window...
> 'Cause tonight I'll be staying here with you

Staying *in here* with you. The world is outside the window - where the wind can howl like a hammer, where it can blow cold and rainy - but him? He's staying in behind her windows. Sharing her bed, her room, her private space. *'Bring that bottle over here'*, and hey, put a *'sign on the window'* saying: *'three's a crowd'*.

A great image this *window* isn't it? It lets me take you from the start to the end of Dylan's great 1960's journey in the twinkling of a few paragraphs; hopefully citing enough songs for you to have snatches of folk, blues, rock and country songs from him floating around in your head. Hopefully, too, having given you an inkling of how prevalent and important windows imagery is in Dylan's songs.

Ah, but I made it sound too easy a journey - for it is certainly not that. Especially not for those without the single-mindedness an artist needs to stay true to his calling. Thankfully, the artist in this case, Dylan, is often there to help the rest of us in the struggle, pointing the way for us all. Nowhere more so than in the magnificent 'Can You Please Crawl Out Your Window?'

Here is the same window-as-aperture-to-the-soul metaphor. But the person he is singing to here - presumably a woman - is trapped in her own space. She is frightened to come out, but she *must* do so because the alternative is to stay in a box (this is a brilliant image - it is not a proper room, or life, because it has no *windows*) as the plaything of a sadistic man.

This man is so far removed from the true world of the Imagination that he thinks he can just grow a third eye when one is needed, a man who would take the moon - the quintessential symbol of Romanticism - only to peel and expose it.

The woman is being urged by Dylan to break free from her dark and hateful world by crawling out of her window. The ungainly image in the chorus depicts the effort needed - this will not be easy, or dignified - but come on out and give it a try, you can always go back, but just crawl out your goddam window and see what happens.[7]

'Can You Please Crawl Out Your Window?' is a crucial song in Dylan's oeuvre for at least three reasons. It hints of the violence and sadism that result from not being true to yourself. Secondly, the mixture of guilt and responsibility over the situation is striking. The guy she is living with may well be an out-and-out bastard but he 'sits in her room' because she opened her window and let him in. Now she has closed it behind him, effectively trapping him as we are told in the line *'Are you frightened of the box you keep him in?'* Responsibility for your actions, for proper give and take in relationships, is a key theme even in the superficially fun and salacious songs on *Blonde On Blonde*. The flowing lines from 'Fourth Time Around' take on a nightmarish hue in 'Can You Please Crawl Out Your Window?':

> But she said, 'Don't forget,
> Everybody must give something back
> For something they get'

Then thirdly, there is the insistence that although the struggle to self-realisation is a hard one it is worth all the efforts and risk. It is no surprise to me that this pivotal song revolves round a chorus involving a window. Nor does it surprise that he reacted so boorishly when Phil Ochs criticised it by saying it did not sound like it would be a hit single. Dylan threw him out of the car they were travelling in at the time, after it had stopped though so he wasn't as upset as he might have been! Ochs was correct about the chances of it becoming a hit, but you can see why Dylan would be so close to such a key work and fantastic rock song and hurt by Ochs' reaction.

Naturally, a window is sometimes just a window, particularly in Dylan's early work. Even then, though, it has its resonances:

> We'll shake your windows
> And rattle your walls

sang the cocky young protester. Yes, indeed, shake them physically because of the 'ragin'' battle outside, but also shake the complacency of the old guard comfortably controlling everything from behind their walls and windows. One thinks, too, of the *cardboard filled windows* in 'North Country Blues'. Again a common phrase, a literal description, but how evocative it is of the town's emptiness and desolation.

A useful word this 'window', whether literal or metaphoric. It is not to be found only in old blues songs. T. S. Eliot was another who exploited it greatly. How often have you read of T. S. Eliot, and old blues songs, influencing Bob Dylan? So many times that it is unsurprising that the word 'windows' occurs in many more Dylan songs than I've alluded to above.

As mentioned in the previous article, the following lines are beautiful, both as an actual visual description and a metaphor for the difficulties the artist feels in communicating:

> Now the wintertime is coming
> The windows are filled with frost
> I went to tell everybody
> But I could not get across

One notes in 'Man of Peace' from *Infidels* that he has not forgotten its power, in a John Donne-like immediacy of opening line that reminds one of 'It Ain't Me Babe's' starting line so many years before:

> Look out your window, baby, there's a scene you'd like to catch

Yet even if I enumerated them all it still wouldn't tell you the full scale of its impact, because that doesn't come from the imagery surrounding windows alone, but also from the interaction of other key images such as eyes. Windows as 'eyes to the soul' leading to Eye-as-window, Window-as-I. Then there is the interplay between windows and light and darkness and many more. In the mid-sixties' songs, underneath all the dazzling wordplay and clever/jokey literary allusions lies a strong and supple web of imagery. Imagery of eyes and mouths, windows and doors, light and dark, lifelessness and self realisation, love and death and sex... all underpinning classic song after classic song.[8] This was an introductory look at one strand of that web; it is up to each listener to follow it further, if they wish, and see where it takes them.

1. Nick Tosches, *Where Dead Voices Gather*, Jonathan Cape, 2002.
2. Until it was closed down the concordance of A.J. Weberman, infamous 'garbologist', was available on his website. The tedious and reductive theory behind this being that you enter a word and up pops what the word really means in 'Dylan's symbology'. This one to one relationship threw up, as you can imagine, some ludicrous suggestions if read back through Dylan's lyrics.
3. Though *roll my dough* is apt and resonant too.
4. Bantam Books, February 1969. Following comments of mine about *Temporary Like Achilles* on the rec.music.dylan newsgroup in the mid 1990's, Christine Consolvo quoted this same passage.
5. Harry Oster, *Living Country Blues*, Minerva Press, 1975.
6. Another old blues line - Sleepy John Estes having used it as an opening line too.
7. The same advice as was given to Baby Blue in 'It's All Over Now, Baby Blue'.
8. This is particularly true of the celebrated mid-'60's period, when Dylan was the 'unconscious' artist.

# Eleven

# If You See Her, Say Hello

### Foreword

With most articles, I can clearly remember why I wrote them. This one is a little vaguer. I know, however, that it was at least partly inspired by two things. Firstly - surprise, surprise! - by listening to Dylan perform it live with a fairly-faithful-to-the-original set of lyrics but with a delicate and deliberate (it has been repeated since) twist to the ending. Secondly, the sudden realization that I had written nothing solely about any track from Blood On The Tracks. And, you know, when push comes to shove and a guy forces you at gun point to take just one non-compilation official release to that desert island - Blood On The Tracks would be that release...

I do, however, recall how much I enjoyed writing this article. Even if it had never seen the light of day I would have been happy at 'putting down in writing what was in my mind'. Once I began writing about the song, it all seemed just seemed to flow - presumably I'd had these thoughts in mind for years. Which is not surprising, as I expect the vast majority of Dylan fans have carried the songs of Blood On The Tracks with them over the years. The column in On The Tracks gave me scope to write it down and the original version of this article appeared there, spread over three issues.

This article stands apart from the book's subtitle of "early and late songs of bob dylan". I could make the claim that its relevance lies in showing the mature Dylan's relationship songs compared to the young man singing 'Don't Think Twice, It's All Right' and 'It Ain't Me Babe' in chapter two. Even then you might still think that I just could not bear to have nothing about Blood On The Tracks in the book. I wouldn't argue if you did.

# TROUBADOUR

### Opening Impact

Do you remember the impact *Blood On The Tracks* made on you when you first played it? It is difficult to recapture those feelings, and in any case your memory plays tricks on you, but I recall it being ages before the labyrinthine pleasures of 'Tangled Up In Blue' and 'Simple Twist Of Fate' allowed me to concentrate too much on anything else. I was already being intrigued by the mystery of 'Lily, Rosemary And The Jack Of Hearts' and aware there was a fully-fledged major statement from the artist present in the form of 'Idiot Wind'. And then there was 'Shelter From The Storm' and...

You get the picture, I'm sure. Yet somewhere in those first few plays 'If You See Her, Say Hello' caught a place in my heart that it has occupied ever since. Why does it stand out even amongst all those other treasures? Well, firstly because of the magical way the feelings and emotions are conveyed by *The Voice*. Then there is the sheer intelligence and insight of a song that so (seemingly) effortlessly took a traditional folk song motif and transformed it into a work of art that magically communicates to us the multi-faceted experience of a man who has lived, loved and lost, with all the attendant emotions and passions this engenders. I say 'a traditional folk song motif' because the first thing that came to mind when I originally heard it was 'Take A Message To Mary', even though Dylan's song is from a different plane of artistic expression.

Prior to looking further into that, let us now go back to the (not quite) beginning - the starting point for most of us - the album version, and look at the story the song tells.

In the unlikely event that this article is being read by anyone who does not know the song well enough to be able to replay it note perfect in their head, here's an instruction: go and play it now. Then play it again, and again and again until every nuance is stored in your mind, available for instant recall.

Most of you will already be in that happy situation, which is just as well for me, because were you to simply remember - or I to recount - the story of the song it would not speak to us of much. It is a plain, common enough tale, unadorned with metaphor and unburdened by many details. But if you hear the story as performed by Dylan - with the emphasis, the elongations, the shading, the textures, the subtle hints of his voice and the music - then you will know that this simple story contains worlds within its endless few minutes.

In the opening verse, the singer speaks to an unidentified third person asking him[1] to say hello to a woman who left *'last early spring'* and may now be living in Tangier, though it seems far from certain. The potential messenger is also asked to tell the woman that the singer is 'OK' - though not completely so, as *'things get kind of slow'*. Finally, the messenger is instructed not to let on that the singer has not forgotten the woman.

The story beneath the story tells us so much more: the music and vocals tell us throughout that this man has not forgotten the woman - nothing could be further from the truth. We already suspect he never will, a suspicion the song soon turns into a known fact.

The lyrics, although economical in the extreme, are full of meaning. The very vagueness of the woman's whereabouts adds to the wistfulness of the singer's thoughts and emphasises his loss. The fact that she left in spring - the season of hope and rebirth - is bitterly ironic, and subconsciously places the singer in a winter of despair.

The deliberate - and delicately portrayed - self-consciously 'brave stance' of the man suffering his loss in heroic silence is also introduced. Simultaneously we are made to realise that what the singer doesn't tell us is, in many ways, as important as what he does. The more the protagonist claims 'look at how brave I am', the more we see that he is falling apart.[2]

In verse two we discover that the woman left after a not-unusual lovers' quarrel. Her leaving was a catastrophe for him, something that becomes ever clearer the harder he tries to avoid admitting it. He tells the third party - and, therefore, us - that despite the searing pain the separation has caused him *'She still lives inside of me, we've never been apart'*. This seems a double-edged blessing as the song progresses; the feeling conveyed mirroring the complex emotions of real life.

The pivotal third stanza is really quite extraordinary. Not least because Dylan presents us with three outstanding versions by the time of the album's release. But mainly, perhaps, because this stanza was soon to be re-written in a manner so extreme as to make its performance one of the most shocking things Dylan has ever done to an audience (and God knows that is something he has often excelled at). However, I run ahead of myself; on *Blood On The Tracks* track eight we get the heartbreakingly poignant *'If you get close to her, kiss her once for me/I always have respected her for doing what she did and getting free'*.

The toing and froing of emotions is expertly conveyed, as is the almost impossible balancing act of trying to say and believe in the 'right thing' while being torn up inside by the hurt of the loss: *'Oh whatever makes her happy, I won't stand in the way/Though the bitter taste still lingers on from the night I tried to make her stay'*.

By this point in the song the whole weight of the churning emotions in the man has been laid bare, and we, the eavesdropping audience, can all but taste the bitterness, a bitterness amplified by this stanza's revelation of the clear necessity of the sacrifice, and echoed by the sour taste of his subsequent fate.

Verse four gives us a partial insight into the singer's life, though why he is going *'from town to town'* we are not specifically told. *'I see a lot of people as I make the rounds'* describes the life, perhaps, of a touring musician, or it could imply that he is 'doing the rounds' of the places he thinks she might be. Alternatively it may just be describing the life of a socialiser. To try to guess is mere idle speculation - but what this glimpse of his life does make clear is that his life is rootless, repetitive and unfulfilled without this woman he can never forget.

We are also told that he hears her name as he travels around, but not why. Perhaps because, when they see him alone, people mention her behind his back as he moves on? We do not know, again there is no firm basis for this interpretation. Rather, I am extrapolating my own scenario from a few scant details, but I include this conjecture deliberately, because the song encourages, no demands, that the listener does so.

Dylan then turns up the poignancy level to a near unbearable degree with *'And I've never gotten used to it, I've just learned to turn it off/Either I'm too sensitive or else I'm getting soft'*.

In all kinds of ways this is almost too much to take - even taken purely as being claimed by an unidentified narrator in the song it really is laying it on a bit thick- and yet somehow it works, indeed works brilliantly, and is possibly one of the best-remembered parts of the album. Part of the reason for that is that it seems such an un-Dylan-like attitude that Dylan is singing about. At various points in *Blood On The Tracks* our knowledge of Dylan's own life cannot help but intrude into the songs, as in the case of these, and related, lines in this song.

Yet never let it be forgotten that this song, on its own, away from Dylan's life, is not affected by these concerns. The mix of emotions is a perfect delineation of the male psyche: there is that ever-present adolescent in every male - particularly in the arena of sexual relationships. It wants to admit it was wrong in trying to make her stay, but it wishes she had; it wants her to be free, but yearns for her to be back in the prison of their relationship; it can admit that they should be living separately, though realising that he is utterly miserable apart from her. 'Gosh if she only knew how reasonable and brave he was being, facing up to all this, maybe she would...'

The spin of emotions is superbly communicated: the bitter regret, the longing, the bravery of accepting the situation, the desire to have this bravery and longing communicated to the woman, the realization that this would nullify the brave stance, therefore the injunction just to say 'hello' but to hope this stoic 'hello' somehow communicates worlds of meaning and feeling... and back round we go again.

The concluding fifth verse opens with the song's only complex, 'poetic' image; *'Sundown, yellow moon, I replay the past/I know every scene by heart, they all went by so fast'*.

Sundown: like the earlier reference to spring, this subtly evokes the perfect mood. The song is coming to an end, she is not coming back and it is the sundown of the singer's life. When she left, the light went out of his life.

Yellow moon: the moon is the traditional lovers' symbol - the pure, white moon or the silver moon that will be appearing in a later, shocking version that is, not this one that is tainted; tainted because of the night she left.

Leaving the singer endlessly replaying the past, remembering all the times they shared and, as in this song, the night they came to an end. And we too replay this past each time we put the song back on, each time we listen to *Blood On The Tracks*. *'Pain sure brings out the best in people, doesn't it?'*

The second line of this verse is a little masterpiece all by itself: *'I know every scene by heart, they all went by so fast'*.

There is a seeming paradox here; if they went by so fast, surely they'd be difficult to remember? But it is only *seeming*; Dylan is using language so effectively here that it is like a coiled spring, ready to burst open and illuminate our understanding. The man is replaying his past like a video in his head, which is one reason he *'knows every scene by heart.'* Another is that each scene is so very precious to him that he can never forget it. Nonetheless they still went by far, far too fast - how could it be otherwise? He desperately wishes they were still sharing that period of happiness - a period that would have seemed to speed by, compared to the long slow days of his loneliness.

This line encapsulates so much in such apparently simple language – what an extraordinary comparison it makes to the lyrics of a mid-sixties classic like 'Visions of Johanna'. There are not many poets (wordsmiths, artists – use whatever word you are most comfortable with) who have shown mastery of such disparate styles – and no other lyricist I can think of.

Back to the song and, fittingly true to life, he still can't let it go. He swings back in mood to end with another plea: *'If she's passing back this way, I'm not that hard to find/Tell her she can look me up if she's got the time'*.

The pretend insouciance of '*I'm not that hard to find*' is not fooling anyone by this time, but he can't stop himself from saying it. Again this is so true to Dylan's character portrayal - by now I feel I know this man. You can bet your life he isn't hard to find, he's the one standing at the top of the road, straining his vision, ever hopeful of catching a glimpse of her, while knowing in his heart of hearts that it's just not to be. (And that it is better for her that way, he knows, but still...)

The lovely fake (but again not fooling anyone for a moment) casualness of the last line increases the poignancy of the whole song as it draws to a close. But what is he really telling the messenger to say to her? Is it just a 'hello'? Or does he really want the messenger to tell her everything? (*'Look, he told me not to tell you, but, he is really cut up about making you leave, his life is pointless without you, he's trying to put a brave face on it but...'*) Does the singer know himself? Does the messenger know? Do we know? No we don't - not for certain, anyway - but we can know, can hear loud and clear, precisely what Bob Dylan wanted us to experience via this song.

Talking of 'Tangled Up In Blue' in 1985, Dylan remarked that he was '*...trying to do something that I didn't think had ever been done before. In terms of trying to tell a story and be a present character in it without it being some kind of fake, sappy attempted tearjerker. I was trying to be somebody in the present time, while conjuring up a lot of past images.*' Dylan goes on to explain his approach to 'Tangled Up In Blue' and other songs on *Blood On The Tracks* in terms of painting. It is a theme he returned to in 1991 when interviewed by Eliot Mintz for *The Bootleg Series*. On this occasion 'Tangled Up In Blue' and 'If You See Her, Say Hello' are specifically linked, and looking at Dylan's description above it is easy to see why. In the less complex setting of 'If You See Her, Say Hello' he succeeds brilliantly in the same aim he had for 'Tangled Up In Blue'.

So that is how the *Blood On The Tracks* rendition of 'If You See Her, Say Hello' affects me. This is what that track, in isolation, makes me feel, think, vicariously experience. However we all know that it does not exist 'in isolation' for me, or I guess, anyone else. For a start the song has developed in various ways since then, and it also has a history prior to that album.

Among the most rewarding things about following Dylan's career is the way in which he is, on the one hand, a walking, singing, jukebox encyclopedia of popular music, while on the other he is endlessly inventive in further developing his own songs. Each song leads to a never-ending trip through variants, influences, artistic creation – let me take you on the voyage that 'If You See Her, Say Hello' took me on. Before we go forwards into Dylan's reworkings of the song, let us step back via Dylan's pre-release version to what I hear as clear antecedents.

I will begin by considering the original, variant, version and the structural precedents, before examining the thorny topic of the relationship of the song to Dylan's private life and how the song has been rewritten in its various live incarnations.

### Before Blood On The Tracks

Before *Blood On The Tracks* there was *Blood On The Tracks* Mark 1 - the initial release that was quickly withdrawn and re-recorded. Many songs had lyrical as well as musical changes. Both of these affect the song under discussion here, giving a closely related but distinctly different experience for the listener.[3]

The lyrical changes range from minor to highly significant. In the first verse the third line originally was:

*Say for me that I'm all right though new things come and go*

This gives a feeling of the pointlessness of new things, increasing the feeling that develops along with the song that his true life ended when she left; not a greatly dissimilar effect to that of the version released on *Blood On The Tracks*.

The third verse has been completely re-written; in the withdrawn original album version it was:

*If you're makin' love to her, kiss her for the kid,*
*Who always has respected her for doin' what she did*
*For I know it had to be that way, it was written in the cards*
*But the bitter taste still lingers on, it all came down so hard.*

The opening of these four lines is just dazzling. I know the album version is splendid too, and conveys the same overall 'message' as this; but the brutal reality - though not brutally expressed - of *'If you're makin' love to her'*, and the self-revealing intimacy of *'kiss her for the kid'* makes it just the perfect line for this song. As a couplet, however, *the Blood On The Tracks* version has the crucial word 'free' as the rhyme, which makes it difficult to choose between them. What a dilemma! At this point you could be tempted to turn to *Lyrics '62-85* for guidance. If you do so you will be given yet another version:

*'If you get close to her, kiss her once for me*
*I always have respected her for busting out and gettin' free'*

I like this very much too. 'Busting out' is an excellent, active, description of her freeing herself from the constrictions of their relationship. What a wealth of riches to write about in one couplet. And more treasures are to follow in future re-writes. My preferred opening line for this verse is definitely the 'original' one, available on *The Bootleg Series I-III*; on the other hand I think the most effective opening couplet is in *Lyrics '62-85*. But goodness only knows the *Blood On The Tracks* version is splendid too!

On the other hand, to close the verse I much prefer the *Blood On The Tracks* second couplet, with its acceptance of personal responsibility as opposed to the idea of pre-ordained destiny.

It is noteworthy, too, that the word 'respected' is present in all these versions, being of as much import as 'free'; this is also true of the perfect phrase 'bitter taste', as the stanza progresses.

Where did this song spring from though, and how is it related to the others on *Blood On The Tracks?*

### Possible Antecedents

Suggesting a possible antecedent for the song, Michael Gray described it as 'a marvellous re-write of "Girl From The North Country"', and other commentators have followed him in this. With good reason: there is a lost true love, there is a messenger who may or may not meet the woman and pass on the message from the still love-struck man. What there is not, however, is the terrible intensity of *needing* to get the message to her, but knowing you cannot or at least *should* not make her aware of the true situation.

A much closer situation is surely present in 'Take A Message To Mary', a song Dylan had covered earlier, on *Self Portrait*. From the very first time I heard 'If You See Her, Say Hello' that earlier song was shadowing it in my mind. The Dylan song on *Blood On The Tracks* is on a whole other level of creation, but nonetheless there are striking similarities.

Again a message is to be taken to a much loved and missed woman. Again the messenger is instructed not to tell the woman the truth; however, by the same 'trick' we, the listeners, learn the true situation - and its over-whelming pathos. Also, again, we have the same struggle between telling her something but ensuring it is *not* the truth, while thinking: 'Oh! If only she knew...'

In 'Take A Message To Mary' the singer encourages the messenger to make up all sorts of fanciful tales to avoid the truth:

> *You can tell her that I had to see the world*
> *Tell her that my ship set sail*
>
> *Just tell her that I went to Timbuktu*
> *Tell her that I'm searching for gold*

Things are really laid on with a trowel in the traditional song. There's a wedding to be cancelled, he's going to pine away in a lonely cell, while his true love is to be told he has heartlessly deserted her. The cumulative effect is a bit overdone, and borders on parody by the time we get to the final lines:

> *You can say she better find someone new*
> *To cherish and to hold, Oh Lord, this cell is cold.*

Why did all this happen? Again a story is only hinted at, all we are told is:

> *Please don't mention the stagecoach*
> *And the shot from a careless gun*

'Careless' gun sneakily deflects the blame; over and above everything else it is suggested that he is perhaps unjustly, or at least unluckily, jailed.

As you would expect, the differences are as illuminating as the similarities. Compare this to 'If You See Her, Say Hello' where the man admits his culpability in something somewhat less dramatic than a scene from the Wild West. A wild scene all the same; few things are more violent than a lovers' row and split-up. In addition this is a scene from our current reality - not a stage-managed scenario from a romanticised past.

The singer in 'If You See Her, Say Hello' is in a metaphorical prison every bit as cold as the lonely cell in 'Take A Message To Mary'. Indeed, being a far more skillfully depicted situation we can fully relate to it, it chills us much more. They both share the same powerful theme, however, that of Love vs. Freedom.

The love sung about so movingly in Dylan's 'If You See Her, Say Hello' reminds us of the destructive *'dark, secret love'* of Blake's 'The Sick Rose' or, more contemporaneously, Neil Young's:

> *Love is a rose*
> *But you better not pick it*
> *It only grows when it's on the vine*
> *A handful of thorns*
> *And you'll know that you've missed it*
> *You lose your love when you say the word 'mine'*

It is this dangerous, stultifying love that brought the protagonists in 'If You See Her, Say Hello' to their (or, his, anyway) sorry state – in any version you wish to name,[4] the woman has *broken free*. She is better off without him and he knows it. His love for her makes him pleased about this on one level, but at the same time drives his need to have her back. So, still he pines.

For another interesting antecedent, listeners are directed to Dylan's magnificent performance of Johnny Cash's 'Give My Love To Rose' in 1988. (A final separation this time, but many of the same messages, techniques and themes.) I say 'magnificently performed' because Dylan really gets hold of the song and inhabits the dying character's persona (just listen to the way he sings 'mistah'), as indeed he inhabits the persona of the narrator/singer in 'If You See Her, Say Hello'. And this is the main difference between this song and the highly orchestrated 'Take A Message to Mary'; 'orchestrated' not only in the lush musical sense (with the strings and girl backing singers), but also in Dylan's detachment from the story.

One thing that could not be said about the love songs on *Blood On The Tracks* is that Dylan is faking anything; particularly if one considers the original (not the released) album. Michael Gray recognised the album's worth immediately upon its release, in a perspicacious review praising its intelligence, maturity and wit.[5]

It is this mature intelligence that suffuses all the songs on the album; not least the one under consideration here. Elsewhere in this book, I write about Dylan's masterful mid-sixties' dissections of the emotional jails that possessive love engenders. But these - however perfectly realised and performed, both solo and with the magnificent musicians he then played with - come across as almost as abstract and theoretical as the Blake poem referred to above, when compared to the songs on *Blood On The Tracks*.[6]

There is an irresistible feeling of intimacy in these songs; it is hard (impossible?) not to believe Dylan is singing about his own feelings and experiences. Even fairly moderate Dylan fans are aware that he was experiencing marital difficulties at the time he wrote these songs; it would not be long before Dylan took to the road and dedicated 'Isis' ('a song about marriage') 'to Leonard'. Leonard Cohen, that is, one of the few songwriters you feel share a similar insight into the pressures involved in maintaining a marriage in the modern Western World. Cohen called a married relationship 'the hottest furnace...'. Dylan's dedication came near the end of his 1975 tour; in 1976 he opened with an acoustic 'Visions Of Johanna' and followed that by playing a singularly personal-sounding version of 'If You See Her, Say Hello'.

Private lives are dangerous waters, waters I have avoided up until now. I can refrain no longer.

### The Artist's Life Rears Its Head

Up until now, I have skirted the subject of how our knowledge of Dylan's own life colours our view of the songs on *Blood On The Tracks*, mentioning it only when it was unavoidable. I have done so for a number of reasons:

- The subject is such a far-reaching one - affecting a whole raft of aesthetic considerations - that it would have led me away from discussing the song as a single track, the main purpose of this piece.

- I am convinced that in the case of the take on the album it is an unnecessary distraction (see below).

- Frankly the subject makes me uncomfortable.

However, to ignore it altogether would be to fail in my duty as a critic ('If You See Her, Say Hello' does after all come from the album that most fuels this debate). In any case, it would be stretching things to discuss the 1976 version without having done so.

Listeners generally assume that the 'pain' they hear in *Blood On The Tracks* comes from Dylan's separation from his wife Sara at this point in his life.[7] In all honesty it is hard to feel otherwise when these songs are contrasted with the songs he recorded during their happier years.

Dylan himself has, unsurprisingly, very strong views on the point. In the interview that accompanied *Biograph* he says:

> 'You're A Big Girl Now' *well, I read that this was supposed to be about my wife. I wish somebody would ask me first before they go ahead and print stuff like that. I mean it couldn't be about anybody else but my wife, right? Stupid and misleading jerks sometimes these interpreters are...*

It is, as we all know, a dangerous thing to quote Dylan, since it is usually possible to find fairly contradictory quotes elsewhere, but I think this one is crucial. Especially the line: *'I mean it couldn't be about anybody else but my wife, right?'* I will return to this below, I hope in a way that is neither stupid nor misleading.

First of all, though, I think it only right to say that it is impossible for either the listener (if at all aware of Dylan's life) or Dylan himself to completely distance his private emotions from the album. Nonetheless, he makes a valiant stab at it later in the same interview.

> *...everything I do is done from the inside out, you know, I'm a mystery only to those who haven't felt the same things I have.. .you can't take my stuff and verbalize it, like I don't write confessional songs. Emotion's got nothing to do with it. It only seems so, like it seems that Laurence Olivier is Hamlet... well actually I did write one once and it wasn't very good - it was a mistake to record it and I regret it... back there somewhere on maybe my third or fourth album.* (Referring, presumably, to 'Ballad in Plain D'.)

These are insightful comments, and the opening seems particularly relevant to the song under discussion. However, I think it goes too far in *completely* denying any confessional quality or presence of personal emotions in the songs. (Understandable, though, given the crass comments he had had to put up with.) A more balanced view can be heard in the Mat Damsker interview:

> MD: *It seemed like* Blood On The Tracks *was a confession, it was real personal, it was a real chronicle. I could see that in your fragmented way, like on 'Tangled Up In Blue', you were sort of telling a story, and I tied it on to your relationship with Sara.*
>
> BD: *Well, here's the thing. There might be some little part of me which is confessing something which I've experienced and I know, but it is not definitely the total me confessing anything. I mean, when Mick Jagger sings 'Beast Of Burden', you know what I mean, there's something in there that's in him confessing, but you just do that.*

This seems to me to get right to the nub of things - the life is undeniably an input to the art but 'it is definitely not the total me confessing anything'. Dylan has actually - inadvertently, I'm sure - increased the feeling for many people that he is singing about himself and Sara in the following exchange with Mary Travers. Hearing the interview[8] one is struck by how much emphasis and feeling Dylan puts into the word 'pain'; clearly the album was borne out of deep emotional pain for him (which is not at all the same thing as saying it is a confessional diary):

> MT: *And one of the things I enjoyed about* Blood On The Tracks, *as an album, was that it was very simple.*
>
> BD: *Hm, hm. Well that's, you know, that's the way things are really, they are basically very simple. A lot of people tell me they enjoy that album. It's hard for me to relate to that. I mean, you know, people enjoying the type of pain, you know.*
>
> MT: *It is a painful album.*

As the interview progresses Dylan backs away a bit

> BD: *So, er...*
>
> MT: *Well, perhaps maybe the word 'enjoy' is the wrong word. Maybe a better word is to say that you're moved. I was moved by the album. You know, there were things that I could relate to in that album that grew as sense to me. You made sense to me on that album. I felt that it was a*

*much more, well, for me, I felt it was much more 'first person' as opposed to third person.*

BD: *Well, it makes it more clearly defined, but it still doesn't necessarily make it any better than, than, doing it, 'cos you can do it in second, third, fourth person too, you know, it's all the same, sure it is...*

But then concludes with:

*...Um, I know what you mean though...*

The above is one of the most famous exchanges in Dylan's interviews and I immediately thought of it while writing about a song from Blood On The Tracks. On re-listening to it I was intrigued to find that the next lines were:

MT: *Yeah. Let's play 'If You See Her, Say Hello' 'cos I think that's a very beautiful song.*

BD: *Very pertinent.*

So Dylan himself feels 'If You See Her, Say Hello' is *'very pertinent'* when discussing the pain evident in the accurately-titled album. We can feel certain that 'If You See Her, Say Hello' was affected by his then-current personal situation.

Nevertheless, anyone who has ever tried to create art – or who has spent time discussing it - will surely be aware that personal emotions are just the starting point of artistic expression. If one were to take, say, 'You're A Big Girl Now' to be a statement from Dylan to Sara one would have to conclude that it was patronising in the extreme. Thankfully it would also be a completely mistaken approach to the song (or any other piece of art). To equate all women with Sara is not only unmindful of Dylan's words quoted above but also flies in the face of all our experience of art.

Art as opposed to journalism. This album is not a diary of Dylan's life with his wife; it may well have resulted from the turmoil their relationship was going through, and I'll even grant that most songs *may* have started out that way, but they have been written and re-written; carefully crafted to universalize the personal.

Don't you think, also, that when one muses on one relationship one cannot help but think of others, some from long ago, some maybe that you wished had happened but didn't; some you wish had happened differently? I sure do, and I cannot but feel that whatever the specific starting point for an artist expressing a particular mood, emotion or sentiment the final creation will come about from a huge variety of influences. I can think of few things more reductive of *Blood On The Tracks* than to say each song is 'about Sara'.

Also, I have two related points on the danger of attributing all the songs to Sara as the subject. Both concern 'Simple Twist Of Fate', another song allegedly about his recent bust-up with Sara. Firstly, in the little red notebook where the original lyrics were written for the songs that made up *Blood On The Tracks* (and others that did not make it onto the album) 'Simple Twist Of Fate' was first listed as 'Simple Twist Of Fate (4th Street Affair)'.

Secondly, if that parenthetical reference isn't enough to convince you that there was more than Sara on his mind (and, for Dylan listeners, it should!), take a listen to Earl's Court in 1981 where he sings of remembering:

> *Suze and the way that she talks* [9]

Out of personal experience Dylan creates a universal art *(...everything I do is done from the inside out, you know);* nowhere is this clearer than in 'If You See Her, Say Hello' on *Blood On The Tracks.* There is no need to bring in one's own views of Dylan's current life and emotional state (which would, in any case, be mostly guesswork; Dylan having until very recently at least kept much of his private life precisely that).

If you do drag your preconceptions in you are being very detrimental to the song and to Dylan himself - turning it into a kind of 'oh look at me how brave I'm being, doing the right thing by my life's true love', while a read of *Behind The Shades*[10] will let you know how far from a balanced viewpoint that would be.

But, but, but... much as I'd like to leave it there, I can't. As we move into the 'live' section of this article I would have to say that no-one who knew anything of Dylan's life in the mid '70s could listen to the 1976 version without thinking it had been affected by - or indeed directly born from - the state of his current relationship(s). Despite all my caveats above, I cannot truthfully tell you that I hear this rendering in any way other than as a direct, personal statement from the artist.

For a master of masks and distancing effects this is an extraordinary performance - no one listening to it can feel anything other than that there is no distance at all between the author-performer and the performance. So what did he sing at Lakeland on April 18th 1976?[11] Something along the lines of:[12]

> *If you see her, say hello*
> *She might be in North Saigon*
> *She left here in a hurry*
> *I don't know what she was on*

*You might say that I'm in disarray*
*And for me time's standing still*
*Oh, I've never gotten over her*
*I don't think I ever will*

*A bright light from me, I saw*
*A shattering of souls*
*Just one of them reckless situations*
*Which nobody controls*
*Well the menagerie of life rolls by*
*Right before my eyes*
*And we'll do the best we can*
*Which should come at no surprise*

*If you're makin' love to her*
*Watch it from the rear*
*You never know when I'll be back*
*Or liable to appear*
*Oh it's natural to dream of peace*
*As it is for rules to break*
*But right now I got not much to lose*
*So you better stay away (awake?)*

*Sundown, silver moon*
*Hitting on the days*
*My head can't understand no more*
*What my heart don't tolerate*
*But I know she'll be back some day*
*Of that there is no doubt*
*And when (the) moment comes, Lord*
*Give me the strength to keep her out.*

There is a rather nasty hint in the opening stanza that the woman was out of control on one substance or another. Clearly, too, the blame is on her not him. In this version, she has rushed off and deserted him for no apparent reason.

The second half of verse one is 'true' in every version but elsewhere is implied, not baldly stated as here. This rendition is clearly going to pull no punches.

In the next verse, the lines:

*Just one of them reckless situations*
*Which nobody controls*

return us to a situation of no blame, like the original '*it was written in the cards*'.

Then we have the whole merry-go-round of life spinning by as he is trying to keep a grip on reality, and a belief in some kind of structured behaviour rather than the sudden inexplicable departure that has left him in 'disarray'.

The most remarkable re-write is of the third verse. Its shocking opening is a complete contrast to the *Blood On The Tracks* version or even the earlier '*if you're makin' love to her, kiss her for the kid*'. This time it is both brutal and brutally expressed. The stanza continues with a dangerous, menacing tone, underpinned by hints of infidelity and hazardous sexual encounters.

The underlying violence even intrudes in the phrase '*hitting on the days*' as the concluding stanza maintains the mesmeric driving spell with:

> *My head can't understand no more*
> *What my heart don't tolerate*

This is magnificent writing. In Lakeland he starts to sing it incorrectly (with *tolerate* where *understand* should be), but quickly corrects himself, instead of just letting it pass. Given that this is a live performance not intended for posterity, it is another sign that he is wrapped up in getting this message out. What a couplet! It is all to do with emotions. The core of the soul is involved in this relationship and no amount of rationalising by the mind can cope with such 'disarray'.

And then there is the ending; a phenomenal articulation of a tension similar to those of previous versions - though with a major difference. The contradiction of 'I want/need/must have her but it is better for her that she's gone' is converted into the despairing 'I want/need/must have her but it'll be the end for me if I ever get her back'.[13]

The song was rewritten once more for the 1978 tour, though again rarely performed; just four times in fact, all in Japan. The lyrics became:

> *If you see her, say hello, she might be in Tangier*
> *She left here last early spring, she's livin' there, I hear*
> *Say for me that I'm all right though things are kind of slow*
> *If she's wonderin' what I'm doin' by now, just tell her that you don't know.*

> *We had a falling-out, like lovers sometimes do*
> *But to think of how she left that night still hurts me kinda through and through*
> *And though our situation, ooh, it hurt me to the bone*
> *She's better off with someone else and I'm better off alone.*

*I see a lot of people as I make the rounds*
*And I hear her name here and there as I go from town to town*
*And I've never gotten used to it and I've learned to turn it off*
*Either I'm too sensitive or else I'm just getting soft.*

*Sundown, yellow moon, I replay the past*
*I know every scene by heart, cause they all went by so fast*
*If she's passin' back this way, most likely I will be gone*
*But if I'm not, just let her know it's best that she stay gone.*

Listening to this, two major differences are immediately apparent: the difficult pivotal verse has been dropped, and the musical arrangement has been transformed again.

The opening stanza ends in a much more offhand way, mirroring the new, jaunty, stop/start musical arrangement. In fact it is almost dismissive but we know - and Dylan knows we know - the previous versions and, even though the crucial 'third' verse has been dropped altogether, there is still enough detail in this version to let us know he's hurting more than he and the music suggest on the surface.

Stanza two lets us know they'll always be together in his heart; the break up in this rendering is portrayed as just one of those things that often happen to lovers. No blame is apportioned. He admits he's hurt but tries to mollify it with that characteristically clever Dylan use of 'kinda', then comes clean over the depth of the hurt in the next line.

Just as we absorb that he turns it around again; when the tension of previous versions is transformed into the astonishing admission:

*She's better off with someone else and I'm better off alone.*

This has changed from the original versions where he needed her but *she* was better off without him; first to 1976's he needed her but *he* was better off without her and then to 1978's she's always in his heart but they are *both* better off without the other!

This leads to a very strange - but nonetheless apt - balancing act in the final verse. What is the point of singing the song (giving her the message) if she is unlikely to come back and, even if she does, he'll most likely not be there (which in is just as well as they are better off apart)? Because it isn't true; or at least it is not the whole truth. This is made clear not only by the lines:

*And though our situation, ooh, it hurt me to the bone*
*She's better off with someone else and I'm better off alone.*

but also because both we listeners and the performing artist are carrying some or all of the previous versions with us as we hear this new one.

And then the song was quickly dropped - shades of '76 - and not resurrected again until 1994. What a pleasant surprise it was when he introduced it in Japan (again), and to this day he still plays the song every now and then. The 'difficult' pivotal verse is still absent and he has returned to the *Blood On The Tracks* version in the main, with occasional couplets from the 1978 version - but the experimentation has not completely stopped. In 1996 he introduced a new ending, a very nice re-write of the last two lines:

> If she's passin' back this way, I'm not so hard to find
> Tell her she can look me up if I'm on her mind

It sounded like he was still hoping![14]

## Afterword

Not long after this article first appeared I received an e-mail from Bev Martin that included the following comments:

> '*In looking for antecedents for this song, I think anyone would be remiss not to include an old jazz/swing song called 'Tell Him I Said Hello'. I do not know who wrote it... similarities in lyric... attitude and song structure also seemed similar but not the melody. The version I heard was by Betty Carter and recorded in 1956.*'

You can imagine how captivated I was by this. A quick trip into the city centre found me scurrying home with a CD entitled *Meet Betty Carter and Ray Bryant* clutched in sweaty paw. This CD was released by Sony/Columbia in 1996 and combines a vinyl release of the same name plus tracks from an earlier Betty Carter compilation called *Social Call*, which is where this performance of 'Tell Him I Said Hello' comes from. And what a great performance it is; leaving aside the Dylan connection for a moment, this is magnificently sung and beautifully played. However, here we are concerned with 'If You See Her, Say Hello', and I can report is that Bev Martin was completely correct. A languorous jazz performance with a strong yet subtle vocal, showcases lines that you feel the radio-hungry teenage Dylan must have heard at some point or another. The song is credited to B. Hagner/J. Canning and goes like this, ending with the breathiest 'hello' imaginable:

> When you see him, tell him things are slow
> There's a reason and he's sure to know
> But, on second thought, forget it

*Just tell him I said hello*
*If he asks you when I come and go*
*Say I stay home 'cos I miss him so*
*But, on second thought, forget it*
*Just tell him I said hello*
*Look into his eyes when you speak my name*
*Maybe there's a spark to start another flame*
*Do I love him? Don't say 'yes' or 'no'*
*If he should ask, but he won't, I know*
*'Cos it's all over and forgotten*
*Just tell him I said hello ... hello*

So still the voyage of discovery continues, a whole world of music with a web of interconnections; because, guess what? There were other things on the same CD that excited me, that connected to other things I listen to - yes, including other Dylan, - and, once heard, Ms. Carter's voice needs to be heard again and again. Thanks, Bev, thanks Betty and thanks, most of all to Bob Dylan for 'If You See Her, Say Hello'.

1. I have always imagined the third person to be a him - something which is implied in other versions and explicit in the live '76 version. There is no evidence to say for sure that it is a he in this rendition, but I will stick to 'him' as we have no dexterous means of expressing 'her/him' in English.
2. Perhaps this was echoed some years later, in the beautiful 'In The Summertime' from *Shot Of Love*: *'Did you respect me for what I did/Or for what I didn't do, or for keeping it hid?'*
3. This original version was later released on *The Bootleg Series*, as were the original version of 'Tangled Up In Blue', an earlier version of 'Idiot Wind' and the very personal out-take 'Call Letter Blues'. *Biograph,* another box set, boasts the original 'You're A Big Girl Now' and the out-take 'Up To Me'.
4. OK - until he dropped the verse altogether that is!
5. *Let It Rock*, London, 01 April 1975
6. I mean no disparagement of the achievements of the younger Mr. Dylan or the genius of Mr. Blake. I am merely trying to point out the contrast, the reason *Blood On The Tracks* hits us right where it matters, every time.
7. Many commentators incorrectly say that it is a result of his divorce - a simple checking of the dates would show that the album came out years before the divorce, but somehow that seems to be beyond their abilities. No wonder this angers Dylan!
8. The *Fiddler Now Upspoke* book series of interviews also has accompanying tapes.
9. Thanks to Peter Vincent and Clinton Heylin for pointing this out.
10. Especially chapter 21 in the updated, 2000 edition *Behind The Shades: Take Two* (Viking Books, published by the Penguin Group).

11. He played this version one more time, at Tallahassee on April 27th.

12. The tape only exists in poor quality; the lyrics above are my attempted transcription with help from others. (In particular, Patricia Jungwirth, Clinton Heylin, Les Kokay and Ben Taylor.)

13. Listeners will recall a similar dichotomy in *Abandoned Love,* a song that is worth comparing to this performance in many ways, for the imagery that is shared, and particularly the terrific - if terrible - tension in both:

> *My head tells me it's time to make a change/But my heart is telling me I love ya but you're strange.*

14. For later live rewrites see this book's supporting website at www.amuir.co.uk/troubadour/

# Twelve

# Nonsense Verse

## Foreword

*Based upon an article from issue 2 of* **Homer,** the slut, *this chapter reminds me of those days of a self-photocopied, free fanzine nearly entirely written by myself (my brother-in-law chipped in with an article on the just-released* under the red sky *too). The same issue carried details of my first exposure to it. I re-read that diary-like entry while updating the main article for inclusion here, and as I did so many memories came flooding back, not just of Dylan-related experiences but of things like my work at the time, the people there, where I was living and so forth. I wish I had similar notes on all my first listens to new Dylan albums; the heightened intensity of one's feelings at those times would open up the way for all the associated recollections.*

*Although it may already have seemed lengthy by fanzine standards, the article - Modes Of Nonsense Verse - was curtailed by time and circumstances into something shorter than the notes I had accumulated could have provided, with even* The Basement Tapes *mentioned only in passing. I will now try to amend that, though the main area of nursery rhymes and their correlation with the folk tradition has already been well and truly mined by Michael Gray in his third edition of* Song & Dance Man. *This fascinating field of study was opened up for me, too, by* under the red sky *and it is one I have been ploughing on and off ever since. Its bountiful acreage provides a seemingly endless crop of education and entertainment in history, literature and all manner of songs - thanks again, Mr. Dylan, for leading me to yet more joys.*

*Another part of the original article and notes, concentrating on the surreal landscapes (and attack on rationalism) of some of Dylan's mid '60s classics is*

*now incorporated into the earlier chapter, 'Too Much Confusion'. To save repli-*
*cation those are only alluded to in the body of this chapter, though this is not to*
*be taken as downplaying their significance.*

*On the other hand, as well as widening the scope of nonsense verse to include*
*more works by Dylan than the original piece had, I have also expanded my look*
*at the* under the red sky *album to include commentary on the songs that do not*
*fully fit within the main nursery rhyme and folk-fable core of that album.*

### Part one: Nonsense Verse

*Met the King and Queen and a company of men*
*A-walkin' behind and a-riding before.*
*A stark naked drummer came walking along*
*With his hands in his bosom a-beating his drum.*
*Sat down on a hot and cold frozen stone,*
*Ten thousand stood round me yet I was alone.[1]*
*Took my heart in my hand to keep my head warm*
*Ten thousand got drowned that never were born.*

The verses above come from the song 'Nottamun Town'. This seems to me
to be the world of *under the red sky*, and not simply because of the felicitous
coincidence of the number 10,000. The mystery, the depth of feeling/meaning
in folk nonsense poetry, the paradoxical sequentiality of the non sequiturs,
the oral/biblical/folk nursery rhyme world; these were what I was after.

The number did, though, set me off on a trail of Dylan associations. The
use of such numbers, (impressive, nice sound, nice round number) is
common enough. Hearing '10,000 Men' on the Dylan album reminded of
these lines and reminded me also that I'd first listened to 'Nottamun Town'
because I had read that Dylan took the tune for 'Masters Of War' from
'Nottamun Town'. I looked for a copy of 'Nottamun Town' at home, only to
discover that I no longer had the Fairport Convention album I had heard it
on. The next day I went to a library near work to look it up and the first
volume of nonsense poetry I came across was *The Chatto Book Of Nonsense*,
edited by Hugh Haughton. Mr. Haughton ends the introduction to his selec-
tions with the following:

> *But of all modern American poets, it is perhaps Bob Dylan who makes*
> *the most memorable use of nonsense in his vernacular-oracular songs,*
> *especially such junkyard do-it-yourself mythological poems as 'Ballad*
> *Of A Thin Man' and 'Desolation Row'.[2]*

Serendipity indeed!

On the other hand, the coincidences and connections are not so far-fetched. Dylan's affiliations with the folk/oral traditions are well known and documented. It is not surprising that he should produce lyrics which set me thinking of 'Nottamun Town'. It is also not surprising that Dylan should appear in an anthology of nonsense poetry. What at first appeared as a 'coincidence' is, instead, the result of a chain of influences.

Dylan has utilised 'nonsense verse' at various points throughout his career, and I propose to highlight these in this article. I should start by saying that the term 'nonsense verse' covers a wide variety of forms and approaches. The songs Mr. Haughton refers to above, for example, are of a different strand to those of *under the red sky*, a different mode of nonsense verse. The field of nonsense verse is far larger than one might at first suppose. Consider this definition from the introduction:

> *Nonsense poetry is less a genre than a possibility, a dimension, a boundary which poetry touches more frequently than we usually imagine. It may take the form of nursery-rhyme, utopian protest, riddle, parody, fable, automatic writing, mad song, limerick, futurist experiment, learned joke, satire or jeu d'esprit, but at its heart lies a playful formal inventiveness and delight in transgression, a protest against the arbitrariness of order and an affirmation of the pleasure principle applied to language.*[3]

With such a wide ranging 'net' it is difficult to see where 'nonsense verse' would stop and non-nonsense verse would start. For example, Mr. Haughton can easily justify the inclusion of 'Ballad Of A Thin Man' and 'Desolation Row' in his discussion of nonsense verse and a further two ('Tiny Montgomery', 'Don't Ya Tell Henry') in his anthology. He is correct to emphasise how many kinds of what we tend to casually group together as 'nonsense' verse there actually are. To appreciate how these impinge on Dylan's songwriting, I need to examine the different modes of nonsense that Dylan utilises. For example, I think it fairly obvious that the last two songs mentioned above inhabit a radically different milieu to the first pair.

In practical terms it is almost impossible to have a definitive definition of nonsense, because the term is used to cover a multitude of different but related things, some of which, as we will discover, can be considered 'nonsense' in a wide sense but would run counter to any strict definition. To delimit a grouping of nonsense verse that matched a philosophical or linguistic exactitude would be to debar a multitude of all kinds of what we

**149**

normally recognise as 'nonsense songs'. That is not my aim; rather, I am specifically interested in the different modes of nonsense, sheltering under that umbrella term, which appear in the songs of Bob Dylan.

I am going to look at Dylan's use of nonsensical verse in the following ways; first I will look at his use of it in a specifically modernist way, then survey the many strands of nonsense verse we can find within his oeuvre, and finally examine his use of nursery rhymes, particularly in relation to *under the red sky*.

### 'Modernism' and nonsense verse

Dylan's admiration for the works of Rimbaud is well known. To quote again from Mr. Haughton's introduction:

> *...Such receptivity to the nonsensical has been a hallmark of much modern culture, with our premium on making it new, and our attraction towards making it stranger and stranger. Rimbaud claimed to have a key to the 'parade sauvage', and the late nineteenth-century Symbolisme of Mallarmé and Rimbaud created a new mystique around French poetic language in its search for the unknown by 'le dérèglement de tous les sens'- ...[4]*

Add to this the great art movements of surrealism, impressionism *et al*, following on from the philosophical and psychological works of such thinkers as Freud and Jung, and you have a very 20th Century feel to certain artistic uses of the nonsensical. This certainly had a direct effect on Dylan's work in the sixties as did, whether directly or indirectly, Sartre and Camus's theories of existentialism and of the absurd. Theories which have generated a peculiarly post-WWII outlook on life, and whose notion of 'the absurd' is at the hub of the type of nonsense verses that Mr. Haughton illustrates in part by including Bob Dylan's lyrics to 'Ballad Of A Thin Man' and 'Desolation Row'.

### Symbolism And Surrealism

One way to achieve, through verse, 'le dérèglement de tous les sens' was to overburden the language of the poem until the referential nature of the language broke under the strain. The 'sense' was buried under an avalanche of images and impressions. See, for example, the following from Oliver Bernard's translation of Rimbaud's *The Drunken Boat* (for Penguin classics):

> *Libre, fumant, monté de brumes violettes,*
> *Moi qui trouais le ciel rougeoyant comme un mur*
> *Qui porte, confiture exquise aux bonns poëtes,*

*Des lichens de soliel et des morves d'azur;*
*Qui courais, taché de lunules électriques*
*Planche folle, escorté des hippocampes noirs,*
*Quand les juillets faisaient crouler à coup de triques*
*Le cieux ultramarins aux ardents entonnoirs*

**Trans.**

*free, smoking, risen from violet fogs,*
*I who bored through the wall of the reddening sky*
*which bears a sweetmeat good poets find delicious:*
*lichens of sunlight [mixed] with azure snot;*
*who ran, speckled with lunula of electricity,*
*a crazy plank with black sea horses for escort,*
*when Julys were crushing with cudgel blows*
*skies of ultramarine into burning funnels*

However impressive one finds this, it is undeniably 'difficult' - to quote a common response to modern poetry. However, when Dylan is overburdening the language in his verse, he has the incalculable advantage of his music. So, when, say, 'Sad Eyed Lady Of The Lowlands' ventures into the realm of nonsense verse for all the wrong reasons, we can still be led on a warm and intriguing emotional and mental journey by Dylan's voice and music and the free floating words, devoid perhaps of an anchor of meaning but attractive as part of the overall soundscape.[5]

Alluring though the charms of 'Sad Eyed Lady Of The Lowlands' are, I am not using them as an excuse to 'write off' what I perceive as seriously flawed - if at times inspired - lyrics. Play 'Visions Of Johanna' from the same album and compare it with 'Sad Eyed Lady Of The Lowlands'. Which do you prefer? For me, and I would find it hard to imagine anyone disagreeing, it is 'Visions'; and the reason is the lyrics. I love 'Sad Eyed Lady' but not as much as 'Visions' which is clearly superior - notwithstanding that they both have exquisite melodies, sublime vocal performances and, to a degree, share a similar lyrical approach. 'Visions' has more precision of referential meaning and this makes it a more enriching experience. I like language to have a certain degree of referential meaning; though I trust I'm not blind to the reasons why sometimes symbolists push beyond this in their struggle with the use of language, with the very nature of language itself.

In every verse there can be good and bad; this is as true of impressionist, symbolist or surrealist writing as any other. Modern poetry is difficult not only for the reader, it is also an immense challenge for the poet, or, post-Dylan, the songwriter. And it is a challenge which provoked an outpouring of unintentional nonsense verse from most trying to ape Dylan's success with these forms. Risible lyrics from an unholy mixture of sub-hippie idealism and sixth form exercises in surrealism seemed to affect everyone from the self-styled 'poets of the inner self singer songwriter school' even to the before-this-could-seem-to-do-no-wrong Beatles. I am not implying that Dylan ever produced anything in this style of writing that was as lacking in taste as any of these, but in the likes of 'Sad Eyed Lady Of The Lowlands' he sometimes strays too close for comfort.

On the other hand, as he was nearly always sure-footed, and since his single-handed creation of the modernist popular song (with his uncanny mastery in combining the likes of the beat of Chuck Berry and the pen of Rimbaud) will probably be remembered by posterity as his greatest achievement, it is perhaps unfair to Dylan to complain about what this inspired in 'artists' following the usual pop formula of copying what is new and successful.

Instead we should dwell on his own achievements in song. The most towering accomplishment of his symbolist verse (and one that has a very strong case for being his best song) is the aforementioned 'Visions Of Johanna'. The melody, the voice and the lyrics are all 'perfect', all contributing equally to the whole. The lyrics here - unusually - would stand as major poetry in their own right, but how much *fuller* the work is when heard. And, incredibly, we have more than one version that reaches these elevated artistic heights. The contemporaneous lyric alternates that we know of are of equal standard to those of the album track. Likewise Dylan's performances on the alternate takes and in the live shows of that time enrich and enlarge the work of art that is 'Visions Of Johanna'. Dylan had produced a song that stood at the forefront of 20th Century artistic thought and practice. To achieve this in a field of popular entertainment aimed at the youth market was an achievement that is still hard to measure, so profound an effect has it had. In Mr Haughton's views this would be a verse fit for his anthology alongside the preceding album's 'Desolation Row'.

His all-encompassing maw could also sweep up three consecutive lyrics from Dylan's official lyric book, *Lyrics 1962-1985*, namely: 'Farewell Angelina', 'Mr. Tambourine Man' and 'Gates Of Eden'. These would be included for their overtly surrealist conceits and are discussed elsewhere in this book. Also discussed, in the chapter 'Too Much Confusion', are the lyrics from that period which attack an over-reliance on rationalist thought.

Mr Haughton writes about 'Ballad Of A Thin Man' and 'Desolation Row', not only for their surrealist wit but also for this reason, which, in his definition, makes them flag carriers in the march of 'non-sense'. Much of that earlier chapter is applicable here, too, and although I want to move on to more recognisable modes of nonsense verse there is one particular strand of modern thought that is highly pertinent to this chapter, that of existentialism. This slant to modern nonsense verse sprang, with apt absurdity, from a Christian philosopher's ruminations on the implications of facing up to the concept of a seemingly meaningless existence.

### Existentialism: philosophy of the absurd

The connection between the existentialists and nonsense verse comes from their concept of the absurd, not for the existentialists in the sense of 'comic' but as an insight brought upon by realising that human life has no order, no underlying structure. Sartre called this experience *nausea,* a perfect term for the effect caused when one recognizes the framework upon which we conduct our daily lives is arbitrary.

Similar thoughts have been pervasive in literature ever since Nietzsche said, 'God is dead', whether or not the writer is thought of as an existentialist. Joseph Conrad - a writer whose work we know Dylan is well acquainted with – provides a prime example of an artistic expression of this moment of recognition and the 'nausea' it induces in his novel *Lord Jim.*

To return to Sartre, however, his belief was that once we have realised that despite there being no point to it, existence is still all we've got (we cannot just withdraw from it - barring suicide), we are totally free. Yet this was a freedom that made 'no sense'. Our 'dreadful human freedom' consisted of being totally free to choose what we think and do because there is no external order, no moral framework to work within. What value then does such a freedom have, how does one then act, or define oneself? The burden of responsibility in making this choice may seem light if existence is meaningless; on the contrary, secular existentialists concluded that man could only progress from his state of nausea by imposing his own arbitrary order on the world and living by that. The consequences from whatever decision he took with his 'dreadful freedom' are then his and his alone. Add this to the inevitable contingencies of life in a community and this was to make each individual assume a burden of responsibility so great it had hitherto only been placed on the shoulders of an omnipotent God.

I am conscious that I am condensing the writings of major philosophers into a few lines, and that this is not a book on philosophy. My concise overview is merely to set the scene for how this impinged on Dylan's writing. You can feel the impact of such thoughts beginning to affect Dylan's verse in songs such as 'It's Alright, Ma':

> *You lose yourself, you reappear*
> *You suddenly find you got nothing to fear*
> *Alone you stand with nobody near…*
> *…A question in your nerves is lit*
> *Yet you know there is no answer fit to satisfy*
> *Insure you not to quit*
> *To keep it in your mind and not fergit*
> *That it is not he or she or them or it*
> *That you belong to*

Also, the world depicted in many of the songs of the seminal mid-sixties' trilogy, *Bringing It All Back Home*, *Highway 61 Revisited* and *Blonde On Blonde*, is often absurdist. Its population includes many people who evade looking beyond a meaningless, 'surface' world, people who are caught, not able or willing to confront their 'dreadful freedom'; not 'crawling out their windows' or 'leaving their stepping stones behind'. It's a nightmare world that Dylan recalls, glancing back, as it were, from the overtly biblical standpoint of 'All Along The Watchtower'. There, Dylan sings:

> *'There must be some way out of here', said the joker to the thief,*
> *'There's too much confusion, I can't get no relief'*

This world of 'too much' confusion was to be found out on Dylan's pop-mythological road, 'Highway 61'. In modern street language tied to a rock beat, this song's opening verse succinctly recreates the starting point of all modern philosophy connected to existentialism. That sounds *absurd* all by itself, doesn't it? Yet consider this. The father of existentialism was the inspired Danish theologian, philosopher and writer, Sören Kierkegaard. Kierkegaard's philosophical thinking led him to believe that man's earthly existence was spent in a meaningless world, a frightening and pitiful existence. Sartre, Camus et al took this view and built upon in secular terms. For Kierkegaard, though, there was no humanist solution to the malaise of this existence. For him, the only thing that could save man was a leap of blind faith that would lead to a wholehearted belief in a God there was no evident reason to believe in. In Kierkegaard's view, God was completely hidden from man, so true believers had to pass the test of believing in Him when they had no reason to do so.

To make the test even harder, God deliberately set out to show the world as completely irrational and belief in him as absurd. This absurdity - the first time the existential theory of the absurd was propagated - was unveiled in his fictional teaching *Fear and Trembling*. The main protagonist of the story has to demonstrate complete faith by carrying out an order from God that is not only absurd, flying in the face of all reason, but also cruel, unjust and an affront to human nature. He must make a leap of blind faith and kill his own son for God to make him a leader that can guide his people to Salvation. The test of faith is the sole reason for this barbarous and absurd request. You may know the story already because this character is called Abraham and his son, Isaac.

> *Oh God said to Abraham, 'Kill me a son'*
> *Abe says, 'Man, you must be puttin' me on'*
> *God says, 'No.' Abe says, 'What ?'*
> *God says, 'You can do what you want Abe, but*
> *The next time you see me comin' you better run'*
> *Well Abe says, 'Where do you want this killin' done ?'*
> *God says. 'Out on Highway 61'*

The existential theory of the absurd seems linked to the comic absurd only in a black-humour sense, but they do share a common root, as the use of the word for this philosophical position suggests. Without order, everything can seem meaningless and in that state the daily routines and tasks that we all undertake, the great political dramas of the day and so forth seem comically pointless. Nor can one assign any particular degree of importance to one thing or another.

Both meanings of the absurd are captured perfectly in the peerless 'Clothes Line Saga' on *The Basement Tapes*. The absurdity of daily surface reality is captured nowhere more pointedly, or delightfully, than in this little masterpiece of a song. The title itself is the first comic touch. This 'saga' is as far removed from the epic Norse tales that classically use that title as one can imagine. Gods, nations and races may rise and fall in the heroic sagas but a clothes line saga? It's a tale about bringing in clothes from the clothes line once they have dried. Great speeches and songs and long tales of wonder fill the Scandinavian Legends but here, well, as the second line puts it: *'nobody said very much'*.

Even when someone does speak it is not with the intention of communicating properly. The merest suspicion of such is immediately challenged, and the speaker almost apologetically explains away his act of speaking as meaningless. The 'meaty action of the saga' is then returned to in silence:

*Mama come in and picked up a book*
*An' Papa asked her what it was*
*Someone else asked, 'What do you care?'*
*Papa said, 'Well, just because'*
*Then they started to take back their clothes*
*Hang 'em on the line*

Yet much is revealed in the song. Like a master short story teller unveiling a whole tableau with great economy, Dylan paints us a scene and populates it with characters that stay with us long after this haunting little number ends. He achieves this mostly through what he has them say and how he sings what they say, allowing the listener to pick up on the implications of what they do *not* say. It is his vocal delivery that imparts the underlying meanings and feelings because, as we have already noted, *'nobody said very much'*.

Over a desultory backing, The Band expertly depicting the required atmosphere with a tune that seems as though it's too tired to actually get anywhere, Dylan delivers this 'not very much' in a deadpan, hick voice that seems to contain not only a fully formed individual identity but also that of the community he lives in. He does something similar, though not in the first person, in 'Po' Boy' from *"Love And Theft"*. There are a myriad of connecting threads that run through *The Basement Tapes, under the red sky* and *"Love And Theft"*, many of them deriving from the use of 'nonsense verse'.

The conversations he sings in 'Clothes Line Saga' are an exercise in what is known as phatic communion. That is when things are said either to fulfil some kind of social convention or simply as a sign of sociability. To follow my short story analogy, perhaps the most splendid use of this in the whole of literature is the question *'is it still snowing'* in James Joyce's *The Dead*.

It is apparent too in daily life. Entire conversations are conducted throughout Britain daily in which the words used have no meaning whatsoever, 'It's a nice day, isn't it?' on a nice day, for example. People say things out of habit, because it is what one does, the meaning of the words has long been stripped bare. Add to all the weather examples that instantly spring to mind daily greetings such as: 'How are you' or 'Long time no see, how's life been treating you?' The answers to these questions are not, 'Glad you asked, as I am ageing I am finding my memory going a bit and my left leg stiffens up in bad weather. In addition I have a rather nasty toothache that comes and goes and...' and 'Well, life has been treating me in a variety of ways over the last seven years, first of all I had a stroke of good luck...' No, the answer is 'Fine, and you?' To which the speaker of the original question replies 'Fine'.

In other words, 'nobody says very much'.

'*Mama, of course, she said, 'Hi*' intones Dylan in a delightful line encapsulating phatic communion's' meaning and purpose. In this song where, naturally, '*everybody was feelin' fine*', people 'communicate' in virtually no other way. The neighbour asks banal questions about clothes drying because that is all there is to ask about, not because he cares which clothes belong to whom. (Realising, like the father did belatedly, that even this small talk is going a bit far he blows his nose to distract from his effrontery, just as the father began taking back the clothes to distract from his.)

The important piece of news:

> '*Have you heard the news?*' *he said with a grin*
> '*The Vice President's gone mad*'

is treated with not much more attention than the question about who the drying clothes belong to. There's a brief spark of questioning but it is not with genuine curiosity, empathy or any degree of engagement and soon all settles back down again into utter mundanity.

> '*Where?*' '*Downtown.*' '*When?*' '*Last night*'
> '*Hmm, say, that's too bad*'
> *Well, there's nothing we can do about it,*' *said the neighbor*
> '*It's just somethin' we're gonna have to forget*'
> '*Yes, I guess so*' *said Ma*
> *Then she asked me if the clothes was still wet*

Clinton Heylin, in researching his *Recording Sessions* book, discovered that the song was originally entitled 'Answer to an Ode [To Billy Jo *(sic)*]'. Thus removing a blindfold from all commentators who had hitherto missed the connection between Dylan's recorded-for-private-listening-only masterpiece and a record that had dominated the charts and airwaves of America in August, 1967.

Bobby Gentry, Capitol Records sixties siren, had recorded a single called 'Mississippi Delta'. The b-side was a song called 'Ode To Billie Joe'. DJ interest in this flip side soon saw it shortened by over two minutes and strings added as it was turned into an A-side. A healthy placing in the UK top 20 was only a fraction of the success this had Stateside, where it topped the charts. The hook was the mystery of the thing, emphasised by the brevity of the tale. A family dinner is the setting for the news that Billy Joe has committed suicide by jumping off the Tallahatchie Bridge. The song tells the tale almost off-stage as it were, it occurs almost as an aside to their dinner table talk, as does the death of the family father in the postscript that is the last verse. The only clue in the song as to why Billy Joe killed himself is that he and a girl were seen throwing something off the same bridge. The nation was obsessed with knowing what that something was and why it drove him to take his own life.

On first hearing it, years later, I thought that the clear intent was that the girl had had an abortion at Billy Joe's insistence and they had disposed of its remains and then the guilt had driven him to commit suicide. I would presume this was a popular interpretation, but it would clearly be wrong to suppose it was what everyone would think. Other people had their own ideas and probably would have thought everyone should think like they did too - hence the debates and hence the attraction of the song. There was even a film made out of the song, *Ode To Billy Joe* (1976), which portrayed Billy Joe throwing his girlfriend's rag-doll over the bridge and gave a homosexual affair as the reason for his suicide. Bobbie Gentry, very smartly, never commented on any of the theories.

She did however, get to the core of the song in an interview for *Billboard* that is quoted by Greil Marcus in his detailed look at 'Billy Joe' in *Invisible Republic*. Among other observations she said:

> *...everybody seems more concerned with what was thrown off the bridge than they are with the thoughtlessness of people in the song...the real message of the song...revolves around the way the family talks about the suicide. They sit there eating their peas and apple pie and talking, without even realizing that Billy Joe's girlfriend is sitting at the table, a* member of the family.

And

> *The song is a sort of study in unconscious cruelty.*

Rather than '*a study in unconscious cruelty*', Dylan presents us with 'a study in unconscious living'. It is a lack of existential awareness that Dylan highlights so magnificently in his song. His characters are absolutely ripe for an existentialist epiphany that will illuminate the pointlessness of their lives to them, inducing in them a nausea that can only be recovered from by taking control of their lives and shaping their individual destiny and all that entails. Somehow you just know that this is not going to happen. It's better maybe not to realise anything ever; yep, the seasons are turning, nights are fair drawing in, time to shut all of them darn doors, settle down for winter and every now and then ask: '*is it still snowing?*'

Dylan's 'saga' is not so much an 'answer' to Gentry's 'ode'; rather he extends it to cover all of America, and by extension all of mankind's absurd existence. The deadpan understatement, the meaningless of actions be they vice presidents going mad or clothes being taken in, and the utter lack of real communication, leading to isolation rather than community[6] (the song ends with the line *'And then I shut all the doors'*); all of this screams out : 'Is this all there really is, is this the sum of our existence?' In this way a little absurdist short story in song imparts a great deal of sense to those with ears to listen to Dylan's words and delivery, a 'nonsense song' talking profound sense.

However, the treasures to be found in this bountiful Basement also contain pure unadulterated nonsense. 'Clothes Line Saga', as we have seen, is a sort of pastiche song, though much more than that (as is Dylan's demonic and almost worryingly personal take on Bobby Bare's 'All American Boy'). Parodies and pastiches are to be found throughout both *The Basement Tapes* and nonsense verse, as are burlesques, satire and inversion. A whole genre of parody and burlesque, that of the carnival with its geeks and grotesquerie, forms one of the most venerable of nonsense verse modes. In 'Ballad Of A Thin Man' Dylan, using plain everyday language, adroitly employs more than one of the modes of nonsense verse I have addressed so far. In stanza three he uses carnival images to marvellous effect.

> *You hand in your ticket*
> *And you go watch the geek*
> *Who immediately walks up to you*
> *When he hears you speak*
> *And says, 'How does it feel*
> *To be such a freak ?'*
> *And you say, 'Impossible'*
> *As he hands you a bone*

Mister Jones is now quite explicitly faced with a crisis of identity - who is the geek and who is the freak? Mister Jones's values are being inverted, for him language and reality are breaking down. The geek, on the other hand, comes across as being perfectly at ease. In 'Desolation Row' the carnival holds up a mirror to 'normal society' that shows it, rather than the carnival, to be a place of inverted values.

### Gibberish

Parody, inversion and the carnival all contribute to a 'nonsense verse' that is the polar opposite of the meaningless nature of absolute nonsense, which I want to look at now. In these mad creations nothing makes an iota of sense. They cannot be rationally analysed or explained in other words, that is their very raison d'être.

It may seem surprising, but songs like these are difficult both to create and to enjoy. When it is successfully done the sheer, overwhelming pleasure both for the creator and the audience is unmistakable and cannot be produced in any other way.

The reason it is so difficult to capture this precious pleasure, so deep it feels like a surge of freedom in our otherwise suddenly grey-seeming lives, is that the artist is a rational being creating something with shape and starting and ending points - yet somehow he has to convey utter gibberish. There's an almost irresistible urge to infuse meaning into the verses; the main way this is overcome is for the creator to be swept away by the pleasure of creation to a point approaching a kind of inspired madness. Once he has captured that near-lunatic burst of exuberant expression we, the audience, can share in the enjoyment. Or at least sometimes we can, because despite the artists' efforts on our behalf to share the liberating joy of his nonsense, we too can spoil it by 'straining for meaning'. It is difficult to stop ourselves because this is, after all, a natural human reaction.

To take a mundane example, first, think of the level of irritation you feel when trying to read or think on a train journey when someone in the carriage is engaged in a mobile phone conversation. These annoy us because we 'strain for meaning', only hearing one side of the conversation means our minds cannot just take the conversation as whole and mentally place it aside. Therefore it is much more irritating than a conversation of equal volume between two people in the same carriage.

In terms of being entertained by nonsense, this inbuilt tendency to reach for meaning is counter-productive. Scholars have pored over the famous nonsense literature of Rabelais to such lengths that linguistic structures have been found to underpin even the most nonsensical of passages. One is not sure whether to admire their scholastic determination or kick their behinds for spoiling the fun.

Later in this article we will be looking at nursery rhymes; again their inherent joy is not enough for some people. Instead, they construct elaborate – but completely without foundation – 'explanations' of the meanings behind innocent outpourings of nonsense verse.

Due to our desire for meaning, these explanations can seem very convincing. Until, due to the release of *under the red sky,* I began reading and listening to nursery rhymes and exploring their history, I had believed the much repeated theory that 'Ring a ring a-roses' was a macabre dance 'celebrating' the great plague. A simple joining up of historical dates I already knew and a glance at the real symptoms the plague caused would have led me to look more closely and see there was no basis for this. Yet this false 'interpretation' seemed not just plausible but *right*, so strongly do we 'strain for meaning'.

How does pure nonsense overcome this need of ours for sense? I have suggested above that it is by a kind of high-spirited, liberating madness. You can hear this not only in new Dylan creations on *The Basement Tapes* but also in his and The Band's over-the-top covers like 'I'm Your Teenage Prayer' and 'You Gotta Quit Kickin' My Dog Around'. You have to listen to them and others like 'Next Time On The Highway' and 'See You Later Alligator/Allen Ginsberg' to hear what I am getting at, the whole point being that I cannot recreate the feeling in rational prose for you, you have to experience them.

Dylan's creations that most encapsulate the purest nonsense are 'Apple Suckling Tree', which we will look at a little later, and 'You Ain't Goin' Nowhere' (the first, unsanitised, *'head of lettuce'* version). This last is true meaningless gibberish; it makes no sense, nor does it 'play' on or off something that does make sense.

> *Now look here, dear Sue (suit? Zoot?)*[7]
> *You best feed the cats*
> *The cats need feedin'*
> *You're the one to do it*
> *Get your hat, feed the cats*
> *You ain't goin' nowhere.*
>
> *(chorus):*
>
> *Oh, oh, ride me high*
> *Tomorrow's the day*
> *That my bride's a-gonna come*
> *Whoo-ee, are we gonna set*
> *Down in the easy chair.*
>
> *Look here you bunch of basement noise*
> *You ain't no punchin' bag*
> *I see you walkin' out there*
> *And you're the one to do it*
> *Pick up your nose, you canary*
> *You ain't goin' nowhere.*
>
> *Chorus*
>
> *Just pick up that oil cloth*
> *Cram it in the corn*
> *I don't care if your name is Michael*

*You're gonna need some boards*
*Get your lunch you foreign bib*
*You ain't goin' nowhere.*

*Chorus*

*Now, look here, you pile o' money*
*You best go to (the) fair to find a file*
*I see out you out there beatin' on your hammer*
*You ain't no head of lettuce*
*Feed that buzzard*
*Lay him on a rug*
*You ain't goin' nowhere.*

*Chorus*

### 'Relative' Nonsense Verse

As opposed to that absolute nonsense verse there is also something we can refer to as 'relative nonsense'. This is where each line or couplet or verse makes sense in itself and it is only by putting two or more beside each other that it creates nonsense. This can be a fun exercise for anybody from children to folk song writers, indeed there are even a number of literary movements that have utilised the same techniques. Noel Malcolm discusses this in detail in his *Origins Of English Nonsense:*

> The 'medley' took up the form of a popular song or ballad and turned it into nonsense by stringing together a series of unconnected lines or couplets. This is a type of poem which seems to have sprung up quite suddenly in England in the mid sixteenth century... The basic principle on which these poems work is clear: they guy the inconsequentiality of popular songs and ballads, suggesting that it makes little difference which order the lines come in, or from which different songs they are derived.

There is an element of this in *The Basement Tapes*, though as far as the lyrics go this is more due to the way they were created, with half-remembered lines being completed or rhythmically matched on the hoof:

> We were doing seven, eight, ten, sometimes fifteen songs a day. Some were old ballads and traditional songs...but others Bob would make up as he went along...We'd play the melody, he'd sing a few words he'd written, then, make up some more, or even syllables as he went along. It's a pretty good way to write songs.

Garth Hudson[8]

What Dylan and The Band do consistently is to achieve the same debunking of popular song by their musical and vocal deliveries. A further twist to the origins of nonsense verse was a later development of the medley into the 'catch', a form of singing lines from various poems or songs in a new arrangement by multiple voices. This form proved popular and endured over a long time, undoubtedly having a deep effect on the development of nonsense balladry, and thus affecting both the folk tradition that has been the bedrock of so much of Dylan's writing and the nursery rhyme tradition he mined for *under the red sky*.

It is also worth noting that the technique of the medley is, as Mr Malcolm points out, itself a pastiche of a serious literary form, that of the *cento*. This school of writing took the lines of classical poets and created new texts from them; the same technique Dylan had employed sporadically with folk material in his earlier career, and would return to fully embrace, with stunning effect, on *"Love And Theft"* and, with more mixed success, in the nursery-rhyme songs on *under the red sky*.

### Bawdy

A somewhat less-exalted, but ever-present and much-loved form of nonsense verse is that of bawdy rhymes and songs. From venerable poets to the local rugby club, bawdy is created, preserved and endlessly enjoyed. So widespread are bawdy songs that they even influence nursery rhymes to a surprising extent. Perhaps because pornographic and satirical new verses appeared along with ballad broadsheets and nurses (nannies) often sang what they remembered of ballads from those broadsheets to what were, after all, non-understanding ears.

In Dylan's work bawdy appears here and there, as you'd expect from someone steeped in the blues, but nowhere more consistently and vividly than in the good-time bonhomie nonsense of *The Basement Tapes*. With a relish that recalls the forays into beer and bawdy of another famous popular poet, songwriter and folk music enthusiast Robert Burns, Dylan and the band go rolling down New Orleans' Bourbon Street and whoop it up in Mrs Henry's combined bar and brothel. The drinking buddies having fun can be heard all over the collection; in 'Silhouette' and 'Bring It Home' the listener is all but dropped into debauched revelry. It's hard, though, for anything to top 'Please Mrs Henry' for bawdy nonsense:

> *Now, I'm startin' to drain*
> *My stool's gonna squeak*
> *If I walk too much farther*

*My crane's gonna leak*
*Look, Missus Henry*
*There's only so much I can do*
*Why don't you look my way*
*And pump me a few ?*

With their double entendres and promiscuous settings bawdy songs form a subset of the most prevalent of all nonsense verses, those of the Comic. Dylan showed himself to be a master of this early in his career, especially in his early talking blues. Examples abound, and I'm sure we all have our favourites - here's the one I chose as my favourite back when I first wrote about this in 1990:

*Well, I wake up in the morning*
*There's frogs inside my socks*
*Your mama, she's a-hidin'*
*Inside the icebox*
*Your daddy walks in wearin'*
*A Napoleon Bonaparte mask*
*Then you ask why I don't live here*
*Honey, do you have to ask ?*
*Well, I got to pet your monkey*
*I get a face full of claws*
*I ask who's in the fireplace*
*And you tell me Santa Claus*
*The milkman comes in*
*He's wearing a Derby hat*
*And you ask why I don't live here*
*Honey, how come you have to ask me that ?*

Comic verse has been important throughout Dylan's career, from the earliest recordings to the latest. (At the time I write this, *"Love And Theft"*; the use of comic verse there is something I will discuss in the chapter on that album.) For now, though, I want to move on, in part two of this chapter, to discuss *under the red sky*. Before even that most basic of all nonsense verse, the comic, we hear, as infants, nursery rhymes. It is these that form the foundation of *under the red sky*, and their influence that provoked so much ignorant derision.

**Part Two: Nursery Rhymes**

So strong was that derision that one almost feels a necessity to rush to the defence of the form, to point out that Blake, one of Western Literature's foremost poets, made use of it, that the closely aligned world of the fairy tale has been shown to contain profound psychic truths. To proclaim, as Michael Gray eloquently does, that:

> ...*nursery rhyme has a value as a venerable yet living, expressive form of folklore - one with its own internal logic and integrity, celebrating the vibrancy of direct yet magical language. When Dylan comes to use it so thoroughgoingly on 'Under The Red Sky' he is exploring one more form of Anglo-American folk culture and another part of his roots.*[9]

There really should be no need to do so, but the prejudice against their delightful contributions to life and literature is so ingrained that it is difficult to begin on any other foot but the back one. Let's look instead at the previous history of nursery rhyme in Dylan's music.

A musician Dylan admires, Buddy Guy, did 'Mary Had A Little Lamb' and Guthrie and Lead Belly both wrote and performed children's songs. Dylan has name-checked Lead Belly's children's songs, as well as mentioning in interview (though one takes his interview comments under consideration only with the usual caveats) that he'd like to do an album of such songs himself. A year after *under the red sky* he did record a delightful version of 'This Old Man' for *Disney For Children* (Disney Records). In his preaching days he also gave us 'Man Gave Names To All The Animals', a surprise hit in France and a jukebox option in much of Southern Europe.

There are all manner of musical echoes of earlier Dylan in this album, and a large number of lyrical echoes too. Examples include the lines:

> *Scale that wall and smoke that vine*
> *Feed that horse and saddle up the drum*

which have got up and left *The Basement Tapes* milieu (see 'Please, Mrs Henry'); as has the delicious pun of '*God knows it's outta sight*'. The repeated questions beginning '*How many*' in the bridges of '2x2' bring 'Blowin' In The Wind' to mind. The description of the wolf in 'Cat's In The Well': '*He got his big bushy tail dragging all over the ground*', is the language of 'Man Gave Names To All The Animals' (as you'd expect it to be).

In Part One of this chapter I spent some time on *The Basement Tapes* as a fount of nonsense verse, so you'll not be surprised to find a strong nursery rhyme connection there too. That collection shares with nursery rhymes a galaxy of eccentrically named individuals (Tiny Montgomery, Skinny Moo, Half-track - though you may know him as T-bone - Frank, Turtle and so forth), the naming being for delight of sound, silliness and perhaps adding a piece of deft characterisation as in 'The Mighty Quinn'. In the liner notes to his *Biograph* collection, Dylan says of that song *'I don't know what it was about, I guess it was some kind of nursery rhyme'.*

I guess it was too, as was 'Apple Suckling Tree'. About the only sure thing in this song is that the lovers will be happily alone under the tree. You can certainly pick up on allusions to various old folk and children's songs, and perhaps, just perhaps, the tree refers to the Garden Of Eden. None of this can be assumed with the slightest degree of certainty, but it matters not a jot. What we experience is the joy of listening to an absolutely charming song. If its lack of specificity bothers you, you're probably one of those bothered by *under the red sky*, because this is the same terrain: children's nonsense verse and nursery rhymes with their disjointed causes and effects, weird lists and recurrence of numbers, underpinned by tales from the Bible and the oral tradition. The last verse of 'Apple Suckling Tree' from *Lyrics* could surely fit straight into *under the red sky*:

> Now, who's on the table, who's to tell me?
> Oh Yeah!
> Who's on the table, who's to tell me?
> Oh Yeah!
> Who should I tell, oh, who should I tell?
> The forty-nine of you like bats out of hell
> Oh underneath that old apple suckling tree

As Paul Williams has written in his *Performing Artist*, volume one:

> *...this is a nonsense song. Dylan is singing in tongues, and no amount of messing with the lyrics could make the song more joyous or more universal than it already is... it demonstrates exuberantly the universal musical principles that underlie and unify folk music and rock and roll... Unquestionably it draws on that great reservoir of mystery that Dylan has spoken of as a characteristic part of traditional folk music. His piano-playing, Robbie's drumming, and Garth's organ on this track are sheer delight, a tonic for depression, a definition of comradeship, an affirmation of the healing power of music and demonstration of how it can be simultaneously totally mystifying and disarmingly simple and direct.*

No one questioned the use of a nursery rhyme song in *The Basement Tapes*. Perhaps because it was a one-off, perhaps because it could be dismissed as Bob and the boys goofing about in what was meant to be private, unreleased fun. By the time of *under the red sky* though, it was the nursery rhyme element that caused the most dissent and division. What's it all about? Why did I, and other commentators go scurrying along to our libraries in search of nursery rhymes? Were we, like the three kings, in need of a key? No, we weren't, because we all know it doesn't work like that if you *care* for the work of art in the first place. The album had invaded my heart and usurped my soul on its own. It had interested me in its connections with nursery rhymes, and made me curious about Dylan's reasons for manipulating this mode of verse. As in the Springsteen references in 'Tweeter And The Monkey Man', or the Humphrey Bogart quotes throughout *Empire Burlesque*, Dylan uses references to other spheres as a backdrop to his songs, giving a reflection that can be deepening, wry, comic and enlightening. In the case of *under the red sky* it goes even deeper, the very structure of some of the songs refers back to/is based upon children's nonsense verse.

Not that this means that the songs cannot be enjoyed without the listener being well versed in nursery rhymes and their histories, although this knowledge undoubtedly adds to the pleasure the songs bring. Nor does it mean - as has been claimed - that Dylan was being 'lazy', far from it. As Mr. Haughton has written:

> One of the first patterns that emerges when we look at nonsense poems of this sort is that patterns emerge. To make nonsense, you have to do more than gabble or scrabble. If anything nonsense is more shapely, more brazenly formalised and patterned than other kinds of language – not the reverse, as is often assumed. Indeed it might be argued that, far from being a very special case of poetry, nonsense represents what makes poetry itself a special case. I suspect there is a pleasure in nonsense at the core of all poetry, a pleasure ultimately rooted in the child's free play with sounds, words, rhythms and patterns of repetition – experiments with which are made in defiance of the obligation to make sense.[10]

Much the same can be claimed for song as well poetry.

It is worth reflecting on what using this mode of nonsense verse as a bedrock for his album opens up for Dylan. What makes nursery rhymes tick?

> ...children's rhymes may serve as chapters of consequences... and miniature ABC's of linguistic order. They deal regularly with the basic constituents of language and number as well as the regular ins and outs and ups and downs of childhood...

*Nonsensical and nursery rhymes are particularly drawn to serial order of one kind or another; number as in 'Green grow the rushes-o'; names such as London churches in 'Oranges and Lemons'; days of the week, as in 'Solomon Grundy'; ...*

*...Inconsequence is of huge consequence in the world of children's rhymes, with their double fascination with sequentiality and non sequiturs.[11]*

The last paragraph there could apply to most of the songs on *under the red sky*; the first two to certain songs, in particular '2x2'. Why though would Dylan want to communicate to us like this? The answer to that may lie in the very gravity of what he is conveying; the world of *under the red sky* is a grim one. The 'bleak wasteland' that Gavin Martin wrote of in his *NME* review of *Oh Mercy* is even more pertinent to this album. We are talking here of a blasted world and, not surprisingly, Armageddon seems just around the corner. Nonsense verse allows Dylan to deal with these concerns, hardly novel in his work, in a new, challenging and entertaining way:

*As the haunting work of Eastern European writers like the Czech Miroslay Holub and the Romanian Martin Sorescu reminds us, nonsense may be a liberating way of dealing with the intolerable, or at least handling the impermissible.*
*To call something nonsensical is normally a way of putting it down. Yet despite this, or maybe because of it, reading a piece of inspired nonsense is curiously rather tonic. It sets us up. It makes desolation row more bearable.[12]*

Earlier in this article I quoted Mr. Haughton on the wide range of verses that could be encompassed by the term 'nonsense verse'. Perhaps more surprising is the scope of origins for nursery rhymes. In their authoritative introduction to *The Oxford Dictionary of Nursery Rhymes*, the Opies inform us:

*Indeed, the farther one goes back into the history of the rhymes, the farther one finds oneself being led from the cot-side. It can be safely stated that the overwhelming majority of nursery rhymes were not in the first place composed for children; in fact many are survivals of an adult code of joviality, and in their original wording were, by present standards, strikingly unsuitable for those of tender years. They are fragments of ballads or of folk songs ('One misty misty morning' and 'Old woman, old woman, shall we go a-shearing?'). They are remnants of ancient*

*custom and ritual ('Ladybird, ladybird', and 'We'll go to the wood'),*
*and many hold the last echoes of long-forgotten evil ('Where have you*
*been all day?' and 'London Bridge'). Some are memories of street cry*
*and mummers' play ('Young lambs to sell! young lambs to sell!' and 'On*
*Christmas night I turned the spit'). One at least ,'Jack Sprat', has long*
*been proverbial. Others (If wishes were horses', and 'A man of words')*
*are based on proverbs. One ('Matthew, Mark, Luke, and John') is a*
*prayer of Popish days, another ('Go to bed, Tom') was a barrack room*
*refrain. They have come out of taverns and mug houses. (Nose, nose,*
*jolly red nose' still flaunts the nature of its early environment.) They are*
*the legacy of war and rebellion ('At the siege of Belle Isle' and 'What is*
*the rhyme for porringer?'). They have poked fun at religious practices*
*('Good morning, Father Francis') and laughed at the rulers of the day*
*('William and Mary, George and Anne'). They were the diversions of*
*the scholarly, the erudite, and the wits (as 'Dr. Wallis on a 'Twister', Dr.*
*Johnson on a 'Turnip seller', and Tom Brown on 'Dr. Fell'). They were*
*first made popular on the stage (Jack Cussans's 'Robinson Crusoe') or in*
*London streets (Jacob Beuler's 'If I had a donkey'). They were rude jests*
*(like 'Little Robin Redbreast sat upon a rail'), or romantic lyrics of a*
*decidedly free nature (as 'Where are you going to my pretty maid?'),*
*which were carefully rewritten to suit the new discrimination at the turn*
*of the last century. We can say almost without hesitation that, of those*
*pieces which date from before 1800, the only true nursery rhymes (i.e.*
*rhymes composed especially for the nursery) are the rhyming alphabets,*
*the infant amusements (Verses which accompany a game), and the*
*lullabies. Even the riddles were in the first place designed for adult*
*perplexity.*

At least the lullaby is safely still within nursery walls. It may well be the
source of all song, as many have claimed; the original rhythm being that of
rocking a cradle rather than a hedonistic or spiritual (or both) dance. The
Bible contains snatches of lullabies from Roman times which, interestingly for
students of folklore:

> *reveals the existence of a folk tradition utterly independent of the litera-*
> *ture of the time. It has, in fact, more in common with the songs sung by*
> *the Italian peasantry of today than it has with the productions of the*
> *contemporary Latin poets of classical times.*[13]

The innocent pleasure of the lullaby is contrasted with the iniquities of
T.V. in 'T.V. Talking Song', by the speaker at Hyde Park:

*The man was saying something 'bout children when they're young*
*Being sacrificed to it while lullabies are being sung*

As for the wide range of sources above, they entered the nursery, as mentioned earlier, through nurses or mothers singing half-remembered snatches of ballads and songs, particularly choruses and opening verses. Once these became part of the nursery rhyme tradition they tended to become fixed in content for astonishing lengths of time. In all of folk music only bawdy songs have remained so well preserved. The latter because the attraction and the 'jokes' never alter, and the former due to children's tenacity in demanding exact repetition night after night. 'You're singing it wrong, mummy', 'You've missed a bit, Daddy' are cries known to all parents and baby-sitters.

I'd like to look in detail now at the songs from *under the red sky* that seem to me to have been most successfully integrated with the nursery rhyme and then to look at the album as a whole and see how they fit within it and come to an overall conclusion about the album's merits (or otherwise). The title track, capitalised unlike the album title, is for this listener the finest on the album. The opening verse of 'Under The Red Sky' is a repeated two lines that place us unequivocally in nursery rhyme land:

*There was a little boy and there was a little girl*
*And they lived in an alley under the red sky.*

These lines come straight from 'Proposal':

*There was a little boy and a little girl*
*Lived in an alley...*[14]

In all the song has only twenty lines, of which eight are repeats. Nevertheless, it contains a concentration of allusion to well-known nursery rhymes. The second verse evokes the man in the moon, who came down too soon. The third verse borrows a line from the following:

*Little girl, little girl, where have you been?*
*Gathering roses to give to the queen.*
*Little girl, little girl, what gave she you?*
*She gave me a diamond as big as a shoe.*[15]

The children being baked in a pie evoke the Hänsel and Gretel story and:

*A bag full of Rye,*
*Four and twenty*
*Naughty boys,*
*Bak'd in a Pye.*[16]

The very next line is yet another borrowing, this one from the palindromic children's verse 'This is the Key of the Kingdom', and so on. From these building blocks Dylan composes a beautiful song with a haunting melody; a small fable of summer's dreams being unfulfilled and hope ending in infertile winter.

A bright future is forecast early and linked to summer:

> *There was an old man and he lived in the moon.*
> *One summer's day he came passing by...*
> *Someday little girl everything for you is gonna be new*
> *Someday little girl you'll have a diamond as big as your shoe*

Then, in a typical nursery rhyme non sequitur the children find themselves (again reasonably typically) *'baked in a pie'*.

Only after this is the 'key' to what went wrong given:

> *This is the key to the kingdom and this is the town*
> *This is the blind horse that leads you around*

Before we end with hope retreated and the ominously dry river:

> *One day the man in the moon went home and the river went dry*

We have apparently reliable information that Dylan meant the song to be a story of his home townsfolk. This information is given by Don Was in *The Telegraph (44)* - a rather foolish move if he wanted to keep in Bob's good books - and, given the circumstances he describes, I see no reason to doubt that this was Dylan's intention. On the other hand what Dylan says about these things needs always to be treated with caution, and what Dylan intended a song to be is of some academic interest (in comparing his intention with what he actually created) but may have little or no bearing on what the song actually is. *'Never trust the artist, trust the tale'* is not D.H. Lawrence's most famous dictum for nothing. Dylan himself has said that the song is *'intentionally broad and short, so you can draw all kinds of conclusions'*. This seems nearer the mark. The lines:

> *This is the key to the kingdom and this is the town*
> *This is the blind horse that leads you around*

certainly encapsulate a 'fable of missed opportunity', and Dylan eloquently conveys the mood that Don Was relates, but without this 'inside knowledge' I doubt we would ever relate it to Hibbing. Dylan clearly states that we aren't meant to look for such specificity.

Before looking further at the song itself, lets examine Mr. Was's interview, in which unfortunately he paints an image of himself that is as impoverished as his production work on the album is enriching. He begins by telling us:

> *I think people are missing it. I see it being dismissed as just nursery rhymes, and that's wrong. It's actually about people who got trapped in his home town. I think it's about Hibbing and about people who never left. I think that that shows Bob's artistry - that as opposed to just saying it literally, like Springsteen's 'My Home Town', he wrote a little biblical story.*

The dismissal of nursery rhymes aside, there's nothing wrong with this, you'll be thinking. Just so, but Mr. Was continues by berating both those 'who don't get it' and nursery rhymes in general with increasing severity:

> *but the one thing that's really bugged me in all the reviews I've read is that people miss the essence of the song. I think it's a really great song and yet people are dismissing it as some nursery rhyme gibberish.*

And

> *It's such a charming, moving piece of music that I can't believe it when I see the reviews, that people don't get it, don't pick up the vibe. They think he's just throwing any words in there, like he's writing bad nursery rhymes.*

On he goes decrying the wonderful world of nursery rhymes along with those too blind to see what he can. Except he was just as blind himself, if not more so until he has a private word with Dylan. His entire original interpretation was 'misunderstood'.

> *When I first heard it, I misunderstood. I thought they baked a bird in a pie and I thought, OK so here's these people, they inherit the earth, great future, and then they baked a bird in the pie. I thought, Aw, it's about ecology. It's about people who are fucking up the earth.*

Even worse, he approached Bob like someone excited that he'd got a clue in a crossword puzzle:

> *So he came in the room. I said, I got it - this thing's about ecology! And he looked at me like I was a total asshole,*

You'd think this would have made him think twice about laying into reviewers who had not had personal contact with Dylan to set them straight. Anyway, after Mr. Was pursued the matter, Dylan replied:

> *It's about my home town.*

With these few words, the scales fell from Mr. Was's eyes:

*So I thought about it and it's such a great little fable. These people have all this opportunity and everything and they choose to be led around by a blind horse and they squander it. It's beautiful and so simple, and he sang it one time through and it was perfect.*

Which I do think is a fair interpretation, though the song is also much more than that. And it is unquestionably a nursery rhyme, and a nursery rhyme completely detached from Hibbing at that. Without Mr Was's reporting that comment of Dylan's no-one would have thought of Hibbing, there's nothing in the song to suggest it, it's a universal 'fable of squandered opportunity'. Apart from anything else, to think of it as Hibbing puts the author and singer of the fable in a horribly smug 'I escaped and you lot blew it' perspective that runs counter to the beautiful achievement of the song.

Michael Gray sees the song as being, at least potentially, hopeful. He points out that many nursery rhyme characters (as well as Jonah in the Bible) survive being swallowed, so perhaps being baked in a pie need not be terminal. His diligent scholarship allows him also to proffer possible positive interpretations of seemingly obvious negative lines and images. However, by the time you read that the blind horse can be seen as a 'benign guardian' the supporting evidence is so very far removed from the experience of listening to the Dylan song that I think it can safely be discounted. All this would be of interest, since Dylan's album clearly points the critic towards a study of the nursery rhyme tradition, *if* the song gave a hint that there could be positives to be gleaned. Yet it does no such thing, the song ends with a dry river and the man in the moon, whose appearance coincided with hope and summer, has gone home. We are told this in the final verse directly following the gloomy line:

*This is the blind horse that leads you around*

It is a wonderful song but it has no happy ending. Nor does the album as a whole, but more of that later.

There is, perhaps, an echo of 'Blowin' In The Wind' as well as a touch of the Bible. The seeming non sequiturs tell a tragic tale. The lack of particularity only increases the sense of devastation of the children being *'baked in a pie'* and the desolation of *'the river went dry'*. This seems to simultaneously evoke the death of Imagination (the spiritual world) and the end of the physical world.

The song has a beautiful melody and Dylan's vocal is marvellously evocative, with shades of regret, wistfulness, care and a multitude of other emotions. All in all a fine song and I can heartily concur with Michael Gray on this comment:

**173**

> *...I don't understand how anyone who much appreciates Bob Dylan's genius can rubbish a song as reverberative, warm and true as 'Under The Red Sky' because it is 'kiddie-stuff' any more than you can validate a song as dead and untrue as 'Trust Yourself' or 'Never Gonna Be The Same Again' on grounds of its supposed 'grown upness'.*

Another, although much lesser, song that works within the nonsense verse/nursery rhyme orbit is '10,000 Men'. Straight from a mixed world of nursery rhyme ('The Grand Old Duke of York', 'The King of France') and the blues, this is a slight piece but irresistibly enjoyable. It is nonsense as fun, and all the better for that. I smile warmly at Dylan's pronunciation of 'blue' ('balloo') at the end of the opening line, I laugh at the cleverness of the conception and marvellous delivery of:

> *None of them doin' nothin' that your mama wouldn't disapprove.*

And at the absurdity of:

> *Ten thousand men looking so lean and frail*
> *Each of 'em got seven wives, each one of 'em just out of jail.*

The fifth stanza seems to come from somewhere else, Dylan's voice verging on the maniacally gleeful and with a very peculiar phrase, 'eat off his head'.

> *Hey, who could your lover be*
> *Let me eat off his head so you can really see*

Dylan makes his image all the more violently forceful by using 'eat' rather than the more usual 'bite'. The novelty of the phrase and the verb's connotation of devouring make it powerful indeed, and make us listen much more closely to what is going on in the song.

From that unsettling image we are led on to the first direct mention of women, in a bridal depiction of 'dressed in white' at that. There are ten thousand women to pair with the ten thousand men, yet they are all:

> *Standin' at my window, wishin' me goodnight*

This sits oddly with the bridal picture, though not as much so as the previous verse does. We feel uncomfortable at this far from settled picture that is emerging. I presume that the person referred to in '*Hey! Who could your lover be?*' is female because of the reference to *his* head. Is this woman one of the ten thousand women? Is her lover one of the ten thousand men? Is the singer? The singular and the ten thousand interchange bewilderingly fast here.

If you are following the thread of numbers through the song and looking for significance in them, you've then got to take into account that each of the ten thousand men has seven wives. I say 'the' ten thousand men but there is no necessity for it being the same ten thousand men each time. (I tend to feel it is the same men at different times and in various circumstances, but you know, *does it matter?*) I'm not going to be joining any hunt for any significance in the numbers. I am aware that 10 and 7 are of special import in many times and cultures (Roman, for example) and feature prominently in the Bible (the description of the Whore of Babylon, for another example) but I just don't believe that we are meant to look for specific meanings and connections. The numbers entered the Bible and the nursery rhyme worlds because of their special import. Dylan picks up on them from there and uses them in the nonsense verse, the absurdity of the '70,000' wives attests to this.

Instead, we are in the land of nonsense and non sequiturs. Why, we ponder, are they 'just out of jail'? Perhaps because they've 'got seven wives', that is presuming it is the men, and not the wives, who've just been freed or escaped. Perhaps the spell the men have had in jail is what has made them so 'lean and frail', or perhaps it is an old nudge-nudge reference to satisfying the sexual demands of seven wives. Perhaps it is a combination of the two. All these 'perhapses'! About the only thing for certain is that the men have gone from being an army on the march to being rather decrepit.

The song presents contrasting views of the male/female roles At first glance Dylan seems to be almost listing archetypal images of the active male and the subordinate female (as you'd expect in nursery world land):

| Men | Women |
|---|---|
| goin' down | dressed in white |
| coming for you | standin' |
| drummin' | spilling my buttermilk |
| on the move | wishin' me goodnight |
| digging for silver & gold | sweepin' my room |
| coming in from the cold | sweeping it up with a broom |
| got seven wives | 'serving' tea |
| just out of jail | being so nice to me |

However, it is not at all that straightforward; the men are also *'lookin' so lean and frail'*, and are *'gonna get killed'* so life is not a bed of roses for them either. Not that it is of any significance, it's just a nonsense song to be enjoyed for what it is. Its original and delightful title of 'hat pin' would have made that even clearer than it already is.

It is important not to force messages or meanings onto songs, which can pertain to certain areas of experience without making dogmatic statements. I believe that most of the songs from *The Basement Tapes* and *under the red sky* are like that and I don't think the less of them for it. Indeed what they are 'saying' - what we get from them - can be as important, relevant and artistic as what we get from songs which set out a specific critique.

In this song you get the feeling that Dylan is just making it up as he goes along, and there's nothing wrong with that, it makes it much like many of the songs on *The Basement Tapes*. Just as the song began with allusions to various nursery rhymes, so it ends. Making cups of tea and sweeping up occur quite frequently, as does 'buttermilk':

> Hie to the market Jenny come trot,
> Spilt all her butter milk, every drop,[17]

Two things which appear frequently in nursery rhymes are food (and drink) and animals (particularly domestic and farmyard ones). So it is on *under the red sky*. For food alone: Track 1 has a bowl of soup and a pail of milk, track 2 has '*baked in a pie*', track 3 has '*feed that swine*', '*milk and honey*' (and '*drive you to drink*'). 'T.V. Talking Song has an egg (albeit an odd one) and '*forbidden fruits*', '10,000 Men' has 'buttermilk' and 'tea', '2x2' has wine, 'Handy Dandy' has 'brandy' plus '*sugar and candy*', as well as brandy being poured and a drink being finished.[18] All of these appear before the last track, as do the following animals: a swarm of bees, a big fat snake, several horses, the bird, bait in a fish's mouth, that beast, that swine, black cats and, by implication, there are more in 'Two by two they step into the ark', 'Something in the moonlight still hounds him'.

In 'Cat's In The Well', as you'd expect, all the themes and imagery of the album come to a head. It is a brilliant composition on all levels; the nursery rhyme, the blues and the Biblical threads brought to a coherent, if dark, finale.

The single phrase: '*the barn is full of bull*' not only refers to a number of nursery rhymes, but does so with a clever inversion that illuminates a number of meanings. On a literal level '*the barn is full of bull*' continues the food theme (full of beef), the phrase also brings to mind the common terms 'full of bullshit' and 'bull in a china shop' as well as metaphorically - and this I suggest is the over-riding image - by calling to mind a very large, animated bull. '*The cat's in the well*' refers back to the ever popular 'pussy's in the well', but in Dylan's song the world has darkened immeasurably and the cat is trapped in the well by a wolf that seems the embodiment of evil. It seems this because the whole album has been underpinned by the familiar Dylan theme of the approaching Armageddon and the Second Coming of Christ.

**176**

Just as food and animals populate the last track as well as the album as a whole, so the biblical strands are completely present in the finale. The closing lines:

> The night is so long and the table is oh so full
> The cat's in the well and the servant is at the door
> The drinks are ready and the dogs are going to war
> The cat's in the well, leaves are starting to fall
> The cat's in the well and leaves are starting to fall
> Goodnight my love, may the Lord have mercy on us all

have been taken as referring to the Last Supper[19] (the full table, the ready drinks, the servant at the door[20]), and the beginning of the Apocalypse (the cat contained by the evil wolf, perhaps symbolising Satan, whilst the '*dogs are going to war*'). This last image, as we'll see, being the latest in a line of impending images of doom and violence, following swiftly on the heels of:

> Cat's in the well and grief is showing its face
> The world's been slaughtered, it's such a bloody disgrace.

All of this gives the already impressive last line a literal meaning as a final prayer for Mercy. You don't have to believe, follow or feel this interpretation to enjoy the song, but the reason so many (all?) commentators have heard them this way is because they climax an album dripping - not uncommonly in Dylan's work - in biblical imagery and commentary.

As closely as nursery rhymes at times are paralleled in the blues, so they have much in common with the Bible, giving you a threefold Dylan web of allusion throughout *under the red sky*.[21] This can lead to a situation where you are not sure which reference you are supposed to have been reminded of. Take for example the phrase:

> Kill that beast and feed that swine

Does this send us back to the nursery rhyme, Curly Locks?

> Curly locks, Curly locks,
> Wilt thou be mine?
> Thou shalt not wash dishes
> Nor yet feed the swine

Or the Bible, The New Testament, The Gospel of Luke, Chapter 15, 11-32 with a nursery rhyme sounding opening phrase?

> There was a man who had two sons; and the younger of them
> said to his father, `Father, give me the share of property

*that falls to me.' And he divided his living between them.*
*Not many days later, the younger son gathered all he had*
*and took his journey into a far country, and there he*
*squandered his property in loose living. And when he had*
*spent everything, a great famine arose in that country,*
*and he began to be in want. So he went and joined himself*
*to one of the citizens of that country, who sent him into*
*his fields to feed swine.*

If the latter, (which in my mind is the one we are supposed to think of, not that it matters too much as they both bring benefits and add to my enjoyment of the album) the servant at the door line brings further echoes of the same passage as it continues:

*And he would gladly have fed on the pods that the swine ate;*
*and no one gave him anything.*
*But when he came to himself he said, `How many of my father's*
*hired servants have bread enough and to spare, but I perish*
*here with hunger! I will arise and go to my father, and I*
*will say to him, 'Father, I have sinned against heaven and*
*before you; I am no longer worthy to be called your son;*
*treat me as one of your hired servants." And he arose and*
*came to his father. But while he was yet at a distance, his*
*father saw him and had compassion, and ran and embraced him*
*and kissed him. And the son said to him, `Father, I have*
*sinned against heaven and before you; I am no longer worthy*
*to be called your son.' But the father said to his servants,*
*`Bring quickly the best robe, and put it on him; and put a*
*ring on his hand, and shoes on his feet; and bring the*
*fatted calf and kill it, and let us eat and make merry; for*
*this my son was dead, and is alive again; he was lost, and*
*is found.' And they began to make merry.*

While Matthew 16:2-4 provides us with a reference for the album as a whole:

*When it is evening, you say, 'It will be fair weather, for the sky is red.'*
*And in the morning, 'it will be stormy today, for the sky is red and*
*threatening.' You know how to interpret the appearance of the sky, but*
*you cannot interpret the signs of the times. An evil and adulterous gener-*
*ation seeks for a sign, but no sign shall be given it except the sign of*
*Jonah.*

There is a biblical feel to many of the lines (as there was on *Oh Mercy*) - of armies moving, lands being wasted and people poisoned. '2x2' overtly refers to the story of the Ark, while 'God Knows' is explicitly a statement of Dylan's faith and a pointer to where we should go for 'another rendezvous'. Curiously relevant - curiously because the rest of the video is either unimaginative or worse (the LSD number plate) - *The Wicked Messenger* (1830) quotes from 'Proverbs, ix 22':

> *Like a gold ring in a pig's snout is a beautiful woman who shows no discretion.*

This strongly echoes parts of the promotional video for 'Unbelievable'.

It is in images of Armageddon, however, that we hear the Biblical voice most acutely, the voice of portent and prophecy. The album is suffused with apocalyptic images, of all things drawing to an end:

> *One day the little boy and the little girl were both baked in a pie...*
> *The man in the moon went home and the river went dry...*
> *It's unbelievable the day would finally come...*
> *It's unbelievable it would go down this way...*
> *Until there were none... they headed for heaven... they step in the dark ...*
> *How many tomorrows have they given away?.. How many more can they afford?..*
> *God knows there's gonna be no more water but fire next time...*
> *God knows it's fragile... it could snap apart right now/Just like putting scissors to a string...*

So we are already in Armageddon mood before 'Cat's In The Well' drives the message home with:

> *'The wolf is looking down... the dogs are going to war....*
> *The world's being slaughtered...*
> *'Goodnight my love, may the Lord have mercy on us all'.*

Attached to this theme of 'the end of all things' is an undercurrent of violence that runs through the album. It ranges from people coming to blows to the destruction of the world, and it begins in the very first track. Beneath the humour are some fairly savage images:[22] '*Wiggle 'til it bites, wiggle 'til it cuts*' and '*Wiggle 'til you vomit fire*'. Violence permeates the album. We have children being baked in a pie, the threat of someone having his head eaten off, people being likened to bait in a fish's mouth, people fighting, people rioting, armies marching. The only songs which maybe escape this are 'Born In Time' (which, as we will see later, does not belong to this album in any case), and

'2x2'. I say 'maybe', because the former involves the cutting pain of love (the lover offers *'what's left of me'*) and the latter's protagonists have had a violent path to their uncertain end.

Another theme connected to that of Armageddon, or at the very least a world out of kilter, with inverted values, which *under the red sky* clearly is (by the time of 'Cat's In The Well' animals have taken over the world) is recurring allusions to Shakespeare's seminal play of a world where order has collapsed, traditional values been overturned, *King Lear*.

The album seems to share a bond with Shakespeare's masterpiece. This is not the first time I've felt this with Dylan's work; both 'Tears Of Rage' and 'Shelter From The Storm', for example, exhibited narrative and linguistic parallels.[23] It could be a direct influence, or it could just betray a shared oral heritage and the language of the King James Bible. Mr. Haughton gives pride of place in his collection of nonsense verse to the scene with the fool on the blasted heath, and points out in his introduction that:

> ...the scene from Lear has as vivid a place in the history of nonsense as in that of madness. The dialogue is shot through with queer, garbled oracular language, and shifts back and forth between reason and madness, pathos and absurdity. It's not only the most vivid representation of the fool in literature, but in its vision of violent social upheaval and broken authority suggests that through the language of madness and adopted madness the characters make touch with truths and feelings outside the pale of their normal language. What they say in their terrible crisis makes sense all right, but it takes a route that zigzags giddily across the border with nonsense...

A passage that is a considerably neater summary of *under the red sky* than most reviewers achieved.

There is also - again perhaps a coincidence, or an indirect influence due to Dylan's recorded admiration of Shakespeare's language - the following exchange in Act IV Scene iv:

> Lear ...Handy, Dandy. Prickly, prandy...
> Lear: 'What, art mad? A man may see how this world goes without eyes. Look with thine ears: see how yond justice rails upon yond simple thief.[24] Hark, in thine ear: change places, and, handy-dandy, which is the justice, which is the thief?'

This in itself points to one of the oldest nursery rhyme based on a 'hand game' for children that we have records of, and forms the basis of numerous variations on 'handy dandy' throughout Europe. Which points me towards the songs on the album I have as yet mentioned only in passing.

Up until now I have discussed three songs that work totally successfully utilising the nursery rhyme mode of nonsense verse: 'Under The Red Sky', '10,000 Men' and 'Cat's In The Well'. Songs deserving of high praise, rather than scornful dismissal as 'nonsense nursery rhymes', with the incorrect assumption that nonsense verse is without merit. Still, just as with the symbolist verse discussed earlier, there are good and not so good examples of this too; simply to use the techniques is not in itself enough. The tracks I have so far lauded are only three from ten and last just under eleven minutes. The remaining seven tracks vary in quality and reflect the dominant themes of the album to mixed degrees. 'Handy Dandy' is probably knocking at my door demanding to be let in to my group of 'total successes', and perhaps he should be. Certainly the utilisation of nursery rhyme is perfect, the handy dandy game already mentioned is combined with common nursery rhyme food and drink fodder: 'sugar', 'candy' and 'brandy' which were combined, for example, in a mid-18<sup>th</sup> century nursery rhyme derived, one presumes, from a song about Bonnie Prince Charlie:

> Over the water and over the lea,
> And over the water to Charley.
> Charley loves good ale and wine,
> And Charley loves good brandy,
> And Charley loves a pretty girl
> As sweet as sugar candy

In addition, Michael Gray has illuminated just how cleverly Dylan has reworked another nursery rhyme staple in the lines:

> He got that clear crystal fountain
> He got that soft silky skin
> He got that fortress on the mountain
> With no doors or windows so no thieves can break in

Which recasts the old 'egg' riddle :

> In marble walls as white as milk
> Lined with a skin as soft as silk
> With a fountain crystal clear
> A golden apple does appear.
> No doors there are to this stronghold
> Yet thieves break in and steal the gold

**181**

It has some of the album's finest vocal gymnastics and cops its melody from the finest rock single of all time, 'Like A Rolling Stone', so its case for inclusion seems overwhelming. What detracts from it for this listener is that after a number of listens the chorus becomes irritating rather than joyful fun, the mystery of 'Handy Dandy's' identity is a game that palls and the melody, although one of my favourites, is a copy and I prefer the original. That may be too personal and harsh as it is certainly another track that deserves applause, not ridicule. So let's say 'Handy Dandy' too is a successful and enjoyable song in the milieu of the album. Four tracks and fifteen minutes then of near unalloyed success, almost half the length of this extremely short album.

Much of the derision poured on the album was allocated to its opening track, 'Wiggle Wiggle'. This is a riot. The humour here is different to that of, say, 'Bob Dylan's 115th Dream':

> Ran out to the street
> When a bowling ball came down the road
> And knocked me off my feet
> A payphone was ringing
> It just about blew my mind
> When I picked it up and said hello
> This foot came through the line

However, I don't understand why, in some quarters, the above should be 'acceptable' while 'Wiggle Wiggle' is so scorned. It's a funny thing to follow up *Oh Mercy* with, a joke on those expecting *Oh Mercy* Part Two, and its play on various pop clichés makes me smile. The idea of Dylan doing the song is funny in itself, its inclusion as opener a bold, if mainly vain, statement to people to cut him some slack and throw off their preconceptions.

However, I am not here to make any grandiose claims for it. It is no more than a routine pop song and its nods to rock and soul tradition as well as children's rhymes and games ultimately do not make it particularly more pleasurable to those who pick up on all those things compared to those who do not. In contrast, 'Under The Red Sky' and 'Cat's In The Well' are magnificent in themselves *and* the enjoyment is deepened by knowledge of nursery rhyme and biblical allusions. It's a throwaway but it does have some good points, one being that the change of mood when 'Under The Red Sky' begins is so dramatic that the second track grabs the listener's complete attention, and then richly repays that attention.

The following track, 'Unbelievable', alas, is as moribund as 'Under The Red Sky' is sparkling. We have, in passing, already noted some of its hints and citations of the nonsense verse and nursery rhyme worlds, and there are more:

*Once there was a man who had no eyes*
*Every lady in the land told him lies*

for instance, yet ultimately any lyrical dexterity is undermined by the lumpen nature of the music. The song is just a slab of auto-rock gunge, sounding all the worse for following on from 'Under The Red Sky'.

'Unbelievable' was also, and ridiculously, chosen as the single from the album. If this is what Dylan or those surrounding him thought of as a potential 'hit', then perhaps they were so misguided as actually to create it for that purpose. Whatever, it deservedly sank without trace. The promotional video was a disgrace, ending as it did with a close up of a car numberplate that read 'LSD', thus linking Dylan with the very past he so often distances himself from, and the very opposite of subtle, of what his life's work has stood for. I know *Oh Mercy* sold disappointingly given its critical acclaim, but this desperate attempt at 'controversy' was pathetic. As was most of the rest of the dire video, still there was the sole inspired touch of the biblical pig (or at least I hope that is what it was).

'Born In Time' has two problems; it is the wrong version and it is on the wrong album. The song comes from the *Oh Mercy* sessions, where it was a plain, unadorned version relying on Dylan's vocal performance alone to make it a thing of majesty and splendour. This is self-consciously trying to be that very thing and therefore completely failing. It is most insensitively placed on the album, and may as well have had a voiceover introducing it: 'here's the big ballad, folks, wait until you hear the sumptuous backing...' Even in its preferable state it would not have 'fitted' on *under the red sky*, but it would then have at least been a thoroughly welcome 'visitor' rather than this egomaniac limelight hogger.

'God Knows' is also from the *Oh Mercy* sessions, and perhaps this is where nursery ideas started. It didn't fit on *Oh Mercy* but, unlike 'Born In Time', it certainly does here. It is a 'list song' like so many nursery rhymes, reflecting, in particular, 'How Many Miles To Babylon', with a nod to 'Jack be nimble, Jack be quick'. It is peppered with biblical allusion too. Yet all this is not to much purpose on the record; the song fails to move or convince. At Vienna, VA in 1993 you can hear what perhaps was in Dylan's mind all along. Despite being as unimpressive live as on record many times, that night he performed a version that was totally convincing. It started with a rather more fitting first line than *under the red sky's* 'God knows you ain't pretty'. The 1993 performance opened with 'God knows I love you'. It was the first of many a transformation; vocally he was in complete control, really living the song, as you can hear by the manner in which his delivery of a word like 'fragile' made sound and meaning identical. Musically the song had been re-worked to pile-drive him toward a superbly scary tone in the last line. Interestingly enough, the same show saw probably the finest live performance of 'Born In Time'.

Still, that only shows what the song could have been on the album, not what it is there. We have a similar situation with 'T.V. Talking Song'. You have to stretch to make this seem appropriate to the album's main themes, but it does mention lullabies, it deals with something, T.V., that has replaced nursery rhymes for many youngsters, and there is a passing biblical allusion. Yet after the novelty of the setting passes, Dylan as observer at Speaker's Corner, Hyde Park, London, there is not much to recommend this performance of the song. Its telegraphed ending is one let-down, but the main problem is that it just doesn't bear repeated listening. I say this performance because there are out-takes of this track from the album sessions that reveal an entirely different song. In those Dylan's performance is way out on the edge, recalling earlier tours de force like 'Sign On The Cross' from *The Basement Tapes*. If only, rather than the insipid cut that made it onto the record, they had selected one of the dramatic renditions that bring out the latent paranoia of the song's best couplet:

> You mind is your temple, keep it beautiful and free
> Don't let an egg get laid in there by something you can't see

The remaining track, '2x2', again fits the album in every respect, another fusion of the nursery rhyme and the Bible. It is an unspectacular if pleasant enough piece, ending in one of the album's many comic touches and reminding us that nonsense verse is fun as well as surprisingly meaningful. It reminds me too that the songs that are spectacular successes make this album 'a dainty dish to set before a king' rather than something to be lightly dismissed or worse, openly derided.

### Conclusion

The harsh criticisms of *under the red sky* were caused by a variety of factors. Firstly, as Paul Williams has rightly observed:

> *This is the recurring problem for Dylan's audience regarding his new work (new albums, new tours): we have trouble hearing it. Dylan is so inventive and so primitive, he operates so far outside anyone else's concept of singing, writing and performing, that learning the language of one set of Dylan performances does not necessarily aid us in learning or acclimatizing to the language of another set. Indeed, it can be the*

*primary obstacle in our listening: our attention is not innocent but expectant, and it's waiting (as it turns out) in all the wrong places.*[25]

In this case many people seemed to be waiting for '*Oh Mercy* Part 2'. Hopefully this article can play a small part in helping us 'hear the language' of *under the red sky*.

Secondly, the lack of specificity is infuriating to those who approach a song as though it were a crossword puzzle. There is no remedy for this, but then there wasn't where 'Sad Eyed Lady Of The Lowlands' was concerned either. Again, Mr Williams has got it right, there are 'different sets of Dylan performances'; sometimes you can summarise what a song is about, sometimes X = Y (though hopefully never that crudely), but not this time.

Thirdly, some people simply dislike the songs: the production or the voice or whatever. Some have dismissed the album after only a few listens, which is a shame, especially if they are contemptuous in their dismissal. Others have persevered but still don't like it; which is fine, they've 'learnt the language' but don't want to hear it again.

Fourthly, all the 'megastars' that were listed as being on the album seemed a waste of time and space. Their inclusion smacked of the same desperation for a hit as the obnoxious video for 'Unbelievable'.

Finally, there wasn't very much of it, people felt short-changed. When I used the nursery rhyme epithet 'dainty', I meant it as a compliment, denoting delicacy and grace, but the word also has the connotation of 'small'. Overall in Dylan's oeuvre the achievement is quite small, but it is a greater one and of more significance than most people have given it credit for. You cannot help but feel that this is not only because of a simplistic view that dismisses all nonsense verse as meaningless rubbish, but also because the author and singer of the songs is Bob Dylan. Once again, preconceptions took precedence over open-hearted approach to an individual creation. However, *under the red sky* is 'dainty' in more than one way: the album is also of small size.

Although the album was only four minutes shorter than *Oh Mercy* it seemed much briefer, and at 35 minutes it was 20 minutes shorter than his next album, *Good As I Been To You*. It struck me years later that the reason I felt that *under the red sky* was so short was that it came out as I made the switch from vinyl LP to CD. *Oh Mercy* at under 40 minutes had seemed a fine length on vinyl, whereas just over 35 minutes on CD seemed a let-down. Now it is not that I am saying quantity is more important than quality. For example, for live Dylan in the 21st Century I'd rather have less shows and more quality to be honest, and I'd also rather have shorter shows if all the songs were performed to the best of his abilities. Similarly, a record of 35 minutes of 'Under The Red Sky' and 'Cat's In The Well' standard would have been more than acceptable by this listener's criteria (so much so that it would have been an album that would have been fitting with Dylan's career's own high standards).

That isn't what we got, however, and given that, despite all my laudatory comments above, the nursery rhyme theme was not seen through to a coherent conclusion, it might have been a proper gesture to put out the NRBQ[26] tracks as a bonus disc. Or, since *Oh Mercy* out-takes were already present in new takes, add more of those as bonus tracks. I would not normally want that mix-match of artistic visions, but *under the red sky* would be very short indeed if the tracks with its core vision were all we had.

What the debate over length highlighted was the more problematic and very important difference between listening to an LP (or pre-recorded cassette) compared to listening to a CD.

*The Telegraph* interview with Don Was brought up that very point.

> *The record clocks in at about 35 minutes, yet a lot of artists - yourselves included - are putting out about 50 or 60-minute albums...*
> DW: *Well, I tell you, I gotta theory. I believe that in the era of CDs, less is better. People listen to the first five songs on CDs over and over, but no-one's got an hour to sit and listen to something. Now in the old days you turned the record over and you just dropped the needle down and went about your business. On cassettes, when one side finished you played the other side. But CDs start at the beginning every time and if you start polling people, you'll find that they can tell you the first five or six songs on every record, but they can't tell you what's on the end. So now I'm advising artists that I work with to make their statements at the front, 'cos no one's gonna get to the back - or rarely will they get to the back. 35 minutes, maybe...*

I am not at all sure I agree with this. I know it is not true for myself listening to any Dylan album on compact disc since *under the red sky*. *Time Out Of Mind* is more than double the length of *under the red sky* and no-one I know only listened to the first five tracks. Surely to goodness the world is not full of listeners with such a limited attention span? However, Mr. Was has considerably more experience of the business than me so perhaps his points are valid in certain audiences, though not I'd argue in those of Dylan, Waits, Young, Springsteen etc., or certainly not amongst the people I know who listen to those singers.

Still the argument that there is an important difference in how one listens to the two formats is irrefutable, and it has had a profound effect on Dylan's art. The album was where Dylan made his artistic statements, and it had fundamentally changed. For Shakespeare it would have been as though the theatre he was working in had changed shape and length of plays had been changed by some law imposed by those who knew naught of stagecraft. He'd have had to adapt.

The sequencing of tracks on Dylan albums was a major 'factor' on all Dylan albums up to and including *Oh Mercy*. It was also something almost always expertly done. Not just in obvious ways like 'Forever Young' closing side one and opening side two of *Planet Waves* (one acoustic, one electric), or the electric/acoustic sides of *Bringing It All Back Home*[27], but in counterbalance, counterpoint, flow, accumulated and reflected meanings and emotions. These all are part of his artistry, part of the reason Dylan was thought of as an 'album artist' in the days when acts were segregated into album and singles camps. Most in the album camp were known for their - usually unspeakably pretentious and musically offensive - so-called 'concept albums'; but Dylan was a trailblazer (as ever) for those who conceived of the album as an organic work of art where everything from dust jacket and liner notes to track sequencing added to the overall 'statement' the LP made.

The LP format was Dylan's canvas, and is sorely missed. The displacement of the once king 12" LP vinyl format has added more fuel to the fire of Dylan's disillusionment with studios and modern recording. The absence of its defining features are evident in every release since *Oh Mercy*, whether one considers these to be brilliant successes, artistic failures or something inbetween.

The concluding chapters of this book will let you know exactly how I consider them, and why I see the writing in *under the red sky* as a continuing influence.

---

1. This reminds one of the 'lonely crowd' of 'I Shall Be Released'.
2. Hugh Haughton (Editor), *The Chatto Book of Nonsense*, Chatto & Windus Ltd. 1988
3. Ibid
4. Ibid
5. Although, as we saw in the earlier chapter, even music is bound by conventions and language-like regulations.
6. This failure of community is seen in a tragic light in the heartfelt loss of 'Tears Of Rage'.

7. It may just be difference in hearing but the common reading of this line as ending in 'Sue' seems to me another potential attempt to infiltrate sense into nonsense. I suspect it may be 'suit' or some other word ending in a consonant - not that nonsense is postponed for long if it is 'Sue'. Clive Barrett suggested to me it could be the proper name, 'Zoot'.

8. Quoted in *Invisible Republic* by Greil Marcus.

9. Michael Gray, *Song and Dance Man III: The Art of Bob Dylan*, Cassell, 2000. Further quotes from Mr. Gray in this chapter are all from the same source.

10. Hugh Haughton (Editor), *The Chatto Book of Nonsense*, Chatto & Windus Ltd. 1988.

11. Ibid.

12. Ibid.

13. Iona and Peter Opie (editors) *The Oxford Dictionary of Nursery Rhymes*,1951.

14. Raymond Briggs (editor), *The Mother Goose Treasury*, Hamish Hamilton 1966.

15. Iona and Peter Opie (editors) *The Oxford Dictionary of Nursery Rhymes*, 1951.

16. Raymond Briggs (editor), *The Mother Goose Treasury*, Hamish Hamilton 1966.

17. Ibid.

18. For more on the food imagery see John Stokes' insightful article on the interlocking themes of food and sacrifice on *under the red sky* in **Homer**, *the slut* issue six. ('Guess Who's Coming To Dinner? A gourmet's guide to *under the red sky*).

19. This being the culmination of John Stokes's point, in the above named article.

20. I seem to be alone in seeing the servant at the door reminding us of the lesson Jesus gave his disciples by having no servants present and washing Simon Peter's feet Himself. He let the disciples jostle and argue for sitting positions before appearing in the doorway and acting as a servant to teach them that all men are equal. Nonetheless, I'm far from seeing the Last Supper as necessarily being the meal in the song.

21. The already mentioned farmyard animals being one thread of that web. The barnyard, the blues, the Bible and nursery rhyme connections link all Dylan's writings since *under the red sky* come to that, and there are particularly strong links between *The Basement Tapes, under the red sky* and *"Love And Theft"*.

22. Again this is something that is shared with *"Love And Theft"*.

23. So much so with the latter that I first heard 'futile horn' as feudal horn' and still wonder if it is a deliberate vocal pun.

24. This puts me in mind of Dylan's ruminations on justice in his 'protest' days.

25 Paul Williams, *Watching The River Flow*, Omnibus Press, 1996

26. Don Was: *There are three songs with NRBQ that didn't make the record. I just heard the tracks yesterday, and they're real strong. Hopefully, we'll...*

*Put them out eventually?*

*I hope so, 'cos they're real good.*

*What are the titles of them?*

*They were like working titles. One was almost like a tango, so we called it 'The Tango'.* (*The Telegraph* interview, op. cit.)

27.This was the most obvious casualty in the barbarism of the cassette releases that 'evened up' the timings of the tracks on each side to minimise the amount of tape needed, destroying an album's structure.

# Thirteen

# Singing The Lexicon

## Foreword

*This chapter concerns itself with the period between* under the red sky *and* Time Out Of Mind: *two albums that bookend the longest period - seven years - in Dylan's career of no releases containing new original compositions. The much trumpeted inclusion of 'Dignity' on 1994's Greatest Hits Vol. 3 does not really invalidate this, as the song dated from the* Oh Mercy *sessions in 1989[1].*

*With the full benefit of hindsight, I will tell a tale of Dylan's song-writing muse deserting him as he turns 50, and his enticing her back by repeating a course of therapy he had used before. The treatment involved re-immersion in the musical roots that nourished him and led to his earlier creative breakthroughs: traditional music, folk, blues, country and rockabilly.*

*Hindsight can be a wonderful thing, but it can also make a complicated path seem simple. It is by no means clear - indeed, he often stated the opposite - that Dylan felt the need to tempt his muse to return. The story of the late re-flowering of his song-writing is inextricably intertwined with his extraordinary dedication to touring, which he has been doing every year since 1986, and his increasing aversion to working in the studio. The latter was something he'd never been fond of, but the modern, digital development of the process had left him feeling repulsed rather than just uncomfortable.*

*As with* under the red sky, *I have notes and correspondence from the years involved, so I can read those, recall how things felt at the time, and so write without relying solely on the sometimes illusory benefits of hindsight. It was a mixed time for Dylan fans, who on the one hand could follow the Never Ending*

# TROUBADOUR

*Tour year in year out, but on the other found years passing without knowing whether there would ever be albums containing new Dylan songs released again.*

*The second part of this book deals with this 'late' part of Dylan's career, the previous chapters having covered his early output (c.62-66) plus 'If You See Her Say Hello' from 1974 (which offers a mature exploration of some of the themes first enjoyed in songs of the young Dylan). These two parts are bridged by the preceding chapter on nonsense songs, which looked both at earlier songs (including 1967's* Basement Tapes, *which formed a reaction to the 1966 period previously discussed) and 1990's* under the red sky. *From here we move on to the last decade of the twentieth century, and the opening year of the twenty-first.*

*The book was not deliberately planned like this, but it was perhaps inevitable that this was how it would work out. Firstly, it is natural that I would have been drawn to those songs which first attracted me to Dylan and which as I grew up became such an influence on and integral part of me. At the same time, having written a book on the relentless touring Dylan has undertaken from his mid-forties into his sixties, I feel similarly impelled to tell the tale of how I feel about Dylan's song-writing drought, and the astonishing rebirth that partly shows itself on the inconsistent* Time Out Of Mind *and comes to full flowering on the near-flawless* "Love And Theft".

*As the latter period has produced only two albums of original Dylan material, I can embrace them fully as albums. By that I mean I can take into account every track on both albums, as well as the albums as a whole. This is something that would have been impractical for me to do in the case of the hundreds of songs from the 1960s, especially as the albums were supplemented by singles, out-takes, compilations and so forth. (A process still on-going, as much of the material from Dylan's earlier career is now being released in various forms by his record company, in particular in their 'bootleg series' volumes.)*

*Before considering those two albums, it is important to see where they came from, what happened in the years between* under the red sky *and their emergence. Dylan may not have been composing new songs during this time but he was most decidedly fully immersed in making music, both on stage and, to a lesser degree, in the studio.*

*My initial thoughts on* Good As I Been To You *appeared in* **Homer,** *the slut issue seven, just after the album came out. Some of the comments on the Never Ending Tour Covers' bootleg box set are from my review of it for* Judas! *issue two. The vast majority of this chapter is, however, new to this book.*

*Those old songs are my lexicon and my prayer book. All my beliefs come out of those old songs, literally, anything from 'Let Me Rest on That Peaceful Mountain' to 'Keep on the Sunny Side.' You can find all my philosophy in those old songs. I believe in a God of time and space, but if people ask me about that, my impulse is to point them back toward those songs. I believe in Hank Williams singing 'I Saw the Light.' I've seen the light, too.*

Bob Dylan, quoted by Jon Pareles
1997 N.Y. Times News Service

As already stated, this chapter tells the tale of an immersion in roots music leading to a rebirth of Dylan's song-writing. To use the terminology of an earlier song, his muse wasn't going anywhere so he 'strapped himself to the tree with roots' in the meantime.[2] It is a story with various parts that intermingle and intertwine. I will attempt to convey the feeling of this by starting with, and returning to, cover songs performed in Dylan's unremitting yearly touring; in between which I will be looking at *Good As I Been To You*, *World Gone Wrong* and Dylan's production of a Jimmie Rodgers tribute album, plus other undertakings.

This is not a new story: Dylan had dipped back into this creativity-enhancing well before. *Self Portrait*, *Knocked Out Loaded* and *Down In The Groove* (plus various other activities around those times) had preceded what were then acclaimed as returns to form[3] in *New Morning* and *Oh Mercy*. There were crucial differences though, as *Self Portrait*, *Knocked Out Loaded* and *Down In The Groove* are all very weak albums by Dylan's standards, as though he were creatively lost. *Good As I Been To You*, though, is anything but weak and *World Gone Wrong* is even stronger; a cohesive, powerful Dylan statement, a Dylan album in effect despite there being no Dylan-penned songs on it.

Also, this time his journey to the well of inspiration was on a much larger scale. Not until 1992 had Dylan ever released an album with no self-penned songs, nor had he ever gone anything like seven years between releasing albums containing new material.

Nor had there ever been the amount of cover songs played on his tours (nor amount of shows year after year come to that). For the Dylan fan there seemed to have been a major shift in approach away from producing albums of his own songs to only putting out covers, while shifting his attention all but entirely away from the studio and onto live performance.

While it was thought by many at the time, and assumed by all looking back on these events, it is not necessarily the case that Dylan was deliberately trying to re-ignite his muse. More than once he said that there were already more than enough songs in the world:

> Bob Dylan...*The world don't need any more songs.*
> Paul Zollo: *You don't think so?*
> Bob Dylan: *No. They've got enough. They've got way too many. As a matter of fact, if nobody wrote any songs from this day on, the world ain't gonna suffer for it. Nobody cares. There's enough songs for people to listen to, if they want to listen to songs. For every man, woman and child on earth, they could be sent, probably, each of them, a hundred records, and never be repeated. There's enough songs. Unless someone's gonna come along with a pure heart and has something to say.*[4]

On the other hand this may have been a convenient belief for him, as he also indicated many times that he was still trying to write songs but was encountering problems. His 1992 comment that:

> 'My songs aren't written like they used to be, which was all the time. They come slower now (laughs).'[5]

was amplified in following years into comments that even those songs that came slowly were abandoned unfinished. Perhaps, though, it all came down to the same thing: maybe he lacked the motivation to finish them because he felt there were too many songs in the world already. It's also hard not to speculate that subconsciously he may not have been at ease with this professed abandoning of writing songs. He had written them all his life, after all, and these interviews suggested that he *was* still trying to write, but becoming frustrated in those attempts.

One can only speculate, though I do find it interesting that he noted in that same interview with *Song Talk* quoted above, where he said there were already too many songs, that:

> The melodies in my mind are very simple, they're very simple, they're just based on music we've all heard growing up. And that and music which went beyond that, which went back further, Elizabethan ballads and whatnot... To me, it's old. [Laughs] It's old.

Interesting in that, alongside compositions from his own career, he was performing some of those old songs on stage. This is not the same as him saying that he was playing them in the hope of rejuvenating his own writing but it is easy to see such an implication, consciously or unconsciously, in his words: *'Music which went back further, Elizabethan ballads and whatnot'.*

Love of and respect for traditional music has been with Dylan from the beginning. Even at the height of his rock star mid-sixties period he was acutely aware of what these songs, this 'old music' meant to him:

> Traditional music is based on hexagrams. It comes about from legends, Bibles, plagues, and it revolves around vegetables and death...All these songs about roses growing out of people's brains and lovers who are really geese and swans that turn into angels...I mean you'd think that the traditional-music people could gather from their songs that mystery... is a fact, a traditional fact... I could give you descriptive detail of what they do to me, but some people would probably think my imagination had gone mad.[6]

But this time his return to it appeared different, more totally engulfing than at any time since the days he was forming the character 'Bob Dylan' from the songs of Lead Belly, Guthrie and so forth.

The quote that heads this chapter shows that it has now become a matter of faith to him. The 'lexicon' he speaks of envelops his work like an intricate, all-encompassing web. The connecting threads of the lexicon create a mesh of associations, picking up more and more by the minute, shedding more and more light on the power and influence of the songs through the years. This was not something he said one day and moved on from, as he has done with so many other things. It was something he was sure of. In another 1997 interview he used much the same language: *'I don't adhere to rabbis, preachers, evangelists, all of that. I've learned more from the songs than I've learned from any of this kind of entity. The songs are my lexicon. I believe the songs.'*[7]

Here again one sees a major difference from previous times - the magnitude of Dylan's affiliation to his lexicon is now so great it is like a religion. The one, true religion at that. In previous phases he had dipped into the traditional stream, but here the immersion was complete. *'I believe in Hank Williams singing `I Saw the Light.' I've seen the light, too.'* He was now singing from this 'prayer book' rather than composing new songs. The spiritual tone of those interviews seemed to paint the picture of a 'Born Again' traditional music believer. Dylan appeared to have a new religion, one he practiced on the Never Ending Tour and in all his recorded work of this period. He embodied the 'light' of the lexicon and it shone through in everything he did. This 'embodying' allowed him to produce a seamless creation of new music from traditional parts, new parables from the old hymn book.

Ah, but that is jumping ahead and using hindsight again; let us first go back to see how this happened. *Good As I Been To You* was the first ever authorised covers-only Dylan album release, but, as I have intimated already, it did not come out of nowhere. For some time in Dylan's live performance the standout tracks had been covers, especially, though not exclusively, traditional songs. These were performed night after night, year after year by a fully engaged Dylan with all the interpretative, transcending genius that implies. He lived the songs both for himself and his lucky audiences. Often - though I am generalising wildly here - while tossing off songs he had penned himself with little attention, far less grace.

The words to these covers rarely troubled Dylan but things like 'The Times They Are-A-Changin' could have him all over the place, pretending to sing off mike, or enunciating correct-sounding noises to replace forgotten words. You could hear bits from various verses repeated or inserted in the wrong place, one of my favourites being a 1991 rendition of 'Blowin' In The Wind' with the question: *'How many seas must a man walk down?'* Perhaps we should just pass it off as a Christ allusion...

Transcendent covers started long before the Never Ending Tour, however. Indeed to trace them back to their starting point would be to review Dylan's entire career. The frequency of touring in his later years seemed to herald in a particular focus on them, however, and 1988 the first of what have become known as the Never Ending Tour years saw a number of traditional songs performed with dignity, power and a resonant engagement. I am referring to songs like 'Barbara Allen', 'Two Soldiers', 'Eileen Aroon', 'Waggoner's Lad' and 'Lakes Of Pontchartrain' among others. As we shall see later in this chapter, so it has continued throughout the Never Ending Tour.

At the moment I am concentrating on the period that brought us the two cover albums, the first of which, *Good As I Been To You*, appeared in 1992. Prior to its release, a number of new traditional, or at least older, songs were added to the growing list of Never Ending Tour covers. The month of March brought 'Little Maggie', 'Female Rambling Sailor' and 'Little Moses' and April 'The Lady Of Carlisle' and 'Delia'. Then, just before the recording of the album, June and July showcased 'Girl On The Green Briar Shore' and 'The Roving Blade' (aka Newlyn Town) respectively. These were grand additions to the burgeoning catalogue of classic songs performed with Dylan's peerless expressive and emotive gifts.

Whether those same gifts were in evidence at another dip into the pages of his lexicon, in a session produced by David Bromberg that June at Acme Recording

Studios, Chicago, I cannot tell you. This session is as yet uncirculating amongst collectors, though we do know that the songs recorded were[8]: 'Rise Again' (Dallas Holm), 'Nobody's Fault But Mine' (Blind Willie Johnson), 'Lady Came From Baltimore' (Tim Hardin), 'Polly Vaughan' (trad.), 'Casey Jones' (trad.) and 'Duncan And Brady' (trad.), plus two Bromberg songs. Exactly the kind of thing that appears on his cover albums, though none of these songs ever actually has. The ultra-Christian 'Rise Again' would be interesting to hear, Dylan having performed it so spectacularly well on the 1980 'Gospel tour'. Well they all would be more than interesting to hear, and two have been played live on the Never Ending Tour: 'Lady Came From Baltimore' (Tim Hardin) and 'Duncan And Brady', the latter sharing a commonality of theme and history with *Good As I Been To You*'s 'Frankie and Albert' and *World Gone Wrong*'s 'Stack A Lee' and 'Delia'.

November found Dylan playing (as a one-off) 'Farewell to the Gold', a song from Nic Jones's *Penguin Eggs* album (1980 vinyl, 1991 CD release). Another song from that same source, 'Canadee-i-o', could be found on *Good As I Been To You*, released the month before. We know it is from the same source because one of the odd things about *Good As I Been To You* was that instead of transforming the songs as he did on stage Dylan played each track clearly copying a specific source.

Not that Dylan can exactly be mistaken for anyone else singing, of course. Nor would it be true to say that he did not bring any of his own unique singing genius to bear on the tracks, but still we can be certain which versions were Dylan's exact sources. It was more a case of 'here is me doing Paul Brady's version of 'Arthur McBride', rather than 'here is me interpreting 'Arthur McBride'.' So we get Dylan performing Mick Slocum's 'Jim Jones', his take on the Mississippi Sheiks' 'Sittin' On Top Of The World' and so forth.

One has to assume Dylan did this in tribute to the originals, though one suspects some accreditation in the sleeve notes and, where relevant, copyright acknowledgement may have felt more like a proper tribute to the original artists and arrangers.

On October 16th at Madison Square Gardens, there was a '30th Anniversary' superstar bash held in Dylan's honour. (No, the date is not actually the anniversary of anything in particular). The star-studded event was on Pay-Per-View TV and later released on record/CD and video/DVD. Dylan's own performance at it was so impoverished that he had to re-record his contribution to the multi-vocal 'video-single'. It sparked 'stories in the press' that the whole event had been quickly put together to praise him while he was still with us.

Anyone catching his own fine shows around the same time would have realised that it was just the characteristically contrary Dylan trick of messing up in front of the cameras and large prospective audience, or his inherent discomfort at these gala events. Take your pick but this one was *his* gala event after all, he could have stopped it. I must admit I have never seen the point of the whole jamboree - why thirty years? Why didn't we have one after twenty-five years or forty years?

Dylan followed up that over-bloated celebration of his incomparable writing talents by releasing, only a couple of weeks later, the first ever album that contained none of his own songs on it. It was excellent to see such impish Dylan perversity wrong-foot everyone again in this manner. Though it is also true that *Good As I Been To You* similarly shone the spotlight on Dylan's past. This time, however, it was highlighting the kind of songs that shaped him and his song-writing craft, rather than that art itself.

Vocally, Dylan was setting himself up for a comparison with his younger self. Much of his range had gone and the caressing sensitivity he brought to bear on covers at the Gaslight Café in 1962 or the Big Pink in 1967 was no longer available to him. He could, however, still pull off a song like 'Tomorrow Night' which has both vocal and historical ties with *"Love And Theft"*, nearly a decade later, as we shall see in that chapter of the book. In addition, most of the songs sat within Dylan's vocal range of the time, as you'd expect with a folk based collection. For the record, though I am expecting everyone who reads this book to know the album well, the track listing was:

'Frankie & Albert', 'Jim Jones', 'Blackjack Davey', 'Canadee-i-o', 'Sittin' On Top Of The World', 'Little Maggie', 'Hard Times' 'Step It Up And Go', 'Tomorrow Night', 'Arthur McBride', 'You're Gonna Quit Me', 'Diamond Joe' and 'Froggie Went A-Courtin'.

A very pleasant surprise was Dylan's sympathetic and lively guitar accompaniment. 'Surprising' because it felt a long time since he had performed so well on the acoustic guitar. In performance he had been strumming rather than picking or embellishing as he did here. Given that *Good As I Been To You* eschewed modern recording protocols some problems are clearly audible but, as Matt Snow noted: *'his few mistakes add to rather than detract from the unforced texture of a sentimental journey.'*[9]

Naturally, despite certain limitations in his vocal range and texture an album of Dylan singing acoustically is going to bring rare vocal treats to bear. His intuitive understanding and love of the songs - something we did not often feel on many of the covers in previous studio albums - and his unparalleled understanding of how to approach them means he projects each song to maximum emotional effect.

His unmatched phrasing ability transmutes even the most commonplace conceit into something very moving. The very way he controls his breathing in 'Tomorrow Night' calls to mind the lustful longing he is singing about. While his enunciation of: *'The day you quit me baby/That's the day you die...'* in 'You're Gonna Quit Me' sends shivers down your spine.

Although one would have to admit to a raw roughness to his tones on many songs, that is all part of the 'warts and all, rough and ready' live feel to the album. Sublime moments appear out of this approach and in the case of 'Hard Times', for example, Dylan produces a sustained, masterly interpretation.

This song looks forward to the minstrelsy roots of *"Love And Theft"*, written as it is by Stephen Foster, the 19th century popular song composer. Although hailing from Pittsburgh and never straying further south than Cincinnati, Foster made his living writing songs of a romanticised, fictional South, amongst which are some of the most popular American songs ever. I am thinking here of the likes of 'Camptown Races', 'O! Susanna', 'Jeanie with the Light Brown Hair' and 'My Old Kentucky Home'. His 'Hard Times', however, provides a pointed contrast between society's haves and have-nots:

> *While we seek mirth and beauty and music light and gay,*
> *There are frail forms fainting at the door,*
> *Though their voices are silent, their pleading looks will say,*
> *Oh, hard times, come again no more*

In Dylan's hands the song becomes something that tells of an unspoken but implicit endurance that is both heroic as well as explicitly mournful. It is one of the album's highlights.

Another highlight is the children's song 'Froggy Went A-Courting' which concludes the album, as usual, on a perfectly fitting note:

> *If you want any more, you can sing it yourself, uh-huh.*

One could not envisage a more apposite final line. It works on many levels; firstly, Dylan having sung popular folk songs from all kinds of places for over an hour leaves it to the folk he has been singing for to continue themselves, if they so wish. It also serves as a stinging rebuke to those who so harshly dismissed *under the red sky*'s nursery rhyme influence.

Here's a song that had a 'political protest' origin – it can be traced back to the 16th century where it appeared as a satirical ballad on the questionable activities in high places of the time and was known as: *'A moste Strange weddinge of the ffrogge and the mowse'*. Many changes of title, content and melody have taken place in the interim and it is now familiar as both nursery rhyme and folk song. In addition it forms a perfectly fitting contrapuntal conclusion - surprising as that may first appear - to all the darkness of an album beginning with a tale of such grisly goings on as the deadly vengeance of 'Frankie & Albert'.

It is yet another example of Dylan's exquisite sense of how to end an album. He had said in interview years previously that he would like to do a children's album one day. Even though you thought then that he was playing mind games with the interviewer you simultaneously could see the validity of the idea, not least because of the Woody Guthrie and Lead Belly's children's songs connection. This is even better than his fine performance of 'This Old Man'.[10] I really love the way he sings it, there is no condescension – it is straight and pure. This already lets us know that the album's closing line is not mainly to be heard as a 'so there'. On one level, as we have seen, it is that, yet it is chiefly a warm invite to join in the folk process the album has exemplified. We can be sure of this because it was not Dylan signing off from singing these kinds of cover songs; the following year brought another, *World Gone Wrong*. The greater achievement of this following album has tended to overshadow the pleasures *Good As I Been To You* affords.

This is a pity as, all in all, it was far from a disappointing album not only in quality but in quantity too - each side being nearly as long as all of *under the red sky*. *Good As I Been To You* was remarkably well received at the time (unexpected for this kind of album, especially from Dylan) by music critics. There were exceptions, naturally, but generally speaking it was given a warm welcome, and the same can be said for Dylan fans too. He may not have included any original Dylan songs but he had chosen to cover a whole new batch of songs, which was great news for the fans. As much as one would have wished for an official 'Female Rambling Sailor', it was all to our benefit to have heard its splendid concert appearances and have 'Canadee-i-o' on the album instead. Good as he'd been to us before, he was being even better now.

'Female Rambling Sailor' and 'Canadee-i-o' are both tales of women serving on ships, disguised as men. Or as Dylan put it, when introducing the former in an Australian show in the spring of that year, these are songs: '*about a sailor. A certain kind of sailor*'. *World Gone Wrong*, 1993's album, consisting again only of cover songs, continued the trend with yet another of these songs: 'Jack-a-roe'.

They are all very moving and Dylan brings his powers to bear on the stories they tell. The two album versions have happy endings – unlike so many of the songs they accompany - but 'Female Rambling Sailor' has a fatal, though heroic, conclusion. Dylan's aged vocals contribute to the poignancy of all three tales, which with 'Golden Vanity', performed in concert in 1991 and again in 1992, form a subset of outstanding songs he has sung relating to the sea. In these, his uncanny and unique ability to conjure up what he is singing about has your senses seeing, smelling and tasting the sea air.[11]

'Jack-a-Roe' may be akin to 'Canadee-i-o', and *World Gone Wrong* seems a similar successor to *Good As I Been To You* on the surface, but there are many differences between the two albums. In some ways, the success of the second outing has retrospectively diminished the appeal of the former and quietened the applause it was greeted by. This may be neither rational nor just, but such is the way of things. As Paul Williams has written:

> World Gone Wrong *is so warm, in fact, that it makes Dylan's previous album (*Good As I Been To You, *which I praised at the time for its unusual intimacy) seem cold and distant. It wasn't, but it is an indication of the extraordinary power of this new set of performances that they set a standard that, unfairly but inevitably, diminishes prior efforts in the same direction. Of course, the creative process is a working-out, involving a great variety of internal and external considerations.* World Gone Wrong *very probably could not have come into existence without the personal and public breakthrough that* Good As I Been To You *embodies...*[12]

The term 'warm' is a perfect one for how listeners who have fallen under its spell feel about this album. This is some achievement, given that its material is even darker in theme than its predecessor's. It is only one of many achievements, though, joining others that combine to make it feel like an original Dylan album, one that had a cohesive, comprehensible overall feel and import. This marvellous sensation of a complete, bona fide Dylan album stood in contrast to *Good As I Been To You*'s (albeit satisfying) collection of covers.

Another difference is that, although Dylan is often faithful to the originals he is covering in *World Gone Wrong*, he is less slavish to them, overall, than he was on *Good As I Been To You*. Also, despite many of the same themes being repeated, this time there is a darker, more underworld texture to it all. This is reflected in a bluesy domination of the sound compared to its more folk-based predecessor. Both were a mixture of folk and blues, but the emphasis had palpably changed.

This was something the more perceptive music critics picked up on:

> *Last year's* Good As I Been To You *was a nice tribute to the master's inspirations, but nothing you would go back to very often. This new one, though, deserves to be considered a major Bob Dylan album, the latest*

*in the series of occasional lightning bolts most recently represented by Infidels (1983) and Oh Mercy (1989). In World Gone Wrong Dylan demonstrates that he can say more in someone else's song than most artists can say in their own.*[13]

Again for the record, the track-list was:

'World Gone Wrong', 'Love Henry', 'Ragged & Dirty', 'Blood in My Eyes', 'Broke Down Engine', 'Delia', 'Stack A Lee', 'Two Soldiers', 'Jack-A-Roe', 'Lone Pilgrim'.

The most dramatic of all the differences between the two releases was that in *World Gone Wrong* the songs were not all we got. In addition, they were accompanied by extensive and exuberant liner notes penned by Dylan himself, entitled: *'About the Songs (what they're about)'*. This is a (partial) red herring, however. These liner notes are about lots of things, but they never are really concerned with telling us what the songs *are* about. You are made immediately aware of that when Dylan opens by telling us McTell's song 'Broke Down Engine', with its use of the familiar blues trope of engine trouble equalling sexual breakdown, really is all about trains:

> *BROKE DOWN ENGINE is a Blind Willie Mctell (sic) masterpiece. it's about trains, mystery on the rails–the train of love, the train that carried my girl from town-*

Dylan's wicked double-shuffle of a title for these notes alerts us to what they are telling us, which is what the songs are 'about' in Dylan's mind; Dylan, the troubadour of old songs, in a modern world that has gone very wrong indeed. He writes of the clash of the two worlds, those of the songs and what they mean to him with how he perceives the world into which he is bringing them.

That we get to know what these songs connote for, and arouse in, Dylan from his *World Gone Wrong* viewpoint forms an important part of the overall impact of the release. Most Dylan fans I know were just delighted he was still writing anything, but the bonus was that the notes are delightful in themselves too. Or at least they were once one overcame the familiar and favoured Dylan style of glorying in the lower-case and avoiding normal rules of punctuation. Thankfully, however, it is not taken to the extent he has sometimes done in the past. Yet it still looks as dated as it does infantile and offers no aid to communication, rather raises a barrier. Hopefully it has not put too many people off trying to follow (I say 'trying' because it is not always an easy matter to do so) his wonderful leaps of imagination and acute insights.

He uses each song as a launching pad for ruminations on the state of the nation(s). By bringing elements of the song into the present he can attack a wide range of modern failings. Two old targets are quickly hit. Love Henry is paraded as 'modern corporate man' and given an all too familiar description:

> an infantile sensualist–white teeth, wide smile, lotza money, kowtows to fairy queen exploiters & corrupt religious establishments, career minded, limousine double parked, imposing his will & dishonest garbage in popular magazines

We may laugh at the accuracy of the portrait but he, 'unable to handle his "psychosis"', does a deal of damage, as do faddish 'alternative lifestyle' advocates, something that Stack A Lee at least is not, according to Dylan:

> neither does he represent any alternative lifestyle scam (give me a thousand acres of tractable land & all the gang members that exist & you'll see the Authentic alternative lifestyle, the Agrarian one)

This agrarian authentic lifestyle permeates the album and in 2001's "Love And Theft" would be portrayed again as the real alternative, the living antidote to the world's malaise. The modern media gets it in the neck too, with the world of popular magazines and the 'boob tube' held up to the mirror of real life.

And so it goes on, the modern world's ill advised evasions of and false panaceas for facing real life are shown to be pitiful when contrasted with the real living in these songs. Delia, we are drily advised, 'would never go on a shopping spree'. Nor, we are told, does she 'ride a Harley Davidson across the desert highway' (in a line that brings to mind Neil Young's 'Unknown Legend' from his 1992 release, Harvest Gold:

> Somewhere on a desert highway
> She rides a Harley-Davidson
> Her long blonde hair flyin' in the wind)

In the midst of this rich explosion of Dylan's thoughts and words are good descriptions of how the album itself sounds and makes you feel. Put together Dylan's comment about the Mississippi Sheiks' songs being 'raw to the bone' and Blind Willie McTell's 'Broke Down Engine' being about 'variations of human longing' and you have a good description of the meat of the album, and from the latter's description you can also read how it is performed: 'the low hum in meters & syllables'.

I have been stressing the differences between the albums, but the similarities are manifold and plain to see. The Mississippi Sheiks provide a strong link between the two. At the same time, both the World Gone Wrong title track and 'Blood in My Eyes' are more affecting and transformed performances than *Good As I Been To You*'s faithful replication of the Sheiks's 'Sittin' On Top Of The World'. Dylan sings the two *World Gone Wrong* songs in a manner altogether more desolate and ascetic than that of the originals.

This reminded me of when I first heard older versions of 'Moonshiner'. They were all so damn cheerful - party sing-a-longs completely at odds with the song's lyrical sentiments. Dylan then, as here, stepped in and uncovered their hidden heart for us. He turned the songs upside down and inside out, revealing laments on the human condition that he projected out to us, his lucky audience.

'Blood In My Eyes' is an extraordinary performance. There is, despite its seedy content, a fragile declaration of something approaching real desire lurking in there. At least inasmuch as he needs her as a man needs a woman in a love song; there is devotion mixed in his longing. Somehow this shines through in what is but a (failed) tawdry money transaction driven by need and a desperate lust for sex.

As Dylan writes in the liner notes there is *'nothing effete about the Mississippi Sheiks'* and this is a song from the dark side of desire, though not without poignancy. It's all in the voice, as he so expressively tells the tale of the man desperate for sex but more frustrated than ever by the song's end as even the already paid prostitute puts him off:

> I went back home, put on my tie,
> Goin' get that girl that money will buy
>
> (chorus) Hey, hey, babe, I got blood in my eyes for you
> Hey, hey, babe, I got blood in my eyes for you
> Got blood in my eyes for you, baby
> I don't care what in the world you do
>
> She looked at me, begin to smile,
> Said, 'Hey, hey, man, can't you wait a little while?'
>
> (variant chorus) No, No, babe, I got blood in my eyes for you
> No, No, babe, I got blood in my eyes for you
> Got blood in my eyes for you, baby
> I don't care what in the world you do
>
> No, no, ma'am, I can't wait,
> You got my money, now you're trying to break this date
>
> (chorus)
>
> Goin' tell you something, tell you the facts,
> If you don't want me, give my money back

This too is a tale *'about variations of human longing'* and *'dupes of commerce'*, as Dylan's liner notes describe 'Broke Down Engine Blues'.

As with the rest of the album, it's heart-breaking stuff with a steel edge. *'Raw to the bone'* indeed, and proving once again that you don't need electric instruments and loud music to produce a devastating effect.

Performances like these are Dylan showing the modern-day musician how it is done and where the magic comes from. In interview after interview he talked of how current music stars had no foundations, no tie to the lexicon he believes in. Gary Hill obtained a revealing and widely circulated interview for Reuters[14]. He reported:

> *Dylan also has a workingman's distaste for many current music stars, saying they can't sing or play but get by on personality and electronic gimmickry.* 'When they electrified the guitar', *he says,* 'that's as far as it needed to go'.

Dylan seems almost on a crusade to turn the new generation's attention back to the past, back to what he sees as the real music. Like the world, popular music itself has 'gone wrong'. In the same interview he contrasts his memories of growing up listening to country music that was close to a pure hillbilly source, something lost in the present day:

> *They were just one step removed from the early ones, and you could hear that. But you can't hear it anymore, it's so polluted and unclean. ...People should go to those old records and find out what the real thing is, because mine is still second generation. My version of 'Broke Down Engine' is maybe third generation from Blind Willie's version of it.*[15]

Third generation maybe, but not for the first - or last - time in his career Dylan 'brings it all back home' to produce a blast of reality amidst the plastic life of MTV, mobile phones, McDonald's and pre-packaged music 'stars' who value auto-cues above authentic emotion.

He gives a real voice, and brings a legitimate knowledge of the world whereof he sings, to what Greil Marcus has termed the 'invisible republic'.[16] Years ago in 'Chimes Of Freedom' he had sung of bells tolling for: *'...the aching ones whose wounds cannot be nursed/For the countless confused, accused, misused, strung-out ones an' worse'*.

Here, nearly thirty years later, he is giving them voice among the grimy squalor and lurid passions of a world gone wrong. He does this despite his older, more restricted vocal range. Experience and mastery of tone allied to subtlety of intonation and phrasing enables Dylan to transport the listener through a wide variety of moods. His baritone alternatively can be the poignant regret of 'Delia' or a disgruntled bleat or angry moan. He conveys all manner and shades of feeling, though they are mostly of the sombre variety. The suppressed anger and frustration of these threaten to spill out at any moment. You can hear a growl that sounds like it is about to turn into a bite or a tenderness that may just be building up to a farewell kiss to all humanity's broken dreams, as the world goes to hell in a basket.

For, despite the shafts of light that heroism and love throw into the picture, it is overall a dark and gloomy proposition. This world is the same one he depicted, at the close of the last album of his own songs, in *under the red sky*'s 'Cat's In The Well':

> *The cat's in the well and grief is showing its face*
> *The world's being slaughtered and it's such a bloody disgrace*
> ...
> *The cat's in the well, leaves are starting to fall*
> *Goodnight, my love, may the Lord have mercy on us all*

Dylan has written many an apocalyptic image and many a song (and many concluding an album, like these) to foretell the imminent destruction of the world. In this album, though, he seems to be actually living in the Final Days, singing his songs/lexicon of human desires and heartbreaks. I am reminded of the images the young Dylan conjured up at the end of the apocalyptic 'A Hard Rain's A-Gonna Fall', some forty years earlier:

> *Where hunger is ugly, where souls are forgotten,*
> *Where black is the color, where none is the number,*
> *And I'll tell it and think it and speak it and breathe it,*
> *And reflect from the mountain so all souls can see it,*
> *And I'll stand on the ocean until I start sinkin',*
> *But I'll know my song well before I start singin',*
> *And it's a hard, it's a hard, it's a hard, and it's a hard,*
> *It's a hard rain's a-gonna fall*

So while there are not any Dylan penned lyrics, it's a Dylan message in spades. Love and heroism engulfed, and all but overwhelmed, by misanthropy, betrayal, lust, and revenge in the bleak landscape of a 'world gone wrong'.

Then, in a beautiful conclusion, 'Lone Pilgrim' lays it all to rest in spiritual tranquillity as death takes the body away from this bleak landscape and the soul rests in peace at last:

> *The tempest may howl and the loud thunder roar*
> *And gathering storms may arise,*
> *But calm is my feeling, at rest is my soul,*
> *The tears are all wiped from my eyes*

It seems impertinent to nitpick at such beauty but there was a downside to the release, and that was in the woeful sound of the CD, a messy production with terrible sound. It sounded something like an old bootleg of him playing somewhere without proper equipment. Which may have been the point, of course. There is an irony in that this much-bootlegged artist would release such a shoddily made artefact in an era when bootleg records came free of surface noise. Only Dylan could release a 1993 official CD that starts off with background hiss.

Allegedly this was Dylan's own doing; on receipt of a perfectly engineered 'final' copy he demanded that a disfiguring background noise be applied, presumably to work against the clean digital sound he rails against in the sleeve-notes and various interviews. Whatever the intent, the execution left it sounding nothing other than a faulty recording.

As with *Good As I Been To You*, the album garnered surprisingly positive reviews. It was far from universal acclaim, it would never be so for Dylan until after his heart ailment in 1997 (which may or may not just be a coincidence). David Sinclair led the nay-sayers in his review for *The Times*:

> *Tired, wizened, and so bereft of inspiration that he has had to resort once again to assembling a grab-bag of old folk tunes rather than write anything new of his own, Bob Dylan is clearly in a state of terminal artistic decline. Even so, he seems more engaged in his work on* World Gone Wrong *than he was on last year's lamentable* Good As I Been To You.[17]

Thankfully others had a less blinkered approach and saw the value and import of Dylan's creation. Don Carnell suggested that:

> *...those who have dismissed it as a 'contract filler' or even as evidence of writer's block are completely missing the point.*
>
> *Both through the songs themselves and in the excellent, self-penned sleeve notes, Dylan spells out his message: strange things are happening. Darkness covers the land. Corruption is everywhere.*
>
> *Big business operates its evil unchecked, Greed and oppression triumph over compassion. All resistance has been crushed. Technology – a big, big evil in Dylan's book – is slowly strangling any creativity in us, replacing real experience with arm's-length 'virtual reality'.[18]*

The two albums of covers, plus the reassuring reappearance of Dylan's writing abilities in *World Gone Wrong*'s liner notes, made a powerful statement and were warmly regarded by a significant proportion of Dylan's hardcore following, impatience for new Dylan songs notwithstanding.

Despite being generally well received in the press they continued the disastrous run of poor sales that had been dogging Dylan for many a long year. Dylan's sales have never been commensurate with his massive influence and import, but ever since his evangelical Christian phase they had gone downhill fast and were not really to pick up until 1997's *Time Out Of Mind*. Scott Marshall reported that:

> ...the post-Slow Train Coming *years were marked by a stunning lack of commercial success. The following studio albums from Dylan had not achieved the minimum gold status of 500,000 units sold, as of October of 2000:* Saved, Shot of Love, Empire Burlesque, Knocked Out Loaded, Down In The Groove, Oh Mercy, under the red sky, Good As I Been To You, *and* World Gone Wrong. Infidels, *released in 1983, was the only exception, and its commercial success may have been attributed to early reports that its songs reflected a reversal of Dylan's Bible-thumping... every single Dylan studio album released prior to 1980 had gone gold, platinum, or multi-platinum.*[19]

It is perhaps dangerous to put all the blame on his conversion; after all *Street-Legal* was a very poor seller in the States, while *Slow Train Coming* sold very well. In addition, there were other reasons not to have rushed back to listening to Dylan - reasons such as *Knocked Out Loaded* and *Down In The Groove* (then again, previous times had witnessed *Self Portrait* and the (unauthorised) *Dylan* album), to say nothing of his lamentable performance and behaviour at Live Aid in 1985.

However, not only the above statistics but also personal experience has taught that the religious conversion lost Dylan his sales potential within a significant proportion of the rock listening community. He was not to regain it until nearly twenty years later. By this larger 'community', I mean a more broad-based rock constituency than just the hard core Dylan fans – (though even many of those were put off when they heard his particular brand of right wing, judgemental salvation for the undeserving elect only Christianity) - the kind of people who would buy a Dylan album every now and again rather than every one.

This wider rock fraternity had always looked upon Dylan as the de facto head man, whether or not they were in love with his voice. They could scarcely believe that a man so famed for insight and innovation had turned to such a clichéd place when he needed help. Dylan's position both as a thinker and as a leading proponent of the sanctity of individual will and experience was suddenly a thing of the past. Michael Gray, the Dylan writer, has been touring with a talk on 'Bob Dylan and The History of Rock 'n' Roll' since the turn of the century. These talks attract not just the Dylan fans who read fanzines, travel to many shows, go to conventions and so forth but many from the wider rock audience. Time and again they have said to him that they 'used to love Dylan but never really got over that Christian period' or words to that effect. Some have been tempted back by reports of the renaissance of his powers in *Time Out Of Mind* and *"Love And Theft"*, plus the passage of time and an (albeit mistaken) widely held assumption that his Christianity was a thing of the past.

Although these fans were not the kind to buy every Dylan release, their sheer numbers meant that their occasional concert ticket or album purchases totalled a sizeable amount. Dylan albums were now selling only to the dedicated. Paul Williams noted this, but as ever, found a positive view to things too:

> Not that anything he does, however welcome, is likely to make the album sell any better than any other disc he's put out in the last ten years – one week at number 30, then off to oblivion. But you can look at it another way, which is that this will almost surely be the bestselling collection of traditional blues and ballads released this year by any American artist.[20]

Unbeknown to all of us then, by the time of Dylan's next studio album this pattern that had seemed set in stone would be broken, but that is the story of the next chapter.

For now, these two albums of covers may not have turned the sales figures round, but through them Dylan had reminded us of the golden treasure that is his 'lexicon'. A lexicon that follows no rules of segregation by race or anything else. Dylan's early defiant rejection of the rules and snobbery of the folk music world is mirrored in the way his favourite music evolved without regard to segregation or regulation.

In these two albums we have songs from British and Irish ballad traditions transported to the Appalachians and on to Dinky Town and Greenwich Village, but we have all kinds of others too. The blues here is a mix of country and city sounds and of (what is thought of as) 'black' and 'white' music. So complete is the mix in some songs - 'Stack A Lee' and 'Delia' for example - that there is no racial boundary left discernible. These are instead vibrant songs of the fabled 'melting pot' of cultures, the oral musical traditions that form the soundtrack of non-mainstream USA. The music that got lost when, as Dylan puts it in the liner notes, *'the insane world of entertainment exploded in our faces'*.

These two cover albums were far from his only promotion of and immersion in his lexicon of songs from before that explosion. As well as the ongoing 'Never Ending Tour', which I'll be turning my attention to again shortly, there were some lost opportunities for spreading the word via film, plus a Dylan-produced tribute album to Jimmie Rodgers on a new record label he had set up specifically for such a release.

After the close of 1993's legs of the 'Never-Ending Tour' Dylan played some special performances at a small-scale New York venue, The Supper Club, on November 16$^{th}$ and 17$^{th}$. Dylan and his regular touring band of the time played both nights as free concerts with two sets each night, each set lasting about an hour. These shows were all acoustic and staged with the express purpose of being filmed for a proposed video release.

MTV had been running, for some time, a very popular and influential series of shows called 'Unplugged' which featured famous musicians playing acoustically (REM, Springsteen, Neil Young, Eric Clapton, Kurt Cobain have all been featured). The Supper Club performances seemed like Bob Dylan's own version of the same idea. Dylan personally funded the professional filming of the shows for an intended release.

It never came, despite some magnificent renditions of his own songs - both well known and obscure - and a fistful of traditional tracks. The opening set had 'Blood In My Eyes', the second had 'Ragged And Dirty' and 'Jack-A-Roe', the third featured 'Ragged And Dirty' and 'Blood In My Eyes', while the final set, Dylan's most impassioned and engaged of them all, had no less than five traditional songs out of the 11 performed: 'Ragged And Dirty', 'Weeping Willow', 'Delia', 'Jim Jones' and 'Jack-A-Roe'.

'Weeping Willow' is an old Blind Willie Johnson song and Dylan does a *Good As I Been To You* on it, by which I mean that he replicates the original, even down to the mid-song expostulation *'Aw shucks'*, which sounded like a sublime, instinctive interlocution from Dylan unless one had heard the original version.

Even so it, and the Supper Clubs overall, had much to recommend them, and I very much regret the non-release of this well planned and executed mix of his songs and songs from the lexicon. It was a glorious reflection of what he was doing on the Never Ending Tour, but in a different setting with a traditional sound.

A year later there was the chance to set this right. Having been dissatisfied with the results of 'The Supper Club' when he reviewed the resultant film, Dylan agreed to appear on the MTV Unplugged set a year later. He turned in a functional, disappointing acoustic run-through of songs he didn't particularly want to play. Given the history and fuss surrounding Dylan 'going electric' in the first place, this return to 'unplugged' should have been a huge coup. Lots of artists, moribund and otherwise, had found their *Unplugged* appearances not only good one-off sellers but career-revitalising. Not so Dylan's damp squib, which was all the more frustrating following on from the year before.

That he did not play anything from the lexicon appears to have been at the root of the problem. Though also one despairs at his own lack of drive in ensuring that he played what he wanted to. In one of his many interviews with *USA Today's* Edna Gundersen:

> *I would have liked to do old folk songs with acoustic instruments, but there was a lot of input from other sources as to what would be right for the (MTV) audience. The record company said, 'You can't do that, it's too obscure.' At one time, I would have argued, but there's no point. OK, so what's not obscure? They said 'Knockin' on Heaven's Door'.*

So neither 'The Supper Club' nor the 'Unplugged' projects yielded anything of note, and the magic of the former is still in the vaults. More successful, and a crucial testament to his ongoing love for and promotion of his lexicon, was his Jimmie Rodgers tribute undertaking.

In February 1928 Jimmie Rodgers released the hugely popular 'Blue Yodel'. The same month 41 years later Dylan recorded 'Blue Yodel' numbers 1 and 5 in Nashville with Johnny Cash. Some 27 years further down the line, he produced *The Songs of Jimmie Rodgers: A Tribute* on his own, newly created Egyptian Records (distributed etc. by Columbia). The label on the CD is a tribute in itself, being a recreation of 'Bluebird Electrically Recorded Phonograph Records'. This was an idea Dylan would replicate, again to pleasing and apt effect, on *Time Out Of Mind*.

Jimmie Rodgers is the main link back to the world of the likes of the Mississippi Sheiks for Dylan. His influence is all-pervasive in the music Dylan grew up with and loves to this day, if you consider Rodgers' influence on Hank Williams and therefore on the rockabilly magic of the mid 1950s. Rodgers both directly and indirectly affected the music of Jerry Lee Lewis, for example, whom Dylan refers to in the liner notes as having said '*...there are only four stylists: Jimmie, Al Jolson, Hank Williams and himself*'. Modesty was not one of Jerry's many vices or virtues, but Dylan joins him in placing Rodgers centrally in the history of popular song, going as far as to say *'Jimmie may very well be "THE MAN WHO STARTED IT ALL"'*. Dylan himself performs 'My Blue-Eyed Jane' on the album, while Bono, Mellencamp, Willie Nelson and Van Morrison are amongst those covering other Jimmie Rodgers songs.

Listening to the album one is struck by the fact that Rodgers also provides a link back to minstrelsy and the popular music of that time. Jimmie Rodgers started out in the days of blackface performers, as did the likes of Gene Autry according to Nick Tosches. That world, seemingly long lost in the mists of time, is really not so very long ago and its immense influence on modern popular music has been neglected until very recently. It is the world that *"Love And Theft"* grows out of, and Jimmie Rodgers' place in its transmission to Dylan is hard to overestimate. In reading Dylan's homage to Rodgers and listening to the tribute he put together, one hears also Dylan's voice from the classic 'Visions Of Johanna', telling us that *'everything's been returned which was owed'*.

In the accompanying liner notes, Dylan acutely defines the style that so impressed Jerry Lee, '(Rodgers') *refined style, an amalgamation of sources unknown, is too cryptic to pin down. His is a thousand-and-one tongues yet singularly his own'*. Not only is this a fitting description of Rodgers, but it could also double as a comment on some of Dylan's own fulsome gifts. As could this extended paean of praise: *'he was a performer of force without prece-dent with a sound as MYSTICAL as it was dynamic. His voice gives HOPE to the vanquished and humility to the mighty'*.[21]

This is what Dylan was doing so often in his non-stop touring - especially when he covered traditional music. Through all his other projects the Never Ending Tour, as its name implies, continued and continues to this day, each year adding more to the long list of songs Dylan has covered.

One enterprising bootleg label went so far as to collect every song covered between the years 1988-2000 and put them out in a 9 CD Box Set entitled the *Genuine Never Ending Tour Covers Collection – 1988-2000*. This is useful in giving you an idea of the sheer scale of Dylan's ongoing spreading of the word of the lexicon. This collection boasts '162 performances and 138 songs'. (The 24 repeated songs are significantly variant versions.) And the two years since have added even more.

These covers are culled from the mists of time right up to the present, as disc 4's title 'Contemporary Competition' attests. Contemporary efforts do not reside only on that disc, however.

'Long Black Veil' is a personal favourite, which I would guess it is for many people. I love various versions of this by other artists (Nick Cave, The Band, Johnny Cash, BR5-49) so you can imagine what Dylan singing it does for me. Its place in 'the lexicon' is an interesting one because, although of the lexicon, it too is based entirely upon 'old songs'.

It absolutely sounds a genuinely old traditional classic, but instead was written by Danny Dill whose stated aim was 'to write an instant folksong'. That quick coffee advert sounding claim may be unsettling but only until one has heard the song - especially as performed by any of the above, far less Dylan. Listening to this you can only be thoroughly captivated by the drama and emotion of this most authentic sounding folksong: instant or not.

'Long Black Veil' is not the only example of a modern writer trying to create an 'old, traditional' song. The never-far-away from the Never Ending Tour presence of the Grateful Dead can be found in this guise on various tracks. Dylan's interpretation of something like 'Black Muddy River' invests it with such grandeur and depth of human spirit that this listener is awed in a manner that probably could only rightly be described as spiritual. Speaking of spirituality, human emotion and contemporary covers, the opening track of 'Contemporary Competition', Leonard Cohen's 'Hallelujah', given a towering rendition here, shows that the lexicon can be composed of new songs too. Though, in this case, 'timeless' would seem a more appropriate description.

Other discs focus on Dylan crooning ballads, or singing established Christian songs. The ones that carry the most spell-binding and deep songs, though, are the ones with traditional folk and country blues material. As is the case on the Never Ending Tour itself, the main strands of the web of the lexicon can be traced back from rhythm and blues and rockabilly through blues to the ancient folk songs.

Traditional music has been with Dylan from the beginning, as we are reminded by the presence of 'Man of Constant Sorrow' on this disk, from on-stage some 40 years after it appeared on his very first record. It, like so many other such songs, shows the connecting threads of the Lexicon, creating a web of associations, picking up more and more by the minute, shedding more and more light on the power and influence of the songs through the years.

Dylan has often spoken out on the importance of all this to his own art:

> *The reason I can stay so single-minded about my music is because it affected me at an early age in a very, very powerful way and it's all that affected me. It's all that ever remained true for me. Everything else changed.*

Talking of traditional folk and blues music, he went on:

> And I'm very glad that this particular music reached me when it did
> because frankly, if it hadn't, I don't know what would have become of
> me. I come from a very isolated part of America and grew up in a very
> innocent time and I'm not affected by the Sixties. I don't care one bit
> about the Sixties. I don't think I'm standing on that foundation. I know
> it was a time of great upheaval in the world, but still I don't care about
> them. What's dear to me are the Fifties, 'cos that's when I grew up. I
> didn't grow up in the Sixties, so Bob Dylan the Sixties protest singer isn't
> me at all.[22]

So it transpires that this bootleg collection has an importance to Dylan's
oeuvre that should not be under-estimated. It is not as though it would ever
be a viable commercial release for Sony to consider, yet it's an essential collection of songs for those interested in the later Dylan. I listen to 'Dust My
Broom' which used to make me think of old bluesmen. It still does, but now
it brings to mind *"Love And Theft"* too. On this collection, it is followed by
'Sally Sue Brown', which takes me all the way back to *Down In The Groove*.
These songs span not only the Never Ending Tour, but all that period of
Dylan's recorded life. These are the kinds of songs that kept him going, that
spawned the two cover albums and that could have lit up the *MTV
UNPLUGGED* show if he had stuck to his guns.

They form a crucial part in understanding and appreciating the Dylan who
got from the mid '80s to *Oh Mercy* and *under the red sky*, and then they were
the bedrock he clung to during the long, long writing gap between the critically panned *under the red sky* and the lauded *Time Out Of Mind*.

Without the exploration of and immersion in the 'lexicon of songs' that
this chapter has addressed, *Time Out Of Mind* and *"Love And Theft"* are
simply unthinkable. As Dylan put it:

> When I survey the horizon, I don't see anyone who has the same influ-
> ences as me and who has stuck to them. Realistically, my influences have
> not changed and any time they have done, the music goes off to a wrong
> place. That's why I recorded two LPs of old songs, so I could get back to
> the music that's true for me.[23]

The fertile earth of the lexicon may have taken some years to yield up its
fruits but when it did, a whole new vibrant phase of Dylan's career opened up
and caught the world by surprise again.

1. The 1994 release was ruined by inappropriate overdubs and the removal of some of the original instrumental tracks. On 2000's *The Best Of Bob Dylan Volume 2*, the outtake from the *Oh Mercy* sessions was used in its original form.

2. *Buy me a flute/And a gun that shoots/Tailgates and Substitutes/ Strap yourself/To the tree with roots/You ain't goin' nowhere.*

3. 'We've Got Dylan Back', as the *Rolling Stone* review hailed *New Morning*.

4. Paul Zollo, *Bob Dylan: The Song Talk Interview* 1991.

5. *The Age*, Friday, 3 April 1992 (Melbourne, Australia).

6. Nat Hentoff, *Playboy interview*, 1966.

7. David Gates, *Newsweek interview*, 1997.

8. Clinton Heylin, *The Recording Sessions 1960-1994*. St. Martins Press 1995, p. 189-91.

9. Mat Snow, *Q*, December 1992.

10. Released on *For Our Children*, Walt Disney Records 60616-2, May 1991.

11. I am thinking of others such as 'House Carpenter', 'Golden Vanity', 'Like A Ship On The Sea'.

12. Paul Williams, *Watching The River Flow*. Omnibus Press 1996.

13. Bill Flanagan, *Musician* Dec. 1993.

14. Gary Hill, 'A Talk With Bob Dylan', *Reuters* 1993.

15. Ibid.

16. Greil Marcus, *Invisible Republic*, Picador, 1997.

17. David Sinclair, *The Times* 19 Nov 1993.

18. Don Carnell, *Jewish Chronicle* 26-11-93.

19. Scott Marshall, *Restless Pilgrim: The Spiritual Journey of Bob Dylan*. Relevant Books 2002 p 159-60.

20. Paul Williams, *Watching The River Flow*. Omnibus Press 1996.

21. As we will see in the chapter on *"Love And Theft"*, this was echoed in 'Lonesome Day Blues'. There Dylan sings: '*I'm gonna spare the defeated/I'm gonna speak to the crowd/I'm gonna spare the defeated, boys, I'm going to speak to the crowd/I am goin' to teach peace to the conquered/I'm gonna tame the proud*'. As discussed there, the line appears to have a very ancient provenance indeed, being an adaptation of lines from Virgil's *Aeneid*.

22. 'Talking to Alan Jackson', *The Times (Magazine)* November 15th 1997.

23. Ibid.

# Fourteen

# Time Out Of Mind

## Foreword

*Fans are the most demanding creatures on Earth. The more you give them the more they want. I think back to the hysteria that greeted the 1978 tour in the UK – remember that barring the 1969 one-off Isle of Wight show Dylan had not toured the UK since the then derided, now legendary 1966 tour - and contrast it with these years of the Never Ending Tour.*

*I remember the queue in Glasgow starting three days and nights before the morning of the ticket sale. I remember the queue being broken up by the police and reforming and slipping back a little once and regaining lost ground the next time. I remember being very cold because I'd been sitting in a pub when the local radio station made a humorous remark about a few sad souls queuing already and walking straight out to join the queue. Thankfully my parents turned up at night with clothing and hot soup but if they had told me then that 20 years later I'd be going to see Dylan every year, sometimes two or three different times in a year, I would have thought they were madder than me.*

*In fact they would have been telling the truth - and had we known that then we would have thought nothing could be better. When heaven is delivered to you on a plate, however, you soon get used to it and find something else to long for. In the 1990's this new holy grail became an album of original Dylan songs. The gap between* under the red sky *and the October 1997 release of* Time Out Of Mind *seemed an eternity. The tension and expectation placed upon its release was immense for all followers of Dylan's career.*

It was with these expectations that I began part one of my look at the album, which appeared in *Dignity* in October 1997. That review was planned in advance. The strategy was a straightforward one; I would note down my impressions of each track on the album as I heard them for the first few times. The thinking behind this was that we commonly have very varied reactions on hearing an album over the first few listens but what we mostly read are critic's views once they have formed solid opinions of an album. So, I was determined to take this opportunity to present *Dignity* readers a diary-like account of how my views changed from my very first exposure to the point where I had a firm, settled view of the songs.

The changes in my views on this particular album turned out not to be too dramatic; there were some as I went along, naturally, but overall what emerges is a deepening of initial attitudes, an expansion of appreciation for the material I liked in the album and a continuing inability to overcome the things I did not. Part two was published in *Isis* the following month and concentrated on the four major songs on the album. As this was reprinted in *The Isis Anthology*[1] I have endeavoured to update it here in this new, overall look at the album, bringing in the new perspective afforded by the release of *"Love And Theft"*. And, since I so often complain of how the songs sound on the album, I have also looked at them in their live setting, away from the suffocating studio artificial echo and ambient sound gimmickry.

A perfect way for this exercise to begin would have been for me to come to the album with no prior conceptions. Alas, that will never happen in these days of information superhighways and Dylan cottage industries. Indeed, even before the advent of such things, a seven-year gap in Dylan releasing self-penned songs, the overwhelming history of what the man has already achieved, wonder at how he reacts to the world in his fifties etc. would all have created preconceptions, however vague.

Any potential vagueness was given unwelcome clarity by a number of factors:

The 'Stormy Season' rumours; Bob has created a masterpiece of a new album depicting the stormy mid-late life crisis season, an album of mature reflections on ageing. You try to dismiss such rumours, of course, but...

Then, more seriously, the musicians who played on the album, plus Lanois and dear Don Was all gave glowing testimonies upon hearing it. I will share with you some of the quotes that whetted our appetites beyond bearing prior to the tapes circulating: it seemed a never-ending stream of people (Don Was, Greil Marcus, Jim Dickinson, Daniel Lanois) were queuing up to tell us that not only was the new album great but that it was on a par with some of the best things he'd ever done. It wasn't just musicians who were doing this; the *Newsweek* reviewer followed a similar tack:

> Bob Dylan *is pulling a move no one could have expected. On his exquisite new album, 'Time Out Of Mind' (Sept 30), the 60s' most ornery survivor embraces his past. These bluesy, folk-splattered tunes erupt with organ sounds right out of 'Like a Rolling Stone' and electricity-charged guitar as fierce as anything since 'Highway 61 Revisited.' His mood is mordant in some songs, heartbroken in others; whatever the reason, he hasn't sounded so fresh and almighty in years. It's enough to give us some faith in the future.*

Now I am fairly resistant to such things, and have been ever since Al Kooper assured us that *Knocked Out Loaded* was Bob back to his very best, sounding like he did on *Blonde On Blonde*, but they are bound to colour one's expectations. Especially when someone as talented and knowledgeable about the blues as Duke Robillard came out with:

> *'I was just completely blown away by the material,' he enthused. 'Just beautiful, incredible songs - in my opinion as good as anything I've ever heard by him. I think he's done an awful good job of blending his new ideas and his old self in these songs. I found myself wanting to hear them over and over after I left the sessions and remembering certain words and melodies. I'm dying to hear it.'*

Thankfully the expectation was slightly dampened by a number of factors. Not least of which was that the producer was Daniel Lanois, whose initial promise and achievement as a producer had by now degenerated into a series of heavy-handed Lanois-template gunge poured over records by artists anxious to reproduce the dollar rush of U2's success. 1995's *Wrecking Ball* even managed to bury the delectable voice of Emmylou Harris under a typical Lanois aural mess. Sad, though commercially successful.

The idea of Dylan singing in front of an R&B sound driven by Duke Robillard was certainly tempting, but also tempered when one read that:

> *Producer Daniel Lanois' instructions to Robillard were simple and the guitarist has a chuckle when he recalls them. 'He basically asked me not to play like me - not play anything familiar, not play anything related to blues, which was kind of interesting because Bob Dylan obviously wanted me there to be who I am and add that to his music. It was an interesting job because I really wasn't sure what to do to please either one of them because of what the requests were. Just the fact that Dylan asked*

*me to be there means he liked what I played but I think Daniel wants things to be a combination of elements that haven't been heard before. We did one blues where I just played blues guitar and was very turned on by it but I think it was not what he wanted because it sounded like blues guitar. I just happen to be a blues guitar-player - I can't help myself![2]*

To hire a blues player that plays how Dylan likes and then tell him to play differently is odd. Doubtless some people will defend this under the banner of 'spontaneity', creating a chaos from which Bob's genius will emerge etc. In other words, the decision of a producer who thinks he is the equal of, if not superior to, the artist. There was also the matter of the Billy Joel single of 'Make You Feel My Love' (which, mercifully, I have never heard) giving us an early preview of a complete song's lyrics. They were worryingly Hallmark card like, reminiscent of 'Emotionally Yours'. Added to these worrying signs were Dylan's defensive sounding quote: *'It's definitely a performance record instead of a poetic literary type of thing.'*

None of these things augured well for the new album; then again you could raise your hopes again by re-reading the Edna Gundersen piece from *USA Today* on July 7th 1997, where her description and juicy quotes made it all sound like the first 'Stormy Season' rumours all over again. Such excitement, such anticipation, such coming and going of hopes and fears...and we hadn't even started yet.

Then there was the album title; sounding like a Philip K Dick title, signifying disjunction and what else, we wondered. We heard there was a 17 minute epic closing it called Highlands. Was this an answer to the 'Lowlands' closer of an album so very long ago that it was almost 'time out of mind'?[3]

Only the tape would tell, and the opening comments in the following discussion were written with the sense of anticipation intact. Now, listening to it again years later, I approach the album differently. Not only, though mainly, because of all the times I have heard it since or heard tracks from it live. Still, one learns new things all the time, and just as I was wrapping up this book for print Dylan began introducing songs from the dying Warren Zevon into his stage show. The two standout renditions amongst these tribute covers were astonishingly powerful and moving versions of 'Mutineer' and 'Accidentally Like A Martyr'. The latter not only has a *Blonde On Blonde* type of title but includes a chorus line with the phrase 'Abandoned Love', the title of a vital Dylan song from the mid 1970s and, perhaps pertinent to this chapter, the phrase 'time out of mind':

> *The days slide by*
> *Should have done, should have done, we all sigh*
> *Never thought I'd ever be so lonely*
> *After such a long, long time*
> *Time out of mind*
>
> *(Chorus) We made mad love*
> *Shadow love*
> *Random love*
> *And abandoned love*
> *Accidentally like a martyr*
> *The hurt gets worse and the heart gets harder*
>
> W. Zevon 'Accidentally Like A Martyr'

Certainly Dylan's pause before carefully and clearly enunciating the line when he first performed it live seemed to indicate he wanted the connection made, and whether it was a connection with hindsight or an original allusion everyone had missed we will probably never know. It will be seen at first glance by a listener to *Time Out Of Mind* that the lyrics quoted above embody many of the main themes and images of Dylan's album: loneliness, shadows, time past and irrecoverable, mad love and love abandoned in more ways than one – the abandonment to love, the love left behind (and later that abandonment regretted), being abandoned by love and by a love. The absence of love (or Love) hangs heavy over an album that begins with an (ultimately unconvincing) outraged cry of one who is sick to death of all this Love business.

Just before I write about the tracks I should ask you to note that I am presuming 'the narrator' of each song to be Dylan. I am fully aware that this is a large presumption and perhaps I should refer to 'the persona Dylan is adopting for these tracks'; however I am mainly going to continue writing 'Dylan', because there is no sense of authorial distance and it is exceedingly awkward to have to write the caveat in every observation. In addition, the *Newsweek* interview makes it clear that Dylan is - for once - not distancing himself from the lyrics. *'It is a spooky record,'* says Dylan, *'because I feel spooky. I don't feel in tune with anything.'*

Further evidence can be found in the *New York Times* interview, a remarkably candid comment by Dylan's standards:

> *'I've written some songs that I look at, and they just give me a sense of awe,' Dylan says. 'Stuff like, 'It's Alright, Ma,' just the alliteration in that blows me away. And I can also look back and know where I was tricky and where I was really saying something that just happened to*

*have a spark of poetry to it. But when you get beyond a certain year,
after you go on for a certain number of years, you realize, hey, life is kind
of short anyway. And you might as well say the way you feel.'*

## Love Sick

I have very few notes from my first listen; not surprisingly as I was so
excited about hearing a new Dylan song heralding a new album. I did note
that it was very atmospheric, quite menacing at times and ended well. I also
noted that the idea we 'were hearing Dylan as we'd never heard him before'
was a preconception that would need support from elsewhere. For all the
world this sounded like you would expect a Lanois-produced Dylan to sound,
it was strongly reminiscent of *Oh Mercy*. I soon learnt that most of the album
had a similar sound; trademark Lanois - swampy, soupy, echoey, reverb
choking - describe it as you will. 'Love Sick' had everything bar Eno's crickets.

Ill advised, gimmicky production aside, I liked bits of the song, and it has
grown on me since that initial Lanois-dominated introduction. The opening
song is apt for what is to follow. Death, mental illness, a missing love are all
present in the lyrically taut opening verse. After that the lyrics seem to alternate between hinting at depths and being unfinished, sloppy notes. Indeed
one would imagine that encountered on the page only they would seem
mainly the latter. As ever, however, it is how they combine with the music and
in particular how they sound when sung by Dylan that is how they need to be
judged. In this, their proper setting, the former seems a fairer judgment of
them.

Dylan's voice adds textural depth to this hint of innocence and vulnera-
bility destroyed:

> *I spoke like a child*
> *you destroyed me*
> *with a smile*
> *while I was sleeping*

While he lightly paints a heart-rending picture of Love visible, but unattainable and obscured for the singer:

> *I see, I see lovers*
> *in the meadow*
> *I see, I see silhouettes*
> *in the window*

The ending with its echo of, say, the narrator of 'If You See Her, Say Hello'
is quite affecting as a bald statement of what has been implicit throughout. Or

at least it would be were the production and delivery not so hammily over the top; triple underscoring a point that would have been (and has been in live performance) harder hitting without such distraction.

As Lanois is so involved in the sound of the album I cannot tell what to praise him or Dylan for. As I admire most of what is clearly Dylan's and despair of all that shrieks Lanois through my speakers, I admit to presuming every good touch is the artist's and every bad one the producer's. It would be unrealistic to think this was 100% the case, although the evidence points to it being something approaching that. Whatever, there are touches to admire, like the slight vocal delay effect on

> I'm sick of love
> I wish I'd never met you

There are, on the other hand, so many false, ham fisted touches to the production that it is difficult to deal with the song as it appears on the album.

Luckily, however, Dylan debuted the song at Bournemouth, Dorset on October 1st 1997, a mere day after the album's official release. Dylan expressed delighted surprise in an interview not long after that the crowd responded to the song instantly on its opening notes, as though they had had time to know it intimately. Well that's pre-release tapes for you - probably just as well that hadn't occurred to him or 'delighted surprise' would not have been the emotion he would have been expressing. That first performance has possibly never been topped, despite many a fine outing up to and including another contender for 'best ever' at San Diego, October 19th 2002, the last I have heard as my time writing this book draws to a close.

The song, freed from melodramatic production gestures, is a dark, atmospheric exposition of a precise psychological state, the only discordant part being the unfortunate thunder-plunder-wonder rhyme. This seems so clearly not to fit that one wonders how it survived whatever editing process the final song went through. It is a real obstacle to full appreciation. Dylan obviously realised this as he often stumbled over these lines - and these lines only - live, as if puzzled as to how to make them fit into his performance or else baffled as to why they were there. After some performances with the words swallowed or whispered, or even a judicious last minute decision to sing off mike at that point of the verse, Dylan simply rewrote the problem lines and allowed the song full rein without this awkward triplet.

'Love Sick' was highly prominent in the Grammy Awards show in January 1998. Not only was it Dylan's single performance of the night - an unusually assured TV performance of a single song from Dylan[4] at that - but it was played at each mention of his name in relation to each award he had been nominated for. It is worth noting that along with two album nominations (best album, best contemporary folk album) the single track Dylan had a nomination for was 'Cold Irons Bound', so the concentration on 'Love Sick' was all the more pointed. This award may seem a tiresome irrelevance to many observers, who (perhaps especially Europeans) eye it with a healthy cynicism for the ultra conservative, anti-rock'n'roll style and position it upholds. (It is enough to say that Dylan had never before been nominated for an album of the year award.)

Nonetheless the show is a big deal market wise, and the winning of the award was a huge shot in the arm for *Time Out Of Mind*'s already impressive sales - increasing them fourfold by one reckoning - and catapulting the album from outside the top one hundred back into the top thirty in the album charts.

'Love Sick' may seem a slight song to bear such heavy emphasis being placed upon it, but its introductory role is a key to the album as a whole. Without reaching the standards of the album's four masterful tracks, it is by some distance the next most effective. And how much more effective it could have been with a more sensible production. The aural damage inflicted upon it was no mistake but rather a deliberate act of vandalism. Daniel Lanois was reported by Michael Gray as having remarked: '*We treated the voice almost like a harmonica when you over-drive it through a small guitar amplifier.*' Indeed so, it sure sounds that way. What a pity no-one thought of treating the voice as, erm, a voice.

You are left thanking whomsoever you may believe in that Lanois did not get his hands on *"Love And Theft"*. A fact underlined when one compares the rockabilly song buried under echo on the second track, 'Dirt Road Blues', with the pure delights of 'Summer Days' on *"Love And Theft"*.

### Dirt Road Blues

On first listen the immediate impact of the second track was its abrupt change of musical style, calling to mind a comment about the sessions producing all different kinds of music. As the rockabilly beat hit home it initially made me think of Dylan performing 'Boogie Woogie Country Girl' on the Doc Pomus tribute album.[5] I then had a sudden hope we'd get some-thing similar to the sublime 'The Big Light' on Elvis Costello's *King Of America*. It was not to be. This sounded an innocuous rockabilly run-through, possibly quite enjoyable were it not so over-echoed.

Puzzling over why that should be, I note the line '*until my eyes begin to bleed'* brings to mind 'Blood In My Eyes', which in turn brings thoughts of an uncomfortable contrast in quality. There are hints of things to come later in the album that you soon pick up on as you hear the album more times - things like the 'chains' and the 'shadow' - but the song seems a harmless little five-fingered exercise in nostalgia smothered in a horrendous mess of a production. According to Lanois one of the atmosphere enhancers at this track was a 1950s track being played - possibly backwards - in the background. The album as a whole is replete with a web of nods, winks and associations to other songs (including other Dylan songs) - it is one of its strengths, though it is not employed as flawlessly as it would be on *"Love And Theft"*.

Once you hear the rest of the album, you realise that this track is the only evidence of more than one style on the album. The more I think about it, the odder the inclusion of this track appears. The sound is very different in an otherwise uniform album, it adds nothing to an album that would be long enough without it - and it breaks up the continuity of the opening tracks. I can't for the life of me think why it is in there, though it's good to see the likeable drummer from his then live band, Winston Watson, get on the album.

Lyrically the track, although slight, fits well enough. It has all the themes of walking, searching for a lost love and a very *Time Out Of Mind*-ish imagery in

> *Gon' walk down that dirt road until my eyes begin to bleed*
> *'Til there's nothing left to see, 'til the chains have been shattered and I've*
> *been freed*

On the album the song ends with Dylan declaring he is going to keep on walking until everything becomes the same and until he hears her holler his name. The official lyrics, however, have a completely different last verse that ends like this:

> *Gon' walk on down that dirt road 'til I'm right beside the sun*
> *Gon' walk on down until I'm right beside the sun*
> *I'm gonna have to put up a barrier to keep myself away from everyone*

It is interesting that this verse was replaced, as the 'sun' is a crucial image in the album and putting this dirt road walker right beside it would resonate meaningfully with other lines throughout *Time Out Of Mind*. I suspect it was dropped because of the last line. Certainly there is a barrier between the album's speaking voice - which we all take to be Dylan - and everyone else, his *'sense of humanity'* as he tells us elsewhere has *'gone down the drain'*. It's a major focus of the entire album, but nowhere else is it stated that this was a situation deliberately created by the speaker. This line would have changed that, had it been included.

As of the end of touring in 2002, 'Dirt Road Blues' is the only *Time Out Of Mind* song that has never been played live, though a live performance on a film set is listed for inclusion in the as yet unreleased film *masked and anonymous*. It is almost as though it slipped onto the album by mistake, and has been overlooked ever since.

### Standing In The Doorway

I must admit that I cannot read most of the notes from my first exposure to this song. I was too busy listening to write much, I was so excited my scribbles went all over the place. What I did pick out was that the opening notes brought 'I Can't Help Falling In Love With You' to mind; that the *'ghost of our old love'* passage made me think he was singing of Sara[6]; I left myself a note to listen carefully to what he was singing about the *'Mercy of God'* and, later, *'the church bells'*; there are then indecipherable comments about how much I was enjoying his singing on certain lines and words. I quote the lovely reference to 'Moonshiner' with glee and, apparently, *'I danced with a stranger, but she just reminded me you were the one'* triggered off thoughts of 'Visions Of Johanna' - of all things - with Louise making it clear that *'Johanna's not here'*. Not that I am saying there is anything particularly relevant in this thought, but that is the kind of thing these notes were designed to capture.

As time passed, I heard all the tracks and realised that allusion to his own songs played a crucial structural role throughout the album. I love this - not my favourite but not far off it. A whole web of imagery and themes now seems to be becoming clear on the album. When they work – which I may as well tell you now I think is fitfully - it knits together and produces something genuinely moving.

What themes and imagery am I talking about? Well: walking, religion, (add those two together and you get a pilgrimage); sickness (particularly mental), dark/light; this world/the next, pointlessness of writing or saying things, time... I'm sure you've all noticed these and others, but this is not the kind of article for me to explore them.

Back to me sitting taking notes on each individual track for my *Dignity* review. And I don't know whether the earlier thought of Sara set off a train of associations or not, but every time I hear the chorus I think of him on the cover of *Street-Legal*. Not an unpleasant image to have, of course, but how young and alive the (already middle aged) Dylan of then seems in contrast to the frankly old and tired sounding Dylan of this bleak record. And bleak it is, though there is the odd crumb of comfort in some lines if you look hard enough, as here in:

*Even if the flesh falls off of my face*
*I know someone will be there to care*

Incidentally, that first line glories not only in gorgeous alliteration but also in a sumptuous vocal delivery.

The opening notes come straight from 'Can't Help Falling In Love'; *'Wise men say...'* is what I hear each time it starts. This is no coincidence. All through the album musical and textual references are made to a whole slew of traditional songs; the usual Dylan touchstones are represented: Guthrie, Johnson, McTell, Elvis, The Stanley Brothers, Rev. Gary Davis and Dylan himself, oh - and whoever that chap who wrote the Psalms was.

Then for the third successive opening - but for by no means the last time on this album - we find our singer walking; this time through summer nights.[7] I like the mention of the jukebox, I can feel the summer night, imagine the scene, Elvis hasn't left my mind - so I can almost hear 'Can't Help Falling In Love' coming from the jukebox. Also I just love it when Dylan makes references to music playing in his songs; *'the last radio is playing'* in 'Shooting Star' gets to me every time.

Whatever anyone thinks of this album, surely we must agree it is extraordinarily depressing (realistically so, but still depressing). The next four lines detail a Dylan in desperate straits:

*Yesterday everything was goin' too fast*
*Today it's movin' too slow*
*I got no place left to turn*
*I got nothin' left to burn*

It was rumoured that these songs would contain Dylan's mid-50s meditations on the ageing process. The rumours were true, what a bleak contrast this is though to the bright fire of Dylan's youth (think of the '65 press conferences, for instance).

For most people, growing older is synonymous with time going too fast - the feeling that Xmas comes every two months; that when you were setting out on life's path you had aeons of time to accomplish all the things you planned to achieve, only to find out that the years have all been eaten up. What could be worse than this feeling that life is speeding by too fast? Dylan knows, and tells us that it is the feeling that even this high-speed career through life is too slow. What comes next, if you are in the situation he depicts throughout the album, is the feeling that you want it to hurry up and be done with. 'Nowhere to turn, nothing to burn' is a doleful thing to hear from one who burned so brightly with the fire of youth. Is this really all that is left? It would seem so here; bereft of the love or loves from the past (loves being real women, his muse, at times it seems all spirituality, too) life is something he seems *condemned* to.

Part of the angst of the album is, of course, this woman (or these women) who he still yearns for even after she (they) have left him. The attraction-repulsion side of love is, as I have discussed elsewhere in this book, something that Dylan has brilliantly delineated throughout his career. He sums it up perfectly in the next line:

*Don't know if I saw you if I would kiss you or kill you*

and then, in a magnificent follow-up that tugs the carpet from under the feet of our preconceptions, shows exactly where he stands in this (long-since-ended, remember) relationship:

*It probably wouldn't matter to you anyhow*

The verse ends with the line '*I got nothin' to go back to now*', taking us back to the previous stanza's closing '*I got nothin' left to burn*'. He can't make it much clearer than this. This track has grown and grown on me the more times I've heard it, and by now I am in almost a hypnotic trance each time it plays. It holds me now as he sings:

*The light in this place is so bad*
*Makin' me sick in the head*
*All the laughter is just makin' me sad*
*The stars have turned cherry red*

As he frequently appears to on this album, Dylan has a mind in trouble as well as '*trouble in mind*'. Mental illness and insanity are disturbing threads through the songs. The third line reminds me very much of that painfully revealing comment he made in an interview about walking by an inn on a cold, rainy night and being attracted by the light and laughter inside. He went in to join the company but they all fell silent and stared at him when he entered. He killed the laughter just by appearing; no wonder he feels fame is a curse.

So what does he do? He strums his guitar and smokes his cigar. Cigars are an important symbol in American folk and blues songs - something Dylan has picked up on. Cigars are often smoked by cruel oppressors: (Maggie's Pa in 'Maggie's Farm', Davey Moore's manager in 'Who Killed Davey Moore?') at the very least they are a symbol of wealth and status ('Catfish'). However they are prevalent in the folk songs of the poor too, almost always, as here, a *cheap* cigar. The poor white trash trying to ape his 'betters' (sic), the slave showing he is a slave no more, the bum on the train trying to convince himself good times are coming, you'll find all of these *'Smokin' a cheap cigar'*. This is one of the many couplets I half expect to have come from some earlier song.

Dan Levy confirmed that this was a reasonable expectation when he brought to attention[8] an occurrence of the second half of it in 'Ten Thousand Miles Away from Home (A Wild and Reckless Hobo; The Railroad Bum)'.

> *Standing on a platform, smoking a cheap cigar*
> *Waiting for a freight train to catch an empty car*

Here we see the lexicon of the last chapter, and Dylan's immersion in it and the resultant impact on his writing in all its multifaceted glory. Not only do we have the *'cheap cigar'*, in the same song we also have a 'Danville Girl':

> *I got off in Danville, got stuck on a Danville girl*
> *You bet your life she's out of sight, she wears that Danville curl*
> *She wears her hair on the back of her head like high toned people do*
> *But if a west-bound train pulls out tonight I'll bid that girl adieu*

A line that gave birth to a variant title of the song - The Danville Girl (performed by Guthrie, Seeger *et al)*. Dylan wrote the epic 'New Danville Girl' (that became 'Brownsville Girl') in the mid-80s. He also has repeatedly covered songs by the Stanley Brothers, who sang this, as more famously did the same Jimmie Rodgers whose relationship with Dylan's music we were looking at in the previous chapter. It is chock-full of Dylan-connected phrases and features one who runs to the call of the passing train and away from the grasp of his girl(s).

Returning to the song at hand, there is a brief gleam of hope and redemption in the lines:

> *There are things I could say, but I don't*
> *I know the mercy of God must be near*

The first is uplifting in that Dylan feels he has things he could say (even if he won't) as much of the album expresses the pointlessness of saying or writing anything at all. (He doesn't contradict that here, but still it's nice to know there was something to say.) The second line is perhaps not surprising to the long-term Dylan listener but it is extraordinarily hopeful in context of this particular album, as we will see when we get to 'Not Dark Yet'.

The verse:

> *I would be crazy if I took you back*
> *It would go up against every rule*

*You left me standin' in the doorway cryin'*
*Sufferin' like a fool.*

is interesting inasmuch as the rest of the song seems to make it clear he's no chance of ever 'taking her back'. Given the 'Can't Help Falling In Love With You' melody line, the phrase 'like *a fool*' irresistibly brings the fools rushing in of that song to mind.

The following verse is my favourite of this track and one of the best on the whole album:

*When the last rays of daylight go down*
*Buddy you'll roll no more*
*I can hear the church bells ringin' in the yard*
*I wonder who they're ringin' for*

As he reflects on a life ruined by the loss of his true love, drawing to a close with him ill and unhappy, he hears the church bells and wonders for whom they toll. If it is not for him this time, the song is telling us they will be soon. It hints, too, at the uncertainty of redemption (a strong theme elsewhere, though much mollified on this track by the earlier line about God's mercy being near), while gently enforcing the stark fact of mortality and the inevitability of death. The 'buddy' in line two is thus Dylan himself, the individual listener, the person the church bells are now ringing for and all of us - all at one and the same time.

The phrase is bleakly humorous too, in that one who is dead most certainly cannot 'roll' anymore. A dip into the great folk and blues heritage that Dylan carries inside him reveals this phrase occurring in a number of settings: the train hopper who meets his end and will not 'roll' on the next train pulling out of the station, the gambler who has thrown his last dice, the itinerant lover who has had his last roll in the hay. Perhaps it is, in fact, another direct quote. I do not know, and I only partly care as this verse breaks my heart regardless.

It is worth noting in passing, especially with *"Love And Theft"* in mind, that the lines are also shadowed by Donne's much quoted passage *'never send to know for whom the bell tolls/It tolls for thee'*.

We are then back to Dylan with a temporary companion who only reinforces the fact that the one he wants, or perhaps that should read 'needs', is not there, before we get the evocative:

*In the dark land of the sun*

At first glance a striking enough phrase that fits well with the anti-life

227

mood; the sun, that symbol of light and life bringing only darkness to the singer's world. Perhaps, like me, you thought of *'Darkness at the break of noon'* when you first heard it. However, later in the album Dylan makes at least one blatant pun on Sun/Son as in the Son of God. This is a traditional double meaning and one Dylan himself has used before, but never quite so forcibly as he does in 'Highlands'. Due to this, the next time you hear *this* line you cannot help but hear the same Sun/Son pun. This immediately brings 'Dark Eyes' to my mind, where Dylan sings of the emptiness of life if religious certainty gives way to doubt - an emptiness starkly realised in these tracks. 'Dark Eyes' would fit well on this album, as would 'Shooting Star', 'Lone Pilgrim' and 'Rank Strangers To Me'. It's an album replete with the themes, images and influences of so many of Dylan's album closers. Then again, what else could be expected of an album so preoccupied with mortality?

The next stanza opens with another quote of another song that would sit well on this album. Namely 'Moonshiner':

> *I'll eat when I'm hungry, drink when I'm dry*

Then there is a line remarkable both for its alliteration and to use Dylan's word again 'bluntness':

> *And even if the flesh falls off of my face*

The alliteration is not just a fancy flash of Dylan's ability with no other motive than to dazzle,[9] there is a gruesome onomatopoeic effect at play that leaves unsettling questions as to who the someone is who will *'be there to care'*. We are still pondering this as he slyly sings *'It always means so much/Even the softest touch'*; I mean, the softest touches are often the most tender anyway, and therefore these are what he would be wanting at this time - would he not? We are slightly wrong-footed and still pondering the import of this 'even' when suddenly we are given another blunt commentary on the inefficacy of words:

> *I see nothing to be gained by any explanation*
> *There's no words that need to be said*

and we leave our singer, where he has been all through the song, where he is staying until the last rays of daylight go down:

> *...standin' in the doorway cryin'*
> *Blues wrapped around my head*

Indeed they are, and he plucks phrases, images and melodies from great blues songs (including some of his own which he seems to regard and treat as songs from someone else) in the other tracks too.

With the exception of the as yet never performed live 'Dirt Road Blues', all the other songs from *Time Out Of Mind* were played on stage relatively soon after the album's release - apart from 'Standing In The Doorway'. For this song we were kept waiting for nearly three years, its appearance in the summer of 2000 being celebrated by a recording of it live being placed for all to hear on the official website at www.bobdylan.com. *Time Out Of Mind* was the first Dylan album that had the support of an official website behind it and fans were treated to live renditions of the songs from various concerts in this manner. Whether coincidentally or not, a number of limited edition singles were also released containing such recordings. Eventually, to coincide with an Australasian leg of the Never Ending Tour in 1998 a two-CD commemorative edition of *Time Out Of Mind* was released. The bonus disc was tracks culled from these singles, including the Grammy Awards performance of 'Love Sick' and both 'Cold Irons Bound' and 'Can't Wait' live in December 1997.

### Million Miles

According to the notes I took as I first listened to it, I liked this one too. I think now that I must have been buoyed by enthusiasm for the previous track. Anyway, back in first-listen-land, I praised the opening and closing verses and really got off on the line:

*People ask about you, I didn't tell them everything I knew*

which is such a Dylanesque one, we are left asking ourselves: 'So what did he tell them? How much did he leave out? What does he know anyway?' It also is tellingly, and beautifully, echoed in the next song on the album.

I was also pleased to be reminded of the splendid versions of the traditional 'Rock Me, Mama' song from the *Pat Garrett & Billy The Kid* sessions by the affectionate recasting of them here in the penultimate 'Rock me pretty baby' verse. The only thing my initial observations complained about was the sound, but there is no point in me re-iterating every detail of the disquiet this causes me on every track, other than to point out when it has a strong effect on my attempted appreciation. Unfortunately that is the case here. I feel that there is a decent song trying to get out, but the overall musical sound is dull and distorted. It is a damn strange thing because lots of the things I love about the two songs on either side of it are present here: the references to Dylan's own past and to traditional songs, the odd bit of phrasing, the general theme even. Yet it just sounds false somehow and the music/sound of it is terribly distracting and off-putting.

Although at times it comes across a little like Robert Hunter writing a Dylan song, there is also a good deal of strong writing here and part of the 'Hunteresque' feeling is because nearly every couplet refers to a previous song Dylan has written, recorded or been associated with in one way or another. Dylan fans can have a little game of 'spot the reference' here, but far more importantly than that these allusions would fit in neatly with the idea that Dan Levy expressed to me; namely that he felt the song was about Dylan's estrangement from his muse.

It certainly is common enough to find Dylan singing to his muse, and throughout this album you are never too sure if the 'love' he is forever searching for is a woman, a number of women, an idealised woman, his muse or his manifest destiny. Maybe he won't be sure either, not until he reaches the 'Highlands'.

I've grown over the years, and with the aid of various live performances, to enjoy this song much more than I did; perhaps my initial reaction was the one to trust after all. The impediment to this being a sustained pleasure would appear to lie with the overall sound, the unnecessary barrier it puts between the singer and the song.

Hindsight also throws a lot more emphasis on the delightfully light-touched jokey pun that appears suddenly out of the general gloom: '*Gonna find me a janitor to sweep me off my feet*'. In the summer of 1999 Dylan told a series of the most appalling pun-jokes on stage - which were kind of great just because of the idea of Dylan telling them - but, as here in 'Million Miles', he was to integrate examples of these perfectly into songs on his next album, "*Love And Theft*".

### Tryin' To Get To Heaven

There wasn't much to read in my original notes. Who could take notes listening to something like this for the first time? I've got scribbled comments on how 'great the Missouri lines are', thoughts of 'Wanted Man' sprang to mind but this was funnier and cleverer and praise poured from my pen for the vocals all the way through, but particularly on 'a-beatin'', 'parlour', '*lose a little more*'. No notes at all on the last two verses and no wonder, I had been transported to some other place. It was easily my favourite so far, much as I had been thrilled by 'Standing In The Doorway'. Inevitably for the Dylan fan, 'Knockin' On Heaven's Door' was never far from one's mind when hearing this song for the first time.

Time passed and this song remained my favourite, despite two more heavyweight contenders on the disc. Everything comes together on this track-all the themes mentioned so far, the quotations from various sources taken to an even greater level, sublime vocals and mercy be, it doesn't even *sound* bad. Everything the early rumours of 'Stormy Season' made one wish for is here.

The writing is witty and resonant - and full of feeling. When, elsewhere, I have criticised the lyrics it has not been because I have been desperate for some 'poetic-literary masterpiece'. Dylan pre-warned us that *'It's definitely a performance record instead of a poetic literary type of thing.'* No Dylan listener I know would mind that at all. It does not however excuse poor lyrics; there is a recognisable difference between good, simple lyrics and sloppy, poor lyrics that are simple in the pejorative sense.

The references to other material are so sure-footed here that it takes your breath away. Indeed it may well be that every line is a direct quote from some previous lyric - oh, but what a quilt Dylan makes of them. The last verse in particular with its explosion of references for listeners to Dylan, Guthrie and the blues is masterly, but then there is not a lyrical or vocal touch that is not.

The lines carry such resonance, and wherever they originate from they are put together with a characteristic Dylanesque eye for the aphorism. The gnomic:

> *When you think that you've lost everything,*
> *You find out you can always lose a little more*

Provides one example and another, perfectly suited to the album's mood comes in:

> *They tell me everything is gonna be all right,*
> *But I don't know what all right even means*

The line that reminded me of 'Wanted Man', Dylan's slight, if enjoyable, song from his late 1960s foray into straight country music:

> *When I was in Missouri, they would not let me be*

is followed by *'I had to leave there in a hurry, I only saw what they let me see'*, which ties in neatly with *'People ask about you, I didn't tell them everything I knew'* from 'Million Miles'. As in the previous song, the listener is left with questions, in this case mainly 'just what in heaven's name was it that they did *not* want him to see?'

Most of the themes I mention at the beginning of this article are to be found here; the imminence of death, underscored by the yearning to get this life over with as quickly as possible, is evident in the very refrain.

Again it is hot, and in the opening lines once again he is 'walking', this time *'through the middle of nowhere'*. He walks so many miles on this album, through the most desperate of places, for nary a smile. The lost love that ruined his life and the irrelevance of words once again stated (a desolate theme in the album, especially given Dylan's reputation) are baldly declared in the middle of the second stanza:

> *You broke a heart that loved you,*
> *Now you can seal up the book and not write anymore*

Again a folk song has been found that is the likely source of this second line. A web of allusion has been created that far outdoes the various film references in *Empire Burlesque* and is even more prevalent than that of the nursery rhymes in *under the red sky*.

From the Rev. Gary Davis title to the beautifully apt Guthrie (and therefore early Dylan) lines:

> *Some trains don't pull no gamblers,*
> *No midnight ramblers like they did before*

the song is built upon the lexicon of song that Dylan seems to have decided is the one thing that cannot be taken from him. We are back to the quote that was so central to the last chapter, it keeps recurring as the crucial touchstone:

> *Here's the thing with me and the religious thing. This is the flat-out truth: I find the religiosity and philosophy in the music. I don't find it anywhere else. Songs like 'Let Me Rest on a Peaceful Mountain' or 'I Saw the Light' - that's my religion. I don't adhere to rabbis, preachers, evangelists, all of that. I've learned more from the songs than I've learned from any of this kind of entity. The songs are my lexicon. I believe the songs.*[10]

No Dylan fan au fait with the Never Ending Tour can help but think of his renditions of songs attributed to Elizabeth Cotton, 'Been All Around The World' and 'Shake Sugaree', when hearing the lines:

> *I've been all around the world boys...*
> *I've been to Sugartown, I shook the sugar down...*

But it is next to nothing just for Dylan to list references and us to have the fun of spotting them. What he has done here is fuse them into a new artistic whole (not just here but most particularly so) because he *has*, as we know, *'been all around the world'* many, many times and this album makes it sound like he is doing it because there is nothing else he can do until he 'gets to Heaven'. Taking our knowledge of Dylan the performer away from this, the line still resonates in its own right as it sounds on this album, as if the singer has walked the circumference of the globe time after time for no apparent reason but just because there may be some point to it if he just keeps walking, walking...

As for *'I've been to Sugartown, I shook the sugar down'*, this may well be a direct allusion to 'Shake Sugaree' but that is only one of many potential references. This line, brilliantly delivered, is positively teeming with possibilities relating to other blues songs, to sugar as 'candy', sugar as 'drugs', sugar as sexual slang, sugar as the sweetness of (usually hedonistic) life, and Bob Dylan did not just go to Sugartown, he damn well shook the sugar down. Yeah, good on you Bob - but that was then, and this is now, when he is simply *'trying to get to heaven, before they close the door'*. Regardless of the originality or otherwise of the line, it becomes Dylan's own in this new setting. As do all the borrowed lines (including the title) in this original masterpiece made from unoriginal parts. The folk tradition in action, directed by Bob Dylan.

Before that wonderful climax, there are the lovely lines about Miss Mary Jane:

> I was ridin' in a buggy with Miss Mary Jane,
> Miss Mary Jane got a house in Baltimore

This triggered a memory or two for me, and Seth Kulick provided the context from that most likely of sources (*'The Folk Songs of North America'* by Alan Lomax).[11] Dig out your old folk anthologies and find the song beginning:[12]

> Ridin' in the buggy, Miss Mary Jane
> Miss Mary Jane, Miss Mary Jane
> Ridin' in the buggy, Miss Mary Jane
> I'm a long way from home

You may be intrigued to find that it continues with such verses as:

> Sally got a house in Baltimo',
> Baltimo', Baltimo'
> Sally got a house in Baltimo'
> And it's three stories high
> Sally got a house in Baltimo',
> Baltimo', Baltimo'
> Sally got a house in Baltimo'
> An' it's full of chicken pie

So what does it all mean? The above reminds me of nothing so much as a lewd *Basement Tape* piece. So much so I can actually *hear* Dylan slyly singing *'chicken pie'*; Clearly Sally ain't got a house, she got a home.

In 'Tryin' To Get To Heaven', though, the lines reek of the elegance of some by-gone time. I am referring to the voice and the music as well as the connotations of 'buggy'. As in much of *Time Out Of Mind* (and *"Love And Theft"*), Dylan is not merely alluding to a previous song. The allusion is instead a point to note, something to bring an additional resonance, an extra bit of pleasure in the midst of one's enjoyment and appreciation of the lines as they appear here in their new setting.

The singing throughout is as exquisite as the lyrics. The way Dylan phrases 'a-beatin'' and 'parlour' and the lines about Miss Mary Jane are triumphantly successful examples of his total control over his material.

'Tryin' To Get to Heaven' offers no easy escape, memories that haunt may be getting dimmer but they have not disappeared, the singer is *'trying to get to Heaven before they close the door,'* but we do not hear that he does. The journey seems long and hope in short supply, the rest of the album continues with Dylan (or the projected figure of the songs, if you prefer) walking through a shadowy world where all seems hollow, towards heaven before they close the door, towards where his heart is, in the Highlands.

In live performances Dylan has taken the song even further. After several years where it featured as a moving live recreation of the album track, Dylan recast the song in a new arrangement. The best version I know of this incarnation was in Wales, at Cardiff in 2000. Dylan in this leg of his ongoing tour was performing the song almost as an orchestrated, conversational soliloquy that the audience was allowed to overhear. There was a devastating wistfulness in his delivery over an understated, minimalist backing. In Cardiff, the audience was treated to a vocalisation of memory, regret touched by a hint of the indomitable questing spirit that brings with it a faint hope that all will be well one day. Not only was the song shown in a new light, but you felt that Dylan was allowing you an intimate glimpse into yet another side of him too, and this brought out in turn hidden parts of your own soul. Dylan was once again, as only he can, communicating the seemingly incommunicable.

Returning to *Time Out Of Mind* itself, everything that is good about the songs on this album is present on this track, but unfortunately everything that is bad is present on the next.

### 'Til I Fell In Love With You

Once again there is hardly a note from my first exposure but this time I was speechless for the opposite reason to that of first hearing 'Tryin' To Get To Heaven'. I could not believe how bad this sounded. I initially presumed that this was the track that had been covered by Billy Joel, but then I realised the title was wrong.

On further listens I even liked the odd line and noticed the usual multitude of resonances, but was (and remain) flabbergasted that this was included on an official release. It beggars belief that the man who has just sung so expressively on 'Tryin' To Get To Heaven' does not realize how insincere this sounds. Without wishing to sound too ageist about it – wasn't Dylan a bit old to be coming across like a love sick teenager? Whatever the answer to that, he completely lacks conviction here.

Everything negative about the album is represented on this one track; sloppy writing, horrendous sound, insincere bluffing of the audience. Compare and contrast the way he sings 'lurve' here and the 'a-beatin'' in the previous song; this is the difference, to use the non-pc phrase from later on in the album, *'between a real blonde and a fake'*.

You hear the line about his eyes falling off his face and hope it was meant as a clever echo of the previous *'when the flesh falls off of my face'*, yet it comes across just as sloppiness. You suspect it has gone onto the album without anyone noticing the double use, especially as it is sung so off-handedly here compared with the tremendously moving appearance in 'Standing In The Doorway', where the *'off of'* was so cleverly delivered and 'flesh' alliterated so gruesomely with 'face'.

I understand the track's role as a minor one, as a 'buffer' between more heavy-duty ones. Some albums need these lighter songs to break up heavier pieces that, if run together, would be impossible to concentrate on or would begin to sound portentous. Many Dylan albums use them to fine effect, although the successor to this would be a notable and noteworthy exception to that layout. It is one thing to have light and witty songs interspersing the masterpieces of the early to mid sixties, for example, and quite another to lurch here from a late masterpiece like 'Tryin' To Get To Heaven' to this ghastly concoction of Lanois at his worst and Dylan sounding like, well I am not quite sure what or who he comes across as - but it is certainly not the artist of the previous or next track.

As ever with Dylan, however, there is always interest in his words. And although the setting may not be to my liking the album's themes are still present, indeed one of them features more palpably here than anywhere else. *'I know God is my shield and he won't lead me astray/Still I don't know what I am gonna do'* Dylan intones dolefully, and this lack of direction despite a belief in God, in the Heaven he is despairingly trying to reach, is echoed throughout this album, where religious faith brings little or no comfort or certainty.

TROUBADOUR

### Not Dark Yet

Those notes I took on my first hearing of the album display a see-saw of emotion; a classic followed by what I thought of as drivel followed by - well it sure sounded like another classic to me. There was the magnificent singing and phrasing - check out *'gay Pareeee'*, if you need convincing that Dylan is still a master of vocal delivery. Taut lines full of compressed meaning shot out at me as I noticed strong links to songs already on the album. On first listen it was right up close to 'Tryin' To Get To Heaven' in my heart.

Now I know that it is nearly everyone's very favourite on the album and it is not at all difficult to see why. Though lyrically and (mostly) musically a desperately sad piece, it is still somehow uplifting and comforting. Not in the sense of 'Don't Think Twice, It's All Right' which, as we saw in an earlier chapter, Dylan described, acutely, as a *'statement you can say to make yourself feel better'*. That isn't true here, if anything the song with its sense of impending death, its lack of comfort (*'don't even hear the murmur of a prayer'*) and slow, funereal music should make you feel worse. It does not though, the delicate guitar work, the church-like organ and the sheer beauty and aptness of Dylan's vocals and razor-sharp words elevate the listener despite the subject matter. When art is this inspired it cannot help but have a positive effect.

The more I heard it the more I liked it. In old fashioned vinyl speak this ends side one, but it would be a fitting last track on Dylan's last album. Actually it could be a fitting last expression for the whole of humanity before the final curtain falls and the stars begin, one by one, to go out.

I am glad it doesn't end this album, though. The ending couplets in each verse are just too desperately forlorn even by this album's standards. Just take the penultimate lines (all rhyme with *It's not dark yet, but it's getting there*):

> *There's not even room enough to be anywhere...*
> *I just don't see why I should even care...*
> *Sometimes my burden is more than I can bear...*
> *Don't even hear the murmur of a prayer...*

That last surely being one of the bleakest things someone who has professed such deep religious faith has ever said. It is a question the inter-viewers have pursued. Jon Pareles in the *New York Times* received an expan-sion on the *Newsweek* comments:

> *Those old songs are my lexicon and my prayer book,'* he adds. *'All my beliefs come out of those old songs, literally, anything from 'Let Me Rest on That Peaceful Mountain' to 'Keep on the Sunny Side.' You can find*

*all my philosophy in those old songs. I believe in a God of time and space, but if people ask me about that, my impulse is to point them back toward those songs. I believe in Hank Williams singing 'I Saw the Light.' I've seen the light, too.' Dylan says he now subscribes to no organized religion.*

The lyrics return to our by now well documented themes. Estrangement from community, *'Well my sense of humanity has gone down the drain'.* Pointlessness, lack of achievement are showcased with a typically well-honed Dylan line, *'I know it looks like I'm movin' but I'm standin' still'.*

The idea of Dylan, of all people, standing still is somewhat shocking by itself. As that line would suggest, this track evinces some of the album's tautest and finest lines. For example:

*I've still got the scars that the sun didn't heal*

is fine as a straightforward descriptive line but it holds strong resonances for the Dylan listener. The 'scars' evokes *Street-Legal's* closing song - 'Where Are You Tonight? (Journey Through Dark Heat)' - the last song before the explicitly Christian albums and tours:

*If you don't believe there's a price for this sweet paradise*
*just remind me to show you the scars*

Once the theme of religious faith, which is never far away, is back in the forefront of the listener's mind, it is difficult to avoid hearing the line as making a great play - not for the first time in his work - of punning Sun with son as in the Son of God.

*I've still got the scars that the Son didn't heal* in turn makes all the more fitting the closing couplet of:

*Don't even hear the murmur of a prayer*
*It's not dark yet, but it's getting there*

The song is packed full of impressive lines, reverberating with meanings that multiply the more you listen to the song and the album as a whole.

If you are surprised to hear Dylan sing that he *'Don't even hear the murmur of a prayer'*, it is not as shocking as the coruscating:

*I was born here and I'll die here, against my will*

This is one of the best lines on the album, I feel, and it seems likely it brings with it a weighty association. The Dylan internet discussion group had more than one correspondent discuss the line in relation to the following passage:

> *And not let your evil inclination assure you that the grave will be a place*
> *of refuge for you – for against your will you were created, against your*
> *will you were born, against your will you live, against your will you die,*
> *and against your will you are destined to give an account before the*
> *Supreme King of Kings, the Holy One Blessed be He.*

This is taken from one of the books of the Talmud, the Jewish *Pirke Avot* (Ethics of the Fathers), 4:29 and the language used is markedly similar to Dylan's. Though we cannot say for sure how conscious an allusion is being made.

This track, uniquely for this album, has some praise for the written word (or artistic expression). It is noteworthy that the writing referred to is not from Dylan himself, however:

> *She wrote me a letter and she wrote it so kind*
> *She put down in writin' what was in her mind*

This too is another doffing of the cap to his lexicon, as the opening line is taken from a couplet that traditionally ends: 'and in this letter these words you'll find' before recounting the letter's contents.

Regarding the music, Dylan told David Gates of *Newsweek* that he had used an old jug-band guitar line in 'Not Dark Yet', and Jon Pareles that he *'structured one song around a guitar line in the Memphis Jug Band's 1929 K.C. Moan'*. As for the singing, well who could resist it? The perfection of the vocal on *'gay Paree'* is one of the reasons we all get so excited by Dylan and pity those who think he cannot sing.

It is not only on the album that the song forms a highpoint. Time and again this song has provided the 'soul' centre of his live shows. Delighted audiences across continents listened in, as it seemed, on Dylan's deep meditation on human mortality. So moving was his delivery and so vocally gymnastic his astonishing delivery of:

> *I can't even remember what it was I came here to get away from*

that the line repeatedly gets a huge cheer all of its own. This acclaim is for more than one reason; firstly for the wit of the line itself, but other fine pieces of writing do not get the same individual approbation. This is provoked also by Dylan's delivery of the line, which enacts someone rushing to get somewhere and then not being sure where he is or why he rushed. Dylan piles the long line of words into the musical phrase and then almost miraculously engineers the space to tail off in bewildered wonderment at the line's end.

The release of tension is palpable; the audience has been holding its breath up until this point, as have you if you are at the show, though all this only becomes apparent in later listening to recordings of the shows. The same process is enacted from this point onwards, the tension again builds up in the listeners and is released in another roar at the song's conclusion. Halls and arenas full of relieved and transformed listeners, on the stage Dylan is already cueing up his band for the next song. Night after night this was a quite extra-ordinary mixture of high art and a populist setting.

### Cold Irons Bound

My first hearing notes took me back to 'preconceptions'; pre-release this title struck me as the most intriguing, it was so full of Dylanesque promise. On that first listen the album had begun to really get a grip on me ("Til I Fell In Love' being forgotten in the buzz from 'Tryin' To Get To Heaven' and 'Not Dark Yet'). This soon dissipated that buzz, though, it just sounded so off-putting. Dylan's voice has been one of the dearest things in my life and to hear it projected like this was a sore experience.

As we will see, he had learned his lesson by the time he came to record *"Love And Theft"*, but it was learnt too late to save songs like this. I am conscious too that some people actually like the sound of all of *Time Out Of Mind*. I can only, as a commentator on Dylan's work, tell you the answer to the question 'how does it feel?' for me. The answer is it feels painful for me to hear Dylan's voice so distorted. In Lanois' defence, the song does seem to lack much of a tune for him to work with.

And it could really do with one. A tune that either matches or plays off the lyrics. I understand the schizophrenic type of dichotomy that is supposed to be going on between the music and the lyrics but I just don't think it works on the record, though it has sometimes while played live.

There I can hear the play between the 'clanginess' and the words, I can enjoy the effect of a driving beat that sounds like he's *being driven* - you can actually feel things getting out of control. At the same Cardiff show as 'Not Dark Yet' above, for example, his exultant cry of 'yeah' after 'Cold Irons Bound' adds to the drama and his relish in his own performance draws me in and engages me in the song. This allows Dylan to punctuate the points of the song that he wants to, like a pugilist throwing knock-out punches.

This is one of those very rare times when it feels like I am finding things to like in the lyrics *despite* listening to Dylan rather than because of it. It opens with another reference to mental illness and has some nice touches lyrically (the Chicago lines for example). The theme again is ageing and lost love:

*It's such a sad thing to see beauty decay*
*It's sadder still to see your heart turned away*

There are flashes too that are up there with the best:
*Oh, the winds in Chicago have torn me to shreds*
*Reality has always had too many heads*

It was not the last time Chicago would appear in late Dylan lyrics. For *Time Out Of Mind* though, next on the agenda is, yet again, love.

### Make You Feel My Love

My primary experience of the song is not noted in any great detail. Clearly, I did not have a lot to say about this one. The greeting-card-like lyrics were well known in advance of the album, so they came as no shock. I quite liked Bob singing it, but then I like Bob singing 'Emotionally Yours' too. I had expected it to be the worst thing on the album but, sadly, I don't think it is.

As time moved on the song failed to do anything for me other than remind me of Dylan singing 'You Belong To Me' from the *Natural Born Killers* soundtrack. Though this Dylan original lacks that song's simple yet elegant beauty:

*See the pyramids along the Nile*
*Watch the sunrise on a tropic isle*
*Just remember, darling all the while*
*You belong to me*

it is a testament to Dylan's peerless interpretative powers that on stage he has transformed this song into something monumentally emotive. So full does he invest the banal lyrics with feelings and depths that the song glows with a poetic aura through sheer power of delivery, the best of its lines especially:

*I'd go hungry, I'd go black and blue*
*I'd go crawling down the avenue*

In turn these live performances make one pay more attention to the song on the album and one can raise a smile at the nodding allusion to 'Blowin' In The Wind' in *'the winds of change are blowing wild and free'*.

Overall though it cannot be held to be of much worth, and it seems sad that the man who single-handedly turned popular music into something other than mindless platitudes about, or banal complaints surrounding, 'love' was moving into his late 50s with an album drenched in the very sentiments he had once vanquished. By now in the album I am sicker of love than Dylan's character in the opening track.

### Can't Wait

My initial impression was yet again of a 'desperately horrible sound'. Presumably Dylan is supposed to sound sly and menacing, but this is not what comes across. The emphases are all so predictable, it is extraordinary that the best phraser we have ever heard is reduced to this unintentionally sleazy come-on.

This meant that I found it very hard work listening to the track at all. If you don't like the music, (most of) the singing or the production there's really not much to entice you. I noted the usual plethora of citations: *'walk the line'*, *'I'm your man'* and even *'How much longer'* which brought *Street-Legal* back to my mind again. There were also the usual themes: trouble in mind recurs and as for lost love, how many of you didn't think of Sara upon hearing:

> *Oh honey, after all these years*
> *You're still the one*
> *Well I'm strollin' through the lonely graveyard of my mind*
> *I left my life with you, somewhere down the line*

And this is preceded by what may very well be the genesis point for all those 'Stormy Season' rumours that long preceded the album's release:

> *I'm doomed to love you*
> *I've been rolling through stormy weather*

Or it may just be a coincidence; whichever, it does tie in with another very open and revealing quote from Dylan on the album's genesis:[13]

> *Environment affects me a great deal. A lot of the songs were written after the sun went down. And I like storms, I like to stay up during a storm. I get very meditative sometimes, and this one phrase was going through my head: 'Work while the day lasts, because the night of death cometh when no man can work.' I don't recall where I heard it. I like preaching, I hear a lot of preaching, and I probably just heard it some-where. Maybe it's in Psalms, it beats me. But it wouldn't let me go. I was, like, what does that phrase mean? But it was at the forefront of my mind, for a long period of time, and I think a lot of that is instilled into this record.*[14]

Both halves of this quote are interesting. The first ties in with other reports that the bulk of the album was written when Dylan was trapped in lodgings by inclement weather in 1996. The second half would appear to be inspired by *John 9:4* (This is the passage where Jesus makes the blind man see):

*I must work the works of him that sent me while it is day; the night cometh, when no man can work.*[15]

The rhyme for 'weather' is provided by:

*I'm thinking of you*
*And all the places we could roam together*

The idea of 'roaming together' is intriguingly divergent from Dylan's normal use of the verb to roam - always up until this point (and then again in 'Highlands' at the close of this album) 'to roam' was an individual action. Indeed it was most usually a declaration of the primacy of the individual, a sign that relationships were doomed. It is usually the bold Bob who is hitting the road and saying goodbye, though his mid-sixties work, in particular, pointed out the inviolability of the individual regardless of sex. So by the time of 1967's 'Santa-Fe', both the female described and the male singer are 'roaming' apart:

*She's proud, but she needs to roam,*
*She's gonna write herself a roadside poem*
*Since I'm never gonna cease to roam,*
*I'm never, ever far from home*

It is highly revealing in terms of the overall tone of this album that now he does have a dream of joint roaming it is something unattainable, something he now is 'doomed to' long for.

Needless to say the apocalypse is never far away, sandwiched between the above two quotes we have a lovely flash of Dylan wit with this wonderfully off-hand delivery of the worst of all news:

*It's mighty funny*
*The end of time has just begun*

On stage, freed from the artificiality of the production, Dylan can give this and other lines a delivery which makes them resonate with meaning and humour, and the cross-references to the album's main songs appear more clearly. (More clearly to me, I mean, those who do not find the production off-putting presumably heard them clearly all along.) So the nonchalance of *'Night or day, it doesn't matter where I go anymore; I just go'* not only raises a smile in its own right but sets off associations with *'I can't even remember what it was I came here to get away from'* in 'Not Dark Yet', both in a show where they both appear as well as on the album. As with some other songs on *Time Out Of Mind* the only way I now listen to 'Can't Wait', unless I am writing about the album itself, as here, is in a live setting where it gains full life, giving strength to Dylan's assertion that album tracks are mere blueprints for songs for him to sing on stage. On the other hand, it would be dishonest of me not to point out that I did not feel the same need for live versions to show me the true worth of any of *Time Out Of Mind* 's four major songs, nor any at all of those on his next album.

### Highlands

Of all the songs this one came with the most preconceptions; as a Scot I was curious if the Highlands were going to refer to the Scottish Highlands, as a Dylan fan the idea of an 'epic closing' song that was called Highlands brought thoughts of 'Sad Eyed Lady of the Lowlands' inevitably to mind.

My initial notes were very extensive, something allowed by the pace and structure of the song itself, which turned out to be a mixture of talking blues and 'Clothes Line Saga' style delivery (so my scribble maintains), perfect for his 1997 vocal range.

The opening verse, I observed, seemed to firmly place the highlands as the Highlands of Scotland. I was a bit concerned by the writing-by-rote second verse but after that my comments were uniformly positive.

My notes of the time continued: 'I love the long scene with the waitress in the Boston restaurant, like the Neil Young reference, adore the contrast between the life that he walks through and the highlands of the choruses. The ending is beautifully written and sung, summing up the album perfectly. The Highlands references become much more diffuse as the track develops - a number of factors moving it away from Scotland and yet the Burns connection becomes more and more apposite'. Expansion of these and other thoughts would have to wait for more listens; I was still laughing my head off at the devastating self put-down of the *'Erica Jong'* reference.

It is curious for me to re-read my notes on first exposure to this song. I wish I had written more so that I could now recapture the feeling more closely. That is impossible now as I know it so well, having played it so often and its spell being so bewitching. And a most pleasing enchantment it is. Simply put, I love this song; I feel like I enter another world when I hear it, or rather a number of other worlds, all of them Dylan worlds – hence the love I feel for it. I hope the following commentary provides you with an insight into why it moves me so much, and I'll begin by addressing the links to the Highlands of the Burns' poem.

As I said above, the opening does seem to place the area as being the Highlands of Scotland (though there are many 'Aberdeens' in the world):

> *well my heart's in the Highlands, gentle and fair*
> *honeysuckle blooming in the wildwood air*
> *bluebells blazing where the Aberdeen waters flow*
> *well my heart's in the Highlands*
> *I'm gonna go there when I feel good enough to go*

On the other hand

> *well my heart's in The Highlands with the horses and hounds*
> *way up in the border country far from the town*
> *with the twang of the arrow and the snap of the bow*
> *my heart's in The Highlands, can't see any other way to go*

would seem to place it very differently. Horses and hounds sounds more like an English fox hunt to me, while the third line brings Robin Hood to mind as much as anything else. Not that horse/hounds/bows & arrows are out of place in the Scottish Highlands - just that they are more readily associated with regions in another country.

To further muddy our highland stream we have the curious line:

> *way up in the border country far from the town*

Now as far as Scotland goes, the Borders are down (south) not up - and are separated from the Highlands (the North) by the central lowlands, a narrow strip of land where upwards of three-quarters of the population live. The geographical distinctions are matched by a long history of cultural, religious and socio-political differences. However Scotland is a small area of a small island to American eyes, and there is no way of knowing if Dylan is still referring to Scotland or to some mythical land in this verse.

Whatever way you look at it, it is certainly more diffuse than the opening references and this, I believe, is all to the good of the song. The lack of specificity is increased by lines like:

> *well my heart's in the Highlands at the break of dawn*
> *by the beautiful lake of the Black Swan*
> *big white clouds like chariots that swing down low*
> *well my heart's in the Highlands*
> *only place left to go*

which further strengthen the impression of a far away realm from 'time out of mind'. The reality of Dylan's Highlands is to be found in the expressly heavenly reference of this verse:

> *well my heart's in the Highlands wherever I roam*

*that's where I'll be when I get called home*
*the wind it whispers to the buckeye trees in rhyme*
*well my heart's in the Highlands*
*I can only get there one step at a time*

And the quite beautifully fitting description of it in the last verse as being: *over the hills and far away.*

Dylan achieves this effect not just by geographical vagueness and 'yᵉ olde worlde' references, but by using verses from another old folk song-writer from the past as a mooring point for his own epic story. In this case a song-writer as famed for taking and re-shaping the oral, folk tradition as himself; the masterly Scottish poet, Robert Burns.

Dylan takes this fun, if trivial, verse and uses it as a touchstone throughout the long song as a realm from time out of mind, an uncertain and undefined heaven. It forms a contrast to what is going on in the rest of the song, which depicts the daily reality of the singing narrator (and we cannot but feel this is Dylan's own perspective) which we are privileged to be shown through his eyes.

Burns' poem is short enough to quote in full:

*My heart's in the Highlands, my heart is not here;*
*My heart's in the Highlands a-chasing the deer;*
*Chasing the wild deer, and following the roe;*
*My heart's in the Highlands, wherever I go. -*
*Farewell to the Highlands, farewell to the North;*
*The birth-place of valour, the country of Worth:*
*Wherever I wander, wherever I rove,*
*The hills of the Highlands for ever I love. -*
*Farewell to the mountains high cover'd with snow;*
*Farewell to the Straths and green valleys below;*
*Farewell to the forest and wild-hanging woods;*
*Farewell to the torrents and loud-pouring floods. -*
*My heart's in the Highlands, my heart is not here,*
*My heart's in the Highlands a-chasing the deer;*
*Chasing the wild deer, and following the roe;*
*My heart's in the Highlands, wherever I go.*

How much Dylan knows of this poem and its composition is something I am not privy to. I first wrote that it would not surprise me if he only vaguely knew it or had maybe heard the refrain in song or ballad (we are talking here of a 'trad. arranged by R. Burns' type of thing). I later came across a reference to an unpublished remark that Dylan made to David Gates during the marvellous 1997 interview for *Newsweek* confirming that it was a deliberate reference.

Whatever the truth behind all this is, it remains a startlingly apt Burns reference for a number of reasons. The opening (and closing) verse is Burns's take on a circulating folk source with a couple of stock traditional images thrown in – much like most of the songs on this album. The verses they enclose are trite, clichéd love lines of the Hallmark greeting card type, much like "Til I Fell In Love With You' and 'Make You Feel My Love' in fact.

Despite the cheesiness (to use a modern expression) of the verses they proved enormously popular (which was unfortunate for Burns' reputation – imagine Bob being judged 40 years from now on 'Make You Feel My Love' rather than 'Visions Of Johanna').

These verses, twee though they were, became a symbol for a mythical place in people's minds. (Perhaps appropriately enough as Burns, like the vast majority of Scots, was not a Highlander.) This could be seen in the way young lovers would quote them to each other after romantic trips to the highlands. ('Walking' holidays away from family and colleagues could have a formative influence on young couples, one would imagine.)

Just to give you an idea of what I mean, I was in an antiquarian bookshop in London the week before the album was released, looking through various editions of Burns' poems. No less than three of them had verses from this (one terribly 'personalised') hand-written in the inside cover commemorating time spent with a lover.

Dylan takes the five verses and spaces them throughout his long mono-logue, the central core that he meanders verbally and physically around before returning to at the end. Not only does the Burns poem provide the opening lines and backbone but it also gives a general feel and coherence of imagery. For example the following phrases would all fit seamlessly into Dylan's song if transposed there:

- *chasing the wild deer, and following the roe*
- *wherever I rove*
- *wild-hanging woods*

The Highlands of Burns' light poem become something far more serious in Dylan's song, forming, as they do, the climax of the whole album. An album through which he has been walking all the time; he's been a million miles away, walking purposelessly and alone. '*With no direction home*' as it were, yet in his heart every now and again, the interspersed 'Highlands' verses tell us, he has the vague but tremendously supportive notion that at the end of all his wanderings he'll find himself in these heavenly Highlands.

This is one of the ways that the final song summarises all that has gone before, while also looking a stage further as so many of Dylan's closing album tracks do. It brings together all the album's major themes (insanity is there, seeing/not-seeing, inability to communicate, breakdown of identity, the question of if there can be hope in a world where the Son/Sun doesn't shine like it used to - fearful echoes of Not Dark Yet's *'Don't even hear the murmur of a prayer'*), building to a close that reflects the almost total bleakness of the album but still holds out a faint, stoic hope of redemption - which is as hopeful as it gets on this album:

> well my heart's in the Highlands at the break of day
> over the hills and far away
> there's a way to get there, and I'll figure it out somehow
> well I'm already there in my mind and that's good enough for now

The ideal state of the Highlands, in a manner not dissimilar to what we saw in the earlier chapter on 'Gates Of Eden', contrasts with the weary distractions and irritations of daily life as evidenced on the rest of the album and in this song's 'non-highlands' verses.

It is, however, a delightfully funny song as well as being profoundly serious, nowhere more so than in the 'waitress scene'. This forms a separate tour-de-force all of its own, within the over-arching achievement of the whole song. Despite this and over and above its wit and gorgeous delivery, the episode is integral to the song - or indeed the whole album. The superb interchange regarding the napkin is a case in point. This is Bob Dylan's life on this (fallen) Earth; meanwhile there may or may not be a heavenly future in the 'highlands' - he won't know for sure until he has walked through this world with its meaningless, disjointed encounters. He depicts one of those encounters here with skill, charm and a self-revealing insight while making us laugh at the same time. It is something that makes 'Highlands' stand out from the rest of *Time Out Of Mind* and point towards *"Love And Theft"*.

That's not to say that there is not humour elsewhere on the album too, but it is generally of a rather grim type. Even here, in the track with the 'lightest' moments there is gravitas behind most lines. The waitress scene is funny while making a number of important points, and it also continues our echoes of the past, as most Dylan listeners are bound to recall the 'waitress encounter' in 'Tangled Up In Blue' while hearing this.[16]

In both cases the woman thinks she knows him from somewhere: *'Don't I know your name?'*, and in 'Highlands': *'I know you're an artist'*. (With an unspoken: 'But I can't remember your name.') This way of greeting him must be a constant in Dylan's life and one cannot help but feel that is why he is partially recognised here, and this claimed acquaintance increases his discomfiture. The restaurant is empty except for him and the waitress. He seems trapped and on trial, she challenges him to justify his life.

There's humour in the way the name Erica Jong comes to the rescue of both the narrator of the song and the lyric writer. The former because he clearly is out of his depth with the waitress and she has clearly deduced his ignorance of feminist thought by his conversation, actions and most particularly his attempts to draw her on the napkin. (A test of his artistry he was, sensibly as it turns out, doing his best to avoid, he is as dubious of his place vis-à-vis women as he is uncertain of his place in the whole album.) The lyric writer because it is damned difficult to think of another word that would give him such a felicitous rhyme, with even the 'bonus' of echoing back to the lovely 'Neil Young' verse from earlier in the song.

All of this is just one part of an exchange that amusingly, but deftly and accurately, demonstrates the character's estrangement from other people, from community itself. The theme of art or writing's inability to bridge that gap is illuminated by this little side scene.

We also have the wit and the very Dylanesque phrasing of lines like:

> *If I had a conscience, well I just might blow my top*
> *What would I do with it anyway, maybe take it to the pawn shop*

He's referring to the conscience and not his 'top', one presumes!

I've already mentioned that 'Highlands' sums up the entire album. Therefore, all of the things I have talked about throughout this article are in the song; according to Dylan this one's melody comes from Charley Patton[17], while guitarist John Perry has pointed it has the same feel, tempo, structure, and vibe as 'Meet Me In The Morning'. When I first heard it I thought of J.J. Cale; those I mentioned that to were dismissive of the idea but I noted at least two other reviewers who wrote the same thing.

We have the usual suspects rounded up:

> Insanity: *Insanity is smashin' up against my soul*
> Isolation: *feel further away than ever before*
> No Direction Home: *Well I'm lost somewhere, I must have made a few*
> *bad turns*
> Ageing: *I wish someone'd come and push back the clock for me*

and that whole verse:

> *I see people in the park, forgettin' their troubles and woes*

*They're drinkin' and dancin', wearin' bright colored clothes*
*All the young men with the young women lookin' so good*
*Well I'd trade places with any of 'em, in a minute if I could*

which takes us back to 'Standing In The Doorway' with its *'All the laughter is just makin' me sad'* and its attendant memories of Dylan-the-legend's inability to share in such carefree laughter. (He was still talking about fame's 'crippling' effect in interviews at the time of *Time Out Of Mind*'s release.)

Dylan spoke of these lines from 'Highlands' to Jon Pareles of the *New York Times:*

*'I can't help those feelings,' he says. 'I'm not going to try to make a fake Pollyanna view. Why would I even want to? And I'm not going to deny them just because they might be a little dismal to look at.'*

'Highlands' often reflects back on previous songs, for example:

*You could say I was on anything but a roll*

takes us back to *'Buddy, you'll roll no more'*. And so it goes on, references within echoes within allusions.

All these songs built on other songs (Dylan's 'lexicon'; what he 'believes in'); all this walking, searching through a world he is isolated from, all this 'trouble in mind', all these tortured memories of lost loves - where does it all lead? It leads to the Highlands.

The last two verses of this remarkable song strike me as being amongst the best written on the album. The sun/Son pun becomes explicit - and, therefore, affects our next hearing of 'Standing In The Doorway' and 'Not Dark Yet' - the reason for his distance from everyday life becomes apparent. He finds that not only is his perspective changed but the very essence of his being. *'I've got new eyes'* seems to play on the old Dylan reading of 'eye' and 'I' that we looked at earlier in this book. Just as the Sun (Son) does not shine for him in the same way as it did then, so the *'new eyes'* he has here are not the same as the ones he acquired then, when he saw everything clearly, in black and white with no distances or grey areas.

There is an upbeat touch to the ending but it is tempered by the gorgeous nursery rhyme/fairy story distancing of *'over the hills and far away'*. This is a quite beautifully apt way of describing the location of his Highlands Never-Never Land of black swans, honeysuckle, horses and hounds, bluebells etc. He does not have a clue when he will get to the Highlands nor even how to get there or where it is. He can visualise it ('I got new eyes') in his mind however and believes he'll get there one day. I wish him the best of luck on his journey.

*The sun is beginnin' to shine on me*
*But it's not like the sun that used to be*
*The party's over and there's less and less to say*
*I got new eyes, everything looks far away*
*Well my heart's in The Highlands at the break of day*
*Over the hills and far away*
*There's a way to get there, and I'll figure it out somehow*
*Well I'm already there in my mind and that's good enough for now*

### The Album as a whole

Good Lord, what mixed initial impressions I had. I adored 'Tryin' To Get To Heaven', 'Not Dark Yet' and 'Highlands', with 'Standing In The Doorway' just behind them. With some reservations 'Love Sick' and even 'Million Miles' seemed redeemable too, but the rest was disappointing. And, given the expectations for and pressures on this album to deliver something of standing, worryingly so. There is no point in beating about any bushes - one of the main problems I had with the album was the damn *sound* of the thing.

I mentioned in 'prior conceptions' that I was worried about Lanois as producer but I was fervently hoping he'd prove me wrong. As it transpired even my most apprehensive thoughts had underestimated the damage he'd do. As far as I am concerned Daniel Lanois is a one trick pony whose trick does not bear endless repeating. Even the RSPCA would agree that this particular pony has had its day.

Still, he was Dylan's choice and with the memories of Lanois' artistic successes with the Neville brothers and on *Oh Mercy,* and the commercial success that has followed the producer, especially since his work with U2, it is perhaps unsurprising. On the other hand what a contrast the bombastic gimmickry of U2's sound forms with what suits Dylan's music and voice best.

Lanois has a number of people in the press who praise everything he does and clearly many fans of popular music like the effects he engenders. I can accept that, though I cannot feel what it is that moves them (this is true of many more producers than just Lanois, there is a whole school of modern production that turns me off while others applaud it, but it is only Lanois who is of relevance here). What I cannot understand is Dylan fans who feel that his smothering, torpor-filling, endless echoing and twiddling is a fitting foil for the great subtleties of Dylan's voice. If you play something like 'Moonshiner' or 'Bob Dylan's Dream' where the young man plays at the wise ol' voice - but oh, what a voice he uses - you experience subtle nuances, pools of thought, intuition and real feeling coming from your speakers or headphones.

Compare that with the complete lack of subtlety, grace or authenticity with which it is projected by the production on most of the songs on *Time Out Of Mind.*

Years later, in an interview with Mikal Gilmore, Dylan revealed that he too had found difficulty in accepting the 'swampy' sound.

> BD: *...I'd been writing down couplets and verses and things, and then putting them together at later times. I had a lot of that - it was starting to pile up - so I thought, 'Well, I got all this - maybe, I'll try to record it.' I'd had good luck with Daniel Lanois so I called him and showed him a lot of the songs... It got off the tracks more than a few times, and people got frustrated. I know I did. I know Lanois did...*
>
> *...I started just assembling people that I knew could play. They had the right soulful kind of attitude for these songs. But we just couldn't... I felt extremely frustrated, because I couldn't get any of the up-tempo songs that I wanted.*
>
> MG: *Don't you think a song like 'Cold Irons Bound' certainly has a drive to it?*
>
> BD: *Yeah, there's a real drive to it, but it isn't even close to the way I had it envisioned. I mean, I'm satisfied with what we did. But there were things I had to throw out because this assortment of people just couldn't lock in on riffs and rhythms all together. I got so frustrated in the studio that I didn't really dimensionalize the songs. I could've if I'd had the willpower. I just didn't at that time, and so you got to steer it where the event itself wants to go. I feel there was a sameness to the rhythms. It was more like that swampy, voodoo thing that Lanois is so good at. I just wish I'd been able to get more of a legitimate rhythm-oriented sense into it. I didn't feel there was any mathematical thing about that record at all. The one beat could've been anywhere, when instead, the singer should have been defining where the drum should be. It was tricky trying to steer that ship.*[18]

I can't deny, after years of being decried for not enjoying the 'swampy, voodoo thing' and being dismayed at the singer not defining 'where the drum should be', finding these words highly gratifying. I just wish he had found the 'willpower' at 'that time', as he was so successfully to do on his next album.

The second negative thing about the album as a whole is the uneven nature of the lyric and melody writing (or adaptations). For obvious reasons I have written more on the successful, quite masterful songs above. Yet there is no escaping the fact that the album contains some desperately poor songs -

"Til I Fell In Love With You', 'Make You Feel My Love', some that one strug-
gles not to so classify - 'Dirt Road Blues' and some that seem beginning
sketches never finished - 'Can't Wait'.

Although this view was not - and to a lesser degree is still not - a common
or popular one, I was not alone in finding these lesser songs and the production so off-putting; or at least not initially. Michael Gray was initially disappointed in the album for these very reasons but he managed to overcome his
initial distaste, to a large degree, by finding positives within the negatives in
rather curious ways.

Michael details the production's flaws with caustic rigour. For example:

> ...Nor is this aural theatricality helpful when this frail question hobbles
> into the frame:
>
> Did I
> hear someone's distant cry
>
> The accompaniment ought to lend a steadying hand, a bit of solid,
> unobtrusive support, allowing the lyric to pass on quickly. Instead, an
> immediate musical 'cry' - a dweepling electronic oooh-oooh - comes up
> behind the singer's querulous wobble towards portentousness and kicks
> away any hope of it not sounding risible. It's so crass, you can hardly
> believe you're hearing it...The sound is elsewhere unhelpful too, isn't it?
> Some tracks have Dylan so buried in the echo that there is no hope what-
> ever of hearing anything of the detailing in his voice... 'Dirt Road
> Blues'... puts Dylan so far away and tiny you just despair.[19]

He argues though that the album sound, despite all his many criticisms,
yields an 'overall cohesion' of sound. It may be cohesive but who wants an
overall cohesiveness of a sound that is 'so crass, you can hardly believe you're
hearing it'?

On the lyrics, Mr. Gray can be no less cutting:

> 'only here and there did Dylan seem authentic about this woe-is-me
> stuff. Mostly it seemed a posture, designed to claim a spurious gravitas...
> a Bob Dylan ducking out of being the serious artist while cynically
> pretending the cynicism is profound...
> ...Portentous self-aggrandisement seemed evident across much of Time
> Out Of Mind, as lines claiming false gravitas wedged themselves
> between slices of self imitation and cliché - ...'[20]

The turn-around in this case rests on the remarkable contention that the
better lyric writing in the 'four good songs' imbues the rest of the album with

some kind of saving grace that allows one to find 'fragments' of worth even in songs like "Til I Fell In Love With You'.

I say 'remarkable contention' and I mean 'remarkable' in the sense that someone as acute as Mr. Gray could come out with something so clearly specious. It just doesn't work like that - even if it did, one could just as easily turn it around and say that the lines that he still abhors (of which he lists many) infect and spoil the good ones by making them seem like lucky coincidences in the midst of an overall lack of acuity.

So for me I am left with four magnificent songs, some songs with much worth but with weaknesses, some songs that are poor by any standards far less Dylan's, and a production that does its best to destroy the experience of listening to Dylan. Understandably therefore, the official album as it stands is not one I often return to. I only play it in its entirety after being on the receiving end once again of someone extolling its virtues so highly that I feel duty bound to give it another shot. However hard I try I cannot refrain from using the skip button.

On the other hand if I extract what I love about the album, 'Standing In The Doorway', 'Not Dark Yet', 'Tryin' To Get To Heaven' and 'Highlands', it makes a disc of stunning quality. Lyrics of the highest order, enchanting melodies and Dylan's voice (it surely can be no coincidence that the songs that really matter are the ones most listenable, least ruined by grotesque sound effects?) carrying me through a splendidly interlocking web of themes, images and quotations. (I could add 'Love Sick' too, it's such a fine opener, and maybe 'Million Miles'. The rest could be out-takes for bootleggers to bring out).

The main four songs alone have a total time of about half-a-minute more than all of those on *under the red sky*, the previous album of Dylan originals. I made myself this edited 'album' and played it repeatedly. All of the themes of the whole disc are present - and best expressed - within these tracks. In addition to the complete clarity in what Dylan is singing about there is no escaping the major concerns as they come back again and again in song after song;

Walking through the valley of death, the fallen world
(sometimes contrasted with a Heavenly alternative, sometimes not)
Uncertainty
Isolation from the community, from human contact
Inefficacy of words
Lost love(s)
Ageing, death, pointlessness of life
Mental illness

Not the cheeriest of pictures emerges, it must be admitted; but with my new slimmed down *Time Out Of Mind* I can marvel at, and be uplifted by, the artistry with which these messages, impressions, sentiments and feelings are conveyed.

I should add too that one theme I have not mentioned in detail, as it is more a background than a theme per se, is the sense of a past community and life that pervades this release. Picking up from *Good As I Been To You* and *World Gone Wrong*, we return to an agrarian dominated time. The label artwork is an old interwar Columbia label reminding one of that of *The Songs Of Jimmie Rodgers: A Tribute*. The transport includes buggies and trains, rather than cars, '*Gay Paree*' means happy Paris and if that is a mini saying all within itself, 'gay' guitar shows Dylan is singing the word as though it were from before it took on sexual orientation connotations. Lamps are turned down low as opposed to lights being switched of. It is perhaps not as strong an old time background as we get in *"Love And Theft"* yet it is a vital element in the overall feel of the album.

I was not alone in creating an edited version of the album. Robert Hilburn wrote:

> At 73 minutes, the length of his classic double album 'Blonde On Blonde,' the package is too long by at least a quarter. The weakest tracks - the empty commentary of 'Million Miles,' ''Til I Fell in Love With You,' 'Make You Feel My Love' and 'Can't Wait' - seem so unfinished that they border on doodling. In those songs, Dylan frequently ruins one good image by following it with a rhyme so predictable that it seems drawn from public domain. Thanks to the ease of CD programming, you can delete the extraneous tracks and create the great 52-minute album that 'Time Out Of Mind' should have been. (Coincidentally, that's the exact length of both 'Highway 61 Revisited' and 'Blood On The Tracks.') By doing so, you'll isolate the songs that you're going to want to hear in concert and celebrate a spectacular return to form.[21]

I am not sure though that it is a matter of being 'too long'; if all the songs were of the quality of the best here I don't see why you wouldn't want as much as possible. Quality seems to me the key issue, one would never think of editing down *"Love And Theft"*. In any case I engineered myself a longer and highly satisfactory CD mixing my favourite studio tracks with some outstanding live versions of 'Million Miles', 'Cold Irons Bound', 'Can't Wait' and, yes, even 'Make You Feel My Love'. Missing now only 'Dirt Road Blues' and ''Til I Fell In Love With You' this forms my *Time Out Of Mind* listening experience. It is 'cheating', I know, but it is my preferred way to enjoy the music.

## Afterword

The release of *Time Out Of Mind* was greeted with almost universal acclaim both from within and without the Dylan fan community. One side effect of this was that people seemed to be forced into taking extreme sides: you (allegedly) had to either love it or loathe it. Whenever I mentioned that I loved or disliked an individual track I was always presumed to be talking about *all* the album. I don't understand why this was so, but I noticed the same thing about the lyric writing. If you mentioned that you found some of it poor or sloppy you were presumed to mistakenly want a return to, say, the surrealistic splendours of *Blonde On Blonde*. It was not accepted that you could just dislike the lyrics for what they are. This is nonsense, one can admire Dylan's writing at many points of this album, good so called 'simple' (sic) writing is as great a wonder as complex, dazzling wordplay, but bad versions of either do not need to be supported in some kind of 'which side are you on?' game.

Nonetheless that is more or less what happened; not to admire the album unreservedly was an act of treason in many Dylan fans' eyes. I would like to think that this has changed in the light of time passing, bringing with it a greater sense of perspective. I certainly hope so, as intolerance of criticism is a very unhealthy state of affairs at any time. As far as *Time Out Of Mind* in particular goes, though, one can now use a comparison with *"Love And Theft"*.

Like *"Love And Theft"*, *Time Out Of Mind* is built upon what Dylan described as a 'grid'; full of inner echoes, lexicon-based, seemingly steeped in a mainly agrarian time from the past. It has seemed to me from the first that *Time Out Of Mind* is partially successful while *"Love And Theft"* is wholly so.

The release of that later album brought some re-assessments of *Time Out Of Mind*. For example, when writing on the release of *"Love And Theft"*, Michael Stephens could not help but compare it with its predecessor.

> Time Out of Mind *was a failed attempt to splice those influences to a modern sensibility, using samples from old blues records, and muddy, ambient mixes. The album's premise seemed to be to evoke the atmosphere of folk recordings, using modern production techniques. Lanois's cosmetic approach worked for U2, a band who always hoped to link their smoke, mirrors and fairy dust stadium-rock to authentic American roots music. But Dylan already was what Lanois hoped to simulate. Nevertheless, Dylan's confidence may have been so shot that he thought he needed the Wizard of Oz to get him back to Kansas.*

> *The three Grammies awarded to* Time Out Of Mind *were not about the music. They were a guilty apology to a sick man from critics who had savaged him mercilessly for 20 years. Most ridiculous of all was the fatuous praise for Lanois's production, which, it was suggested, had somehow saved Dylan from his outmoded sound and made him 'relevant' again. Far from being innovative, Lanois's production was a weak imitation of the Dust Brothers' work with Beck. Lanois did not revolutionize Dylan's sound, he simply made it conform to the arbitrary conventions of '90s pop. For the critics, however, Dylan with samples and loops was a good excuse to bring Dylan back in from the cold.*[22]

There were precious few such views aired at the time and the common phrase was that *Time Out Of Mind* was 'the best Dylan album since *Blood On The Tracks*'. This was quite a claim, and completely unsustainable in my eyes. For a start the next four albums to *Blood On The Tracks* were *Desire, Hard Rain, Street-Legal* and (a well produced one for once) *Slow Train Coming*. I didn't see how the new album could be glibly elevated above any of them, or *Oh Mercy, under the red sky* or *World Gone Wrong* for that matter.

That is without going into the realms of absurdity, shades of the initial over-the-top acclaim for *Oh Mercy* all over again, of those who claimed 'it is right up there with his best'. Now aside from the insult being done to what is commonly considered 'the best' (*Blood On The Tracks* and the 65-66 triumvirate) the staggering injustice this does to albums like, for example, *John Wesley Harding* and *Freewheelin'* baffles me. Comparison games are odious but unavoidable and will always crop up, but there seemed to be no sense of perspective. And this builds up a resistance, I have to force myself not to hear the reasons why this is not so rather than enjoy the album on its own terms. None of my criticisms meant that I disliked all of *Time Out Of Mind*, very far from it, as you have seen from the above. I did, though, have mixed reactions and could not place the album with Dylan's top work, could not countenance it as being a candidate for, say, one of his ten best albums. *"Love And Theft"*, however, was to prove an altogether stronger contender.

1. *ISIS: A Bob Dylan Anthology*, Ed. Derek Barker, Helter Skelter Publishing, 2001.
2. *Rhythms magazine*, Aug 97 issue, Duke Robillard interviewed by Brian Wise.
3 1966's *Blonde On Blonde's* 'Sad Eyed Lady of the Lowlands' was an over eleven minutes album closer, the whole last side of a double LP.

4. Despite a 'performing artist' called Soy Bomb disrupting it with a one man demonstration.

5. *Till The Night Is Gone: A Tribute To Doc Pomus*, Rhino Records, 1995.

6. It is hard at times not to read biographical details of that relationship into Dylan's songs – no matter how often intellect and discernment advise against doing so.

7 One of the references that sits ill with the idea of a snow-storm bound Dylan holed up with nothing to do but write.

8 Posting to Dylan newsgroup, October 1997.

9 There is not an instance of that anywhere on this album - a point Dylan is at pains to stress in the *Newsweek* interview below.

10 David Gates, *Newsweek*, 10/6/97 "Dylan Revisited".

11. Seth Kulick runs an internet site, 'Roots of Bob' at *http://www.cis.upenn.edu/~skulick/edlis.html*

12. Peter Stone Brown advises me that 'Alan Lomax Presents Folk-Song Saturday Night.' is a good one to check out. It was on the KAPP Label (KL 1110) and featured Alan Lomax, Peggy Seeger, Guy Carawan and a harmonica player named John Cole playing alone and together. The album is replete with Dylan connections and includes 'Ridin' In The Buggy'.

13. It is quite amazing how much Dylan has revealed in interviews throughout the years and how many he has given. Amazing because one still reads in the newspapers of the new century how reclusive he is (despite all his touring), how he never talks about his work and even 'Dylan never gives interviews'. Myth is far more powerful than fact.

14 Jon Pareles, A Wiser Voice Blowin' In The Autumn Wind, c. 1997 N.Y. Times News Service. Sep. 27 1997.

15. King James Version.

16. *She was workin' in a topless place*
*And I stopped in for a beer,*
*I just kept lookin' at the side of her face*
*In the spotlight so clear.*
*And later on as the crowd thinned out*
*I's just about to do the same,*
*She was standing there in back of my chair*
*Said to me, 'Don't I know your name?'*
*I muttered somethin' underneath my breath,*
*She studied the lines on my face.*
*I must admit I felt a little uneasy*
*When she bent down to tie the laces of my shoe,*
*Tangled up in blue*

17. Jon Pareles interview/review *New York Times*.

18. Mikal Gilmore, *The Rolling Stone Interview; Rolling Stone 882* - Nov. 22, 2001.

19. Michael Gray, *Song and Dance Man III: The Art of Bob Dylan*, Cassell, 2000 (p. 790).

20. Ibid (p. 786).

21. *L.A. Times* review of *Time Out Of Mind* Sunday, September 28, 1997.

22. Review of *"Love And Theft" PopMatters* Music Review by Michael Stephens.

# Fifteen

# "Love And Theft"

## Foreword

*The idea of taking notes as I first listened to* Time Out Of Mind *had worked so well for me - and for others who commented on how much they liked that approach - that I thought it would be a good idea to do the same again for "Love And Theft". As it transpired, my very first impressions were needed for an issue of* Freewheelin' Quarterly *which would be coming out around the same time as the album's official release. As is customary, fans had copies of the album prior to release so we could let people know our first thoughts, rather than have to wait three months until the next issue before it was even mentioned within those pages.*

*In that brief article, I talked of my relief at some of the initial things to strike. The very first being that it was not* 'Time Out Of Mind 2'. *In the past Dylan had never followed up a success (critical or commercial) with a copycat follow-up, so I really should not have worried. However, as he was 'so much older now' and after the savage reception given to* under the red sky, *in part because it was not* 'Oh Mercy 2', *I did worry. Thankfully there was no need to have done so.*

*If you have already read the preceding chapter on* Time Out Of Mind *you will know that I feel that only the four masterly tracks fully survive being drowned in Lanois' demeaning muddy soup of a production. I found out in many a 'conversation' afterwards that this was, to put it mildly, an unpopular stance to uphold on that production. However, it was - and still is - my response to 'how does it feel?' - four great tracks, most of the rest a struggle to listen to. If that over-meddling approach is compared with the clarity and freshness here, in "Love And Theft", perhaps more people will be inclined to agree with my earlier assessment.*

*I went on to say something more than just this initial relief. I also said straight-out that 'I love this album'. This is as true today as it was from those first listens, except that it is even more so now that I have lived with it for over a year.*

*My first writings on it found me saying: 'I love it for the many funny and fun elements, as well as some very moving moments. It is not setting out to be 'profound' (at least not in a self-conscious manner, it has its own depths, not least in the astonishing closing track, but also in the album's overall effect) but will only not stand up to critical analysis if that analysis has already decided what it wants. Bob is having fun and making great music. I'm all for that.' I contrasted this with what I feel to be the at times too self-conscious and often manufactured 'profundity' of* Time Out Of Mind. *It says much of our culture that to admit to ageing is seen as something deep and daring, or that to acknowledge mortality is seen as profound per se.*

*Many years before a young Dylan, impatient with inane journalists' questions, had said that we all do our work and live our lives with the one binding certainty that one day we will all be dead. It's how we go about our life and work in the light of this knowledge that counts. It seemed strange now to hear and read reviews of* Time Out Of Mind *that seemed to think the album was groundbreaking just for referring to the inevitability of death, the one obvious given we can all surely agree on from a very early age. It was akin to a re-enactment of the 'Emperor has no clothes' with the whole of society playing the part of the Emperor and Dylan being accredited with being the precocious soul who pierced the veil of deception.*

*One has to hope this sorry state of affairs amused him on some level, especially as those that harked on about Dylan's own mortality irked him greatly; it was, as he once again forcibly pointed out, something we all shared after all. As he said in an interview for a handful of selected journalists in Rome, 2001: 'what ties us all together, the one basic characteristic of all of us is mortality... nothing else really makes us similar to each other'. The same subjects of ageing and death are present on* "Love And Theft" *but they are handled in a different way, as we'll see later when discussing the album itself. Prior to that, it is beholden upon me to write some words on the fateful day that the album was officially released. Mortality, as it transpired, was to be much in everyone's mind on that day - September 11th 2001.*

*At first I was not going to mention the horrors of that day here but that would just be an evasion on my part. Whether it should be or not, the release of* "Love And Theft" *is inextricably linked to the atrocity through its release date. Over and above that specific date coincidence, everything of that general time, especially in America, is touched by the shocking events.*

*The tragic events became important in how "Love And Theft" was received in America and how people reacted to the songs. This is something I have to take on board, product of mere coincidence though it be. To return then, to that dark day, I arrived home to see the same horrific and mesmerising TV pictures that were shocking the entire globe. The images being broadcast were unbelievable yet I knew that somehow I was going to have to believe it. The unthinkable had happened, and was being repeated every few minutes on every station.*

*It is one thing hearing about atrocities, intellectually one can recoil in horror, one can extend sympathy, one can try to emotionally engage to a certain degree. However, the sheer visceral effect of the sights and sounds captured by the video cameras that day was searing - and joined us all with the victims on an emotional as well as intellectual level.*

*Images of horror: my parents speak of the horror on seeing, for the first time, the dead bodies and the emaciated ones of the pitifully few survivors as the concentration camps were liberated after WWII. Since growing up I have seen those images many times; repellent though they are, they don't affect me like they affected my parents. Incredulous though they were, they knew what they were watching was true. On an intellectual level I know the same; yet I never feel it - the scale of the horror is too much, the footage doesn't even seem real, one feels it cannot be, even as one knows it is.*

*Film reels gave way to television and I remember the sense of something terrible having happened after John F. Kennedy was shot, and in the mad ensuing days. Still, I was too young to do anything other than pick up the never before felt fear and apprehension in the household. Again looking at the footage now it is a different time, it is not my world. I know what is happening but I don't really feel it.*

*So, for me, only the replaying - this time in colour - of videos of the liberation of concentration camps in some part of what had been known as 'Yugoslavia' a few years back can compare with the utter horror, the way your very gut moaned 'nnnnnnoooooooooooooooo' as you watched that unspeakable second plane circle, then strike...*

*I don't even know which side it was in the former Yugoslavian case that had done what to whom. All I remember was the human pain and suffering I saw, proving - though you feel such a thing should not be credible - that as a race we have learned nothing from the horrors my parents watched on the cinema news. I have not one earthly clue in my memory as to which 'ethnic group' was being shown; but I will always remember the ribcages sticking out through the thin layer of pallid skin, I will always know the horror that such a thing was happening in my world.*

*Now I had another series of hideous images replaying before my impossible-to-avert eyes. New York, New York, king of cities - under attack.*

*You could hardly imagine anything moving you more than this graphic film evidence. Yet the personal stories that emerged over the following days most certainly did just that. As in the case of the Balkan atrocity, it was the human effects that hit home the hardest. The scrambled phone call to say 'I don't have long...I wanted to tell you that I love you...kiss the kids' ...(you can hardly recall it without crying in sympathy and anger) ...the woman who was even told what had happened to the planes that hit the World Trade Centre, by her husband as she phoned him to tell him she was on a hijacked plane and wanted to send her love and say goodbye forever. All those people who tried to give their loved ones their love and strength in the face of oncoming death. Every single death was a loss, celebrity or not; still there was something deeply cutting in hearing that the creator of 'Frasier', who had brought such joy into so many lives, was 'repaid' with an unspeakable period of knowing death was coming and then an unspeakable death.*

*September the 11ᵗʰ, 2001, humanity was stained by acts of infamy. Bob Dylan released an album with the wrong title. This was the time for one called:* World Gone Wrong.

*It was inevitable that this would all become influential in how the disc was greeted in the States, which is Dylan (and Rock music in general's) main commercial and artistic market place. I am sorry if that sounds unfair to the rest of us but it is true, and* "Love And Theft" *is perhaps the most American album from a man who specialises in delivering them:*

> "Every one of the records I've made has emanated from the entire panorama of what America is to me. America, to me, is a rising tide that lifts all ships, and I've never really sought inspiration from other types of music." [1]

*Musically and lyrically this is one of many pertinent quotes that Dylan gave us in interviews to coincide with the release of the album. For reviewers in the States the album could not help but be seen as speaking to America in its post September 11ᵗʰ daze. Reviewer after reviewer spoke of the album in the light of their and the world's reaction to those events.*

*At first, playing a note of music after that fateful day had seemed immoral somehow. I kept seeing those pictures, whether there was a TV on or not. For the first - and, I dearly hope, last - time I lost interest in music. Although it seemed amazing at the time, the world kept turning and I did return to listening to music and there was, naturally, no doubt about what I first started to play. And I have not stopped playing it since. It was, though, very much like starting all over again and this caused two different sets of first impressions, "Love And Theft" was changed forever now. Not that it should be, but the association is there, nothing we can do about that.*

*By the time of my review of the album for* Isis, *it is no exaggeration to say that the world was a changed place. It becomes, in turn, difficult not to respond to the album in the light of ongoing events, in fact it is impossible not to. There is a danger in this that needs to be guarded against, though, as the album is not a response to those events. People already have been told so often that they must believe it, that* Blood On The Tracks *was written as a consequence of Dylan and Sara divorcing; and that* Time Out Of Mind *was written after his life threatening illness. The last thing we need is the lines:*

> *Sky full of fire, Pain pouring down...*
> *When I left home the sky split open...*
> *...Some things are too terrible to be true...*
> *Coffins droppin' in the street like balloons made of lead...*

*being taken as a response to the events of September 11th 2001. The fact that the songs were written before the mass murder (in at least one case many years earlier) may not deter many journalists from claiming this, given the depressing disregard for easy-to-check chronology in the previous examples. You can see how these myths occur - pressed for a deadline, reporters quickly have to scan other reviewers, recent items in other papers etc. They read and repeat that, for example, Dylan has played whole concerts with his back to the audience, or that Bruce Springsteen plays four-hour shows. Indeed so prevalent are these two absurd and easily dismissible claims that they have appeared in books and are regularly repeated in all varieties of media. Therefore their repetition by a new reporter now could be the result of diligent background research.*

*It is also, to counter the more lunatic fringe, clearly not a prophecy, alarmingly apt though certain lines appear. Then again the same could be said from the following lines that appeared on* Time Out Of Mind:

> *The air is getting hotter*
> *There's a rumbling in the skies*

*These, too, are lines that would seem to be apposite to the events of September 11th 2001 but they were written - as were the lines from 'Mississippi' - at least five years earlier.*

*Notwithstanding this, people made the connection and found it fitting and helpful afterwards, which is why I have raised the subject here. All the world shared the grief, but it was in particular an American thing and had a traumatic effect on the nation's psyche. 'Strange things had happened, like never before'.*

**A**s one returns to talk of the album itself, one notes that while it was not as overtly gloomy as a *'Time Out Of Mind 2'* it follows on with many similar themes, and the 'Lexicon' that the second half of this book has perforce kept returning to is once again everywhere you listen. The complete change of overall feel was apparent to everyone. I mentioned earlier that I instinctively used the word 'Joy'. Here are a selection of words used in the first reviews to hit the newsstands: 'relaxed' 'earthy' 'warmth' 'humour' 'loose' 'charm' 'funny' and so forth. In an e-mail to me after first hearing it, critic Michael Gray used words like: 'jolly' 'perky', 'unpretentious', 'pleasurable'.

These point up quite a contrast to the mood of *Time Out Of Mind.* Another major difference from not only *Time Out Of Mind,* but most albums in the now lengthy Dylan catalogue is the way it is put together - and therefore the way it affects the listener.

Dylan called *"Love And Theft"* a 'greatest hits album without the hits'. This remark can be taken cryptically or jokily, yet in a more straightforward manner it holds the essence of what I am referring to here, and it is of central significance in how the album is so stunningly successful in communicating an entire world to the listener.

Traditionally in a Dylan album, 'heavy' tracks are interspersed with 'light' ones. In other words 'hits' (of a particularly 'Dylan' variety at least) with non-hits. I am generalising here and it is not, of course, always so. Nor is it necessarily the case that the 'lighter' tracks are less worthy or enjoyable than the 'heavy' ones. In the best albums they will all contribute crucially to the whole.

For example, it would diminish *Blood On The Tracks* greatly if one were to omit 'Buckets Of Rain' or 'Meet Me In The Morning', though I would be astonished if anyone were to make a case for them being as fine achievements as 'Tangled Up In Blue' and 'Idiot Wind'. In *Time Out Of Mind* 'Tryin' To Get To Heaven' and 'Not Dark Yet' sandwich "Til I Fell In Love With You' which can surely be seen as an extreme case of overdoing the contrast, yet the basic premise is the same.

This is not how *"Love And Theft"* is structured. Nor, I should hasten to add, has it always been the case. One of Dylan's finest albums is 1968's *John Wesley Harding* and it does not follow such a pattern either. Interestingly enough, that was another album that came out of a period where Dylan had dipped into the river of his 'lexicon' and it, too, would have been an album of *'greatest hits without the hits yet'* had Jimi Hendrix not taken his guitar to 'All Along The Watchtower'.

Both *John Wesley Harding* and *"Love And Theft"* are very much albums where the overall impact is greater than the sum of the parts. Actually, this is always true of great Dylan albums, he is the quintessential album artist. Yet there is still a palpable difference with these two albums in that they are more than is normally the case even with Dylan greater than the sum of their parts.

*"Love And Theft"* is different again from *John Wesley Harding* in that the latter achieved its coherence through an overall unity of sound as well as a consistent musical and lyrical approach (the last two tracks alter this but that is for a thematic effect, they are the result of what has gone before). *"Love And Theft"* on the other hand achieves its overall coherence despite what would superficially seem a disconcerting change of musical style for pretty much every track. How it does this is one of the keys to its success in imparting Dylan's vision into the hearts and minds of his audience.

As already stated, *"Love And Theft"* does not work like an album with major and minor tracks. All the tracks play an equal part in the whole with the exception of 'Honest With Me', without which I think it would be flawless. In addition, 'Honest With Me' is meant to play a part in the whole too, it just doesn't sound as good as all the magnificence that surrounds it – and that may well be because the style of music it represents, although the most recent in chronological terms, is the most hackneyed and played out in musical terms.

The range of styles present is quite staggering. The Dylan quote I used in the foreword to this chapter about the album emanating 'from the entire panorama of what America is' to him is fully reflected in the range of music present. You will find blues, pop, rock, crooning, bebop, Texan swing, country boogie, balladeering, rockabilly and more.

When I have mentioned this all-parts-play-equal-part to people, a number have said they agree with the exception of the rockabilly recreation of Sun Records' halcyon period, 'Summer Days'. I do not believe this track is an exception at all; it does not sound, feel or strike me as such. 'Summer Days' may initially seem throw-away due to its overpoweringly fun element, but is as 'serious' in dealing with the album's main themes as any other track, apart that is, from 'Sugar Baby' which is the 'big statement at the end'.

A clue as to how the album can be so coherent and yet so varied at one and the same time was given by Dylan himself. This came in his brief, but directly on the mark, comments to *USA Today:*

> The music here is an electronic grid, the lyrics being the substructure that holds it all together.

Not only does it all *'hold together'* but the tracks all interlock to create a vibrant community all of this album's own. It reminds me of Sherwood Anderson's *Winesburg, Ohio* (another classic depicting the struggle of authentic Americana trying to survive in the machine age) where each short story is part of the *'substructure'* that grows to encompass a myriad of cross references holding together the electronic grid that makes up the fictional town. Like that collection of stories, this collection of songs in disparate styles is very well balanced and has a gorgeous overall feel.

My instinctive act of reaching for a literary analogy to convey the effect the album has on me was echoed in many reviews. Critic after critic latched onto an example from literature to describe the effect *"Love And Theft"* had on them. Greil Marcus went so far as to pen a 'review' that was more of a short story. It is an interesting illustration of the depth and complexity of the experience the album gives the listener.

So while I approached *Time Out Of Mind* in a track by track manner, that will not happen here. Starting with the implications of the title, I am going to travel that electronic grid, navigating around its many crossroads and following such major roads as Minstrelsy, Lexicon, Ageing, Humour and so forth; as well as visiting lots of the fascinating side roads, while not neglecting to drive down the major Dylan Highways of vocal and lyrical performance and treats.

### Minstrelsy

The inclusion of speech marks in the album title led to speculation that it was a tip of the hat to a 1993 book by university professor Eric Lott, about minstrelsy, entitled: *Love and Theft: Blackface Minstrelsy and the American Working Class*

Lott's book focuses on how working class (mainly northern) whites exploited southern blacks while secretly envying them in an ambiguous attraction-repulsion relationship in post civil war USA. His study is considerably more detailed and complex than that brief summary can convey, but that is his main theme.

There are four things that give credence to the view that Dylan means the title to allude to this book. Firstly and most importantly, Dylan has taken some customary minstrel show elements and integrated them fully into *"Love And Theft"*. Secondly, the correlations the minstrel tradition and history has with his own career and his relationship to his 'lexicon'. Thirdly, the initial tip off, the title being in speech marks, itself a further underlining of the theme of borrowing and quotation and lastly, further evidence that minstrelsy was in Dylan's mind came in the pre-release interview he gave to Edna Gundersen of *USA Today:*

> ...And 'Desolation Row'? That's a minstrel song through and through. I saw some ragtag minstrel show in blackface at the carnivals when I was

*growing up, and it had an effect on me, just as much as seeing the lady with four legs.[2]*

Whether or not the title is a deliberate connection to the book has not been confirmed - or denied:

> Gadfly: *Has there been any acknowledgment from Dylan, or people close to Dylan, that he did in fact use the title of your book* Love & Theft *for his new album* "Love And Theft" *and was perhaps even inspired by it?* Eric Lott: *The only word I've gotten on the issue is from Dylan's publicist, who told a writer doing a piece on the relationship between Dylan's title and my book that Dylan 'does not deny a connection' between them. Beyond that, he doesn't want to talk about it.[3]*

The title resonates well beyond the minstrelsy connection, central though that is. When I first heard of it I thought of (and the thoughts came so suddenly I cannot tell you in what order) Tolstoy, Dostoyevsky and Woody Allen. I just put this down to my own tastes and would not have mentioned it here except that I have since read the same thing from others. Perhaps inevitably given Allen's hilarious tribute-parody to Tolstoy's *War And Peace, Love And Death.* Whenever Tolstoy is brought to mind for me Dostoyevsky follows, and so *Crime And Punishment,* as another pair of connected polarities, also came to mind. Once I heard the album, steeped in America as it is, the obvious connection - as I did not know of Professor Lott's book at this time - was Leslie Fiedler's *Love and Death in the American Novel,* that standard of US literary criticism. So I was interested to read, much later, Professor Lott saying that:

> *...My title is actually a riff on one of Leslie Fiedler's; he wrote a famous book of literary criticism called* Love and Death in the American Novel, *and, among other things, it suggests that classic U.S. fiction is continually possessed by the idea of two men, one white and one dark, alone together in the wilderness or on the open sea, like Huck and Jim, Natty Bumppo and Chingachgook, Ishmael and Queequeg - on up to Captain Kirk and Dr. Spock, Mel Gibson and Danny Glover in the Lethal Weapon movies, and beyond, I suppose. I think the minstrel show isn't too far from this notion; with white men putting on blackface to mimic and lampoon black people and black culture, there's the same kind of imaginary proximity of white and black men. So Love And Theft it was: the fascination with and heisting of black cultural materials... he knows full well his musical indebtedness and is playing with it in the songs as well as title of* Love and Theft.[4]

The interviewer took the implications of this further, and voiced a common view when proposing that:

> *...in much the same way that Love And Theft ...sums up the concept of white expropriation of black culture in the form of minstrelsy - what you refer to as 'minstrelsy's mixed erotic economy of celebration and exploitation' - for Dylan symbolizes his relationship with the old blues/country artists? In other words, is what Dylan does in performing the blues/country stuff and borrowing from it in any way a modern equivalent of blackface?* [5]

While seeing some positives in this approach it seems to me that it carries an accusation of racism that cannot be levelled at Dylan, whatever the rights and wrongs of levelling it at the traditions in question.

As we have seen already in regard for example to *Good As I Been To You* and *World Gone Wrong,* Dylan mixes black and white cultural influences, highlighting their inextricably intertwined musical roots as part of the 'entire panorama of what America means to him'. It is not that the *Gadfly* interview misses the point completely, but it raises points at a very simple level and leaves them attached to Dylan's album in a way that avoids the more complex full picture and demeans him and it by the unpleasant connotations it ascribes to both minstrelsy and the folk tradition.

Without wishing to turn this entire chapter into a sociological look at the musical traditions behind the album, I think it important to counter the simplistic approach quoted above, as it is important to see clearly Dylan's relationship to the lexicon he so believes in and, therefore how that may be taken to equate or otherwise with the minstrel tradition that forms part of the bedrock of *"Love And Theft"*.

To start with the minstrel tradition itself, Professor Lott's book is fascinating and illuminating in many ways but it is only one view of a highly complex tradition. It is hotly contested by Nick Tosches, to whom, admittedly, academics are akin to red rags to a bull. However his almost inevitable disagreement eloquently raises all the points that troubled me upon reading the otherwise very useful *Gadfly* interview quoted above.

> *(Eric Lott) sees minstrelsy as emblematic of 'cross-racial desire,' as 'less a sign of absolute white power and control than of panic, anxiety, terror, and pleasure.' The* New York Times *captioned its review of Lott's book 'Minstrel Tradition: Not just a Racist Relic,' as if to imply that the blackface caricatures of minstrelsy were somehow more racist than the insidious stereotype of today's popular entertainment; as if to imply the playing of*

*blacks by whites to be more demeaning or momentous an absurdity than the playing of Italians by Jews and WASPs, from Little Caesar to The Godfather, and every other manner of ethnic fraud upon which our popular culture has to this day been based.*

*Yes. Minstrelsy was a form of stage entertainment in which men blackened their faces, burlesqued the demeanor and behavior of Southern blacks, and, above all, performed what were presented as the songs and music of those blacks. But it was not so simple as that. Not all minstrels were white: many of those who blackened their faces in burlesque were black. And while the songs and music of minstrelsy were indeed usually far from black in origin, the impact of those songs and that music was profound upon the inchoate and gestative forms of blues and jazz. As for the grotesquerie of minstrelsy, there were many, both black and white, who found it no more offensive than the comedy built upon any exaggerated ethnic stereotyping. As late as 1922, a debate was carried on in earnest in the pages of the* New York Herald *as to whether blacks or whites were better at playing blacks...*

*...And it must be remembered that minstrelsy was born in the anti-slavery climate of the emancipatory North, in the most sophisticated and cosmopolitan city of America... If minstrelsy is to be understood, it must be seen neither with myopic simplicity, as a 'racist relic' nor as a textbook manifestation of ideology or psychology.[6]*

Which is exactly what Mr. Tosches proceeds to do in his tale of the minstrel singer Emmett Miller, whom he sees as the missing link in the formation of popular music in America via Jimmie Rodgers, Hank Williams, Jerry Lee Lewis and ultimately Bob Dylan.

While strongly arguing against a simplistic 'it was all just racism' approach to the history of minstrelsy (he raises the matter of its popularity in England as a counter to the thesis regarding ambiguous attraction-repulsion racism in white Americans, for example) Mr. Tosches is convinced that the situation *is* simple and straight-forward vis-à-vis the folk movement of the early sixties stealing from black musicians:

*...But no good at all can be said of those, the great deluded consumer generation, the children of the Beats, who replaced the truth of substance with the lie of posture, who refused to accept reality without masquerade. The demeaning coon show of the celebration of the primitive, the romance of rusticitas - the donning of overalls and tattered caps - came only later, when young, 'liberal,' white America, seeking escape*

*from vacuousness through the delusive pseudo-negritude of the 'raw, hard truth' of the blues, brought about the grossest and most degrading of all minstrelsies. A few old forgotten black guys made a few bucks by putting on the requisite act; and in those few dollars, at least something good, if low, came of it. But what came of it, above all and most devastating, was the lie of a picture of the blues as they never were. It was a fine thing that Mississippi John Hurt (1893-1966) was able to have revived a career that had been stillborn in 1928; a shame that, in doing so, he was compelled to assume the persona of a backwards cotton-field coon imposed upon him by a young white America that saw itself as a force for racial equality and brotherhood. It is this same America, a few years older, balder, and more ridden with the scabies of academic nonsense, that now seeks to find psycho-sociological meaning in the minstrelsy of another era.*

*The truth is that it is those who damn, those who seek the answer to the chimerical question of racism in minstrelsy, who are themselves both the damnable and the answer; they who themselves are the purveyors and consumers of a truly insidious minstrelsy that they refuse or are unable even to recognize as such. If the new minstrelsy, the white folks in the black folks' yard, can be viewed as an outgrowth of the so-called folk-music 'movement' - which began with the Almanac Singers of 1941, approached its commercial heyday in the late fifties, with pop hits such as the Kingston Trio's 'Tom Dooley' (1958), and reached its apogee in the mid-sixties, when Bob Dylan, who had ridden its wave rather artfully and disingenuously, made his brilliant leap from the comfortably fraudulent to the devastatingly real - it is fitting that one of the most popular of the so-called folk-music, the New Christy Minstrels, took their name from a blackface minstrelsy troupe, the Christy Minstrels, of nearly a hundred and twenty years before.*

The difference with Dylan lies in Mr. Tosches' astute comparison of the *'comfortably fraudulent'* and the *'devastatingly real'*. Even before his move to electric music Dylan broke through the folk clichés and regulations. This in turn highlights a crucial point - how you use the sources you are lifting, be that northern whites performing black-faced minstrelsy or urban, northern whites covering delta blues.

Dylan has always been a fierce foe of hypocrisy, even before his 'brilliant leap'. The Tom Paine Award dinner speech showed this - however drunkenly - in political terms, and it was always true musically. Story after story tells how

Dylan did not fit in with the hidebound rules and regulations of the folk music scene that preceded him.

He shook them up and then left them in his trail. The first stage of the *'brilliant leap'* mentioned above symbolises Tosches' whole point. The reason Pete Seeger had the axe he is alleged to have tried to cut the power cables allowing Dylan to play electric music with (at the Newport Folk Festival) is that he was using it for fake 'authenticity' for a songwriting workshop on 'work songs'. As Michael Gray has, with heavy sarcasm, mentioned, perhaps it would have been more apt if he had got his servant to run his workshop.[7] Pete Seeger, an axe-wielding work songs teacher - 'comfortably fraudulent' indeed.

Well aware of a deadly combination of musical and political 'holier than thou' types, decades before he ran up against the same in Christian circles, Dylan refused to play by their rules:

> *I was never part of... There were other folk-music records, commercial folk-music records, like those by the Kingston Trio. I never really was an elitist. Personally, I liked the Kingston Trio. I could see the picture. But for a lot of people it was a little hard to take. Like the left-wing puritans that seemed to have a hold on the folk-music community, they disparaged these records. I didn't particularly want to sing any of those songs that way, but the Kingston Trio were probably the best commercial group going, and they seemed to know what they were doing.[8]*

One recalls the story of him being rejected because he wouldn't sing the proper type of folk song, Appalachian, hillbilly, or whatever only in the time, place and style allocated by these 'puritans'. For Dylan it was always a case of what helps him sing what he wants to sing in the way he wanted to put it across. As he said in a relatively recent interview, this pursuit of 'purity' of tradition is an impossible one in any case: *'It's all mashed up, like the influence isn't in its given form anymore.'* Faced directly with the question:

> *Do you think Dylan's "Love And Theft" might be an attempt to recognize and acknowledge the twisted up forms of racism and cultural thievery that make up America's musical heritage? Might alluding to your book be a nod in that direction?*

Professor Lott answered more guardedly:

> *I don't know; to some extent maybe. Dylan knows how embedded in his culture he is, but I don't guess he thinks of himself or most musicians as only thieving ...he may think of himself as being in the burlesque vein of minstrelsy, but not so implicated in its crimes.[9]*

The reason he would not see himself 'implicated' in what *Gadfly* and Lott (partially at least) see - which Tosches and I would dispute - as its 'crimes' is because he and his art are not 'implicated' in any wrongdoing[10].

Perhaps a more fruitful area for investigation would be why, despite this, his audience is virtually all white. It is a sad fact that at Dylan concerts, conventions and other gatherings there are rarely black faces to be seen. Stevie Wonder's introduction of him as 'our good friend and hero' at the Martin Luther King Tribute where Dylan performed a marvellous one-off rewrite of 'I Shall Be Released' was heartfelt, but he's a 'friend' unvisited when it comes to his fan base.

The comment, *'Dylan knows how embedded in his culture he is'* is more to the point in the case of Dylan's work on *"Love And Theft"* and the decade leading up to it (indeed his whole career come to that) and I include the Jimmie Rodgers' tribute album in that. It would appear Dylan does too, as he echoes his liner notes from there, *'His voice gives hope to the vanquished and humility to the mighty'* in 'Lonesome Day Blues' with *'I'm going to teach peace to the conquered, I'm going to tame the proud'*. Indeed the very next two sentences in those liner notes are a neat description of the bewildering succession of musical styles on *"Love And Theft"* and his own successful deployment of all the traditions he 'thieves' from:

> *Indeed, he sings not only among his bawdy, upbeat blues and railroading songs, but also tin pan alley trash and crooner lullabies as well. He makes everything unmistakably his own and does it with piercing charm.*

Professor Lott's remarks quoted earlier ended on a perceptive note too, when he said Dylan was *'playing with'* his *'musical indebtedness'* – that is very much part of the way *"Love And Theft"* operates.

Dylan had some connections with the minstrelsy tradition before *"Love And Theft"*. His comments on 'Desolation Row' and the carnival are at least partly applicable to 'Ballad Of A Thin Man', for example, and his interest in Jimmie Rodgers is a connection back to that same world, the world Rodgers grew out of. Long before the 1996 tribute album, in February 1969 in fact, Dylan could be found singing 'Blue Yodel' nos 1 and 5 in a Columbia recording studio and no. 8, more commonly known as 'Muleskinner Blues', has popped up throughout his career from his days at The Purple Onion in St Paul in 1960 onwards.

Also in 1969, released on 1970's *Self Portrait* double album, at the Isle of Wight Festival Dylan sang a song called 'Minstrel Boy', which has lines that would not be out of place on *"Love And Theft"*:

*Oh look, he's driving a long, long time*
*There he still sits on top of the hill*
*Well aching and jumping with all laid down*
*With all of them ladies you know he's lonely still*

*With all of these travelling but I'm still on that road*
*Who's gonna throw that minstrel boy a coin?*
*Who's gonna let it roll?*
*Who's gonna throw that minstrel boy a coin?*
*Who's gonna let it down easy to save his soul?*

A connection to that song surfaces in 'Tweedle Dee & Tweedle Dum' with its line, '*Throw me something, Mister, please*'. According to the research of Christopher Rollanson:

> *The words 'Throw me something, Mister, please!' may suggest a dog, but they are also a verbatim reproduction of the traditional parade slogan from the Mardi Gras carnival in New Orleans (connecting with the 'parade permit' in the next stanza) My thanks to 'VanGrod' for putting me on to the Mardi Gras connection. One Mardi Gras website, at http://www.holidays.net/mardigras/, states: 'If you go to a parade, you are surely to go home with some of the famous catches. You can easily obtain any of the following by shouting the famous phrase, "Throw me something, mister!": [beads, doubloons, cups and trinkets].'*[11]

Then in 1975 there was the Rolling Thunder Revue, a travelling minstrel show led by a white-faced white singer in a curious mirror of the blackfaced black singers Nick Tosches was writing about.

Some of his 'lexicon' singers and songs have had connections with minstrelsy too, and many a story is intertwined with various traditions that have shown up in Dylan's work before, but nothing would have prepared the Dylan listener for the extent of the influence minstrelsy has on *"Love And Theft"*.

This is perhaps most evident, musically, on 'High Water (For Charley Patton)' especially with the sound of the banjo. Not long after *"Love And Theft"* came out, a video of an early Dylan TV appearance began to circulate amongst collectors of his 'hard to find' material. It was a show where Dylan was just one of a number of guests and we can see the early Dylan in the context of his 'lexicon'. A banjo featured effectively as part of the backing on one of his songs.

It does so again on 'High Water (For Charley Patton)', though more prominently. This song takes us down in the Delta in more ways than one. A reminder of 'Down In The Flood' and the great Mississippi flood, it is the engine room song of the album. References and themes central to the rest spin off at a dizzying rate, fuelling all the songs around it until they are brought to a conclusion in the final track.

Later on I will be looking at both the humour of the album and the theme of ageing. Many of the jokes are like those that old people tell to youngsters, but at the same time they, and others, are redolent of minstrelsy jokes too.

In 'Floater (Too Much To Ask)' you are treated, amongst many other things in this rich and complex song, to the wit and outrageous Dylan-only rhyming of:

> Romeo, he said to Juliet, 'You got a poor complexion
> It don't give you an appearance of a youthful touch.'
> Juliet said back to Romeo, 'Why don't you just shove off
> If it bothers you so much.'

This isn't the only time Shakespeare appears in a diminished, modern standing - like a living example of Joni Mitchell's reductive term, 'Willie the Shake'. In 'Po' Boy,' Othello's immortal tale is reduced to:

> Othello told Desdemona 'I'm cold, cover me with a blanket'
> 'By the way, what happened to that poisoned wine?'
> She said 'I gave it to you, you drank it'

Richard Jobes tells us that it was common practice for Shakespeare's play to be transformed into something bawdy and farcical in this manner and continues:

> The same song borrows its opening verse directly from an 1866 minstrel performance of Othello, written by George Griffin. 'If for my wife - your daughter - you are looking,' Othello says to Brabantio, 'you'll find her in the kitchen busy cooking.' Dylan takes these lines, and with very little variation, transports them into 'Po' Boy':
>
> Man comes to the door - I say, 'For whom are you looking?'
> He says, 'Your wife', I say, 'She's busy in the kitchen cookin'.'
>
> Productions of Othello were highly popular amongst blackface minstrelsy's audience, unsurprisingly because of the play's racial themes. The manner in which George Griffin used music in his 1866 production of Othello indicates the liberties that were taken with Shakespearean texts to make them appeal to the minstrel audience... Rather than transforming the principal characters of Othello, Hamlet, or Macbeth into plantation workers or urban characters living in social margins, the Ethiopian sketchwriters reduced royalty to common folk and translated the grand tragedies of life into short sketches about

> *courtship, mixed-race marriages, or conventional domestic life. Minstrel shows were mass entertainment, and were 'America's first new form of non-elite culture.' Certainly this attitude to popular culture appears particularly relevant when associated with* "Love And Theft"'s *own cut-and-paste attitude.*

The minstrelsy tradition also has many indirect effects on *"Love And Theft"*. Later, in the passage looking at literature, we will be discussing the influence of the work of Mark Twain, in particular *The Adventures of Huckleberry Finn*. Twain had great enthusiasm for blackfaced minstrelsy and its influence on his classic novel is evident. We will be looking again at the tradition of folk and country music that Dylan has called his 'lexicon' and remembering his two cover albums from the early 1990s. At various times in this book I have mentioned Walt Whitman in relation to Bob Dylan; as both Lott and Tosches tell us Walt Whitman too was an aficionado of the blackface singers. They also write at some length about Stephen Foster, whose 'Hard Times' was so prominent a track on *Good As I Been To You* and whose history was entwined with that of minstrelsy.

Indeed, Stephen Foster - a northerner who wrote songs of a romanticised, rural South - leads us to the next subject area that permeates *"Love And Theft"*: that portrayal of the Southern States and what bearing it has on the album.

### The South

Much of the album is set in the South of the United States; three sets of three references are made explicitly:

Three states - Florida, Georgia and Mississippi
Three cities - Clarksdale, Kansas City and Vicksburg
Three rivers - Cumberland, Ohio, and Tennessee

There is also a lot more that is implied; New Orleans is a clear setting on more than one occasion and the scenic descriptions repeatedly invoke the South almost throughout the album.

In 'Honest With Me' we hear of *'The Southern Pacific leaving at nine forty-five'* and very memorably in 'Mississippi' Dylan sings *'I got here following the Southern Star'*.

The album is not a geography lesson however, nor is it restricted only to the South. Rather it is that the South provides, overwhelmingly, the general ambience. There are lots of non-Southern references too, both musical and textual but then again many of the northern references - Chicago blues for example - have strong Southern links.

For Dylan, who, let us remind ourselves, attests that: *'Every one of the records I've made has emanated from the entire panorama of what America is to me'*, his albums have a sweep that encompasses the nation geographically, historically and mythically. As he said of 'Mississippi': *'I tried to explain* (to Daniel Lanois) *that the song had more to do with the Declaration of Independence, the Constitution and the Bill of Rights than witch doctors...'*

Chicago is strongly present musically in the album, and I take it that the city that 'never sleeps' in 'Honest With Me' is Chicago both for specific mention of a 'Southside', which it has physically and musically, and because of the early 1950's John H. Auer film called *The City That Never Sleeps*. This was not only set in Chicago but 'starred' its dimly lit streets as a major element of the film's atmosphere. The story line is not a million miles away from a number of Dylan songs either; it is one of a moral choice between going on the road for a life of lust and adventure in the entertainment world or staying at home with one's family.

It fits the album's musical 'grid' and textual 'substructure' that Dylan is singing in this hard city electric blues number about the Chicago that so many poor blacks migrated to from the plantations of the South.[12]

Lines and images conjure up a past, rather majestic, sunny and slow moving, country ambience.'Tweedle Dee & Tweedle Dum' has its *'stately trees'*, 'Mississippi' has *'leaves falling from the trees'*, 'Summer Days' boasts *'hogs out in the mud'*, 'Bye and Bye''s *'going where the wild roses grow'* and the *'endless days'*, *'honey bees are buzzing'*, *'summer breeze'* and *'grove of trees'* from 'Floater (Too Much To Ask)', plus pretty much all of 'Moonlight' all combine to create this ambience. Even the cooking references, I have been told, add to the Southern flavour.

And that is a flavour of a generally mythical place. A romanticised, timeless (but definitely pre-modern) South; an agrarian community with solid, conservative values of tradition and family. The South of the northern songwriters in the time of the minstrel shows, in other words. So it was a mythical place especially in and for the minds of the masses of people in the urban, modern, shifting North; for those looking for roots to cling to and a place to long for. A dream, an uplifting fantasy - just like the Highlands of Scotland. A mostly romanticised 'other place' that contrasts with the modern lowlands. The same Highlands as a mythical realm of some majestic past that were used in a poem by Robert Burns. And then picked up and used centuries later as the leitmotif of a magnificent vision in the closing song of *Time Out Of Mind*, 'Highlands', by a Bob Dylan who was *'already there in my mind'*.

Very often the last song in a previous Dylan album foreshadows the next, though we never realise it at the time. It happened again with 'Highlands' and *"Love And Theft"*. The evidence is everywhere: a mythical otherland that provides the setting for a musical treat that lets us see life as Bob Dylan experiences it. Or at least he allows us the privilege to feel that this is what we are doing, both on 'Highlands' and throughout *"Love And Theft"*. I didn't particularly take note of this until writer and Dylan commentator Nigel Hinton pointed it out explicitly. I must have apprehended it on some level, I suppose, but it was with a shock of 'of course' that I first read him mention it in an e-mail to me. It was a point he later expanded in print:

> ...the warmth and joy and silliness and observed detail of everyday life and capacity for wonder that he reveals here. He's re-discovered that you can be complex: serious and comic, cynical and loving, despairing and hopeful all at the same time. And, as we've noticed in the past, this new mood was somewhat prefigured in the last song of the previous album: 'Highlands'. He was unable to change places with all the young women and men but he's discovered that there is another kind of pleasure and reconciliation to be found in his sixtieth year.[13]

On *"Love And Theft"* the legendary region is an agrarian one rather than the mountainous one of Burns's 'Highlands'. Yet the effect is the same, just as the vision of the Highlands was set off against the daily reality of life in Boston so *"Love And Theft"* plays a seemingly languorous country life off of that of busy city existence.

One of the recurring themes in the album is that of the 'country boy goes to town'. It can be almost like the bumpkin barman Woody in the *Cheers* TV comedy (which, like 'Highlands', is set in that historically crucial town of Boston).[14] Indeed the 'po' boy' and Woody could seem all but interchangeable. At other times in the record, though, it can be that the country values stand the traveller in good stead amidst the city corruption. Overall though, you feel danger is lurking everywhere and that the move from the country at best is a perilous journey survived, for now at least.

In 'Honest With Me' the corrupt city style wins the day hands down but 'Mississippi' tells a complex tale on every level, including the country-city one. The song is built upon scenes that move in a sequence - just not quite in the one you might expect. Take the last line of verse one, followed by verse two:

> ...We're all boxed in, nowhere to escape.

> City's just a jungle, more games to play

*Trapped in the heart of it, trying to get away*
*I was raised in the country, I been working in the town*
*I been in trouble ever since I set my suitcase down*

The close proximity of *'boxed in'* and *'city'* evokes the windows of a multi-storey building; all the people in their allocated boxes. How did he come to be trapped there? Dylan jumps us from the city back to a country beginning. Then from country to town to being *'boxed in'* in the inauthentic (*'games to play'*) city. Where did he go wrong? Clearly it's more than just the chorus line of having *'stayed in Mississippi a day too long'*. Everything has gone wrong since he stopped travelling, or maybe even since he left the country, since he packed the suitcase far less put it down.

This gives the song a wider sweep than the - soon to be central - individual focus. It is as though Dylan is speaking about much more than one person here; perhaps this man embodies the state of Mississippi or the whole of the South, or even the United States themselves in some way. It seems a bit fanciful, I know, but here's what Dylan himself went on to say about the song in the interview, partly quoted earlier:

> *Polyrhythm has its place, but it doesn't work for knifelike lyrics trying to convey majesty and heroism...I tried to explain that the song had more to do with the Declaration of Independence, the Constitution and the Bill of Rights than witch doctors, and just couldn't be thought of as some kind of ideological voodoo thing.*[15]

Time and again it seems that 'majesty and heroism', if it is to be found anywhere, is to be found in or of country roots - both in the sense of the mythical South and in the music.

Explaining to Mikal Gilmore what really moved him in the early 60s, Dylan is very clear on the traditions that were most important to him:

> *The people I knew - the people who were like-minded as myself - were trying to be folk musicians. That's all they wanted to be, that's all the aspirations they had. There wasn't anything monetary about it. There was no money in folk music. It was a way of life. And it was an identity which the three-buttoned-suit post-war generation of America really wasn't offering to kids my age: an identity. This music was impossible to get anywhere really, except in a nucleus of a major city, and a record shop might have a few recordings of the hard-core folklore music. What I was most interested in twenty-four hours a day was the rural music. But you could only hear it, like, in isolated caves [laughs], like, on a few*

*bohemian streets in America at that time. The idea was to be able to master these songs. It wasn't about writing your own songs. That didn't even enter anybody's mind.*[16]

You can hear the thought process behind some of *"Love And Theft"* in this interview; mastering the existing songs is clearly relevant and the 'ideal of the rural' raised its head in another interview too - the one in Rome to a handful of European journalists to promote the album.

As we discussed in the chapter 'Singing The Lexicon', the land of *World Gone Wrong* is a rural one; the ties with *"Love And Theft"* are binding. The agrarian world is depicted as the authentic alternative to all that has 'gone wrong'. Dylan was reminded, at that Rome interview, of the remarks he made in the *World Gone Wrong* liner notes:

> *...neither does he* (Stack-A-Lee) *represent any alternative lifestyle scam (give me a thousand acres of tractable land & all the gang members that exist & you'll see the Authentic alternative lifestyle, the Agrarian one)*

He was asked if the 'agrarian alternative life style' was something he thought could work. Dylan replied that *'yes I believe that'* but then spoke of the forces against such a possibility, talking of *'corporate entities'* that force farmers not to grow things, before re-affirming, *'I'm partial to the land'*. This contrast of inauthentic (scam) and authentic (agrarian) ways of life is reflected in the music of *"Love And Theft"*; music that is created rather than somehow manufactured with 'tricked up vocal tracks' and other artificial additives.

Another very specific way in which the South is evoked is through references to the Confederacy in the days of the American Civil War. In 'Honest With Me', Dylan sings:

> *I'm not sorry for nothin' I've done*
> *I'm glad I fought - I only wish we'd won*

This is strikingly similar to a passage from a Civil War folk song 'I'm A Good Old Rebel':

> *For this fair land of freedom*
> *I do not care a damn.*
>
> *I'm glad I fought against it*
> *I only wish we'd won.*
> *And I don't want no pardon*
> *For everything I've done.*

This connection brings to mind the *Time Out Of Mind* version of 'Not Dark Yet' that Daniel Lanois claimed sounded like *'an old Civil War ballad'*.

It's interesting too that at the time I write this Dylan has written a song for the forthcoming Civil War film *Gods And Generals*. Called 'Cross the Green Mountain', it is reported to be '*a haunting, moving ballad, reminiscent of his earliest works with the added insights of a lifetime*'.[17]

More obscure, however, and if Peter Vincent had not pointed it out I would never have known of it[18], is a potential allusion to a heated statement from the then (1863) Confederate cavalry commander, Nathan Bedford Forrest. Angered by having his command interfered with and on more than one occasion taken away, this controversial Civil War soldier (hero or murdering criminal depending on your point of view[19]) has been reported as speaking out in the following way:

> *You have threatened to arrest me for not obeying your orders promptly.*
> *I dare you to do it, and I say to you that if you ever again try to inter-*
> *fere with me or cross my path it will be at the peril of your life.*[20]

Dylan's lines in 'Floater (Too Much To Ask)':

> *If you ever try to interfere with me or cross my path again*
> *You do so at the peril of your own life*

are so very similar that it would appear to be impossible for this to be a coincidence, given the other Civil War references and ambience.

**Lexicon** - strap yourself to the tree with roots

Overarching everything in the later part of Dylan's career, as evidenced by the second half of this book, is what he calls his 'lexicon'. It does not diminish, but rather places in full context, minstrelsy's influence on *"Love And Theft"*, to remind ourselves that it is but a subset of this continuing wellspring of Dylan's art. Indeed, so steeped in the lexicon is *"Love And Theft"* that a number of reviewers took the lines:

> *Well, the future for me is already a thing of the past*
> *You were my first love and you will be my last*

from 'Bye And Bye' to be addressed to his love of the music he grew up with as much as about a particular individual.

Certainly *"Love And Theft"* feels at the moment like the culmination of all that the second half of this book has been discussing. The next album may change the finality of that feeling but as I write this *"Love And Theft"* is Dylan's 'last' album which affords it a special, if temporary, status. Naturally, this is a status that has been enjoyed by every album in turn up until now and the way each is perceived does change after the next one is released[21]. The way it is perceived by fans and critics I mean, not Dylan himself, who understandably views each new album as a completely unique and 'stand-alone' entity and always finds it puzzlingly irrelevant when interviewers refer to his back catalogue.

Whatever the next album brings, however, it will not change the dominance of the influence of the lexicon in *"Love And Theft"* where it is, if such a thing is possible, even more prevalent than in *Time Out Of Mind*.

In addition, in the interviews promoting the album on its release, Dylan was still proclaiming the centrality of the folk tradition in his work:

> Mikal Gilmore: *It seems that some of your most impassioned and affecting performances, from night to night, are your covers of traditional folk songs.*
>
> Bob Dylan: *Folk music is where it all starts and in many ways ends. If you don't have that foundation, or if you're not knowledgeable about it and you don't know how to control that, and you don't feel historically tied to it, then what you're doing is not going to be as strong as it could be. Of course, it helps to have been born in a certain era because it would've been closer to you, or it helps to be a part of the culture when it was happening. It's not the same thing, relating to something second- or third-hand off of a record.*[22]

This last point, stressing the primacy of the live experience over listening to records, has been repeatedly made by Dylan since Greil Marcus's book *Invisible Republic* made so much out of the six disc Harry Smith *Anthology Of American Folk Music* collection of folk, country and blues recordings from the decades between the world wars. Dylan has made a point of denying the significance attached to this set, stressing instead the importance of having seen such songs and performers live when he was starting out.

This takes us back to his comments at the time of the release of *World Gone Wrong* when, talking of the likes of Blind Willie McTell and Charley Patton, he said:

> *These people who originated this music, they're all Shakespeares, you know? They're Thomas Edisons. Louis Pasteurs. They invented this type of thing. In a hundred years, they'll be notable for that. The people who played that music were still around then* (when Dylan was young), *and so there was a bunch of us, me included, who got to see all these people close up - people like Son House, Reverend Gary Davis or Sleepy John Estes. Just to sit there and be up close and watch them play, you could*

*study what they were doing, plus a bit of their lives even rubbed off on you. Those vibes will carry into you forever, really, so it's like those people, they're still here to me. They're not ghosts of the past or anything. They're continually here.*[23]

Back in the Gilmore interview, Dylan continued to make his point by impishly pointing out to his fans that he rates one of his top album achievements to be a harmonica bit part:

*I think one of the best records that I've ever been even a part of was the record I made with Big Joe Williams and Victoria Spivey. Now that's a record that I hear from time to time and I don't mind listening to it. It amazes me that I was there and had done that.*[24]

Those memories and the attendant music that nurtures Dylan is a theme he continually returns to:

*'To me, music either expresses ideas of liberty, or it's made under the oppression of dictatorship,' he says. 'The only stuff I've heard that has that freedom is traditional Anglo-American music. That's all I know. That's all I've ever known. I was fortunate to come up at a time when the last of it existed. It doesn't exist anymore.'*[25]

Given this he sees himself as more or less the last of his kind, which perhaps helps explain the evangelical tone to his commitment to the 'lexicon' as seen in the previous chapters.

*'People who came after me, I don't feel, were ever my peers or contemporaries, because they didn't really have any standing in traditional music,' he says. 'They didn't play folk songs. They heard me and thought, 'Oh, this guy writes his own songs, I can do that.' They can, of course, but those songs don't have any resonance.'*[26]

Last in the lexicon line he may be but Dylan cannot ignore his own part in changing the course of popular music; albeit that the way some of the changes he helped set in motion have turned out has dismayed him. Dylan brought into popular music a modernist sensibility and high literary seriousness. His late career quotation of folk music and lyrics is of a different nature to the post modernist allusions in his celebrated mid-sixties period, but there is a link there. The new way he is writing must be important to how he sees himself in relation to the folk tradition that he feels *'doesn't exist anymore'*.

Part of what he is doing by utilising the lyrics of those who have gone before him rather than writing his own lines is to give to them the status that 'lyrics by Bob Dylan' are now accorded. He has no doubt of the high worth of the pantheon of figures such as Sleepy John Estes, Blind Willie McTell, Lonnie Johnson and Charley Patton: *'They invented this type of thing. In a hundred years they'll be notable for that'*. Notable not least because Bob Dylan has thrown his weight behind making sure we do not forget them and what they achieved, and has embedded their legacy in his latest creations, *Time Out Of Mind* and *"Love And Theft"*, after playing them directly in *Good As I Been To You* and *World Gone Wrong*.

Dylan's fusion of the modernist and the traditional is evident too in his live shows, where tapes of Aaron Copeland's orchestral interpretations of folk and country roots music play in the halls before he takes stage. It is a tellingly ironic comment on high and low art as well as a signifier of his serious intent.

To list every reference to earlier songs in *"Love And Theft"* is impracticable here, especially as you are forever discovering more of them. However, it is worth a quick trip through the album to note the wide range of musical styles employed and to give an idea of the extent of quotations to the 'lexicon':

'Tweedle Dee & Tweedle Dum' nods to Robert Johnson's 'Love In Vain' as well as having an Elvis Presley connection we will look at later. In addition, Christopher Rollanson suspects that the line *'All that and more and then some'* is a reference to the title of a Billie Holiday song 'Tell Me More, and More and Then Some'. This was covered in 1965 by Nina Simone, who has, in turn, a number of Dylan connections.

'Mississippi' is based on the traditional folk song 'O Rosie', something Dylan makes sure we connect with by including 'Rosie' in his song. Variations of 'O Rosie' abound, but all of them include the *'one thing I did wrong ...stayed in Mississippi just a day too long'* conceit and bemoan the situation to Rosie in the chorus.

Its opening line, *'Every step of the way we walk the line'* may be an allusion to long time pal Johnny Cash's hit 'I Walk The Line' from the terrific early days of Sun Records; an era Dylan will re-create on the next track on *"Love And Theft"*. In addition, 'Mississippi' was originally intended for *Time Out Of Mind* and a song that was included on that album, 'Can't Wait', has the line *'It's late; I'm trying to walk the line'*.

'Summer Days' is discussed in terms of its rockabilly links below, and shares its title with a Charley Patton song, though this could very well just be a coincidence.

In 'Bye and Bye' we move further back in the history of American popular music, from fifties rockabilly all the way back to pre-war pop. As with the previous song, the title is such a commonplace that its use as the title of other songs is only to be expected. That one is by Blind Willie Johnson encourages the thought that a deliberate allusion is being made, but that is as far as you can take it. Once you start thinking this way, all the titles start to appear as if they are a tip of the cap to earlier songs.

'Lonesome Day Blues', for example, shares its title with a Blind Willie McTell song. Its appearance on the album signals yet another change of musical genre. Most of "Love And Theft" is steeped in the Southern States, but here we have jumped from Memphis to Chicago, following the re-location of Southern bluesmen to the electric blues of the great northern city of Chicago.

'Floater (Too Much To Ask)' brings yet another style into play, that of the 1930's favourite, Western Swing. It is an appropriately elegant, light piece with Bob crooning à la Bing Crosby on a hit of that time, 'Snuggled On Your Shoulder'. Crosby melody and phrasing, Dylan lyrics and singing. What could be better? Not much, going by this as evidence.

You may recall that Dylan has mentioned Crosby on more than one occasion in interview, most notably in 1985 for Mikal Gilmore's revealing piece for the *L.A. Herald Examiner*. I'll quote his statement in full as it is so relevant to "Love And Theft" in general, as well as ending on a note wholly pertinent to 'Floater (Too Much To Ask)':

> The Delmore brothers - God I really love them. I think they've influenced every harmony I've ever tried to sing... This Hank Williams thing with just him and his guitar...man that's something isn't it? I used to sing these songs way back, a long time ago, even before I played rock 'n' roll as a teenager... Sinatra, Peggy Lee, yeah, I love all these people; but I tell you who I've really been listening to a lot lately - in fact I'm thinking about recording one of his earlier songs - is Bing Crosby, I don't think you can find better phrasing anywhere.

Anywhere except right here, that is.

'High Water (for Charley Patton)' wears its allusions openly on its sleeve, or in its title to be precise, Patton's own song being 'High Water Everywhere'. There are more references in this song that we'll look at soon, but it's worth mentioning in passing that another Robert Johnson song is given the nod by the line 'I believe I'll dust my broom'.

'Moonlight' brings the influence of Hoagy Carmichael into the beguiling stew of the album's musical genres. Not only are certain of his songs evoked musically but the line in Dylan's song *'Doctor, lawyer, Indian chief'* was a Carmichael title (taken in turn from a nursery rhyme, in keeping with this intertwining 'love and theft' process).[27]

In 'Honest With Me' the Southern blues have gone North again; we are back in the electric city blues of Chicago, this time with a direct link to 'Highway 61 Revisited'.

The possible accreditation within Dylan's titles to previous song titles would reach ludicrous dimensions in the case of the next song, 'Po' Boy', so popular a title has that been over the years. Much more direct is Dylan's mark of respect to Blind Willie McTell in his lines:

> *Time and love have branded me with its claws*
> *Had to go Florida, dodgin' them Georgia Laws*

The second line recalls Blind Willie singing *'You'll have to dodge your ma, dodge your pa, go down to Florida to dodge the Georgia law'* in the September 1956 version of 'Kill It Kid'.[28] Dylan's homage is made all the more touching by coupling this with a line that resonates not only with the title of the album but also throughout much of his canon. It is a line of beauty and insight and delivered with a vocal from the heavens.

The odd stop-start melody is the first thing to strike home in 'Cry A While' as is the use of the made-famous-by-Sinatra hook line from 'I Cried for You (Now It's Your Turn to Cry Over Me)'. (See above, *'Sinatra, Peggy Lee, yeah, I love all these people'*). While the penultimate line namechecks the title of a Sonny Boy Williamson song: 'Your Funeral, My Trial'.

'Sugar Baby' is another title that has seen use before, perhaps most notably for a Dock Boggs number. The song's, and therefore album's, extraordinary closing lines are taken verbatim from an old song called 'The Lonesome Road' (again most famously sung by Sinatra). Among the other songs name-checked in the culminating track is Shelton Brooks' 1917 song 'The Darktown Strutters' Ball'. A half way house between the sounds of minstrelsy and jazz, this song is another that has been covered by many singers.

One of those who did so was Dean Martin, a name that can be added to those of Bing Crosby and Frank Sinatra as influences on this album. In late 2002 a gossip columnist in a US tabloid excitedly reported that Dylan had confided in someone at a party how much he admired Dean Martin. Watchers of the innovative TV programme *The Sopranos* would already have heard Dylan sing a song associated with Martin, 'Return To Me', in one of the episodes. It seems as though nearly all of popular US music forms the palette Dylan paints *"Love And Theft"* from.

This was just a quick sprint through the tracks, enumerating some of the more obvious allusions. As I travel the 'grid' and take different turnings to examine the 'substructure' more will become apparent. However, I should pause here and stress that, despite *"Love And Theft"* being a so referentially rich album that it necessitates such a lengthy listing of quoted material (though this has only been a partial top-level listing so far), we should not take our eye off the main boon of the album, which is pure enjoyment of the songs as they stand, in and of themselves.

All these references are interesting *per se* and because Dylan is drawing our attention to them either specifically on an individual basis or in general due to his overwhelming utilisation of them. Yet none of us would be interested in following them up were it not for the pure joy of listening to the album. If you remember from the foreword my bald statement of 'I *love* this album' - that exhilarating delight was partly from knowing instinctively that here was another landmark album that I would have the rest of my life illuminated by, but first and foremost it was that direct thrill of the music, the vocals and the lyrics that step by step grew to be ever more familiar.

Terry Kelly began the kind of review that has you nodding in agreement as you read, with a warning that acknowledging your instinctive reaction is crucial:

> *Our first duty is to acknowledge the pleasure principle. The new album should hit us, pleasurably, in the solar plexus, or not at all. Remember when you were a child, and could respond to music in a pre-literate, unselfconscious fashion? Well, if any of that innocent, unalloyed responsiveness remains, employ it to listen to the gorgeous mouth-music Dylan creates...* "Love And Theft" *is the sound of Bob Dylan having fun.*[29]

The lexicon is not a dead thing to Dylan. It may not exist anymore for new singers, but it does for him and he has fun with it. It lives in the music and newly re-worked, re-situated, differently connected lyrics that he is performing for our enjoyment. Richard Jobes expands on this:

> *It seems that the deliberate name-checking of some key folk and blues songs is another aspect of the song's humour. So many of Dylan's musical sources such as blues, folk and country have now become so enshrined that they appear to be little more than the property of academics. The enjoyment of a Blind Lemon Jefferson record now seems almost secondary to its importance within folk traditions. What so many fail to acknowledge is that this was popular music, to be enjoyed by the listeners, not to be dissected in a vacuum. While Dylan may cherish and*

*respect the foundation upon which he creates his work, he never treats them with gloved hands. If such things were sacred to him "Love And Theft" would be nothing more than an antiseptic contemporary folk/blues album. The creativity with which Dylan attacks his sources renders them so alive to the moment that a listener can approach them with the same sense of joy they originally would have brought.*[30]

One of the paradoxes we keep returning to is how fresh and new something based in the archaic (in recorded popular music terms) is. Dylan is not living in the past, he is engaged in the present; I don't miss the fun by following all the lexicon links. The album's instinctive joy in music-making could not be further from cataloguing the dusty shelves of a library of recordings. Following the links brings an *additional* enjoyment to the real fun that is overwhelmingly present in nearly every track for those with ears to listen and hearts to be moved. Naturally, many of the links here and to literature deepen the experience and enjoyment dramatically; but the starting and central point is the fun in listening to the songs.

What Dylan achieves in *"Love And Theft"* is akin to what Hank Williams achieved by pushing country music until it bordered on what we loosely refer to today as 'rock'. Hank had a plenitude of blues, minstrel and early country influences, but instead of sounding 'retro' he came across as thoroughly modern. He made a popular and contemporary sound while keeping true to those roots. Dylan does the same in *"Love And Theft"*, and one of the strongest of the roots he straps himself to is a genre of music that lit up his formative, mid-teen years.

### Rockabilly

Various links to rockabilly were mentioned above - Elvis, Johnny Cash and all of 'Summer Days' - however, I thought it best to deal with the rockabilly part of the 'lexicon' references all in one place. *"Love And Theft"* continues his affectionate ties with that period, following on from *Time Out Of Mind*, with 'Dirt Road Blues' as a well-intentioned but poorly executed homage to the early days of Sun Records, and Dylan's comments to *Guitar World* on feeling Buddy Holly was with him throughout the making of that record:

> *Buddy Holly. You know, I don't really recall exactly what I said about Buddy Holly, but while we were recording, every place I turned there was Buddy Holly. You know what I mean? It was one of those things. Every place you turned. You walked down a hallway and you heard Buddy Holly records like 'That'll Be the Day.' Then you'd get in the car*

*to go over to the studio and 'Rave On' would be playing. Then you'd
walk into this studio and someone's playing a cassette of 'It's So Easy.'
And this would happen day after day after day. Phrases of Buddy Holly
songs would just come out of nowhere. It was spooky. [laughs] But after
we recorded and left, you know, it stayed in our minds. Well, Buddy
Holly's spirit must have been someplace, hastening this record.*[31]

Elvis Presley - not for the first time - is another who is not that far away as
a presence on a Bob Dylan album. *"Love And Theft"* opens with a song that
harks back to Elvis's early days. In 1954 Elvis was singing a song called
'Tweedle Dee', of which a typical verse went:

*Tweedle tweedle tweedle dee,
I'm a lucky so-and-so
Mercy, mercy, pudding pie,
You got something that money can't buy
Tweedle tweedle dee*

Unfortunately, he sang it in a way that was apt to these lyrics on a literal
level; there was no hint of irony, sarcasm or real feeling. On the generally
excellent *'50's Masters'* set you can hear a live 1954 performance of it that
makes Elvis sound like the least threatening singer imaginable. He epitomises
the 'twee' in 'Tweedle Dee.' Lavern Baker, however, recorded it with a real
rock 'n' roll abandon and had a huge hit with it in the opening months of
1955. The B-side of this was 'Tomorrow Night', another song sung by both
Presley and Dylan.

It is no wonder that the sound of the opening track evokes the 1950s.
Stephen Scobie informed me that the music of 'Tweedle Dee and Tweedle
Dum' is a note for note recreation of Johnny and Jack's minor hit from that
decade, 'Uncle John's Bongos'. This duo's most famous song was
'Hummingbird', which Dylan has used as the opening song on some Never
Ending Tour shows. Although there is no lyrical connection to 'Uncle John's
Bongos', Johnny and Jack's music again features as an opener to a Dylan 'set'.

Notwithstanding all of the musical and lyrical rockabilly connections of
'Tweedle Dee and Tweedle Dum', it is on 'Summer Days' that rockabilly
comes completely to the fore. The track is on one level a tribute to Sun
Records as he recreates those legendary sounds and 'days' - *'You can't repeat
the past? Of course you can!'* Indeed. It follows on nicely, too, from Dylan's
magnificent performance of Warren Smith's Sun hit 'A Red Cadillac And A
Black Moustache' earlier in the year on *Good Rockin' Tonight: The Legacy Of
Sun Records.*

'Summer Days' takes us back to that same time, to Dylan's own 'summer days', with pure, old-fashioned rockabilly music. The lines:

> Well I got eight carburetors and, boys, I'm usin' 'em all
> I'm short on gas, my motor's startin' to stall

Bring to mind Arlen Sanders' 1964 hit 'Hopped-Up Mustang', which includes the following:

> Let me tell ya about my new steed,
> built for comfort, just my speed.
> Ford Mustang, modified to set the pace,
> Man, I could hardly wait to get out'n'race.
> It's got a 289 motor, with a special Cobra kit,
> there ain't nothin' on the road that can even touch it.
> It's got eight carburetors and it uses them all,
> with a four-speed stick that just won't stall.

Dylan is here continuing a classic tale of 'love and theft'. In this case it is one from the seamier side, where the 'theft' far outweighs the 'love'. The 1964 hit is a none-too-subtle lyrical rewrite of Charlie Ryan's earlier 'Hot Rod (Race) Lincoln' with 'Lincoln' changed to 'Mustang'. This new version was then narrated over an Astronauts' LP track ('Movin''). The Astronauts are not only uncredited but you'll find the record label states: 'Music by the Pacifics'. There was lots of theft and a dubious amount of love here.

In his high school yearbook Dylan wrote that his ambition was to *'follow Little Richard'*. It could be that the 'Aunt Sally' who I'll later mention in regard to both nursery rhymes and Mark Twain is a nod to Little Richard's 'Long Tall Sally'. It would not be the first time Little Richard's lines from there:

> Old Aunt Sally, old and grey
> Do the Georgia Crawl till she died away

were alluded to in Dylan songs. On *Slow Train Coming*'s 'Gonna Change My Way Of Thinking' he made a neat and contextually telling reference to both sides of Little Richard - the rock 'n' roller and the preacher:

> She can do the Georgia Crawl
> She can walk in the spirit of the Lord

The strong rockabilly influence on *"Love And Theft"* is also evident in the higher presence of cars and car imagery when compared to the predominantly walking and train-riding filled preceding albums. Speaking of Dylan's previous albums brings me to another major tree in the 'lexicon'.

### Dylan's Own Back Catalogue

Dylan, as always in the post production glow of a new work, was antipathetic to any comparisons of it with his earlier material. He declared to Mikal Gilmore, when the interviewer tried to draw such comparisons, that *"Love And Theft"* *'plays by its own rules'*. Indeed it does, so much so that it took all Dylan followers aback when they first heard it. That is not the same, though, as saying that his own back catalogue was not as ripe for referencing as the rest of his 'lexicon'. On *"Love And Theft"*, as in his nightly shows, Dylan displays no difference in attitude towards his own past songs and the whole pantheon he selects songs from.

So, if we can say of Dylan, as was famously said of Homer; (he whom we presume sang songs woven from the fabric others had left for him or, if you prefer, he who stole from those he loved), *'Our poet came late and had supremely gifted predecessors'* then these predecessors would, in Dylan's case, include earlier incarnations of himself. (The same could be true of Homer for all we know.)

One of the most telling of the references to his own back pages comes in two sets of lines about the wind. Firstly, in 'Lonesome Day Blues' we hear:

> *Last night the wind was whispering something*
> *I was trying to make out what it was*
> *I tell myself something's coming*
> *but it never does*

It is one of the many key references to the 'wind' in this album. Whatever *'answer is blowing'* here, he cannot determine it, nor does he know if it is an *'idiot wind'* or not. One thing for sure though, is that it is not howling in apocalyptic portent as in 'All Along The Watchtower'. Instead, here it just 'whispers,' and nothing happens, no 'slow train' ever comes. This seems a far more dexterous and meaningful reference to his own past lyrics than the rather ham-fisted 'The winds of change are blowing wild and free' from *Time Out Of Mind*'s 'Make You Feel My Love' (even though that may be name checking both the early anthems discussed in chapter one of this book).

That reminder of winds that blow brings me to a second set of lines from *"Love And Theft"* that refer to his past via the use of wind. This time they are from *'Floater (Too Much To Ask)'*:

> *A summer breeze is blowing*
> *A squall is settin' in*
> *Sometimes it's just plain stupid*
> *To get into any kind of wind*

Andrew Davies writes of this:

> *In this verse, an all-encompassing glance at the words written on the page seems to clearly suggest one thing: 'Blowin' In The Wind'. This Dylan standard subtly hidden away in the text could, quite reasonably, be a coincidence but Dylan is so precise as an artist that this is perhaps unlikely. Especially as the last line is a tad nonsensical if taken literally, why on earth is it just plain stupid to get into any kind of wind? If he means 'wind' as in 'argument', then there are surely other words he could have used to make the point other than 'wind'. The name checking of 'Blowin' In The Wind' seems deliberate because, as we shall see, the final lines and words of Dylan verses are often tailored either in turn of phrase or performance to make a point.[32]*

To anticipate my later discussion of some of the vocal treats on the album, I would point out, in passing for now, that it is worth noting how he sings the word 'blowin'' in the above passage, in the light of what I wrote about the same pronunciation in chapter one.

Before running ahead to looking at the vocals on *"Love And Theft"*, there is many a reference to his own back pages. With its deliberate over-stating, doubling effect, *'Some people they ain't human, they got no heart or soul'* from 'Cry A While' is a very Dylanesque line. It also uses heart and soul as two different, but essential, definitions of humanity in a way that harks all the way back to 'Don't Think Twice, It's All Right', as observed in chapter two. These people are also the antithesis of Jimmie Rodgers as described by Dylan in the liner notes to the 1996 tribute album.

Another reference to his back catalogue, perhaps more oblique though very obvious to Dylan listeners, is his triumphant revival of, and revelling in, the trait of inventing new sayings by reworking old aphorisms and coining couplets that cut to the core of what is going on in the world at large.

Fancy a little reminder of the glory days of 1965? Try this on for size:

> *They got Charles Darwin trapped out there on Highway 5*
> *Judge says to the High Sheriff, I want him dead or alive*

This works so well because not only is it a deft couplet and a tip of the hat to the past, but it touches on an important issue of the day too. Some Americans are much vexed by the question of whether to teach what rational minds believe to be the truth of evolution, or to inculcate their youth with the ravings of those bible-thumpers whose egos cannot bear being descended from the same ancestor as that of monkeys and apes. It seems that Dylan -

although himself a sometime bible-thumper - has not lost his ability to comment obliquely on questions of the day. It reminds me of the sudden introduction of 'Drifter's Escape' into the Never Ending Tour set lists in 1992 as the Rodney King outrage was being repeatedly broadcast.

The flawless touch of his rhyming wit also recalls past glories. I knew an example of this before I even heard the album. Michael Gray sent me an e-mail detailing his initial impressions that included the warning:

DON'T READ THE NEXT SENTENCE IF YOU DON'T WANT TO READ A NUGGET OF LYRIC.

So, naturally, I read on:

*There's a rhyme of 'crimson' with the tree's 'limbs 'n'' - that's as clever and adroit and surprising and agile and un-Recent Dylan as can be, and as fine and classic as ANYTHING those Porter people ever did.*

More direct self history referencing can be heard on 'High Water (For Charley Patton)' with its echoes of Dylan's versions of 'Po' Lazarus' and 'Tupelo', as well as the already mentioned ghost of 'Crash On The Levee (Down In The Flood)' from *The Basement Tapes*. You can hear on that same collection similar hick voices and connotations to those that 'Po' Boy' exploits so adroitly. As we saw in the chapter on Nonsense Verse, there are many connections between *The Basement Tapes* and *under the red sky*; the same can be said for both of those albums and *"Love And Theft"*.

With *under the red sky* the similarity is strengthened by its being chock-full of musical echoes of Dylan's own previous melodic output. Without denying Dylan's righteous claim that *"Love And Theft"* 'plays by its own rules' one cannot help but hear musical echoes of his past, in particular the blues-based songs from *Blonde On Blonde*.

Unsurprisingly the Dylan albums that *"Love And Theft"* seems to share most with include the two Dylan-penned albums that immediately precede it in his canon. Looking back from *"Love And Theft"* you can see many a connection with *Time Out Of Mind* and *under the red sky*.

As you would expect, comparisons between the albums show both interesting similarities and illuminating differences. We have already noted how different in feel the, generally speaking, perky *"Love And Theft"* is to the gloomy *Time Out Of Mind*. Both, however, are underpinned by the theme of movement, as are so many of his songs and albums. Through most of his career there is a pressing need to be moving on. In the second chapter of this book, in 'Don't Think Twice, It's All Right' the 'she' of the song was the reason he was *'travellin' on'*. This was because she wanted his 'soul', (his muse, his destiny, his individuality, call it what you will). This was Dylan's imperative to move on through to post 1966; and once again, after he 'reappeared' in the '70s, the signature line in a signature song was that he was *'still on the road/heading for another joint'*.

Certain songs bring out more specific echoes. 'Mississippi' was originally intended for *Time Out Of Mind* and it shares many of that album's major themes: days are numbered and time is short, the singer is trapped, his writing is ineffectual, it is based on an old folk song. Both 'Sugar Baby' and 'Tweedle Dee & Tweedle Dum' use the image of the sun in ways that refer back to 'Highlands', 'Standing In The Doorway' and 'Dirt Road Blues'. This is most effective and significant in the astonishing opening lines of 'Sugar Baby'.

'Lonesome Day Blues' throws up some memories of *Time Out Of Mind;* soon after the singer's mind is described as being a *'million miles'* away, we hear:

> *When I left my long-time darling, she was standing in the door*

One cannot help but wonder if she has *'blues wrapped around her head'*. While the lines from the previous album's, 'Tryin' To Get To Heaven':

> *The air is getting hotter*
> *There's a rumbling in the skies*
> *I've been wading through the high muddy water*
> *With the heat rising in my eyes*

would not be out of place on 'High Water (for Charley Patton)'. This mention of Mr. Patton reminds us that Dylan said that the melody for 'Highlands' came from him[33], thus further strengthening the already compelling bonds between the closing track of *Time Out Of Mind* and *"Love And Theft"* as a whole.

No matter how many likenesses one finds, the two releases are more noteworthy for their illuminating differences. The most important one is that it would never occur to me to make a compilation of some of the tracks of *"Love And Theft"*, far less would I feel compelled to do so as I was with *Time Out Of Mind*. The rich diversity of musical style on *"Love And Theft"* paradoxically creates a much more binding unity than on *Time Out Of Mind*. Here, all the songs truly work together to create a whole far exceeding the already impressive sum of its parts.

Looked at side by side in the light of this, *"Love And Theft"* harshly shows up *Time Out Of Mind's* lack of both humour and authenticity; the previous album looks like an uncertain stab at a finished idea draped in unnecessary distractions to disguise that very fact. Not that this is necessarily a fair way to judge *Time Out Of Mind*, but if you do so, it is obvious that *"Love And Theft"* has a confidence that much of *Time Out Of Mind* lacks.

This probably has a lot to do with Dylan's hands-on approach to the more recent record. As we saw in the conclusion to the preceding chapter, Dylan knew what he wanted on *Time Out Of Mind* but did not *'have the will power'* to make sure it was his vision that went on to the record and thus into history. This was all changed for *"Love And Theft"*, as the tense modern ambience of *Time Out Of Mind* gave way to a cool, clear sound. This time he had the willpower and he did, at least, have enough during *Time Out Of Mind* to refuse to allow Lanois's normal ham-fisted production on 'Mississippi' to be released on that record:

> *The song was pretty much laid out intact melodically, lyrically and struc-turally, but Lanois didn't see it. Thought it was pedestrian. Took it down the Afro-polyrhythm route - multi-rhythm drumming, that sort of thing. Polyrhythm has its place, but it doesn't work for knifelike lyrics trying to convey majesty and heroism. ...But he had his own way of looking at things, and in the end I had to reject this because I thought too highly of the expressive meaning behind the lyrics to bury them in some steamy caul-dron of drum theory. On the performance you're hearing, the bass is playing a triplet beat, and that adds up to all the multi-rhythm you need, even in a slow-tempo song.*[34]

It is also clear that Dylan was aware that if he had brought in a producer for *"Love And Theft"* his vision would have been 'compromised', to use his descrip-tion of what had happened to his previous albums. Mikal Gilmore put it to him that:

> *'This album holds ruminations every bit as dark as those found in* Time Out Of Mind, *but this time you put them across without the previous album's spooky musical ambience. Since you produced this album your-self, you must have wanted a different sound'.*

Dylan responded:

> *The way the record is presented is just as important as what it's presenting. Therefore, anybody - even if they'd been a great producer -would only have gotten in the way on this, and there really wasn't a lot of time. I would've loved to have somebody help me make this record, but I couldn't think of anybody on short notice. And besides, what could they do? For this partic-ular record it wouldn't have mattered.*

These crucial differences do not deny the many similarities, from the little things, like the way Chicago pops up on both and how he sings the 'long line' in summer days and the 'long line' in 'Not Dark Yet', to the themes and resonances that are everywhere on both from the shared well spring of the underpinning 'lexicon'.

And it is that lexicon that takes us back to where the second half of this book began, with *under the red sky* and nursery rhymes. Coincidentally *under the red sky* shares a September 11th release date (*Oh Mercy* was a day later) with *"Love And Theft"*, but that is far from the only thing the two albums have in common. Due to their agrarian settings they are both replete with domesticated animals, along with various nursery rhyme and Bible references. Cats, dogs, pigs, horses, mules, and various birds inhabit the worlds of the two records.

There is also a strong similarity in the way that musical echoes of his own previous work play under the surface of both albums, and then there are lyrical likenesses too. The previously mentioned '*doctor lawyer Indian chief*' line could have got up and walked straight off the tracks from *under the red sky*, and the same could be said for the 'High Water (For Charley Patton)' couplet:

> *I can write you poems, make a strong man lose his mind*
> *I'm no pig without a wig, I hope you treat me kind*

It is in 'Tweedle Dee & Tweedle Dum' that the *under the red sky* connection is strongest. So much so that what we saw in the chapter on nonsense verse as reductive attempts to allegorise away nursery rhymes rears its head again here, with a number of commentators positing the idea that the two characters are Bush and Gore and the song is 'about' the last U.S. election.

This theory is given support by a reference to Gore and Bush as 'Tweedledum and Tweedledee' in one media report at the time of campaigning. Certainly, the nasty and farcical nature of the election itself would fit in with the sour, dry cynicism of some of the lines. Other than that, however, I find little support for the interpretation within the song itself. Actually, outside of a few lines, none at all. I far prefer to take it on its own terms and allow it to take me back to the land of nursery rhymes. The characters became more famous for their appearance in Lewis Carroll, but in yet another example of 'Love And Theft', Carroll was utilising an earlier source. He quotes this as:

> *Tweedledum and Tweedledee*
> *Agreed to have a battle*
> *For Tweedledum said Tweedledee*
> *Had spoiled his nice new rattle.*

> *Just then flew down a monstrous crow,*
> *As black as a tar-barrel;*
> *Which frightened both the heroes so,*
> *They quite forget their quarrel.*

This was the version common at the time, but was only the latest in a number that stretch back to the beginning of the eighteenth century and may well go back a lot further.[35]

Throughout *"Love And Theft"* familial characters appear, and that reminded me of something Michael Gray wrote about *under the red sky* that is, if anything, even more applicable to *"Love And Theft"*:

> When I first heard Dylan's 1990 song 'Cat's In The Well', I misheard the line 'Back alley Sally is doing the American jump' and thought Dylan had combined two Little Richard song references here, putting 'Good Golly Miss Molly' and 'Long Tall Sally' together to make 'By golly Sally is doing the American jump'. 'Long Tall Sally', …'saw Aunt Mary coming and 'e got back in alley' - is a reminder that The Aunt is a figure of nursery rhyme or pantomime dimensions in the blues, as in other folksong. Perhaps mythologising your own family, the neighbours, accounts for some of the 'Old Mother Hubbard' rhymes we have.[36]

The naming of family members throughout the album is only one of a number of ways that the tracks of *"Love And Theft"* talk to each other. All the threads I have and will mention intertwine to provide us with the whole rich tapestry. All kinds of links echo meaningfully back and forth throughout the album tracks, as the 'grid' and 'substructure' combine to sound effect. For example, the following quotes all resonate with each other:

> *Well, I'm preaching peace and harmony,*
> *The blessings of tranquillity,*
> *Yet, I know when the time is right to strike.*
>
> ('Moonlight')

> *I'm preachin' the word of God, I'm puttin' out your eyes*
>
> ('High Water (For Charley Patton)')
>
> *Well, I'm gonna baptize you in fire so you can sin no more*
> *I'm gonna establish my rule through civil war*
>
> ('Bye And Bye')

> *I'm going to teach peace to the conquered, I'm going to tame the proud*
>
> ('Lonesome Day Blues')

We also hear *'so give me your hand and say you'll be mine'*, from 'Mississippi', echoed in 'High Water (For Charley Patton)' by: *'Don't reach out for me,' she said, 'Can't you see I'm drownin' too?'* This last comment is a very effective way of showing the shattering effect the flood has had on the whole Sherwood Anderson-type community. A community that we see through the eyes of an aged narrator, or a succession of same.

### Ageing

One of the many contrasts with much of *Time Out Of Mind* is the much more insightful way *"Love And Theft"* portrays ageing and its effects. Though, to be fair to *Time Out Of Mind*, I am talking about the weaker songs, not the likes of 'Not Dark Yet' nor 'Highlands'. Indeed the poignantly sung lines that always makes my heart skip a beat:

> *All the young men with their young women looking so good*
> *Well, I'd trade places with any of them*
> *In a minute, if I could*

are the starting place for what I write about now. In addition, 'Mississippi' was originally recorded for possible inclusion on that album. Its line: *'Your days are numbered, so are mine'* baldly states what Dylan has said was one of the messages he was hoping that album would convey. *"Love And Theft"* doesn't just talk about ageing, it makes the listener *feel* it.

As we shall see later, literary quotations and references are peppered throughout the album, less so than the overwhelming presence of those referring to the lexicon of folk and popular music, but still important and prevalent. From 'Summer Days' comes one such quote, a statement lifted almost verbatim from *The Great Gatsby* that is seemingly core to *"Love And Theft"* and is always quoted as such in the reviews that mention it:

> *She says, 'You can't repeat the past,' I say 'You can't? What do you mean you can't? Of course you can.'*

The ingenuity of the lines chosen is matched by the wit of Dylan musically proving their very point here and throughout the album. Or at least so it may appear on first listen. In fact, a truer statement came in the preceding song:

> *You can always come back, but you can't come back all the way*

Dylan may well be reliving his 'summer days' musically and verbally in lines like:

> *Well, I'm drivin' in the flats in a Cadillac car*
> *Well, I got eight carburetors and, boys, I'm usin' 'em all*

But those lines are immediately followed by, respectively:

*The girls all say, 'You're a worn out star!'*

and

*I'm short on gas, my motor's startin' to stall*

Fun this track most certainly is but its message is:

*What looks good in the day, at night is another thing.*

If his 'summer days' are being forced further into the past by inevitable ageing then he is not letting them go without a struggle, or until he absolutely must. Like a certain other Dylan, this one has no intention of 'going gentle' into that night; instead, as he proudly growls in 'Cry A While': *'I'm gonna buy me a barrel of whisky, I'll die before I turn senile'*.

The sudden changes of mood from line to line that are apparent throughout the album are also indicators of an ageing mind flitting from subject to subject and memory to memory.

In 'Sugar Baby' the earlier themes of memory and the past are brought to a conclusion shorn of earlier optimism:

*Can't turn back, you can't come back*

*Some of these memories you can learn to live with*
*And some of 'em you can't*

'Sugar Baby', like most last tracks on Dylan albums, echoes what has gone before, and that last quote recalls *'these memories I got, they can strangle a man'* from 'Honest With Me'.

The hotchpotch of recollections in some songs depicts how our internal thoughts flow. This is especially so with the overlay of an older person's mixture of memories from different times and oddly connected associations. So, at times the lyrics come across like an old person talking. The interaction of memories, the vocalisation of inner impressions, the repeated references to people that seem to come from another time/place/story and the way family members are referred to throughout the album, all contribute to this effect.

In 'Honest With Me', Dylan sings:

*Well my parents warned me not to waste my years*
*And I still got their advice oozing out of my ears*

Dylan fans cannot but help be reminded of the time he accepted the Grammy Award in 1991. With delicious devilment Dylan topped off a surreal appearance by quoting a rabbinical saying as advice his father had passed on to him.[37]

Asked by Edna Gundersen about the *Lonesome Day Blues* line *'I wish my mother was still alive'*, he declined to discuss her death the previous year, saying: *'Even to talk about my mother just breaks me up.'*[38]

However, when asked in the Rome 2001 interview if her death had affected the writing here and in 'Po' Boy', Dylan replied *'probably* (pause) *I don't see how it couldn't be'*. Indeed so, such a powerful event is bound to affect his work consciously and/or subconsciously. In 'Lonesome Day Blues' in particular the effect is close to miraculous. Nigel Hinton wrote of this:

> *...isn't the 'Lonesome Day Blues' verse about remembering his mother, just wonderful? And so true about how these moments happen. You're in your car/truck, about forty miles from the mill. You drop it in to overdrive, turn on the radio and - out of nowhere and for no perceptible reason - comes a sudden feeling of longing and that it would be just great to see your dead mother again and tell her about all the things that have happened since she's gone. I was driving in my car yesterday when this verse came on and it made me miss my mother so much. So powerful is his evocation of such a moment, he evoked such a moment in me.*[39]

Michael Gray, whose monumental study of Dylan came out before *"Love And Theft"* was produced, has since given a series of talks entitled 'Bob Dylan & The History of Rock'n'Roll'. In the one I attended he talked about this line in similar terms, describing how he felt listening to it and how it made him wish his mother was still alive. After a pause, he continued, *'And, you know, the thing is - she still is.'* After the laughter subsided I thought how fitting a tribute to Dylan's lyrics and delivery this was.

There is another side to Dylan singing of ageing and his setting an album in a past, agrarian world amidst musical styles from long ago. All this brings to mind his own age and his relationship with - or estrangement from - the modern world. One thing that has never hampered Dylan is an overly scrupulous attention to the modern concept of 'political correctness'.

So it is no surprise to find that this album ignores it. That term has come to convey the stultifying deadness of over-conforming to anything, even things of inherent virtue. What is now a term of scorn was born out of concepts that were inarguably good, no discrimination on basis of sex or race, for example. The human ability to create evil out of good seems never-ending. However, none of this impinges on the land of *"Love And Theft"*, a land from before it was ever heard of, after all. This is part of its charm, which is not to say that everything about old fashioned attitudes is charming; the iniquities they inspired were the whole reason 'political correctness' came into being, after all.

Dylan is a man of the past as well as a man singing of the past, his formative years were in the Fifties, a point he often stresses. If he doesn't say the Fifties he says the Forties but never the Sixties, the second half of which he seems to despise and always makes a point of distancing himself from. Talking of the 'summer of '67' et al in the Rome interview he flatly stated that he was not *'part of that culture'*. For him, yet again, it was his formative years that mattered: *'I think whatever time you are born and raised in has a tremendous influence on whatever your personal and private life is...'*

Christopher Rollanson, in his review of the album, is engaging on this topic in its linguistic incarnation, or rather its absence, due to what he calls Dylan's *'sublime lexical disregard'* for *'the fashionable niceties of... political correctness'*. There are not, as it happens, many offensive terms on *"Love And Theft"* but there are some attitudes which upset people who have taken sixties and post-sixties liberal thinking as their own and think that Dylan shares those views. This happens on 'Sugar Baby', in particular.

Being the final track, it stands slightly apart from the others. It is not as big a jump to this closer as it was to 'Dark Eyes' on *Empire Burlesque*; more like the half-step to 'Shooting Star' on *Oh Mercy*.

In true last track Dylan tradition this sparse, but poignantly beautiful, song sums up the entire album and points the way to further explorations of his muse. In here you will find lost love, lost youth, some sadness, some joy, some bitterness, some defiance, some hope, some anger, some faith.

The rest of the album may be spoken via the mouths of a cast of characters (notwithstanding that they reveal to us Dylan's view of life) but this is Dylan speaking to himself; to thoughts of his loves, his past, his twin, *'that enemy within'*. Perhaps you hear him sing to demons that have haunted him, of addictions both female and chemical, perhaps sometimes also to his muse. Then you listen to the song again and hear it very differently; it is like a coiled spring full of impacted meanings. When they are sprung free, the connotations and references take you down many a different path, led by that unmistakable voice of Dylan in full prophetic and personal modes. The wonder is that he lets us listen in to this statement of how he feels now, at the moment he recorded this.

I know from a number of friends, though, that they feel uncomfortable with this song because, not for the first time, Dylan's words upset their beliefs regarding the place of women. Dylan's uncompromising:

*There ain't no limit to the amount of trouble women bring*

- as well as the opening chorus lines - have re-opened an old debate. To me there is no argument, Dylan is not only not a supporter of the 'women's lib' movement; he doesn't even seem to understand it. Dylan is not a flower power child of the sixties, he grew up before the sixties in a Jewish family in a small Midwestern town. He does not - and never has - shared many of the beliefs of later generations.

If you let that put you off his work, that's your loss. I don't agree with his attitudes to women, but then I often find his views on other subjects (religion, for example) also run counter to mine.

More importantly than all this though is the simple fact that a literal reading of the lyrics brings a very limited view of the song. Even if taken at a basic level you can hear that Dylan is singing about more than woman troubles, as is suggested by a line like:

> *Every moment of existence seems like some dirty trick*

The verses are also clearly speaking from more than one perspective; it seems to me there is a clear shift from the verses to the chorus, perhaps I'd go as far as to say I most commonly hear them as call and response which suits the religious context that I think all important to this song.

Clearly though this is a barrier for some to their appreciation of the song, and therefore the album as a whole. The book's supporting website deals with this digressionary topic in some detail (www.amuir.co.uk/troubadour). Barriers to appreciation were conspicuous by their absence in the slew of enthusiastic reviews that greeted the release of "Love And Theft", with people revelling in the humour of the album.

### Humour

Humour, as evidenced in earlier comments about how the album was received upon its release, is one of the first things that hits the listener to *"Love And Theft"*. The album is shot through with jokes of all kinds; from the corniest to the self-deprecating, via some with a leer, some with a twinkle in his eye. All kinds of jokes abound.

It is difficult not to see the opening track 'Tweedle Dee & Tweedle Dum' as, in part at least, a joke on Dylan reviewers and critics. Reviewers because there had been speculation that a Lanois produced 'masterpiece' *Time Out Of Mind* would, like its predecessor *Oh Mercy* be followed by a dud, as *under the red sky* was so cruelly perceived. You have to imagine this may have been in Dylan's mind when he opened this album with a nursery rhyme set of characters transported into a violence-ridden, modern world setting.

The joke on the Dylan scholars that he lashed out at in the Rome interview is to pack the song chock-full of references: to the Bible, to his past, to various other artists and so forth. You can imagine Dylan smirking as he threw in another one to have people poring over reference material to track down what he was alluding to. Many of the usual Dylan suspects are given a 'nod' (sic) and with '*Living in the land of Nod*' he manages to refer to both the Bible and James Dean.

There is something funny, too, in changing the leading characters' names round from how they usually appear. Is there any significance to this? How could there be as the whole point of these characters is that they are so inter-changeable you can't tell one from the other?

There is lots of nudge, nudge bloke-ish humour on the album. Following on from the '*I'm short on gas, my motor's starting to stall*' impotence metaphor noted already in 'Summer Days' he then sings in the following verse:

> *I got my hammer ringin', pretty baby, but the nails ain't going down*

The line from 'Floater (Too Much To Ask)' '*I'm in love with my second cousin*' sounds like it has popped out of a ribald joke and the frankly lustful '*jump into the wagon, love, throw your panties overboard*' from 'High Water (For Charley Patton)' seems to come from the same world as that of 'Blood In My Eyes', as do the lines:

> *I need something strong to distract my mind*
> *I'm gonna look at you 'til my eyes go blind*

Here however there's more of a smirk and a sneer than the desperate lust of the *World Gone Wrong* song.

On a less smutty level, the comment '*The future for me is already a thing of the past*' from 'Bye And Bye' can be heard as a joke at how he is fashioning his new songs from old material and the remark in 'Sugar Baby', '*some of these bootleggers, they make pretty good stuff*' may mainly be about moonshiners but there is no way Dylan would be unaware of how it would be taken by an audi-ence who in large numbers listen to bootlegged Dylan music. Especially during a period when his own record company is releasing some of these under the umbrella term *The Bootleg Series*.

'Po' Boy' boasts one of the many flashes of mordant wit on the album:

> *I say 'how much you want for that, I go into the store'*
> *Man says 'three dollars' 'all right', I say, 'will you take four?'*

For the '*po' boy*' three dollars is an unattainable amount so why not sarcastically offer four. It's like if a friend were to say to you: 'I need a million dollars,' and you replied: 'Really? Is that all, here have two.'

The following lines:

> *Po' boy, never say die*
> *Things will be all right, by and by*

are a testament to his robust spirit as exemplified by the cheeky *'will you take four?'* and the hope that one day such an answer will not be sarcastic, that he will one day no longer be 'poor boy'.*'*

There's something impishly Dylanesque, and very much in the spirit of this album, about concluding this sublime performance with a lame *'knock knock'* joke.

Similarly terrible jokes were a feature of his shows in the summer of 1999, when he regaled audiences with such witticisms as his bus getting a flat tyre because they came across a fork in the road, or specially-tailored-to-the-locations ones like his comment when he played a gig in Normal: *'I can't believe I am here. People always say I am a long way from normal'*.

So *'sitting on my watch so I can be on time'*, *'Freddy or not here I come'*, and *'I'm hunting bare'* were forewarned. There are more puns dotted throughout the album, smutty and otherwise, right from the opening track where we hear the two brick company businessmen:

> *They're lyin' low and they're makin' hay,*
> *They seem determined to go all the way*

And

> *I've had too much of your company*

Puns, bawdy, 'knock, knock' jokes etc. all play an important role in the overall atmosphere of the album, even the lines about the 'Englishman, Italian and Jew' - apart from other meanings - cannot help but sound like start of a joke. At times it seems that the usual Dylan apocalypse is more of a cosmic joke. It isn't that the situation has become any less serious, but what else can you do except crack a joke and shrug your shoulder?

There is a degree of dark humour even in 'High Water (For Charley Patton)'. It reminds us of the humour of people trying to survive bombings during the war. As we say in Britain of tough cities to grow up in with a reputation for humour - 'well you have to laugh, otherwise you'd cry'. The grim side of humour is flatly stated in the chilling line from 'Sugar Baby': *Every moment of existence seems like some dirty trick*.

So it was not surprising to find Dylan at pains to correct Mikal Gilmore's over-emphasis on the humour in the overall tone and effect:

MG: *C'mon, there are some pretty funny lines on this album - like the exchange between Romeo and Juliet in 'Floater (Too Much to Ask),' and that knock-knock joke in 'Po' Boy.'*

BD: *Yeah, funny...and dark. But still, in my own mind, not really poking fun at the principles that would guide a person's life or anything. Basically, the songs deal with what many of my songs deal with - which is business, politics and war, and maybe love interest on the side. That would be the first level you would have to appreciate them on.*

That being said, the initial impression one gets from the album is that it is suffused with open-hearted humour. This remains with the listener, despite its 'darker' side. As Nigel Hinton put it:

*There is, in addition to all the other tones and themes and seriousness, an approachability, a warmth, a sense of fun that is nice to be around. The silly jokes are so self-consciously silly. He's like an old grandfather cracking corny jokes to the kids who groan and laugh simultaneously. It makes the no-more-serious* Time Out Of Mind *sound like the work of a monotonous old grouch.*[40]

In his liner notes to the album he put together on his own new label, Egyptian Records, *The Songs of Jimmie Rodgers, A Tribute* Dylan wrote: 'at the heart of it all...a seriousness and humor that is befuddling'. Not for the first or last time, lines written there are brought to life on *"Love And Theft"*.

### Sinister

Throughout the album, beneath the humour, lurks some things much more sinister. The very title sees 'love' undermined by deception and wrong-doing, 'theft'.

As ever, the opening track, 'Tweedle Dee & Tweedle Dum' gives us a fore-taste of what is to come. The arboreal delights that so often feature in these tracks is under attack here as the two miscreants are to be found *'throwin' knives into the tree'* right at the beginning of the album. It is the first hint of the dark streak of violence throughout an album that on the surface is jokey, upbeat and of a sunny disposition.

Dylan's 'modern nursery rhyme' is a highly sinister tale; there is no happy ending here - or at least not for the rest of us with these two running loose. It's not the first time Dylan has mixed the ominous and the nursery rhyme; we have seen it in this book already in 'Subterranean Homesick Blues', 'Maggie's Farm' and throughout *under the red sky*.

Things that appear randomly thrown into the lyrical mix of 'Tweedle Dee & Tweedle Dum' make much more sense when you have heard the whole album, as many of the themes re-appear more clearly in later songs. The sinister element first seen here creeps in all over the album, even in those songs that sound (and lyrically start) so sweet.

'Bye and Bye', for example, begins with Dylan *singing love's praises with sugar-coated rhyme* and though the music stays in tune with this sentiment it is not long before there are hints of something far from *'sugar-coated.'*

This change of lyrical tone is first heralded by the phrase: *'I'm walking on briars.'* This is picked up soon after in *'...going where the wild roses grow.'* Not the rose of *'sugar-coated love'* but the *wild* rose. These quotes sandwich a verse where the singer has to tell himself he has found happiness (somewhat different from actually having found it) and try to convince himself he has at least one dream that *'hasn't been repossessed'*. (A particularly powerful image given the young Dylan's involvement in helping his father repossess goods from payment defaulters.)

All these hints of foreboding combine to move the song from its opening stock phrases proclaiming uncomplicated love in standard pop phrases to:

> *Papa gone mad,*
> *Mama, she's feeling sad*
> *Well, I'm gonna baptize you in fire*
> *So you can sin no more*
> *I'm gonna establish my rule*
> *Through civil war*

This is not the kind of thing you expect to hear being half-crooned in lounge music style. This is pre-war pop refracted through Dylan's lyrical and vocal genius. As he menacingly puts it in 'High Water (For Charley Patton)' *'I can write you poems, make a strong man lose his mind'*.

'Lonesome Day Blues', the following song, picks up this menacing touch and runs with it, barrelling along in rough road-house blues and growing lyrically ever more ominously severe.

'Floater (Too Much To Ask)' may bring relief in its total change of pace, but just like 'Bye And Bye', the sinister stuff soon sneaks up on you. After you've been lulled into a false state of security by the opening description of an endless summer day when the *'honey bees are buzzing'* the song starts to change. Odd touches lead to a warning that *'a squall is setting in.'* People seem oblivious to the warnings, the singer himself is ignoring them.

As the song progresses, Dylan conjures up mysterious images and blithely delivers lines about how bad times are getting. The sense of complacency before a storm leads to the singer issuing the warning:

> *If you ever try to interfere with me or cross*
> *my path again, you do so at the peril of your life*
> *I'm not quite as cool or forgiving as I sound*
> *I've seen enough heartache and strife.*

Again, as in 'Bye And Bye' the change of mood from the song's opening could hardly be more marked. The same thing happens in 'Moonlight'. This song leads us back to a pre-war romantic tune, Dylan allowing us to *'hear again the songbird's sweet melodious tone'* as one of the early lines puts it. By now though we are accustomed to the pleasant taking an ominous turn and it happens here too, when we hear of an *'earth and sky that melts with flesh and bone'*. The sinister signs then pile up until mid-song we get:

> *The clouds are turning crimson*
> *The leaves fall from the limbs an'*
> *The branches cast their shadows over stone*

The foreboding in the lyrics is overwhelming, notwithstanding the *'sweet melodious tone'* of the melody and vocal performance. What started as a standard romantic invite is now downright scary. It may even be that rape is threatened. Certainly if you go to meet this guy *'out in the moonlight alone'*, you are taking one hell of a risk.

Threatening images appear throughout the album. This short selection:

> *I'm preachin' the word of God, I'm puttin' out your eyes...*
> *I'm gonna establish my rule through civil war...*
> *I'm breakin' the roof, set fire to the place as a partin' gift...*
> *When I left my home the sky split open wide...*

is already enough to demonstrate the menace that co-exists with the good feeling. The mixture of the two is very lifelike and is a major part of what makes the album so instantly credible.

### Literature

'Lifelike' as it is, the album makes numerous connections with the world of fiction. That oh-so-quickly-dismissed-by-many first track is a good opener not just in introducing humour, menace, 'the lexicon' (via Rockabilly) and Dylan's own back catalogue (the *under the red sky* connections), but also in heralding the beginning of many literary references.

Some of these are so direct that we can be confident - as Dylan clearly intends us to be - of them and their relevance. Others are less certain, either more oblique or else too ambiguous to be certain of. Perhaps these last could even become contentious if you allow them to develop into that, though there is no need to let that happen. In a short while, we will be looking at some of these 'referential grey areas' that are the inevitable outcome of such relentless quoting and alluding as Dylan has employed. Meantime, we can look at some of the more obvious literary allusions, beginning with the album's opening track.

'Tweedle Dee & Tweedle Dum' has more literary meat to it than just the obvious sharing of two characters most famed for their appearance in Lewis Carroll's *Alice In Wonderland*. There is also, for example, the blatant namechecking of Tennessee Williams's *A Streetcar Named Desire*. This is something he addressed from stage in March 1986 in one of my all time favourite *'onstage raps'*. In this, his quote from Williams could serve as a remarkably acute summary of what his own art asks of its listeners:

> *'Alright, hmm. Anybody here who hasn't heard of Tennessee Williams? I guess everybody knows who that is. Anyway, he wrote these incredible lines you know, he said, what he say again? Yeah:*
>
> *'I'm not looking for your pity. But just your understanding. Not even that, just your recognition. Of you and me and the beginning of time in all of us.'*
>
> *I used to think about those lines a lot.*
>
> *Anyway, you can't hear stuff like 'A Streetcar Named Desire' and 'Fugitive Crimes' anymore. A few years back he died in New York City in a hotel room all by himself. And nobody found him until the next day. He was there because he couldn't get a job...'*

The nitty-gritty of real life; so many artists die in similarly straitened circumstances. The Stephen Foster of minstrelsy song fame that we looked at earlier died in hospital with just a few cents to his name, despite the huge popularity of his songs.

As well as namechecks, some lines are so close to direct literary quotation that it would be hard to put them down to mere coincidence. For example, the lines mentioned earlier as being from *The Great Gatsby* certainly seem to be directly from the following passage, one of lyrical splendour and deep import, aptly enough.

I have put the specific quotation in capital letters, but have also let the quote run on to some following paragraphs that seem to me to be linked first to 'Moonlight', then more loosely to other songs like 'Po Boy', but more importantly to *"Love And Theft"* as a whole:

> *He wanted nothing less of Daisy than that she should go to Tom and say:* 'I never loved you...' *After she had obliterated four years with that sentence they could decide upon the more practical measures to be taken. One of them was that, after she was free, they were to go back to Louisville and be married from her house - just as if it were five years ago.*

> 'And she doesn't understand,' *he said.*

> 'She used to be able to understand. We'd sit for hours -.' *He broke off and began to walk up and down a desolate path of fruit rinds and discarded favors and crushed flowers.*

> 'I wouldn't ask too much of her,' *I ventured.*

> 'YOU CAN'T REPEAT THE PAST.' 'CAN'T REPEAT THE PAST?' *he cried incredulously.*

> 'WHY OF COURSE YOU CAN!' *He looked around him wildly, as if the past were lurking here in the shadow of his house, just out of reach of his hand.*

> *...one autumn night, five years before, they had been walking down the street when the leaves were falling, and they came to a place where there were no trees and the sidewalk was white with moonlight.*

> *They stopped here and turned toward each other. Now it was a cool night with that mysterious excitement in it which comes at the two changes of the year. The quiet lights in the houses were humming out into the darkness and there was a stir and bustle among the stars. Out of the corner of his eye Gatsby saw that the blocks of the sidewalks really formed a ladder and mounted to a secret place above the trees - he could climb to it, if he climbed alone, and once there he could suck on the pap of life, gulp down the incomparable milk of wonder.*

> *His heart beat faster and faster as Daisy's white face came up to his own. He knew that when he kissed this girl, and forever wed his unutterable visions to her perishable breath, his mind would never romp again like the mind of God. So he waited, listening for a moment longer to the tuning-fork that had been struck upon a star. Then he kissed her. At his lips' touch she blossomed for him like a flower and the incarnation was complete.*

> *Through all he said, even through his appalling sentimentality, I was reminded of something - an elusive rhythm, a fragment of lost words, that*

*I had heard somewhere a long time ago. For a moment a phrase tried to take shape in my mouth and my lips parted like a dumb man's, as though there was more struggling upon them than a wisp of startled air.*

*But they made no sound, and what I had almost remembered was uncommunicable forever.'*

At its best *"Love And Theft"* communicates the seemingly incommunicable, as does Fitzgerald, paradoxically enough by this presentation of a character who does not articulate it (directly, anyway).

The similarity to the words in capital letters in the above quote to Dylan's:

*She says, 'You can't repeat the past.' I say, 'You can't? What do you mean, you can't? Of course you can.'*

from 'Summer Days' seems too close to be anything other than a reference we are supposed to 'get'; just as we were intended to pick up on 'Mississippi' alluding to 'O Rosie'. In addition, as you can see from the excerpt quoted, there are thematic and imagistic resonances here. The same can be said with at least some of what appear to be potential Mark Twain references. Twain, like Fitzgerald, (like 'The Coo Coo Bird' too) has featured in Dylan's work before.

In his liner notes to *Planet Waves* Dylan begins by quoting from Twain's *The Adventures of Huckleberry Finn*. He does so again in 'Lonesome Day Blues'; where Huck claims *'the wind was trying to whisper something to me I couldn't make out what it was'*, Dylan sings: *'Last night the wind was whispering something, I was trying to make out what it was'*.[41]

Again the quote is almost verbatim and again it is from a classic American literary text; *The Great Gatsby* and *The Adventures of Huckleberry Finn* - you cannot get more quintessential American novels.

In 'Sugar Baby' Dylan delivers a line that could come straight out of the mouth of Huck himself:

*I'm staying with Aunt Sally, but you know she not really my aunt*

This Aunt Sally may bring to mind *'back alley Sally'* from *under the red sky* (and the other connections discussed throughout this chapter), but I think one should be directed (and I am supported in this by the numerous other references throughout the album) to our old Dylan 'friend', Huck Finn, who did stay with Aunt Sally, and who was not related to her.

In one of the most crucial lines in Mark Twain's writing, Huck says:

*...because Aunt Sally she's going to adopt me and sivilize me, and I can't stand it. I been there before.*

Twain's influence is a major one on how I hear the album, how it affects me. There is a lot of his fiery and humorous character in many of the narrators on *"Love And Theft"*; the eye for the women still bright in the old rascal's mind, the insight yet the corny jokes, the mood changes and the erudition mixed with earthy humour all seem Twain-like.

Like most of Twain's novels, the majority of the tracks are based in the South; Twain was fascinated by the minstrel shows (and this is most apparent in *The Adventures of Huckleberry Finn*) that feature as such a core part of the 'substructure' of *"Love And Theft"*.

Ralph Ellison's famous exposition of Jim as being born directly out of minstrelsy is incontestable in its basic tenets. It is important to point out on Twain's behalf that Jim grows from this blackface caricature figure into a moral being of no little dignity. Being a novelist himself this does not escape Ellison, though it has not stopped the novel being banned from schools in at least one American State:

> Writing at a time when the blackface minstrel was still popular, and shortly after a war which left even the abolitionists weary of those problems associated with the Negro, Twain fitted Jim into the outlines of the minstrel tradition, and it is from behind this stereotype mask that we see Jim's dignity and human capacity - and Twain's complexity - emerge.[42]

Dylan's connections to Twain's classic creation go way back to when he was wearing a Huck Finn cap and singing the songs from his lexicon for the first time. A time when he was performing songs like 'I Was Young When I Left Home' at the Gaslight Cafe, which was released on the *"Love And Theft"* 'limited edition' set as one of two bonus tracks.

Moving far away from canonical texts of US literature to a more obscure reference (in the sense of being connected to the world of *"Love And Theft"*) - though nothing in literature could match the Nathan Bedford Forrest Civil War reference for obscurity - we find in 'Lonesome Day Blues':

> I'm going to spare the defeated, boys, I'm going to speak to the crowd
> I'm going to teach peace to the conquered, I'm going to tame the proud

This fits in with other grandiose gestures throughout the album, but it also echoes very closely the passage in Virgil's *Aeneid*:

> Remember, Rome, that it is for thee to rule the nations. This shall be thy task, to impose the ways of peace, to spare the vanquished, and to tame the proud by war.

Or at least it is very close in the particular translation I have used here.[43] One moves from areas of the obvious, with sure and illuminating quotations and allusions and references to areas of referential uncertainty and ambiguity. This is as true when Dylan is referring to the world of literature as it is when he is doing so to historic, popular music. (Or 'high' art and 'low' art, to use distinctions that his career in general and this album in particular render more and more meaningless.)

One area of such uncertainty occurs when there is more than one potential source being quoted. The Bible, as ever in Dylan's work, as well as being a primary source in itself, underpins everything else that his songs are built upon. Folk music, the blues, minstrelsy, literature, nursery rhymes all stem from and/or are inextricably interlinked with the Bible. Therefore it is everywhere on *"Love And Theft"*, both directly and indirectly.

This can create confusion as to which, if any, area Dylan is pointing us to. One example of how deep this goes can be found in Dylan's line in 'Po' Boy', *'Washin' them dishes, feedin' them swine.'* One could take this as an allusion back to Dylan's own writing in 'Unbelievable' in *under the red sky*:

> Kill that beast and feed that swine
> Scale that wall and smoke that vine

Or, if I may refer you back to the chapter on Nonsense Verse, we saw there that the Bible[44] and nursery rhymes are interconnected and both constantly alluded to by Dylan on *under the red sky*. The feeding of swine occurs in both. The nursery rhyme *Curly Locks* places the common domestic activity of dishwashing right beside the once-common one of swine feeding, just as Dylan does in 'Po' Boy'

Given the amount of quotation going on in *"Love And Theft"* you can often find yourself in a similar quandary over multiple potential reference points for the one phrase. For example, we have so far seen that the 'Aunt Sally' of *"Love And Theft"* could be a figure from nursery rhyme, rock 'n' roll or Mark Twain's Huckleberry Finn, or all of these - or none of these.

All these connections and allusions, these references within references can multiply until you are no longer sure if they are really there or if you are imposing them on to the songs when there is no need or call to do so. Or, given the plethora of potentially meant allusions, whether you are picking up on the 'correct' one; correct that is in artistic appropriateness, which may or may not be the same thing as the conscious authorial intention or a sub-conscious link on Dylan's part (just to open can after can of worms for you there).

Whether you find this troublesome or not probably depends on how you approach the record; if you approach it on its own terms you will not find it bothersome. Richard Jobes wrote:

> ...'*The Coo Coo Bird*' *which appeared on the Smithsonian Anthology Of American Folk Music, a set of six discs that brought together ancient country and blues recordings from the Twenties and Thirties...As Dylan slides these titles into his current compositions it not only reflects his deep understanding and love of such music, but also gives a sly wink to such critics. While Dylan would be the first to claim that he would never sink so low as to write for critics, lines such as* '*The Cuckoo is a pretty bird, she warbles and she flies/I'm preachin' the Word of God/I'm puttin' out your eyes*' *appear to play up to such restrictive readings of his work, and mock their limitations.*'[45]

Later on we will be looking at the humour that is prevalent throughout the album, and a little malicious glee here for Dylan in this manner would be in keeping with that.

However it is still, additionally, a very apt use. Its place in the lexicon is well known. There is a reference to it in 1796 that suggests it existed in printed form much earlier than that. It was in the early Dylan performance repertoire, he was playing it back in the days of the Gaslight Café, he was playing it when he played 'I Was Young When I Left Home' as featured on the bonus CD accompanying "*Love And Theft*". Further to all that, what could be more appropriate for an album called "*Love And Theft*" that celebrates the minstrel and country-blues traditions by using their material to build new art, than including this reference to a song about a bird that steals the nests of others to raise its own offspring in?

So while I take the warning that it may be alluded to as a joke on Dylan's part - and you can almost visualise the glint in his eyes at the very thought - it seems altogether too apt a reference to be only that.

Were a dubiety over how seriously to take that reference to discomfort you however, the next quote I want to concentrate on would probably perplex you greatly. It is from 'High Water (For Charley Patton)' and it is bound up with a literary connection I heard in my first few playings of the album. I thought I could hear echoes of the novelist known as George Eliot. Those echoes are too faint to be certain of, too faint perhaps to be anything other than creations of my own imagination.

What turned my imagination that way, though, was the number of literary allusions. Such as the specific name 'Bertha Mason' that appears in 'High Water (For Charley Patton)'. The only 'Bertha Mason' I have ever heard of is the madwoman who bites her brother in Charlotte Bronte's *Jane Eyre*. Whether Dylan means this as a reference or just alighted on the name for some reason I cannot tell you. What I can say is that it is bound to evoke the same connection in many listeners' mind as the novel is so well known and, like most of the classics, has suffered TV and film adaptations and so is widely recognised even outside the reading public. You would have to think too that even if Dylan did not consciously intend that connection to be made when he first wrote the line then he must have realised it would be by the time the album was released.

I am presuming here that there is no other Bertha Mason, but perhaps someone will discover an old blues or folk singer by that name. Or, maybe, Dylan just liked the sound of the name, thought it fitted. Even if that were true, for me and tens of thousands of others it will be the figure from *Jane Eyre* that is evoked here. Once the connection is made, as long as there are valid reasons for it, (and the Bertha from the novel is suitably menacing for the tone of 'High Water (For Charley Patton)') it enhances your appreciation and therefore it stays with you forever.

So partly it was this general referencing to literary classics that made George Eliot came to my mind elsewhere, but there is a more specific reason and this one gets to the heart of the grey areas of uncertainty that so much allusion inevitably engenders.

Three verses after the mention of 'Bertha Mason' come the lines:

> *Well, George Lewes told the Englishman, the Italian and the Jew*
> *'You can't open your mind, boys*
> *To every conceivable point of view.'*

This particular passage is the centre of much confusion and differing interpretation. You may wish to dismiss it by claiming that it doesn't really matter what the words are referring to, yet when you listen to it, you cannot. It sounds too important; once you have heard the verse you realise that it matters greatly and you want to know.

I initially took the Englishman, Italian and Jew to represent Newton, Galileo and Einstein, and did so because of what I heard as the George Lewes connotation. I presumed that the George Lewes I was hearing about to be the famed nineteenth century Rationalist, who left his wife and caused a scandal by living with Mary Ann Evans, who was known to the reading public by the male pseudonym of George Eliot. The close proximity of Charles Darwin was probably another reason I thought along these lines.

However, two separate reviews I read soon after the album's release took Englishman, Italian and Jew to stand for Protestantism, Catholicism and Judaism. I suspect that these reviewers were alerted to the religious take by the important ethical questions this passage of the song raises. Christopher Rollanson, however, heard 'George Lewes' the same way as I did, so his thoughts followed the same track:

> Why is it specified he told 'an Englishman an Italian and a Jew'? As he was an Englishman himself, why phrase it so? Is it because the Englishman, Italian and Jew are supposed to reflect a specific mind set? (Say the scientific one as all I can come up with here would be Newton-Galileo-Einstein.) Is George telling them they need to take sides between the rationality of Darwin and the blind faith of the closed minded judge? So many questions, such a complex verse.

> Maybe I am dwelling too much on it, perhaps it is another George Lewes ('Jorg Lewis', say, or any made up name you fancy) and the Englishman, Italian and Jew don't represent anything. Yet listening to it, and especially taking the verse as a whole that is very hard to believe. This sounds far from a teasing set of references thrown in as a jape on Dylan's part.[46]

Others following the name checking of Dylan's lexicon did indeed alight on another 'George Lewis'. This was a jazz musician from New Orleans; a perfect figure to be found in the tracks of *"Love And Theft"*. 'George Lewis' is the spelling in the official lyrics, incidentally, though as even a casual acquaintance with those betrays they cannot be treated as reliable.

Does it matter who Dylan is alluding to here? Perhaps not, the music, vocals and large number of clearly intentional references are more than enough to provide the richest of fares. There is a danger is of going too far and losing touch with the original work of art itself. If becomes train-spotting, it is not art appreciation nor entertaining. Undoubtedly things like the *Huckleberry Finn*, *Great Gatsby*, minstrelsy and folk references do add to both our pleasure and understanding. The question is where does this stop?

The Nathan Bedford Forrest allusion would appear to be totally relevant, an inspired choice that deepens the song and the album as a whole. Yet it is so obscure that it is only by chance I ever heard of it.

However, perhaps this is not a problem. You 'get' the obvious ones, and miss the obscure until maybe some future date when you come across one in a novel, poem or song and cross-refer two pleasurable experiences in life.

This happens all the time when you read literature and indeed in the rich lyrics of Bob Dylan's songs throughout the many styles of writing he has employed.

Speaking of enjoyment and learning, I get much of the former and achieve the latter via his vocals. These are a tour de force, albeit within a restricted range.

### Vocalisation

With hindsight, you would think that there should have been no surprise at the vocal style that dominates *"Love And Theft"*, given some of Dylan's previous performances. However, when it was released, the style of 'Moonlight', 'Po' Boy', 'Bye And Bye' and 'Floater (Too Much To Ask)' in particular took everyone aback.

Once we had recovered we remembered the hints of some similar styles that we had heard before. I am thinking of things like Gershwin's 'Soon', which is not the kind of song you associate with Dylan. Yet he gave a beautifully sung, heartfelt and heart-rending performance of it at the 1987 Gershwin Gala event.

Then there was the moving live tribute to Stevie Ray Vaughan, after his tragic death. Dylan poignantly sang a one-off 'Moon River'. There have been other live songs like 'Confidential To Me' and 'Answer Me, My Love' that implied the possibility of his *"Love And Theft"* voice. Crooning had appeared before, much earlier in Dylan's career; the full *Basement Tapes* as well as *Nashville Skyline* attest to that. Then there was his renditions of 'Tomorrow Night' both on *Good As I Been To You* and live. One of the CD's in the collection of Never Ending Tour covers we looked at in the 'Singing The Lexicon' chapter was entitled *Crooning 'Neath The Moon*.

It is not only that he sings a variety of styles so well on *"Love And Theft"* but the way he carries them all off so confidently. If I can refer you back to chapter two and 'Don't Think Twice, It's All Right', Dylan then said that:

> *I don't carry myself yet the way that Big Joe Williams, Woody Guthrie, Leadbelly and Lightnin' Hopkins have carried themselves. I hope to be able to someday, but they're older people.*

For years now he has been one of those 'older people' who can carry themselves; one thinks back to his assured performance of 'Pretty Boy Floyd' on the 1988 Leadbelly/Guthrie tribute album, *A Vision Shared*. The same authority and control of phrasing is evident throughout *"Love And Theft"*. Dylan's confidence in himself and his material is absolute and this adds a certain relish to various parts of *"Love And Theft"*. In 'Cry A While', for example, the

Mr. Goldsmith who is so lambasted in line two, is facing a fighting character:

*I don't carry no weight, I'm no flash in the pan...*
*...Feel like a fighting rooster, feel better than I ever felt*

As noted earlier, there's also something defiantly grand in his declaration of 'I'm gonna buy me a barrel of whisky, I'll die before I turn senile.' It is conveyed in his voice as well as the words. The vocals make the lyrics work and the lyrics inspire the vocals, two sides of the one coin.

'Lonesome Day Blues' powers along with swaggering growl, the way Dylan alights on the word 'boys' reminds one of the camaraderie evident in the 'male' jokes throughout the album.

With Dylan revelling in his own abilities as vocalist, confidence apparent in every utterance, we listeners have no option but to be deeply interested in what these utterances are saying. The reason I am so keen to know which 'George Lewis' he is referring to is because the way he sings the passage makes me need to know. It is the same reason that a question was raised about the suitcase in 'Mississippi' in the Rome interview. Actually the singing throughout that song is as good an example as any of how the meanings and emotions behind these tracks are conveyed by a voice that manages to be simultaneously restricted and resplendent.

We have already noted that Rosie is central to this song. You cannot escape knowing that once you have heard the following beautifully sung by Dylan with a mixture of the wistful and the sensuous:

*I was thinking about the things that Rosie said*
*I was dreaming I was sleeping in Rosie's bed*

You can hear in the timbre of his voice that his mind is back in time, away from the present (the preceding line is *'Say anything you want to, I have heard it all'*) when things were fresh and new. His *'summer days'*, perhaps; and I can't help but feel he has to dream he was sleeping in Rosie's bed because he missed the chance of really doing so, by *'staying in Mississippi a day too long.'*

His voice betrays touches of anger in the song, too. Moods change, you can hear sorrowful desolation and then feel joy when his voice 'lifts'.

Every emotion in 'Mississippi' is evident in the 'grain of his voice' just as in all classic Dylan. Alan Davis, in the following quote, instinctively feels what Dylan is singing to him about. How does he know this? He *feels* it, like I do, like you do:

*'Having painted myself into the corner of my own life, can I find a way out? Sometimes I think I can. I know all about those bursts of*

*sentimental optimism, expressed here with penetrative insight, though it looks at first sight like pop pastiche: 'give me your hand and say you'll be mine'. It could be a line from a Beatles' song - quite out of place in a song such as this. But here, sung with the passion of the moment, it's perfect. We do slip into cliché, all of us; we do respond to sudden upsurges of sentimental feeling. But such a bubble can easily burst...Listen to the cold horror in the voice as it experiences the endless emptiness in the last verse of the song, as he realises that you can't swim in the same water twice.'*[47]

I have already mentioned in this book that one of Dylan's notable skills as a vocalist is his ability to make words that he sings enact their meaning. It is a skill he has not lost. You can hear his voice as well as the leaves stir in 'Floater (Too Much To Ask)'; he makes the word 'room' sound roomy. One of the most telling of these occurrences is in a line we have looked at already: *'a summer breeze is blowing...wind'*. The connection I discussed between these lines and 'Blowin' In The Wind' is made not only textually but also through the way he sings the word 'blowing'. As on the original you can hear the wind, though it is much subtler here, after all it is only a breeze.

Dylan is bringing it all back home once again; his vocalisation and rhyming on his latest album turns our minds to his first big 'hit' nearly forty years before.

Nigel Hinton drew attention to a similar vocal feat in 'Lonesome Day Blues':

*'And what about the wind whispering verse, where in the repeated line he suddenly drops in the additional 'something' (half-heard) like the something he half heard when the wind was whispering? Oh so simple and so perfect. He doesn't just describe it, he makes it happen to the listener, too.'*[48]

Some of the other vocal delights are very characteristic of Dylan. I am thinking of things like the way he compresses the following dialogue from *The Great Gatsby* into the short musical phrase:

*She says, 'You can't repeat the past,' I say 'You can't? What do you mean you can't? Of course you can.'*

Or, as in his heyday, the way words and lines stretch out or squeeze in with tour-de-force Dylan mastery of control. 'Cry A While', for example, opens with an astonishing feat of vocal gymnastics:

> *Well, I had to go down and see a guy named Mr. Goldsmith*
> *A nasty, dirty, double-crossin', back-stabbin' phony I didn't wanna*
> *have to be dealin' with*

Then there is the texture of his voice in 'Bye And Bye' as he sings: 'I'm not even acquainted with my own desires'. To list all the vocal finery would be impractical yet I want to point out how some words - not always the ones you'd expect - are caressed. I want to talk about how well the Minnesotan deadpan style that worked so effectively on *The Basement Tapes* does so again here. Or how in 'High Water (For Charley Patton)' he sings 'I don't care' so that it is both menacing and nonchalant. Such singing is core to the song's import, as are the sinister 'heavy breathing' effects that underscore the song's dark elements. In many ways all you need to guide you through the emotions of the album is that ever expressive voice. Compare the way he sings 'care' in the following verse to the one about the High Sheriff. Same word, same place in verse, completely different meaning conveyed.

And the manner in which Dylan's voice communicates his meaning is even more crucial in two of the album's finest tracks, 'Sugar Baby' and 'Po' Boy'. 'Sugar Baby' would seem a pitiless song without what his voice brings to it. It still sounds wounding, but the insight that he transmits vocally tells us it is no simple put-down.

'Po' Boy' is a total vocal triumph; an extraordinary feat of describing a cuckolded loser - a loser to the *nth* degree - with merciless lyric dissection and yet treating his situation with tremendous sympathy. The warm, compassionate empathy in the music and the vocals transforms the song into something magical. Dylan's voice imparts a love of humanity in all its befuddled state. It is there throughout the song, peaking in places - like the implied feeling behind his voice at the end of '...and I won't forget him' when singing of the uncle. It is there, too, in the way he caresses the word 'cars', at the end of the fourth stanza. Perhaps it is there most of all in the heart-tugging rendition of:

> *All I know is that I'm thrilled by your kiss*
> *I don't know any more than this*

### Work

Despite all the themes I have discussed thus far, there are still others for the listener to follow that I have not covered. Part of the album's appeal is its depth and complexity, bearing more repeated and intent listens than I have yet to see an end to. I doubt I ever will. For example, there are political, business and work related comments that may not be numerous but which resonate throughout the album as a whole. From the first two tracks onwards (Tweedle Dum and Dee's 'company' and 'games to play' in 'Mississippi') you can hear things that are important to Dylan's summation of the album as:

> 'The whole album deals with power. If life teaches us anything, it's that there's nothing that men and women won't do to get power.'[49]

This shows up on a day-to-day level with an attention to detail that surprises given that Dylan's position in life shields him from such situations:

> One of the boss's hangers-on
> Comes to call at times you least expect
> Try to bully ya - strong arm you - inspire you with fear
> It has the opposite effect
>
> 'Floater (Too Much To Ask)'

Such insights add to the feeling that these songs are for and about ordinary folk going about life. And doing so with love, lust, deceit, stoicism and much fun but also lots of work, work that often is part of a power-play, everyone in a struggle to 'get on'. This struggle doesn't rob them of all their humanity, however; you can feel that through the singing:

> It's a realm of the felt rather than the analyzed, where the vibe becomes part of the poetry. Unafraid to be romantic, Dylan's characters plunge in headfirst, make shrewd calculations of their chances, and then cry in their beers. Though they might not be fully acquainted with their own desires, they haven't surrendered yet. They'll do anything to steal a kiss or a blissful moment of intimacy - even make like the troubadours of a bygone age, following up an eerie death rattle with some winking old-time soft-shoe.[50]

The characters come to life with some detailed background of working life. Notice the observation within these already fine lines in the verse that follows on from the one above in 'Floater (Too Much To Ask)':

> There's a new grove of trees on the outskirts of town
> The other one is long gone
> Timber two foot six across
> Burns with the bark still on.

From politicians running for office to the nitty-gritty of the workplace; again we see the scope and authenticity of Dylan's *'panorama of what America means'* to him.

So many themes in one album, it is bursting with life. Themes that cohere and add to the unity and realism of a recognisable world, despite it being built upon so many varied musical styles and set mostly in the past. Dylan creates something novel and stately for the new century, built on the groundwork of what had gone before, an 'American panorama', indeed.

### 'All that and more and then some'

Minstrelsy, the lexicon, the South, ageing etc. etc. - what does it all add up to? It adds up to listening to this album, to being (willingly) sucked in, to being transported, to being impelled to return again and again to its world. To enjoy it and, yes, to learn more with each visit. Like all great art, *"Love And Theft"* appears to those enraptured by it to be, as Nigel Hinton was quoted as remarking, 'a miracle'. This is why we either do or should revere our poets - for this seemingly miraculous ability to move us and let us see the world with new eyes.

Dylan has performed many such 'miracles' before, of a variety of kinds. They all had in common an authenticity which was felt immediately and instinctively by the listener able to appreciate the power and beauty of Dylan's singing. This is why I said in the introduction to this book that I have always apprehended his expressive genius first through his voice, no matter the power and worth of the music and lyrics.

Then there is the detail beneath the authentic voice of *"Love And Theft"*. The genuiness comes from everything I have been talking about from the chapter on nonsense verse onwards. This is a creative album, not a manufactured one. Despite all the album's themes and interests, the first and lasting impression is one of joy. The joy we feel from art that is soundly crafted; standing, in this case, on solid and multi-various foundations. Dylan is the creator of that joy, I merely share my thoughts on some of the ways he achieved his creation and why it inspires such feelings in myself.

This authenticity is at the core of how *"Love And Theft"*, following on from 'Highlands' works. You feel you are sensing the world through Bob Dylan's emotions and thoughts. It either is so or the artifice is so convincing that it is indistinguishable. To quote again from Nigel Hinton:

> *"Love And Theft" is about the experience of being a sixty year old Bob, without ever talking about the experience of being a 60 year old Bob. It is how he sees the world, how he feels the world... He doesn't talk about what it's like to be an old guy with grandchildren to whom you say silly things to make them laugh, he is the old guy saying silly things to make us laugh.*

**319**

*There's a marvellous example in 'Summer Days'. The summer days and summer nights of his life might be gone, people might think he's a worn-out star but he knows a place where it's still going on - the music he's playing. And when he enjoins us to lift up our glasses and sing, he really is, through this wonderful reconstruction of Sun-tinged rockabilly, proposing a toast to the King. The medium is the message, The message is the medium. Extraordinary art.*[51]

Mikal Gilmore picked up on an earlier comment Dylan had made to the effect that he saw *"Love And Theft"* as autobiographical and probed for more information on this. Dylan obliged:

*Oh, absolutely. It would be autobiographical on every front. It obviously plays by its own set of rules, but a listener wouldn't really have to be aware of those rules when hearing it. But absolutely. It's not like the songs were written by some kind of Socrates, you know, some kind of buffoon, the man about town pretending to be happy [laughs]. There wouldn't be any of that in this record.*[52]

Feeling for a moment like Woody Allen wheeling in Marshal McLuhan, I also draw attention to a Dylan comment in the same interview that cuts to the core of *"Love And Theft"* and 'Highlands' before it: *'A song is a reflection of what I see all around me all the time.'*[53]

You have to treat Dylan interview comments with a large degree of caution, but the way he repeatedly brings up the autobiography angle belies the idea that it was just a passing fancy:

*'I've never recorded an album with more autobiographical songs,' he says. 'This is the way I really feel about things. It's not me dragging around a bottle of absinthe and coming up with Baudelairian poems. It's me using everything I know to be true.'*[54]

One of the things Dylan sees 'around me all the time' is his live show and all that surrounds his 'never-ending tour'. As in the best of those performances, *"Love And Theft"* sees Dylan jump from style to style with a controlled touch and a sense of exuberance. He is like a master jumper along a train, carriage by carriage, covering the mileage of American popular music as a train would eat up the miles - and he never looks likely to fall between the cars.

Over and above all I have said about 'Tweedle Dee & Tweedle Dum', the opening track acts as a kick-start to get the whole thing up and running. This is just like the opening song he and the band tear into onstage. As Dylan rampages through whatever show opener it may be, I am often thinking of what the second song will be; I've long felt it is a good indicator for how good a show will be - a fine performance here and the whole show is usually special. If this album were a show, I'd be sure of a cracker, as the second song is a classic.

Reminders of the Never Ending Tour are apposite as on *"Love And Theft"* he is backed by his then touring band. Much to fans' delight *"Love And Theft"* songs were ripe for live outings. It took no imagination at all to see where various songs would fit in a Dylan set list. Once the album was released, so the songs appeared.

Live performances of *"Love And Theft"* songs are for another book, this one has mainly been looking at Dylan's song-writing. The most striking thing about his writing on *Time Out Of Mind,* and even more so on *"Love And Theft",* is the way he is now integrating quotes from others into his songs, if not building entire songs from others' words. It is something that has always been present in his song-writing but it has now taken on an all encompassing role; the 'theft' has become as total as the 'love'.

I confess to feeling disappointed in the past when I have discovered that some of the lines I most admired were not written by Dylan but copied from older songs. Now I always knew about the folk process and that there is an art to copying other people's work and making a new song of it, but nonetheless I was deflated that some of my favourite lines in mid-sixties songs that I had thought for years were Dylan originals turned out not to be. I felt something similar when I realised that my favourites passages in 'Trying To Get To Heaven' were not written by Dylan either.

I do not feel the same about *"Love And Theft"*. Until writing this chapter I had not thought about that so I am not entirely sure why it is the case, but I have some good pointers that it is more than just me growing accustomed to the practice. Firstly, as I have mentioned before, especially in relation to the sound of Hank Williams, it is because Dylan makes his past ingredients sound so fresh on *"Love And Theft"*. The album seems to look both to the past and the future, it feels original in spite of everything it 'steals'. Secondly this new form leaves people like me unable to 'categorise' it, something that would rightly please Mr. Dylan and therefore energises me too, with the novelty of it all. As Professor Lott remarked in the *Gadfly* interview we looked at back near the beginning of the chapter:

> 'What's fascinating when it comes to the music is that it's usually tricky to specify where minstrelsy or obvious cultural appropriation stops and

*something different and fresh begins. Sometimes they co-exist outright, in (say) Biz Markie or the Beastie Boys. The Michael Boltons of the world are always there to give us the worst-case minstrel show example; but it's far easier to spot a lame plunderer like Kenny G or Robert Palmer than it is to say how an obvious borrower like Dylan or Elvis nevertheless somehow makes the music his own.'*[57]

He is speaking there of minstrelsy in particular but the same thing is true in the wider sense of borrowings from the whole 'lexicon'. It isn't exactly the same thing as Dylan was doing earlier in his career when he took a cheery drinking song like 'Moonshiner' and transformed it into a lament of poetic depth solely on the basis of his playing and singing. It is also not the same as the post-modernist borrowings and allusions of his mid-sixties period. It shares similarities to both but it is a new form, created out of his lexicon, minstrelsy, literature, his own iconic career and those of trailblazers before him. It is literary, it is burlesque, it is a type of modernism and it is 'low art', it is popular music; it is *"Love And Theft"*.

I cannot see any Dylan fan who approaches it with an open mind not enjoying it, only false expectations or personal agendas demanding the artist be something other than he is could lead to disappointment. For all others this album will be a thing of joy, a breath of fresh air and a treasure trove to keep returning to. They, like me, can say to this 'sugar baby':

*Your charms have broken many a heart and mine is surely one*

## Afterword

The overwhelmingly referential nature of *"Love And Theft"* brought the best out of the internet Dylan community. I was well on my way to filling a notebook with (some of) the multitude of references in these lyrics when I was directed to a website that was collecting them all in an online annotated set of lyrics. I presume that the idea here is to put every possible reference up and allow the individual to decide which ones s/he thinks is appropriate. It is a very worthwhile project and included many I had not, nor ever would have, thought of. Some of these have directly affected this chapter. It is to be found at: www.republika.pl/bobdylan/lat/

After my initial reviews a lot of things were written about the album and other reviews and articles have obviously had an influence on me. I have striven to acknowledge these wherever possible by quoting the writer who first brought something to my attention, or who simply put it best. My thoughts on the album have been coloured in particular by the writings of Nigel Hinton, Richard Jobes and Christopher Rollanson, the last of whose work promises to be ongoing at his website (www.geocities.com/Athens/Oracle/6752/).

Dylan's interviews included comments from him showing distaste for 'manufactured music'; *"Love And Theft"* is an antidote to that but it was not the only breath of fresh, yet archaic, air felt since the turn of the millennium. With the success of the film *O Brother Where Art Thou* more attention is being paid to earlier forms of American popular music. Nick Tosches' campaign on behalf of the legacy of Emmett Miller, allied to the aforementioned Greil Marcus's *Invisible Republic* and the re-release of the Harry Smith anthology, are testament to a whole growth of interest that has come to fruition in the early years of the new century.

Dylan, as we have seen, had long been at the vanguard of respecting and keeping alive the music of this older world. He is on record as an enthusiast of *O Brother Where Art Thou* and you have to think there were other developments that pleased him too. The new millennium found much of the music world looking back further into the past than before, it was a climate in which a seven-CD 'complete recordings' Charley Patton box set could be released in the same year as *"Love And Theft"*.

I have lived with *"Love And Theft"* for well over a year now and it still totally captivates me. It is still the record I play most each and every week, unofficial ones included. This has never happened before in my life, though it undoubtedly would have happened with *Blood On The Tracks* had I not then been discovering Dylan's entire back catalogue, both official and bootleg. (Something still ongoing when *Desire* was released). Were I even older than I already am I would have had previous experience of one album dominating my listening for this long. The way it has turned out for me, however, puts *"Love And Theft"* as the leader in that regard and it is still the first album I pack for any journey.

A more suitable point to leave my book on the troubadour that has so illuminated my life is hard to imagine. Yet it is only the ending at this point in time; Dylan has written for and starred in an about-to-be-released film, he has written a new song for a big feature release on the US Civil War and he is gearing up for the beginning of another tour. After that, who knows? Hopefully another album, but it would need a braver man than me to predict what that would sound like.

I wanted to end by writing something to sum up my feelings on *"Love And Theft"* in particular and Bob Dylan in general. Dylan beat me to the first when he wrote in his liner notes to the Jimmie Rodgers tribute album:

> *He sings not only among his bawdy, upbeat blues and railroading songs,*
> *but also tin pan alley trash and crooner lullabies as well. He makes*
> *everything unmistakably his own and does it with piercing charm.*

He beat me to the second too. In the same piece, Dylan said of Rodgers
what I would say of him:

> *A blazing star whose sound was and remains the raw essence of individ-*
> *uality in a sea of conformity, par excellence with no equal.*

1. Mikal Gilmore, 'The Rolling Stone Interview' 882 - Nov. 22, 2001.
2. Edna Gundersen *USA Today*, August 2001.
3. 12-10-01 www.gadflyonline.com.
4. Ibid.
5. Ibid.
6. Nick Tosches, *Where Dead Voices Gather,* Jonathan Cape 2002.
7. Talk on Bob Dylan & The History Of Rock'N'Roll, 2002.
8. Mikal Gilmore, 'The Rolling Stone Interview', *Rolling Stone* 882 - Nov. 22, 2001.
9. 12-10-01 www.gadflyonline.com.
10. Lott shows himself as aware of this later in the same interview. I am conscious that by extracting parts of his thought to reflect on Dylan only I may be presenting an incomplete version of his views. I would urge the reader to read his book for the full picture. After all I would be loathe to falsely portray a man who when asked what he thought of Dylan calling his album *"Love And Theft"* replied, 'I'm thinking of calling my next book *Time Out Of Mind.*'
11. Christopher Rollanson, The Critical Corner, http://www.geocities.com/Athens/Oracle/6752/
12. I realise the phrase 'the city that never sleeps' is commonly used to refer to New York and it would not change the emphasis much if that were the case but to me Chicago is the better fit.
13. Nigel Hinton, 'Things Come Alive', *Judas!* 1.
14. Though it's probably best for your blood pressure not to think of Carla or Diane being the waitress in 'Highlands'
15. David Fricke, 'The Making of *"Love And Theft"' Rolling Stone* 878.
16. Mikal Gilmore, 'The Rolling Stone Interview', *Rolling Stone* 882 - Nov. 22, 2001.
17. Ron Maxwell: www.ronmaxwell.com/ggenerals.com.
18. This level of obscurity of an allusion raises questions as to its relevance, Dylan's intent and the relevance or otherwise of that too.
19. Since he made his money pre War as a slave trader and is alleged to have been a Grand Wizard in the Klu Klux Klan after it, controversy can be found throughout Mr Forrest's life.
20. Full details of this quotation and its context can be found at: http://members.aol.com/GnrlJSB/NBFmurder.html
21. In writing this one cannot help but also be pointing out the fact that one day there will be a final album which will take on a completely special status. This may not be the way things should be appreciated or judged but it is a fact of life that they are. We can only hope that the final album is still many years in the future.
22. Mikal Gilmore 'The Rolling Stone Interview', *Rolling Stone* 882 - Nov. 22, 2001.
23. Gary Hill, Reuters, 1993.
24. Mikal Gilmore, 'The Rolling Stone Interview', *Rolling Stone* 882 - Nov. 22, 2001.
25. Edna Gundersen, *USA Today,* August 2001.
26. Edna Gundersen, 'Dylan Is Positively On Top Of His Game', *USA Today* Sep 10 2001.

27. With thanks to Arthur J at http://www.republika.pl/bobdylan/lat/ for this - see Afterword for fuller details and accreditation.

28. Thank you, Duncan Hume, for the e-mail pointing this out.

29 Terry Kelly, 'Bob Dylan's Songs of Innocence and Experience', *The Bridge* 11, Autumn 2001.

30. Richard Jobes, 'Po' Boy, Dressed In Black', *Judas!* 3.

31. *Guitar World* Magazine, *Maximum Bob,* March, 1999.

32. This comes from an article that is intended to appear in *Judas!* 5, April 2003

33. Jon Pareles interview/review *New York Times.*

34. David Fricke, 'The Making of *"Love And Theft"'* *Rolling Stone* 878.

35. Christopher Rollanson in a detailed essay on the song at:
(www.geocities.com/Athens/Oracle/6752/magazine.html) traces the origin of the two characters: 'Martin Gardner, a commentator on Carroll and editor of 'The Annotated Alice', traces our two heroes back to the eighteenth century, to a comic poem written in 1725 by John Byrom which lampoons the public rivalry between two composers. One of these was none other than George Frederick Handel; the other, rather less famous today, was Giovanni Battista Bononcini: Some say, compared to Bononcini/That Mynheer Handel's but a ninny./Others aver that he to Handel/Is scarcely fit to hold a candle./ Strange all this difference should be/Twixt tweedle-dum and tweedle-dee. Martin adds: 'No one knows whether the nursery rhyme about the Tweedle brothers originally had reference to this famous musical battle, or whether it was an older rhyme from which Byrom borrowed in the last line of his doggerel'. Be that as it may, Byrom's lines confirm the COD reference to 'the stock names of rival musicians', and also supply the earliest example of the phrase given by the OED. It is interesting to note additionally that Bononcini and the composer of 'The Messiah' were, like Dylan's Tweedle brothers, a pair of business partners who did not always see eye to eye: the 'Concise Oxford Dictionary of Music' tells us that 'in 1719 Handel, in association with Bononcini (…), was a musical director of the so-called Royal Academy of Music (not a college but a business venture to produce Italian opera' - which lasted eight years, finally closing in 1727 'because of lack of support'.

36. Michael Gray, *Song & Dance Man III: The Art of Bob Dylan,* Cassell, page 649

37. See my own *Razor's Edge* p. 74-75, Helter Skelter Publishing, 2001. I discuss Dylan's comments in the light of *Psalms* 27:10 and the startling similarity of Dylan's apparently improvised speech to the words of 19th century Rabbi Shimshon Rafael Hirsch: "Even if I were so depraved that my own mother and father would abandon me to my own devices, God would still gather me up and believe in my ability to mend my ways."

38. Edna Gundersen, *USA Today,* August 2001.

39. Nigel Hinton, 'Things Come Alive', *Judas!* 1.

40. Ibid.

41. My own review in *Isis* was followed up by others both there and elsewhere that quickly added to my initial comments on the Twain links. As far as I am aware this one was first mentioned by Matthew Zuckerman also in *Isis.*

42. The Negro Writer in America: an Exchange, *Partisan Review,* XXV (1958)

43. Those more familiar with the Dryden translation will know this as:
> But, Rome, 't is thine alone, with awful sway,
> To rule mankind, and make the world obey,
> Disposing peace and war by thy own majestic way;
> To tame the proud, the fetter'd slave to free:

44. 'The Gospel of Luke'; Chapter 15, 11-32.

45. Richard Jobes, 'Po' Boy, Dressed In Black' *Judas!* 3.

46. Christopher Rollanson, www.geocities.com/Athens/Oracle/6752/lat.html

47. Alan Davis, 'Staying in Mississippi', *Isis* 100 Dec. 2001.

48. Nigel Hinton, 'Things Come Alive', *Judas!* 1.

49. Mikal Gilmore *The Rolling Stone Interview* 882 - Nov. 22, 2001
50. Philadelphia Newspapers Inc.
51. Nigel Hinton, 'Things Come Alive'. *Judas!* 1.
52. Mikal Gilmore *The Rolling Stone Interview* 882 - Nov. 22, 2001.
53. Ibid.
54. Edna Gundersen, 'Dylan is positively on top of his game', *USA Today*, Sep.10th 2001.
55. 12-10-01 www.gadflyonline.com.

# Thanks And Acknowledgements

Thanks and Acknowledgements

(Jailhouse) John Alexander, Joel Bernstein, Bob Bettendorf, Mitch Blank, Jim Brady, David Bristow, Jim Callahan, Mark Carter, Nick Carrruthers, Alan Davis, Jim Devlin, Dangerous Daniel, Glen Dundas, Chris & Stephan Fehlau, Robert Forryan, Alan Fraser, Andy Goldstein, Michael Gray, Jim Heppell, Clinton Heylin, Alex and Olive Hill, Nigel Hinton, Duncan Hume, Richard Jobes, Catriona and John Kennedy, Raymond Landry, C.P. Lee, Dan Levy, Joe McShane, David Moodie, James Muir, John Perry, Ed Ricardo, Shakin' All Over yahoogroup, Stephen Scobie, Nigel Simms, Lucas Stensland, Ray Stavrou, John Stokes, Manny & Philly Vardavas, Peter Vincent, Roy Whiteaker, Paul Williams, Dave Wingrove, Ian Woodward, Keith Wootton, Andy Wright and all friends, contributors and supporters of **Homer**, *the slut* and *Judas!* magazines.

Thanks to *Dignity, Isis, Freewheelin'* and *On The Tracks* for carrying some of the chapters in their original form.

Many thanks for comments on draft chapters to Peter Vincent in particular and also to Robert Forryan, Pia Parviainen, James and Olive Muir and Keith Wootton.

The author and publisher wish to thank Jeff Rosen and all the relevant copyright holders for permission to quote from the lyrics of Bob Dylan. The best location for up-to-date copyright information on each Bob Dylan song is in the 'song section' of the wonderful official website at: www.bobdylan.com/songs/index.html

In addition, detailed copyright acknowledgement for every song quoted in this book is available at *Troubadour*'s website at: www.amuir.co.uk/troubadour

# TROUBADOUR

Bibliographical Notes

The two things I first read that treated Bob Dylan as a serious artist were the first of Michael Gray's books and a dissertation for Strathclyde University by Jim Brady. Their influence on this book will therefore be profound. The Dylan library has grown exponentially in the years since I started reading about him; being what one might term 'slightly obsessed' with the man, I have read every one I could, some of them more than once. To list them all here would seem impractical and this general acknowledgement hopefully suffices when combined with the specific acknowledgements in each chapter. A fully detailed bibliography is available at *Troubadour*'s website. Special mention should be made, however, of Michael Gray's *Song & Dance Man III: The Art of Bob Dylan*, Paul Williams' *Performing Artist* books and Clinton Heylin's *Behind The Shades: Take Two*.

*The Fiddler Now Upspoke* by Desolation Row Promotions Ltd., (19b Gravenhurst Road, Campton. Beds., SG17 5NY, UK) is an invaluable series of collected Bob Dylan interviews.

I edit a Dylan magazine, *Judas!* whose stated aim is to treat Dylan with the respect and intelligence his work demands and deserves. With a mixture of well known and new writers the emphasis is always on quality; quality of writing and quality of presentation. You can find out more about this magazine at: www.judasmagazine.com

Other English language Dylan Fanzines at the time of publication (in alphabetical order)

*The Bridge*
www.two-riders.co.uk/
*Dignity*
19b Gravenhurst Road, Campton. Beds., SG17 5NY, UK
*Freewheelin'*
www.freewheelin-on-line.info
*Isis*
www.bobdylanisis.com/
*On The Tracks*
www.b-dylan.com/

# Index

*Italicised entries are for songs by Bob Dylan. Entries for songs not written by him are not italicised, whether performed by him or not. Endnotes to the chapters are not indexed. As Dylan is discussed mainly through the medium of his songs, references to him personally, as opposed to the songs, are also not indexed. Other persons who are cited or discussed extensively are indexed.*